New Perspective in German Studies

General Editors: Michael Butler is Emeritus Professor of Modern German Literature at the University of Birmingham and Professor William E. Paterson OBE is Professor of European and German Politics at the University of Birmingham and Chairman of the German British Forum.

Over the last twenty years the concept of German studies has undergone major transformation. The traditional mixture of language and literary studies, related very closely to the discipline as practised in German universities, has expanded to embrace history, politics, economics and cultural studies. The conventional boundaries between all these disciplines have become increasingly blurred, a process which has been accelerated markedly since German unification in 1989/90.

New Perspectives in German Studies, developed in conjunction with the Institute for German Studies and the Department of German Studies at the University of Birmingham, has been designed to respond precisely to this trend of the interdisciplinary approach to the study of German and to cater for the growing interest in Germany in the context of European integration. The books in this series will focus on the modern period, from 1750 to the present day.

Titles include:

Peter Bleses and Martin Seeleib-Kaiser
THE DUAL TRANSFORMATION OF THE GERMAN WELFARE STATE

Michael Butler and Robert Evans (*editors*)
THE CHALLENGE OF GERMAN CULTURE
Essays Presented to Wilfried van der Will

Michael Butler, Malcolm Pender and Joy Charnley (*editors*)
THE MAKING OF MODERN SWITZERLAND 1848–1998

Paul Cooke and Andrew Plowman (*editors*)
GERMAN WRITERS AND THE POLITICS OF CULTURE
Dealing with the Stasi

Wolf-Dieter Eberwein and Karl Kaiser (*editors*)
GERMANY'S NEW FOREIGN POLICY
Decision-Making in an Interdependent World

Jonathan Grix
THE ROLE OF THE MASSES IN THE COLLAPSE OF THE GDR

Gunther Hellmann (*editor*)
GERMANY'S EU POLICY IN ASYLUM AND DEFENCE
De-Europeanization by Default?

Margarete Kohlenbach
WALTER BENJAMIN
Self-Reference and Religiosity

Charles Lees
PARTY POLITICS IN GERMANY
A Comparative Politics Approach

Hanns W, Maull
GERMANY'S UNCERTAIN POWER
Foreign Policy of the Berlin Republic

James Sloam
THE EUROPEAN POLICY OF THE GERMAN SOCIAL DEMOCRATS
Interpreting a Changing World

Ronald Speirs and John Breuilly (*editors*)
GERMANY'S TWO UNIFICATIONS
Anticipations, Experiences, Responses

Henning Tewes
GERMANY, CIVILIAN POWER AND THE NEW EUROPE
Enlarging Nato and the European Union

Maiken Umbach
GERMAN FEDERALISM
Past, Present, Future

New Perspectives in German Studies
Series Standing Order ISBN 0–333–92430–4 hardcover
Series Standing Order ISBN 0–333–92434–7 paperback
(Outside North America only)

You can receive future titles in this series as they are published by placing a standing order.
Please contact your bookseller or in case of difficulty, write to us at the address below with
your name and address, the title of the series and the ISBN quoted above.

Customer Services Department, Macmillan Distribution Ltd, Houndmills, Basingstoke,
Hampshire RG21 6XS, England

Germany's Uncertain Power

Foreign Policy of the Berlin Republic

Edited by

Hanns W. Maull
Chair of Foreign Policy and International Relations
University of Trier, Germany

First published in 2006 by
PALGRAVE MACMILLAN
Houndmills, Basingstoke, Hampshire RG21 6XS and
175 Fifth Avenue, New York, N.Y. 10010
Companies and representatives throughout the world.

PALGRAVE MACMILLAN is the global academic imprint of the Palgrave
Macmillan division of St. Martin's Press, LLC and of Palgrave Macmillan Ltd.
Macmillan® is a registered trademark in the United States, United Kingdom
and other countries. Palgrave is a registered trademark in the European
Union and other countries.

ISBN-13: 978–1–4039–4662–1 hardback
ISBN-10: 1–4039–4662–0 hardback

This book is printed on paper suitable for recycling and made from fully
managed and sustained forest sources.

A catalogue record for this book is available from the British Library.

Library of Congress Cataloging-in-Publication Data

Germany's uncertain power : foreign policy of the Berlin Republic / edited by
Hanns W. Maull.
    p. cm. —(New perspectives in German studies)
    Includes bibliographical references and index.
    ISBN 1–4039–4662–0
    1. Germany – Foreign relations – 1990– 2. Germany – Foreign economic
relations. 3. Germany – Foreign relations – European Union countries.
4. European Union countries – Foreign relations – Germany. 5. National
security – Germany. 6. Germany – Military policy. I. Maull, Hanns, 1947–
II. New perspectives in German studies (Palgrave Macmillan (Firm))

DD290.3.G49 2006
327.43009′049—dc22   2005044662

Transferred to digital print 2007

Printed and bound in Great Britain by
CPI Antony Rowe, Chippenham and Eastbourne

Contents

List of Tables and Figure

Tables

Figure

Notes on Contributors

Martin Beck is a Senior Fellow at the German Institute for Middle East Studies and a Senior Lecturer at Hamburg University, Germany. He also taught at Denver University, United States and Birzeit University, Palestine. In spring term 2005, he filled a position as acting professor for international relations at Helmut Schmidt University, Hamburg. He has published several books and numerous articles on international relations, political theory and comparative politics of the Middle East.

Andreas Falke is Professor of International Studies at the Business and Economics School of the University of Erlangen-Nürnberg. He specializes in trade policy, transatlantic relations and US Politics, subjects on which he has published widely. From 1922–2002 he worked as an economic specialist at the American Embassy in Bonn and Berlin.

Jörn-Carsten Gottwald. *Dr. habil. (*1970)*, studied political science, economics and Chinese in Muenster, Munich, Leiden (Netherlands), Tianjin (People's Republic of China) and the University of Witten-Herdecke. He received a Master of Arts from LMU Munich and a PhD from Free University Berlin. Having completed his PhD thesis on the politics of regional development of China, he recently finished a study on the politics of financial market regulation in the European Union as *Habilitation* and has thus acquired the qualification for a professorial position. His main areas of research are politics and economics in East Asia, especially the PRC, and the politics of financial market regulation in the United States and Europe. Since 2000, he is assistant-professor at the Department of Political Science, University of Trier.

Sebastian Harnisch is Associate Professor of International Relations at the University of Trier. His research interests include German and American Foreign Policy, non-proliferation issues as well as theories of international relations. His recent publications on Germany include *Germany as a Civilian Power. The Foreign Policy of the Berlin Republic* (co-ed with H. W. Maull, 2001); *Deutschland im Abseits? Rot-grüne Außenpolitik 1998–2003* (co-edited with H. W. Maull and C. Grund, 2003), and Deutsche *Sicherheitspolitik. Eine Bilanz der Regierung Schröder* (co-ed. with C. Katsioulis and M. Overhaus, 2004).

Dr. Günter Joetze, born 1933, was President of the Bundesakademie für Sicherheitspolitik from 1955–1999. He studied at various German universities and at the Johns Hopkins Center, Bologna, and London School of Economics. Dr. Joetze then joined the German Foreign Service in 1963. Besiders serving at the embassies in Moscow, Phnom Penh, Saigon, and

Niamey from 1975–1984, he participated as director for East–West relations in all CSCE meetings. After three years as Consul General in Los Angeles he became head of the German delegations at various Arms Control negotiations in Vienna. In 1987 he was made Permanent Representative to the CSCE. He teaches and publishes widely on issues of conflict prevention, regional stability, and conflict diplomacy, and has published a book on German diplomacy and the Kosovo conflict. He is currently preparing a similar volume on Iraq.

Hanns W. Maull is Professor of Foreign Policy and International Relations at the University of Trier, Germany. He has also taught at the universities of Munich and Eichstätt in Germany and at the Johns Hopkins University, Bologna Center. He has published extensively on German foreign policy, comparative foreign policy analysis, and issues of East Asian and international security.

Alister Miskimmon is Lecturer in European Politics and International Relations at Royal Holloway, University of London. He is also currently a postdoctoral fellow of the European Foreign and Security Policy Studies Programme of the Compagnia di San Paolo—Riksbankens Jubileumsfond—VolkwagenStiftung. His research interests include German foreign policy and the Common Foreign and Security Policy of the European Union.

Peter Molt is honorary Professor for International Relations and Government at the University of Trier, Germany. After a career in Germany's public service and the United Nations, he teaches since 1984 development policy, relations with developing countries, and governance in Africa and Latin America. He has published extensively on German and European development policy, and African and Latin-American affairs.

Friedemann Müller is the chairman of the Research Group "Global Issues" at the German Institute of International and Security Affairs (SWP) in Berlin. Previously he worked as a visiting fellow at Moscow State University and at various US think tanks. His professional expertise focuses primarily on energy security, international energy policy, and climate policy. He also serves as director of the International Network To Advance Climate Talks (INTACT).

Harald Müller is Director of Peace Research Institute, Frankfurt, Germany, and Professor for International Relations at Frankfurt University. He is also visiting professor at Johns Hopkins University, Bologna. Since 1999, Prof. Müller has been serving on the Advisory Board on Disarmament Matters of the UN Secretary General. One of the worlds leading specialists in arms control and non-proliferation, he has also widely written on international security issues and the theory of international relations.

Marco Overhaus is research assistant at the Chair of Foreign Policy and International Relations at the University of Trier and is heading the internet-project "deutsche-aussenpolitik.de" on German foreign policy. He studied political science at the universities of Potsdam, Germany, and San Diego, USA. He is currently writing on his doctoral thesis on German NATO-policy since the end of the Cold War.

William E. Paterson is Chairman of the German British Forum and Director Emeritus of the Institute for German Studies at the University of Birmingham. He was formerly Director of the Europa Institute at the University of Edinburgh and Professor of Politics at the University of Warwick. He has published extensively on all aspects of German politics, environmental policy and comparative social democracy and is a co-editor of the *Journal of Common Market Studies*.

August Pradetto, PhD, is a Professor of Political Science at the Helmut Schmidt University/University of the Armed Forces, Hamburg. He has taught at universities in Berlin, Vienna, and Hong Kong. He has published widely on International/ European security and NATO, German foreign policy, and transformation of postcommunist countries.

Peter Rudolf is a senior research associate at the Berlin based Stiftung Wissenschaft und Politik (SWP), the German Institute for International and Security Affairs. He worked as an APSA Congressional Fellow in Washington, DC and held research posts at Frankfurt Peace Research Institute and Harvard's Center for Science and International Affairs. In addition to his research post at SWP, he has taught at the University of Augsburg and at the Free University Berlin. He has published widely on US foreign policy, transatlantic relations, German foreign policy, arms control and other international security issues.

Siegfried Schieder is Lecturer and Research Associate in International Relations at the University of Trier. He has lectured at the University of Dresden and at the Free University of Berlin. He has published works on the Theory of International Relations and International Law, European Integration as well on German and European Foreign Policy. His publications include "Pragmatism as a Path Towards a Discursive and Open Theory of International Law," in *European Journal of International Law*, 11 (2000), 3, 663–98, "Theorien der Internationalen Beziehungen: Eine Einführung," UTB: Leske Burdrich (co-edited with M. Spindler, 2003), and "Theorien der Internationalen Beziehungen," 2nd edition, Wiesbaden: VS-Verlag (co-edited with M. Spindler, 2006).

Detlef F. Sprinz is a Senior Fellow with the Postdam Institute for Climate Impact Research (PIK) and teaches international relations and social science methodology at the Faculty of Economics and Social Science, University of

Potsdam, Germany, as well as in the international joint MA program in International Relations of the Free University of Berlin, Humboldt University of Berlin, and the University of Potsdam. His research and publications encompass international regimes and their effectiveness, international environmental policy, and modeling political decisions. He is co-editor of *International Relations and Global Climate Change* (The MIT Press, 2001, with Urs Luterbacher) and of *Models, Numbers, and Cases: Methods for Studying International Relations* (The University of Michigan Press, 2004, with Yael Wolinsky-Nahmias) in addition to numerous journal articles. Detlef Sprinz is a member of the Scientific Committee of the European Environment Agency, Copenhagen, Denmark, and a member of the European Academy, Bad Neuenahr-Ahrweiler, Germany.

Hans Stark has been the General Secretary of the Study Committee for Franco–German Relations (Cerfa) since 1991 and research fellow at the Ifri since 1989. He teaches contemporary history and European studies at the University of Sorbonne, Paris III. His professional expertise focuses primarily on contemporary Germany: internal policy, foreign policy; Franco–German relations: security issues, European construction; South-Eastern Europe: political and security issues, regional cooperation; European integration: European Security and Defence Policy, institutional debate.

Stephen F. Szabo is Professor of European Studies at The Paul H. Nitze School of Advanced International Studies, The Johns Hopkins University. He held the Steven Muller Chair in German Studies at the Bologna Center of Johns Hopkins University in 2004–2005. He teaches in the areas of European security, European politics and leadership, with a specialization on contemporary Germany. He has taught at the National War College and has also served as Chairman of Western European Studies at the Foreign Service Institute, US Department of State. His publications include *The Successor Generation: International Perspectives of Postwar Europeans* (London: Butterworth, 1983), *The Bundeswehr and Western Security* (London: MacMillan, 1989), The Changing politics of German Security (New York: St. Martin's press, 1990) and *The Diplomacy of German Unification* (New York: St. Martin's press, 1992) and *Parting Ways: The Crisis in German–American Relations* (Washington, DC: The Brookings Institution Press, 2004).

Martin Wagener is Lecturer at the Chair for International Relations and Foreign Policy at the University of Trier, Germany. He has also taught at the University of Goettingen. He is currently working on a dissertation project concerning the security policy of the USA in Southeast Asia. He has published works on the German Armed Forces and issues of East Asian and international security, with particular emphasis in the last few years on terrorism in Southeast Asia.

Reinhard Wolf is Professor of International Politics and Area Studies at the University of Greifswald, Germany. He is a co-editor of both "Politische Vierteljahresschrift" and the new "Handbuch der deutschen Außenpolitik." He has published works on German foreign policy, great power cooperation and on issues of security and international political economy.

List of Abbreviations

AA	Bundesministerium des Äußeren (Federal Foreign Office)
ABM	Anti-Ballistic-Missile
ACP	African, Caribbean and Pacific states group (associated by agreement with European Union)
ACTORD	Activation Orders
AIDS	Acquired immunodeficiency Syndrome
ASEAN	Association of South East Asian Nations
AVE	Association of German Retailers
AWACS	Airborne Warning and Control System
bb	billion barrels
BDI	Bundesverband der deutschen Industrie (Federation of German Industry)
BGA	Bundesverband der deutschen Groß- und Außenhandels (Federation of German Wholesale and Foreign Trade)
BMU	Bundesministerium für Umwelt, Naturschutz und Reaktorsicherheit (Federal Ministry of Environment)
BMWA	Bundesministerium für Wirtschft und Arbeit (Federal Ministry for Economics and Labour)
BMZ	Bundesministerium für wirtschaftliche Zusammenarbeit und Entwicklung (Federal Ministry for Economic Cooperation and Development)
BWC	Biological and Toxic Weapons Convention
CAP	Common Agricultural Policy
CBD	Convention on Biological Diversity
CCD	Convention to Combat Desertification
CDG	Carl Duisberg Gesellschaft (Carl Duisberg Society)
CDU	Christian Democratic Union (Christlich Demokratische Union)
CEE	Central-Eastern Europe
CEO	Chief Executive Officer
CESDP	Common European Security and Defense Policy (of the European Union)
CFE	Conventional Forces in Europe
CFSP	Common Foreign and Security Policy (of the European Union)
CIA	Central Intenligence Agency
CODUN	Committees on disarmament in the United Nations
CONOP	Committee on Nonproliferation of Weapons of Mass Destruction
CPI	Counterproliferation Initiative

CSCE	Conference on Security and Cooperation in Europe
CSU	Christian Social Union (Christlich Soziale Union)
CWC	Chemical Weapons Convention
DAC	OECD Development Assistance Committee
DEG	Deutsche Investitions- und Entwicklungsgesellschaft (German Investment and Development Corporation)
DIH	Deutscher Industrie- und Handelstag (German Association of Chambers of Commerce)
DPG	Defence Policy Guidelines
DR	Democratic Republic
DSE	Deutsche Stiftung für internationale Entwicklung (German Foundation for International Development and Cooperation)
DSO	Division Spezielle Operationen
EADS	European Aeronautic Defence and Space Company
EC	European Community/European Communities
ECB	European Central Bank
ECJ	European Court for Justice
ECR	Electronic Combat and Reconnaissance
ECSC	European Community for Coal and Steel
EEC	European Economic Communities
EMU	Economic and Monetary Union
ERM	European Exchange Rate Mechanism
ERRF	European Rapid Reaction Force
ESDI	European Security and Defense Identity
ESDP	(Common) European Security and Defense Policy (of the European Union)
ESDU	European Security and Defense Union
EU	Eurpean Union
FCC	Federal Constitutional Court
FDP	Free Democratic Party (Freie Demokratische Partei)
FRG	Federal Republic of Germany
FSAP	Financial sector Assessment Program
FSF	Financial Stability Forum
G-7/8	Group of Seven/Eight
GATT	General Agreement on Tariffs and Trade
GDP	Gross domestic product
GDR	German Democratic Republic (DDR)
GEF	Global Environment Facility
GHG	Green House Gases
GNP	Gross National Product
GTZ	Deutsche Gesellschaft für technische Zusammenarbeit (German Society for Technical Aid)
HIPC	Highly Indebted Poor Countries
HIV	Human Immunodeficiency Virus

IAEA	International Atomic Energy Agency
IDA	International Development Association (of the World Bank Group)
IEA	International Energy Agency
IFI	International financial institutions
IGC	Intergovernmental Conference
IMF	International Monetary Fund
ISAF	International Security Assistance Force
KAFOR	Kosovo Force
KEDO	Korean Energy Development Organization
KfW	Kreditanstalt für Wiederaufbau, German Credit Bank for Reconstruction
KSK	Kommando Spezialkräfte (Special Forces Command)
KVM	Kosovo Verification Mission
LDC	Least developed countries
LICUS	Low income countries under stress
LNG	Liquefied Natural Gas
mbd	million barrels per day
MDG	Millenium Development Goals
MEADS	Medium Extended Air Defense System
NATO	North Atlantic Treaty Organization
NBC	Nuclear, Biological, and Chemical
NePAD	New strategic partnership for African Development
NGO	Non-govermental Organization
NPT	Non-Proliferation Treaty
NRF	NATO Response Force
NTBT	Nuclear Test Ban Treaty
ODA	Official Development Assistance
OECD	Organization of Economic Co-operation and Development
OPCW	Organization for the Prohibition of Chemical Weapons
OPEC	Organization of Petroleum Exporting Countries
OSCE	Organization for Security Co-operation in Europe
PA	Palestinian Authority
PAA	Partnership and Assisiation Agreement
PBA	Program-based approach
PDS	Party of Democratic Socialism (Partei des Demokratischen Sozialismus)
PLO	Palestinian Liberation Organization
ppm	parts per million
PRC	People's Republic of China
PRSP	Poverty Reduction Strategy Papers
PRT	Provincial Reconstruction Teams
PSI	Proliferation Security Initiative
ROSC	Reports on the Observations of Standards and Codes

SPD	Social Democratic Party (Sozialdemokratische Partei Deutschlands)
TACIS	Technical Assistance to the Commonwealth of Independent States
TRIPS	Agreement on Trade-Related Aspects of Intellectual Property Rights
UCK	Ushtria Çlirimtare e Kosovës (a paramilitarian Organization in Kosvo)
UNCED	United Nations Conference on Environment and Development (Rio de Janeiro, 1992)
UNFCCC	United Nations Framework Convention on Climate Change
UNMOVIC	United Nations Monitoring, Verification and Inspection Commission
UNOSOM II	United Nations Operation in Somalia II
UNSCOM	United Nations Special Commission
WEU	Western European Union
WMD	Weapons of mass destruction
WTO	World Trade Organization

Introduction

Hanns W. Maull

Since the unification of Germany on October 3, 1990, German foreign policy has represented a paradox: while the end of the east–west conflict transformed Germany itself, its European environment, and even the world at large, German foreign policy has insisted on continuity, and has indeed by and large determinedly stuck to its old course. Thus, Germany has embedded itself even more deeply in the European Communities and has continued to embrace membership in NATO (North Atlantic Treaty Organization) and participation in its integrated military structures, willingly trading aspects of its regained sovereignty for other foreign policy objectives, such as reassuring its partners. By supporting both the "deepening and widening" of existing international institutions and the creation of new ones, Germany remained faithful to its almost "reflexive" multilateralism. As for the participation of the Bundeswehr in military operations outside the traditional alliance context, Germany accommodated the demands of its allies and the new realities of international relations with visible reluctance and only after considerable soul-searching. Germany, in other words, continued to adhere to its traditional "culture of reticence" toward the use of force.

The paradox still persists, but the tensions, even contradictions, between its traditional "grand strategy"—or foreign policy role concept as a "civilian power"[1]—and a Germany, a Europe, a world of international relations so radically different from what they had been before 1990 have become increasingly apparent. To be sure, German foreign policy has tried to adjust, most visibly in the context of using Bundeswehr forces to prevent, through collective action, genocide and to secure peace and international stability. Yet, up until 2001, overall policy adjustment remained incremental. Even the country's participation in the NATO war against Serbia over Kosovo, without the international legitimacy provided by a UN Security Council Resolution authorizing the use of force (an action that has been characterized as a "coming of age" of the new Germany), represented in fact a mere modification of (West) Germany's traditional foreign policy role concept as a civilian power.[2]

Then came September 11, 2001, and in its aftermath another decisive shift in international relations. Eighteen months later, German–American relations experienced their most serious crisis since 1949, NATO was in deep trouble, and the European Union (EU) was split between an "old" and a "new" camp. Berlin readily seemed all but to abandon its traditional policy of maintaining equidistance between Washington and Paris, and moderating between the two whenever tensions threatened to undermine Germany's multiple alliances and the two countries' respective institutions. German foreign policy even showed signs of abandoning its reflexive multilateralism: in the autumn of 2002, Chancellor Gerhard Schröder ruled out any support for military action against Iraq even in the case of a UN Security Council Resolution authorizing the use of force. In late 2004, Berlin refused to permit German NATO officers to participate in a NATO-led mission to train Iraqi security forces, threatening the viability of some of NATO's planned operations in that context.

Will the paradox of German foreign policy—of policy continuity in a different world—thus come to an end in the era of Chancellor Schröder? It is too early to tell, but signs of change are clearly in the air. First, German foreign policy has shown signs of a loss of coherence, consistency, and above all effectiveness from about 1995 onward,[3] and with accelerating speed since mid-1999 (i.e., after the country's very successful diplomacy during and immediately after the Kosovo war). Moreover, the multiple crises in Germany's principal alliance contexts, the European Union and NATO, in 2002 and 2003 were not only, and not even principally, the result of incompatible political personalities or specific, unusual configurations, but rather the cumulative result of deep-seated, structural changes in transatlantic relations. In a nutshell, the crisis brought to light how much the world had changed—and how insufficient had been Germany's foreign policy adjustment to this new world.

The background: what we know about German foreign policy

Since unification, analysts of German foreign policy have been of two minds about their subject. During the Cold War, a broad consensus of scholars had stressed that the foreign policy of the postwar "Bonn Republic" displayed several distinctive characteristics, reflecting the heavy burden of Germany's wartime history and the "semisovereign" (Peter Katzenstein) nature of the Federal Republic.[4]

In contrast, after unification, there ensued a lively debate, both political and scholarly, about the likely future trajectory of German foreign policy.[5] Two catalysts triggered this debate: first, historical memories came back to haunt Germany's European partners and even Germans themselves; the question arose as to whether a unified German nation-state could live in peace with its neighbors. Second, there was a widespread view that German unification heralded a major shift in the European power equation, not only vis-à-vis the former Soviet Union with respect to Russia, but also within Western Europe.

This debate turned around the issue of "normalization." Protagonists of normalization argued that the end of the Cold War had altered Germany's position in the international system. The country had grown in territory, population, and economic output; it was now surrounded by friendly nations and—after the implosion of the Soviet empire and the Soviet Union itself—without a plausible strategic competitor on the continent. Thus, Germany was bound to become the "central power in Europe" (H. P. Schwarz),[6] a "world power by destiny" (C. Hacke),[7] or a "power state longing for hegemony" (G. Schöllgen).[8] Using a variety of realist and neorealist theoretical approaches, these authors held that Germany would shed its multilateral past, would become more competitive both in Europe and beyond, and would seek to maximize its gains within (but also increasingly beyond) international institutions.[9]

Skeptics of the normalization hypothesis, on the other hand, posited that Germany's postunification foreign policy would not really divert from its traditional trajectory. Continuity, rather than change, was expected because of Germany's embeddedness in international institutions and its particular foreign policy culture of restraint, which would survive changes both in the strategic environment and in the material base of its foreign policy. In this view, the Berlin Republic's foreign policy reflected that of a "tamed power,"[10] still seeking to shape its milieu rather than maximizing its positional goals,[11] a "trading power"[12] or a "civilian power"[13] that continued to be committed to deepening European and transatlantic integration, enhancing cooperative and multilateral conflict resolution, and resorting to force only as a last resort—and strictly within the framework of the United Nations.[14]

By the late 1990s, this debate had petered out, and a new consensus was emerging: broadly speaking, Germany had indeed remained a civilian power, though there clearly had been some adjustments in the Berlin Republic's foreign policy.[15] Just when this debate seemed settled, however, German foreign policy displayed unexpected signs of independence, assertion, and recalcitrance, triggered by the shockwaves of September 11, 2001, and the "Bush revolution" in US foreign policy.[16] First, Germany decided to deploy, for the first time ever, ground forces (namely, Special Forces, albeit in very small numbers) in combat missions in Afghanistan to help destroy remnants of Al Qaeda and the Taliban regime—admittedly with a mandate by the UN Security Council, but without the kind of normative, human rights justification that until then had driven Germany's willingness to resort to force; rather, the decision was motivated by the desire to demonstrate solidarity with the United States. Then, the issue of alleged Iraqi possession of weapons of mass destruction and how to deal with it divided both NATO and the European Union, and brought about Germany's defiance of the United States, its refusal to support coercive action even with a UN mandate, and the categorical rejection of any form of military participation in operations on Iraqi territory to subdue the old regime or pacify the country afterwards.

This unexpected departure from established patterns of German foreign policy behavior triggered a lively new debate among German academics and policy analysts.[17] Some academic observers interpreted these events as demonstrating that the "mainstream analysis" of German foreign policy since unification had tended to ignore important developments in the country's foreign policy that neither contradicted nor confirmed the hypothesis of foreign policy continuity; they argued that these developments were of an altogether different nature. While the earlier debate about "normalization" had turned around the substance of German foreign policy—that is, its self-ascribed norms, its perceived interests and objectives, its basic orientations and strategies, and its preferred instruments—the changes now becoming apparent seemed related to a shrinking resource base and to the policy process, as well as to fundamental disagreements with the United States over the future of world order.

What forces of change have been identified in this most recent debate about German foreign policy? Realist scholars have challenged old notions about German gains in relative power in Europe[18] and have pointed to diverging interests, values, and preferred strategies between Germany and the United States.[19] Another set of structural factors that has been identified to account for the Red–Green coalition's foreign policy conduct has been erosion of both material and immaterial resources for its foreign and security policy.[20] Thus, budget allocations for the foreign policy sector have diminished by about 40 percent in real terms from their peak in the late 1980s,[21] and serious structural weaknesses in Germany's economic performance have begun to affect the conduct and also the direction of the country's foreign policy.[22] Arguing that parallels exist between foreign policy making and the deep structural impediments to reform in German domestic politics, these authors stress the growing mismatch between the challenges of a rapidly globalizing international environment to foreign and security policy and, by comparison, its rather modest response, constrained by escalating fiscal burdens and misguided political priorities in the allocation of resources through the federal budget. Hence, as illustrated by a continually postponed reform of the Bundeswehr,[23] or more recently by German efforts to loosen the fiscal constraints of the European Stability and Growth Pact, on which it had itself insisted when arrangements for introducing the euro were negotiated, Germany is increasingly ill-prepared to deal with pressing new international problems.

Constructivist and institutionalist scholars have stressed processes of policy learning and socialization to account for changing behavioral patterns such as increased Bundeswehr participation in out-of-area missions. Thus, Adrian Hyde-Price and Charlie Jeffery argue in their analysis of the "normalization" of the Schröder government's European policy that, in Germany, policy learning took place against the background of the failure of Western (and, specifically, German) efforts to contain violent conflicts in the former Yugoslavia. Similarly, several authors have stressed the importance of "processes of socialization" through Germany's membership in the European Union.[24]

This literature also taps the much broader research on the "Europeanization" of member states—that is, the "emergence and development at the European level of distinct structures of governance"[25]—arguing that "Europeanization" has changed nation-states, their domestic institutions, and their national political cultures.[26] There is indeed evidence that membership in the European Union has modified Germany's foreign and security policy by limiting policy choices, shifting competences, and creating new understandings of common purpose and institutional mechanisms of compliance,[27] and also by enhancing the reach of national foreign policies.

Finally, another development that may account for a more comprehensive change in the Berlin Republic's foreign policy outlook is generational change. This argument holds that Germany's leading policy makers, especially those in prominent positions in the Red–Green coalition, do not share the same postwar experiences of "loss and shame" as their predecessors and that they are thus more candid and assertive in expressing German national interests.[28] While this "generational hypothesis" has also been applied to the foreign policy positions of other nations, such as the United States, the argument may have particular explanatory power in the German case since the country's wartime history has played a prominent role in several recent accounts of German foreign, European, and security policies.[29]

A changing German foreign policy: the puzzles

In this book, we have started with the premise that German foreign policy has indeed undergone subtle but important mutations, some of which seem to go against the grain of the country's traditional foreign policy orientation as a civilian power. In our view, the debate on whether Germany is a normal country or not has diverted attention away from three persistent and increasing problems in German foreign policy making: first, the growing complexity and intractability of the country's foreign policy environment and the erosion of the material, institutional, and "soft power" foundations of Germany's foreign policy both abroad and at home (i.e., the weakening of the EU, NATO, the OSCE (Organization for Security Co-operation in Europe), but also of the Bundeswehr and the diplomatic corps); second, a declining commitment to foreign policy substance by the political class, which allowed subnational actors to capture more aspects of foreign policy and thus produced uncertainty about the purposes of German foreign policy; and, third, a loss of coherence and consistency resulting from the proliferation of actors and interests in foreign policy.

The evolution of Germany's relative power since unification, and the implications of any shift in power in Europe, are far from obvious. This is our first puzzle: has unification really made Germany more powerful? While there has been a widespread assumption that Germany's power has increased since 1990, even a cursory glance at indicators of the country's relative power base (e.g., the development of the gross national product, of military spending and capabilities, or of demographic trends) suggests that this is dubious.[30] Comparing power resources, however, in any case is a notoriously difficult and crude form of measuring power. In this volume, we will pursue a different approach, that of analyzing *policy outcomes*. That is, we will ask: what has been the influence of Germany within its principal institutional contexts?

Our second puzzle concerns the purposes of German foreign policy, its role concept. Is Germany's foreign policy still following its traditional basic guidelines ("never again," "never alone," and "politics before force")? In other words, does the country still behave like a civilian power? Are the changes in foreign policy behavior only minor modifications, reflecting adaptation and adjustment to a different external environment and changed expectations by others? Or have they begun to affect the core substance of German foreign policy, foreshadowing a new, fundamentally different role concept? In other words: how does German foreign policy see itself, and what does it want?

The third puzzle concerns the policy process. How has the performance of German foreign policy been affected by changes in its domestic, regional, and international environment? What has been the effect of resource constraints? How has German foreign policy tried to adjust?

From a theoretical perspective, our arguments will try to shed light on some gaps in recent accounts of Germany's foreign policy. The first gap is the tendency to assume a unitary Germany foreign policy that pursues a coherent strategy, while in fact more and more domestic policy areas are addressed and administered by international institutions such as the European Union, and, partly as a consequence, domestic actors have become much more important for policy makers.

Second, there has been a trend in recent literature on Germany's foreign policy to suppose that there is a stable and somewhat congenial institutional international context and reliable partners for Germany's peculiar foreign policy orientation as a civilian power. However, as international institutions had to address new challenges, such as the proliferation of ethnic conflicts, or weapons of mass destruction, the difficult question arose as to how these institutions should be reformed, which institution should fulfill which task, how the moderation of policy conflicts within the institutions could be managed effectively, and where the necessary political and financial support for these institutions might come from as they are asked to shoulder ever more policy responsibilities from national governments. As a result, international institutions have experienced serious difficulties in adjusting to a new world, weakening their capacity to underpin international cooperation. Similarly, Germany's most important partners—the United States and France—also had to adjust to this new environment. This resulted in a loss of reliability and predictability in those countries' policies toward Germany. The United States, in particular, under President George W. Bush, seemed increasingly reluctant to rely on institutionalized forms of conflict resolution,[31] and in the aftermath of 9/11 embarked on a new, radically different foreign policy course.[32]

Third, while Germany's traditional foreign policy style has included a strong proclivity toward cooperative and common security, expressed by initiatives such as the OSCE, the Balkan Stability Pact, the Petersberg Process for Afghanistan, these and other regional and international institutions have often been incapable of coping effectively with protracted violent conflicts and the complexities of humanitarian intervention and state building, conflict resolution, and the prevention of the proliferation of weapons of mass destruction. Many analysts of German foreign policy have tended to underestimate the persistent problems of violence between and within states and the difficulties of containing and resolving them.

Structure of the book

The research objectives of this book will be approached through a series of policy case studies, which are designed to give a comprehensive picture of the evolution of German foreign policy in the decade since the mid-1990s. Part I deals with domestic and European sources of German foreign policy, exploring both constraints and opportunities. The contribution by August Pradetto focuses on the evolution of foreign policy norms and public attitudes; Alister Miskimmon and William Paterson explore the implications of domestic economic constraints and the implications of the Europeanization of German foreign policies. In Part II, we take a closer look at the foreign policy sector in which changes have been most visible and perhaps most far-reaching: (military) security policy. Harald Müller analyzes German nonproliferation policies and finds both substantial changes in the early 1990s and remarkable continuity since then; Martin Wagener explores changing German policies toward the use of force, which he interprets as a process of "normalization," and Marco Overhaus looks into the difficult balancing act German security policy has been trying to conduct between NATO and the efforts to develop a European Security and Defense Policy.

Part III deals with the key core bilateral relationships in German foreign policy with France and the United States, each of which lies at the heart of a broader, multilateral framework for cooperation and integration, the European Union and NATO. Taking up some of the themes developed by Miskimmon and Paterson in their chapter, Sebastian Harnisch and Siegfried Schieder assess and evaluate new elements in Germany's policies toward the European Union; Hans Stark takes stock of the ups and downs of the Franco–German relationship, while Stephen Szabo and Peter Rudolf look, from their respective sides of the Atlantic, at the turmoil in German–American relations. Ambassador Günther Joetze concludes this part with a reflection on Germany's policies toward the Balkans and Russia, which have been driven by the search for ways to bring stability and prosperity to those as yet unstable parts of the pan-European theatre.

Part IV addresses environmental and economic policy issues (though we are acutely aware of the linkages between economics, the environment, and security, and certainly reject the old distinction between "high" and "low" politics), with Andreas Falke examining changes in German foreign trade policies, Reinhard Wolf assessing policies toward financial markets and exchange rates, Detlef Sprinz analyzing Germany's claim to international environmental leadership, and Friedemann Müller exploring the failure of German and European energy policies to integrate energy, environmental, and security objectives.

Part V starts with an assessment by Peter Molt of German foreign economic assistance policies to promote development in what used to be called the Third World. Martin Beck explores whether German policies toward the Israeli–Arab conflict have been compatible with the role concept of a civilian power, while Jörn-Carsten Gottwald explores a dimension of German foreign policy in which Germany has behaved like a trading, rather than a civilian, power: bi- and multilateral relations with Pacific Asia.

In the course of this project, I have had the good fortune to find much support and assistance, and I am profoundly grateful to all those who have made this book possible. My thanks go above all to my colleagues at the University of Trier, Marco Overhaus, Siegfried Schieder, Martin Wagener, and above all Sebastian Harnisch, who has worked on this with me from the beginning. In many ways, this book is his as much as mine. I also gratefully acknowledge the manifold support of Constantin Grund, Bettina Hauptmann, Christos Katsioulis, Ruth Linden, Nicole Molitor, and Veit Swoboda and, last but certainly not least, Christine Ann Rupp in Trier. We were able to bring together many of the authors, as well as a number of other scholars and experts from Germany and abroad, to discuss earlier drafts, as well as other issues relating to German foreign policy. This has been a wonderful opportunity to take stock of that policy, with our cues taken from a keynote speech given by one of the parliamentary stalwarts of Germany's foreign policy in the past, Karl Lamers. We appreciate very much his willingness to share his thoughts with us and to inspire us intellectually. The conference was made possible by the generous financial support of the *Stiftung Volkswagenwerk*, the *Arbeitsstelle Internationale Beziehungen* at the University of Trier, and the *Bundeszentrale für politische Bildung Brühl Conference Centre*, which also graciously hosted the conference. Alfred Schmidt from *Volkswagenstiftung* and Christoph Müller-Hofstede from the *Bundeszentrale* have also given much valuable support and advice. We also recognize gratefully the organizational wizardry and intellectual wit of Stephan Böckenförde in bringing us all together in Brühl. Debi Howell-Ardila has greatly improved the readability of our sometimes somewhat teutonic English, and despite major upheavals in her own life has sub-edited the whole volume with unstinting dedication and truly professional skill. Alison Howson has been infallibly supportive, charming, competent, and patient in shepherding this project through the editorial process. They all deserve much of the credit for what we have achieved together in this volume; blame for errors or omissions, however, should as usual be addressed solely to the editor.

Notes

1 For an exploration of the theoretical background of the use of role concepts in analyzing foreign policy generally, and the "civilian power" concept in particular, see Knut Kirste and Hanns W. Maull, "Zivilmacht und Rollentheorie," *Zeitschrift für Internationale Beziehungen* (referred to hereafter as *ZIB*) 3: 2 (1996): 283–312; and Knut Kirste, *Rollentheorie und Außenpolitikanalyse. Die USA und Deutschland als Zivilmächte* (Frankfurt am Main: Lang, 1998).

2 See, for a thorough analysis of the evidence, Hanns W. Maull, "Germany and the Use of Force: Still a 'Civilian Power'?," *Survival*, 42: 2 (2000): 56–80; and Kerry A. Longhurst, "Strategic Culture: The Key to Understanding German Security Policy?," PhD dissertation, Birmingham University, Institute for German Studies, 2000.

3 Cf. Hanns W. Maull, "Quo vadis, Germania? Außenpolitik in einer Welt des Wandels," *Blätter für deutsche und internationale Politik*, 42: 10 (1997): 1245–56.

4 Cf. Peter J. Katzenstein, *Policy and Politics in West Germany: The Growth of a Semisovereign State* (Philadelphia: Temple University Press, 1987). See also Hans-Peter Schwarz, *Die gezähmten Deutschen. Von der Machtbesessenheit zur Machtvergessenheit* (Stuttgart: dva, 1985); Helga Haftendorn, *Sicherheit und Entspannung. Zur Außenpolitik der Bundesrepublik Deutschland 1955–1982* (Baden-Baden: Nomos, 1983); and Wolfram F. Hanrieder, *Deutschland, Europa, Amerika. Die Außenpolitik der Bundesrepublik Deutschland 1949–1994* (Paderborn: Schöningh, 1995).

5 Thus far, there has been no comprehensive and systematic overview of this debate. For an introduction see, Philip H. Gordon, "The Normalization of German Foreign Policy," *Orbis*, 38: 2 (1994): 225–43; Gunther Hellmann, "Goodbye Bismarck? The Foreign Policy of Contemporary Germany," *Mershon International Studies Review* 40/S1 (1996): 1–39, and Gunther Hellmann, "Jenseits von 'Normalisierung' und 'Militarisierung': Zur Standortdebatte über die neue deutsche

Außenpolitik," *Aus Politik und Zeitgeschichte*, B 1–2 (1997): 24–33. Cf. also A. James McAdams, "Germany after Unification. Normal At Last?," *World Politics*, 49 (1997): 282–308, and Ingo Peters, "Vom 'Scheinzwerg' zum 'Scheinriesen'. Deutsche Außenpolitik in der Analyse," *Zeitschrift für International Beziehungen*, 4: 2 (1997): 361–88. Cf. also Douglas Webber, ed., *New Europe, New Germany, Old Foreign Policy? German Foreign Policy since Unification* (London: Frank Cass, 2001); Adrian Hyde-Price and Charlie Jeffery, "Germany in the European Union: Constructing Normality," *Journal of Common Market Studies*, 39: 4 (2001): 689–717.

6   Hans-Peter Schwarz, *Die Zentralmacht Europas. Deutschlands Rückkehr auf die Weltbühne* (Berlin: Siedler, 1994).

7   Christian Hacke, *Weltmacht wieder Willen? Die Außenpolitik der Bundesrepublik Deutschland*, Second edition (Berlin: Ullstein, 1993).

8   Gunther Hellmann, "Rekonstruktion der 'Hegemonie des Machtstaates Deutschland unter modernen Bedingungen'? Zwischenbilanzen nach zehn Jahren neuer deutscher Außenpolitik, Beitrag zum 21." Kongress der Deutschen Vereinigung für Politische Wissenschaft in Halle/Saale, October 1–5, 2000. Available at: http://www.soz.uni-frankfurt.de/hellmann/mat/hellmann-halle.pdf. Accessed February 2, 2004; Inge Schwammel, *Deutschlands Aufstieg zur Großmacht. Die Instrumentalisierung der Europäischen Integration, 1974–1994* (Frankfurt am Main: P. Lang, 1997).

9   Cf. John J. Mearsheimer, "Back to the Future. Instability in Europe after the Cold War," *International Security*, 15: 1 (1990): 5–56; Kenneth N. Waltz, "The Emerging Structure of International Politics," *International Security*, 18: 2 (1993): 44–79; Rainer Baumann *et al.*, "Macht und Machtpolitik. Neorealistische Außenpolitiktheorie und Prognosen über die deutsche Außenpolitik nach der Vereinigung," *Zeitschrift für Internationale Beziehungen*, 6: 2 (1999): 245–86.

10 Peter Katzenstein, *Tamed Power. Germany in Europe* (Ithaca: Cornell University Press, 1997).

11 Cf. Andrei Markovits and Simon Reich, *The German Predicament. Memory and Power in the New Europe* (Ithaca: Cornell University Press, 1997); Simon Bulmer, Charlie Jeffery, and William Paterson, *Germany's European diplomacy. Shaping the regional milieu* (Manchester: Manchester University Press, 2000).

12 Richard Rosecrance, *The Rise of the Trading State. Commerce and Conquest in the Modern World* (New York: Basic Books, 1986), and Michael Staack, *Handelsstaat Deutschland. Deutsche Außenpolitik in einem neuen internationalen System* (Paderborn: Schöningh, 2000).

13 Hanns W. Maull, "Germany and Japan: The New Civilian Powers," *Foreign Affairs* 69: 5 (1990/91): 91–106; Sebastian Harnisch and Hanns W. Maull, eds, *Germany— Still A Civilian Power? The Foreign Policy of the Berlin Republic* (Manchester: Manchester University Press, 2001); and Henning Tewes, *Germany, Civilian Power and the New Europe. Enlarging NATO and the European Union* (New York: Palgrave, 2002).

14 Cf. Thomas Berger, *Cultures of Anti-Militarism. National Security in Germany and Japan* (Baltimore: Johns Hopkins University Press, 1998); Thomas Banchoff, *The German Problem Transformed. Institutions, Politics, and Foreign Policy, 1945–1995* (Ann Arbor: MIT Press, 1999); Longhurst, "Strategic Culture: The Key to Understanding German Security Policy?" (see note 2); Volker Rittberger, ed., *German Foreign Policy since Unification. Theories and Case Studies* (Manchester: Manchester University Press, 2001).

15 Cf. Stephen F. Szabo, *Germany: Strategy and Defense at a Turning Point* (Washington, DC: American Institute for Contemporary German Studies, 1999).

16 Ivo M. Daalder and James M. Lindsay, *America Unbound, The Bush Revolution in Foreign Policy* (Washington, DC: Brookings, 2003).

17 The debate was conducted in journals such as *WeltTrends*, 42 and 43 (2004); *Die Internationale Politik*, 58: 9 (September 2003) and 60:1 (January 2005), *Aus Politik und Zeitgeschichte*, B 11/2004 (March 18, 2004), among others. Cf. Gunther Hellmann, "Sag beim Abschied leise servus. Die Zivilmacht Deutschland beginnt, eine neues 'Selbst' zu behaupten," *Politische Vierteljahresschrift*, 43: 3 (2002): 498–507; Gunther Hellmann, "Agenda 2020. Krise und Perspektive der deutschen Außenpolitik," *Internationale Politik*, 58: 9 (2003): 39–50; James Sperling, "The Foreign Policy of the Berlin Republic. The Very Model of a post-Modern Major Power?" *German Politics*, 12: 3 (2003): 1–34; Hanns W. Maull, "Auf leisen Sohlen aus der Außenpolitik?," *Internationale Politik*, 58: 9 (2003): 19–30; Hans-Peter Schwarz, "Von Elefanten und Bibern. Die Gleichgewichtsstörung deutscher Außenpolitik," *Internationale Politik*, 58: 5 (2003): 31–38; Christian Hacke, "Deutschland, Europa und der Irakkonflikt," *Aus Politik und Zeitgeschichte*, B 24–25 (2003): 8–16; Hanns W. Maull, Sebastian Harnisch, and Constantin Grund, eds, *Deutschland im Abseits?* (Baden-Baden: Nomos, 2003); Kerry Longhurst, *Germany and the use of force, The evolution of German security policy 1990–2003* (Manchester/New York: Manchester University Press, 2004).

18 Cf. Sperling, *German Politics* (see note 17).

19 Cf. Stephen F. Szabo, *Parting Ways, The Crisis in German–American Relations* (Washington, DC: Brookings Institution, 2004).

20 Cf. Maull, *Blätter für deutsche und internationale Politik* (see note 3); see also Hanns W. Maull, "Die deutsche Außenpolitik am Ende der Ära Kohl," *Jahrbuch für Internationale Sicherheitspolitik 1999*, Erich Reiter, ed. (Hamburg: E. S. Mittler, 1998), pp. 274–95; also Maull, *Internationale Politik* and Hellmann, *Internationale Politik* (see note 17).

21 Frank Sauer, "Daten zu den Ausgaben des Bundes für die deutsche Außenpolitik im Zeitraum 1981–2001, zusammengestellt für den Beitrag von Gunther Hellmann 'Agenda 2020,' " *Die Internationale Politik*, 58: 9 (2003): 39–50. Available at: http://www.soz.unifankfurt.de/hellmann/mat/IP_09_2003_Daten_www.pdf.

22 Cf. Szabo, *Parting Ways* (see note 19).

23 Cf. Johannes Varwick, "Die Reform der Bundeswehr, Konturen und Defizite einer nicht geführten Debatte," *Gegenwartskunde* 3/2000: 321–32.

24 Cf. Hyde-Price and Jeffery, *Journal of Common Market Studies* (see note 5).

25 Maria G. Cowles, James Caporaso, and Thomas Risse, eds, *Transforming Europe. Europeanization and Domestic Change* (Ithaca, NY: Cornell University Press, 2001).

26 Cf. Michèle Knodt and Beate Kohler-Koch, eds, *Deutschland zwischen Europäisierung und Selbstbehauptung, Mannheimer Jahrbuch für europäische Sozialforschung*, Bd. 5 (Frankfurt am Main: Campus, 2000).

27 Axel Lüdeke, *Europäisierung der deutschen Außen- und Sicherheitspolitik. Konstitutive und operative Europapolitik zwischen Maastricht und Amsterdam* (Opladen: Leske, 2002).

28 Cf. Hellmann, *Politische Vierteljahresschrift* (see note 17).

29 Cf. Berger, *Cultures of Anti-Militarism* (see note 14); also Jonathan Bach, "Between Sovereignty and Integration. German Foreign Policy and National Identity after 1989" (Münster: Lit Verlag, 1999. See also Banchoff, *The German Problem Transformed* (see note 14) and Longhurst, *German Strategic Culture: The Key to Understanding German Security Policy* (see note 2).

30 What a systematic comparative analysis of the power resource base of major countries shows is mostly the implosion of Soviet/Russian power. Excluding that

factor, Germany's relative position vis-à-vis other Western countries has declined. (Rainer Baumann, Volker Rittberger, and Wolfgang Wagner, "*Macht und Machtpolitik: Neorealistische Außenpolitiktheorie und Prognosen für die deutsche Außenpolitik nach der Vereinigung,*" Tübinger Arbeitspapiere zur Internationalen Politik und Friedensforschung, No. 30 (Tubingen, 1998).

31 Cf. John van Oudenaren, "What is 'Multilateral'?," *Policy Review,* 117 (2003). Available at: http://www.policyreview.org/feb03/oudenaren/print.html. Accessed on February 1, 2004.

32 Cf. Daalder and Lindsay, *America Unbound* (see note 16).

Part I

Domestic and European Sources of German Foreign Policy

1
The Polity of German Foreign Policy: Changes since Unification

August Pradetto

Introduction

As with all politics, the study of German foreign policy needs to consider not only the policies themselves but also the politics and the polity behind them. This chapter will focus on two specific aspects of polity—namely, the norms and the political culture behind German foreign policy. "Polity" encompasses basic normative, usually constitutionally enshrined, elements, as well as certain other structural elements of politics that—as the result of historically grown "condensed politics"—channel political processes and thus are essential prerequisites for political actions.[1]

For the purposes of this chapter, the norms behind German foreign policy consist of those enshrined in the *Grundgesetz* (Basic Law) of the Federal Republic of Germany (FRG), in its laws, and in the rulings of the Bundesverfassungsgericht (Federal Constitutional Court, FCC). The foreign policy culture is formed according to the orientations of the country's elites and the general population; it reflects Germany's specific historic experiences and the conclusions drawn from them and finds expression in relatively stable attitudes and positions taken vis-à-vis other nations.

Normative premises of German foreign policy

Germany's constitutional order not only defines the fundamental parameters for the conduct of politics, but it also expresses its political culture and translates it into basic legal norms. The Basic Law of 1949—which, with several amendments, has been retained as the constitution of the Berlin Republic—contains a number of key principles for the country's external relations. They are found in Articles 1 and 9, paragraph 2, as well as in Articles 23 through 26. Among those, the following four major maxims stand out:[2]

First, the Basic Law obliges state authorities and all citizens to work for the maintenance of international peace in their relations with other countries under all circumstances. This is most clearly expressed in the provisions of

Article 26, in which "acts tending to and undertaken with the intent to disturb peaceful relations between nations, especially preparations for aggressive war" are deemed unconstitutional and are considered a punishable offense.

Second, the Basic Law commits German foreign policy to cooperative internationalism; to this end, the constitution explicitly provides for the possible transfer of sovereign powers to intergovernmental institutions. These principles of the Bonn Basic Law have been rightly interpreted as a constitutional task to pursue an active European policy.[3] Article 24 specifically allows the integration of the Federal Republic of Germany into NATO, as the FCC clearly underlined in its ruling of July 12, 1994, concerning missions of the Bundeswehr abroad.[4]

Third, the Basic Law obliges all state authorities and citizens to respect human rights. A fourth basic principle, unification, was dropped as of October 3, 1990. Instead, Article 23, as well as the revised preamble to the Basic Law, underline the close ties of reunited Germany with the European Union and commit it to the realization of a united Europe. Article 23 also defines the preconditions for a further transfer of sovereignty.

The need to revise and reinterpret the Basic Law became apparent in the 1990s as a result of three overlapping developments. The first development concerned political change in Europe in the context of unification; the second resulted from the ongoing European integration in which the FRG had played an active part under the coalition governments of both the Christian Democratic Union (CDU), the Christian Social Union (CSU), with the Free Democratic Party (FDP) and the Social Democratic Party (SPD), with Alliance 90/The Greens. The third development had to do with the dismemberment of multinational states after the collapse of communism from the late 1980s onward, and the humanitarian interventions of the international community in some of the pursuant conflicts. In this context, the Bundeswehr was deployed in several peacekeeping and combat missions in the former Yugoslavia (Bosnia–Herzegovina, Kosovo, Macedonia). The terrorist attacks of September 11, 2001, on New York and Washington created yet another dimension of Bundeswehr missions abroad, with controversial consequences.

Unification and its normative consequences

Internationally, Germany's reunion took place in the context of the Two-Plus-Four Treaty. In it, the four occupation powers—the United States, France, the United Kingdom, and the Soviet Union—as well as the FRG and the German Democratic Republic (GDR) jointly agreed in Moscow on September 12, 1990, to terminate the rights and responsibilities of the allied powers and to reestablish the complete sovereignty of the reunited Germany over its internal and external affairs.[5] In this Treaty, Germany renounced the manufacture and possession of nuclear, biological, and chemical weapons and committed itself to reduce its armed forces to 370,000 within four years, as well as to the recognition of Poland's western border. In the German–Polish Border Treaty of November 14, 1990,[6] the Oder–Neisse line was confirmed as being the border line between the two states.

European integration

After tough negotiations, the Treaty on the European Union was adopted at the European summit in Maastricht in December 1991.[7] With the establishment of the European Union as the new framework for the European Communities (EC), integration gained a new quality. Thus, with the Economic and Monetary Union, one of the key elements of national sovereignty (the power to issue and manage one's own currency) was transferred to a supranational institution and a number of new policy areas—namely, the Common Foreign and Security Policy (CFSP) and cooperation in justice and home affairs—became part of the second and third of the three "pillars" of the new European Union (EU).[8]

Fears that the Maastricht decisions could interfere with the basic rights and the competences of the German *Länder* prompted several German members of the Green party in the European Parliament to oppose the amendment of Article 23 of the Basic Law and the Maastricht Treaty by bringing the case before the FCC, claiming that those passages were unconstitutional. In its so-called Maastricht ruling of October 12, 1993,[9] the Court found that democratic rights could indeed be violated "if the exercise of the powers of the German Parliament (*Bundestag*) passed to such an extent to an EU/EC organ established by the governments that the [...] indispensable minimum requirements for democratic legitimation of the sovereign power vis-à-vis its citizens were no longer met." But the FCC rejected that this had been the case. In its arguments, it evoked the "uninterrupted chain of legitimation" from the people through the democratically elected national parliament and the government in power to EU institutions and noted that the Maastricht Treaty enhanced the competences of the European Parliament. In essence, the FCC thus confirmed the prointegration orientation of German foreign policy. The Law on the Treaty of Amsterdam (of October 2, 1997) promulgated on April 16, 1998 brought further new legal norms to German foreign policy.[10] The new Title IIIa of the EC Treaty on visas, asylum, immigration, and free movement of people established rules for transposing into community law the right to asylum, the mutual recognition of EU member states as "safe" countries of origin, and—with the integration of the Schengen agreements—the shift of border controls from the internal to the external borders of the European Union. Other provisions concerned the strengthening of the CFSP by making the Western European Union an integral part of the European Union, by the appointment of the Secretary General of the EU Council as High Representative for CFSP, and by changes in external trade relations. With regard to EU institutions, agreement was reached, inter alia, on the strengthening of the competences of the European Parliament through extending the co-decision procedure, the extension of qualified majority voting in the council, the consent of the European Parliament to the appointment of the commission president, and the possibility of enhanced cooperation between certain member states. On June 15, 1998, the law for the introduction of the euro[11] was promulgated. The changeover date for the introduction of the euro currency and the end of the deutsche Mark as legal tender was set for the turn of the year 2001–02.

Changes for German foreign policy also occurred after ratification of the Treaty of Nice signed by the FRG on February 26, 2001.[12] The Treaty included new rules on weighting votes in the council, on the future size and composition of the commission, on extending the areas for decision making by qualified majority voting, and on the CFSP, in particular in the area of the European Security and Defense Policy (ESDP).

Security policy

In addition, since 1990 a number of new legal rules and obligations were established through international agreements concerning security policy. First of all, the Treaty on Conventional Armed Forces in Europe[13] signed in Paris on November 19, 1990, set limitations for the five most important categories of conventional weapons systems (battle tanks, armored combat vehicles, artillery, combat aircraft, and attack helicopters) and established a verification regime ensuring compliance with the provisions by exchange of information and inspections. On March 24, 1992, Germany participated in the signing of the Open Skies Treaty in Helsinki,[14] which opened the air space of the parties to this Treaty (NATO states and former Warsaw Pact countries) between Vancouver and Vladivostok and outlined procedures to conduct observation flights over the territories of states parties. As a participant of the Conference on Security and Cooperation in Europe (CSCE), Germany signed the Convention on Conciliation and Arbitration within the CSCE[15] in Stockholm on December 15, 1992, which stipulated the establishment of a Court of Conciliation and Arbitration for the peaceful settlement of disputes between member states of the CSCE in Geneva.

At their Prague summit in January 1994, NATO members decided to institutionalize security policy and military cooperation with the former Warsaw Pact countries and the successor states of the Soviet Union, as well as with other European nations, in a "Partnership for Peace" program.[16] On this basis the FRG engaged in a great number of military cooperation efforts with the neighboring countries to the east. The law on the NATO accession of Poland, the Czech Republic, and Hungary promulgated on April 14, 1998 was a further important step toward the intensification of relations with the neighboring states to the east.[17] Lastly, the basis for German foreign and security policy was affected by the ratification of the law on the protocols to the North Atlantic Treaty of March 26, 2003 concerning the accession of Bulgaria, Estonia, Latvia, Lithuania, Romania, Slovakia, and Slovenia.[18]

With regard to the fight against terrorism, new legal bases had already been created prior to the terrorist attacks of 2001, and the provisions of the agreement of the UN General Assembly on fighting terrorism, dated December 15, 1997,[19] had been incorporated in the constitution.[20] Moreover, on July 20, 2000, the FRG signed the International Convention of the United Nations for the Suppression of the Financing of Terrorism, dated December 9, 1999.[21]

The law on the Rome Statute of the International Criminal Court, dated July 17, 1998,[22] was also of relevance to Germany's future foreign policy decisions and for its position vis-à-vis the United States against the backdrop of an increasingly acrimonious debate with Washington on this subject. The statute provides for the establishment of the International Criminal Court as a permanent institution with its seat in The Hague; the United States refused to join the Court.

As far as the areas of arms control and disarmament are concerned, the Chemical Weapons Convention, which bans the development, production, stockpiling, and use of chemical weapons, was signed in Paris on January 13, 1993.[23] The convention, which Germany has joined, requires parties to destroy all chemical weapons in their possession and all chemical weapons production facilities. At an international conference of states held in Oslo on September 18, 1997 and at a conference of signatory states on December 3, 1997, the FRG also participated in the creation of a Convention on the Prohibition of Anti-Personnel Mines.[24]

The Bundeswehr (Federal Armed Forces)

Although the Federal Armed Forces had already participated in numerous humanitarian aid missions—for example, in Cambodia in the years 1991–93 and Somalia in 1993—it was only in the middle of the 1990s that the scope of Bundeswehr missions was extended to include "robust" peacekeeping and peace-enforcement missions under the roof of the United Nations or NATO. The FCC played a critical role in this context: after respective actions had been brought against the German government in connection with the control of the weapons embargo against former Yugoslavia by the German Navy and Air Force, the monitoring of the flight ban over Bosnia by German AWACS (Airborne Warning and Control System) crew members and the participation in the UNOSOM II (United Nations Operation in Somalia II) mission in Somalia, the Court ruled on July 12, 1994[25] that the deployment of the Bundeswehr in peacekeeping operations was permissible within the framework of systems of collective security, as long as such systems were "strictly bound to the preservation of peace."[26] In its ruling, it referred to Article 24, paragraph 2 of the Basic Law, which allows the FRG to join such a system in support of the participation of the Bundeswehr in operations exceeding self-defense and alliance defense within the framework of NATO, and where the judges made reference to the preamble to the North Atlantic

Treaty, whereby the alliance constitutes a security system in which the members unite their efforts for collective defense and for the preservation of peace and security.

For a Bundeswehr mission under United Nations or NATO command to be legal, the Federal Constitutional Court imposed another condition: the federal government may not decide alone – the *Bundestag* must endorse such a decision.[27] On that basis, decisions were taken on *Bundeswehr* missions and their prolongations in Bosnia–Herzegovina (1995), in Kosovo (1999), in Macedonia (2001), and in Afghanistan (2001) as well as on measures to fight international terrorism.

In connection with the participation of German soldiers in NATO AWACS missions in Turkey in March 2003, the Free Democratic Party parliamentary faction in the Bundestag filed a complaint with the FCC with the intention of forcing the government to involve the *Bundestag* in this matter. The Court, however, dismissed the case on the grounds that an involvement of the *Bundestag* in the decision making on the deployment of German soldiers would be required when combat actions were imminent.[28] Since NATO's only mission in this case was to control the air space and to protect Turkey against attacks from Iraq, no armed engagement was expected. The Court also evoked the government's freedom of decision making in matters of foreign policy: as long as it did not violate parliamentary law, it was up to the government to decide how Germany would participate in executing the decision of NATO's Defense Planning Committee of February 19, 2003.

Another ruling of the FCC (on November 22, 2001[29]) displayed a similar reasoning, when it dismissed the case brought by the Bundestag faction of the Party of Democratic Socialism (PDS, the successor to the Communist Party), challenging the legality of the federal government's decision to adopt NATO's new strategic concept of April 1999 without *Bundestag* approval. This concept had been adopted by the NATO Council to develop NATO's ability to cope with the full range of crisis management tasks, including military crisis response operations. The PDS saw in the new NATO concept an inadmissible extension of the alliance's purpose beyond collective defense as defined in Article 5 of the North Atlantic Treaty, an extension not covered by the NATO Treaty and the related law of approval of the Bundestag. But the Court rejected this position; in its view, the new NATO concept did not entail any amendment to the NATO Treaty and therefore did not need Bundestag approval.

Overall, since 1994 the Federal Constitutional Court has sought to pursue a complex balancing act. On the one hand, the Court sought to protect and enhance the government's decision-making power and limit possible international damage—for example, if international commitments need to involve participation of German armed forces in NATO operations abroad.[30] On the other hand, the FCC has been wary to break with the established, restrictive interpretation of the Basic Law. Thus, in its detailed statements explaining its decisions, the Court has hinted that it might refuse legitimation in analogous situations in the future. In the end, it is a game of give and take between law and politics. If a Bundestag majority supports the government, the Court will be guided by this in its rulings – that is, politics influences judicial decisions. On the other hand, the judicial norms governing the use of force have developed in the course of a long historical process, and a culture of reticence concerning the interpretation of the law has been established, which serves as a guideline for policy makers and works as a factor of continuity.

The foreign policy culture of the Federal Republic of Germany

The concept of political culture was developed originally by Gabriel A. Almond and Sidney Verba.[31] They understood political culture as being made up of a multitude of attitudes, values, and feelings that give the political process order and meaning; political culture is thus the subjective psychological dimension of politics. Applied to foreign policy, political culture may be understood as the "totality of the historically grown, (foreign) politically important, and over time relatively stable attitudes and modes of behavior of society" vis-à-vis foreign policy.[32] Political culture thus legitimates foreign policy and determines the orientation of its actions. It manifests itself in the form of guidelines for action that are inherent in the role concepts of the decision makers.[33] Values are crucially important in this context, as they define goals and interests of a nation's foreign policy.

Definition of Germany's foreign policy culture

The beginnings of a postwar foreign policy culture in Germany lay in the hands of a small political elite and the occupation powers. Germany's new foreign policy culture was shaped by the experiences of National Socialism, war, and defeat. The new foreign policy culture developed through consensus building in the political elite before it took hold, and through socialization in the population as a whole. By the 1960s, the foreign policy culture of what Hanns W. Maull termed Germany's "civilian power" had largely consolidated. The foundations for political culture laid at that time still exist today. Studies reveal that only a few partial areas have undergone modifications; otherwise, there is a high degree of continuity.

According to Kerry Longhurst,[34] Germany's foreign policy culture is based on the rejection of National Socialist policies; on coming to terms with the German past; and on a commitment to the West and the renunciation of any German *Sonderweg* (special path). Germany thus became firmly rooted in the "community of Western democracies"; it strives for predictability and reliability, but continues to nurture skepticism as regards the use of military power as a means of affecting foreign policy outcomes. It overcame nationalism by integration and the transfer of (some) sovereignty to the European Union. Germany has looked toward economic growth and social prosperity as a substitute for territorial expansion, increase in power, and superpower status, but until 1990 it also insisted on leaving open the German question with a view to achieving the desired unification. On that basis, Germany's foreign policy culture consisted of the specific normative premises for foreign policy in the Basic Law; in reparations and special relations with Israel; the commitment of foreign policy to fight massive violations of human rights; in disapproval of Bundeswehr missions that go beyond self-defense and alliance defense; and in a liberal attitude toward international economics. Germany's foreign policy conduct has been characterized by what Lothar Rühl calls a "principled multilateralism," a commitment to institutionalize and put international relations on a legal footing; the desire to deepen and enlarge the European Union and NATO; in efforts to promote stability, détente, and cooperation in all of Europe (CSCE/OSCE); in a willingness to give up and/or transfer sovereign rights; in generally "keeping a low profile" avoiding claims to leadership and the impression that Germany was pursuing narrowly defined national interests. Bonn preferred to overcome differences between its partners and push forward cooperation by mediating as the "honest broker"—and to be seen in those terms as a member state able to "see both sides of a problem."

Changes in the foreign policy culture since the 1990s

After German unification, two previously mentioned developments influenced Germany's foreign policy culture—(1) the dissolution of the bloc structures and the necessity of reshaping Europe through their integration in the European Union and NATO, and (2) the wars of succession in former Yugoslavia. Most analysts agree that, despite these far-reaching events, no real break occurred within the long-standing foreign policy culture of the old FRG. To the extent differences were noted, these constituted shifts of emphasis and modifications below the threshold of fundamental change. Such modifications were most apparent in the area of military security policy.

During the nineties, one shift of emphasis in German foreign policy culture concerned European integration and EU enlargement. Through unification, Germany had become one of the catalysts of the end of bipolarity and the "Europeanization of Europe." This led to a broadening of the foundations of Germany's foreign policy culture centered on Europe. At the same time—beginning with the unilaterally pursued policy of recognition of the secessionist Yugoslavian republics of Slovenia and Croatia in 1991—a debate began on whether German foreign policy aimed at a European Germany or a German Europe.

While opinion polls show that, with steady advances of European integration, the attitudes of the German population and elites have become more differentiated and ambivalent since 1990, with their own interests increasingly playing a role, only approximately one-fourth of the Germans (24 percent) believed at the end of 2003 that EU membership held more disadvantages for Germany than advantages. (In 1998, 30 percent had been of this opinion.)[35] Another 31 percent saw more advantages (in 1998, this figure had been 18 percent), and 42 percent believed that advantages and disadvantages more or less balanced each other (in 1998, 52 percent held this view). On the whole, the basic, pro-European consensus in the population continued to hold.

Growing self-confidence and international responsibility

The second, closely related dimension of a shift in emphasis in foreign policy culture had to do with the Europeanization of German foreign policy, which had already become noticeable since the 1970s. This was a consequence of Germany's newly acquired sovereignty and of a successive repositioning of its politics in a rapidly changing environment, which was characterized by a steadily growing self-confidence. German political elites and the population accepted this new role with growing self-confidence, although it took them a while. (This was variously interpreted as "cautious reflecting" or "hesitation to assume more foreign policy responsibilities.")

In 2002, the Mannheim-based ipos Institute found that Germans were on the way to "dropping their long-time cultivated anti-national attitude and joining the ranks of the self-confident and equal nations of the international community." Among the respondents, 71 percent stated that they were now proud of being German; 85 percent stated that Germans could be as proud of their country as American, French, and English nationals.[36] According to Gregor Schöllgen, Chancellor Gerhard Schröder's rejection of so-called checkbook diplomacy and the critical stance of his government toward the US policy on Iraq clearly expressed this new self-confidence.[37] Wilfried von Bredow considered this stance to be "the breakthrough of a new self-image and a new understanding of the external [...] that differed largely from American priorities and goals." He saw this as an indication of the "sharply increasing willingness [of Berlin] to shape world politics."[38]

This new self-confidence resulted not least from Germany's perception of being indispensable to European and global integration and of playing a key role in the EU enlargement process; but at the same time, Germany felt the need to promote the integration of Europe and of Germany in Europe even more strongly than before.

The Bundeswehr as an instrument of foreign policy

The most important modifications concerning Germany's foreign policy culture concerned the use of force. Up to the mid-1990s, the Bundeswehr participation in peacekeeping and peace-enforcing missions outside NATO was mostly rejected by the population as well as by political elites. But in the course of the 1990s, German foreign policy engaged in a step-by-step extension of Bundeswehr activities through participation in the UN's so-called blue-helmet missions. Even before it had assumed office, the Red–Green government was confronted with the Kosovo crisis of 1998–99; then came the "war against terrorism" proclaimed by the US administration in September 2001.

The extension of Bundeswehr missions in the decade following the FCC ruling of 1994 was accompanied by fierce and controversial discussions. This led to a change in attitudes across all political parties (with the exception of the PDS), which was "felt particularly painfully"[39] in the Social Democratic Party, the Alliance 90, and the Greens. A growing number of people favored Bundeswehr missions outside the traditional areas of responsibility since the wars in former Yugoslavia. While only 17 percent of the German population had approved of Bundeswehr participation in the second Persian Gulf War in 1991, by September 1995 a majority of the population (54 percent) considered NATO missions in Bosnia–Herzegovina necessary. Bundeswehr support of the United States in the fight against international terrorism was endorsed by 69 percent in the immediate aftermath of the attacks on New York and Washington.[40]

In part, this shift in public opinion reflected a heightened perception of threats such as terrorism. Yet, this change in attitude did not constitute a fundamental break with the principle of rejecting Bundeswehr missions outside traditional defense assignments. Implicitly, the continuity of Germany as a civilian power and the recourse to traditional parameters of German foreign policy were proven by the intensity of the discussion about the legality and legitimacy under international law of Bundeswehr missions abroad. Although the population had approved of supporting the United States in the fight against terrorism, the majority of Germans (58 percent) in spring 2003 wanted to see their country participate only "indirectly in combat missions within the framework of NATO, for example by giving logistic support." Just over one-fourth (27 percent) of respondents backed a "direct participation in combat missions within the framework of NATO."[41] Altogether, a clear majority (59 percent) of Germans said in June 2003 that the task of the Bundeswehr should be confined to the defense of its own territory and of NATO allies." Only 39 percent held that "the task of the Bundeswehr should also include the containment of crises outside NATO."[42]

Thus, after the end of the Cold War, major differences between German and American foreign political culture have emerged rather clearly. Gregor Schöllgen, for example, saw Schröder's policy in the Iraq crisis as part of the long overdue emancipation of Germany from the United States and the emergence of a European counterpower under German leadership.[43] Werner Link similarly saw a "NATO first policy" as "internationally anachronistic because the United States were marching off in another direction." Common efforts within the framework of an "intensified" and "structured" European cooperation could help to gradually "create a balanced European–American partnership that could also make an important contribution to world politics."[44] On the other hand, Christian Hacke maintained that, with greater distance from the United States, German policy would end up being "insignificant" and "provincial."[45]

The change in Germans' attitudes concerning the international position of their country, the use of military force, and issues of war and peace in general reflect to some degree modifications in the perception of other important actors on the international political stage. As a consequence, the traditional principle of seeking both closer European cooperation (especially with France) and a close transatlantic partnership with the United States lost some of its relevance. Schröder justified his rejection of the Iraq war in February 2003 asking, "whether there is (or rather should be) a single power determining the course of the world." A joint communiqué with President Jacques Chirac spelled out the joint ambition to promote a "Europe puissance" in a "multipolar world."[46]

The differences with America were reflected in the changed attitudes of the people. The number of those who believed that Germany had more in common with the United States than with its Western European neighbors had sunk since 1996, from 26 percent to a low of 17 percent in September 2003. During the same period, the number of those who saw more common ground with the European countries increased from 65 percent to 75 percent. Nonetheless, the question "Do you like Americans?" was answered affirmatively by 62 percent of the Germans in November 2003.[47] This shows that a differentiation is indeed made between the assessment of the US administration policy on the one hand and "the Americans" on the other. However, the opinion poll also revealed that the French were much more popular among German respondents; 80 percent answered affirmatively that they like the French.

Thus, the Iraq war seems to have left deep scars in the confidence toward the United States. While in the year 1996, 64 percent of Germans still considered the United States a reliable partner, only 28 percent held this opinion at the end of 2003. On the other hand, France was thought to be reliable by 56 percent of those questioned in November 2003 (in 1996, this figure was 23 percent). Moreover, at the end of 2003, 82 percent of those polled agreed to the statement that America would pursue its interests without any regard for other nations. Yet 85 percent of the Germans favored the continued existence of NATO,[48] which points to a high degree of confidence in the institutionalized security policy integration of Germany.

Conclusion

In sum, after the end of the Cold War, at the normative level German foreign policy was confronted with a fundamentally changed foreign policy environment, in particular in the field of European and security policy.

The normative adaptations undertaken since have reflected new orientations and operational measures taken by German foreign and security policy in response to perceived new challenges. These adaptations nevertheless retained their roots in the normative and politico-cultural traditions of the former Federal Republic and were viewed by decision makers as new interpretations of existing premises brought about by changed circumstances and by Germany's new role resulting from such changes, rather than as constituting a break with the past.

While Germany's foreign policy culture today no longer can be called specific but rather has become part of the European credo, which most other EU member countries act in accordance with, Germany still remains acutely aware of its precarious situation arising from the country's size and power, and hence of the need for constantly exercising self-control and assuring others that Germany does not intend to go its own way. On the other hand, the country's increasingly self-confident behavior in Europe and on the international stage is also significant. In the context of specific political events, Germany has sometimes been willing to set multilateralism aside. The country's pressing ahead with the recognition of Slovenia and Croatia in 1991 was an early case in point. This development culminated in Schröder's statement in 2002 that Germany would not participate in any military action against Iraq even if a UN Security Council resolution were taken.

While in some foreign policy areas politics have been characterized by strong continuity, in others—those, for example, concerning the adherence to international law with regard to Bundeswehr missions abroad—consensus is no longer reached in the way it used to be. Germany's Europeanization and stronger leadership role in Europe, as well as its simultaneous acceptance of a more active role—not least militarily—in world affairs, are an expression of a new self-confidence. At the same time, the country continues to have reservations with regard to a German leadership role and about using the Bundeswehr as an instrument of foreign policy. Thus, Germany has been attempting to harmonize foreign policy traditions of the old Federal Republic with the new requirements emerging particularly in the area of military operations.

These characteristics may, in specific instances, give the impression of controversial foreign policy discussions. Yet, for a truly constructive German role in Europe and in the complex post-bipolar world as a whole, this may well be the most appropriate and useful foundation.

Notes

1 See Dieter Nohlen and Rainer-Olaf Schultze, eds, *Lexikon der Politikwissenschaft. Theorien, Methoden, Begriffe*, 2 (2002): 656.
2 Manfred Knapp, "Die Außenpolitik der Bundesrepublik Deutschland," *Einführung in die Internationale Politik*, Gert Krell and Manfred Knapp, eds, Fourth edition

(Munich: Oldenbourg, 2004), pp. 135–200; see pp. 141–46. The following remarks on the premises of the Basic Law for German foreign policy are based on this text.
3 Ibid., p. 143.
4 In its ruling, the Court argued that alliances of collective self-defense could also be regarded as systems of mutual collective security in the meaning of Article 24, paragraph 2, "if and when they are strictly committed to keeping the peace." Ibid., p. 144.
5 *Bundesgesetzblatt* (referred to hereafter as BGBl), 1990 II, 1317.
6 Printed in *Bulletin des Presse- und Informationsamtes der Bundesregierung*, November 16, 1990, No. 134, 1394.
7 BGBl, 1992 II, 1253.
8 Ibid., 1251.
9 Bundesverfassungsgericht, 89, 155 of October 12, 1993.
10 BGBl, 1999 II, 1024.
11 BGBl, 1998 I, 1242.
12 BGBl, 2001 II, 1666.
13 BGBl, 1991 II, 1154.
14 BGBl, 1993 II, 2046.
15 BGBl, 1994 II, 1326.
16 BGBl, 1999 II, 465.
17 BGBl, 1998 II, 362.
18 BGBl, 2003 II, 1386.
19 BGBl, 2002 II, 2506.
20 Amendment of Article 16, paragraph 2, Basic Law.
21 BGBl, 2003 II, 1923.
22 Ibid., 293.
23 BGBl, 1994 II, 806.
24 BGBl, 1998 II, 778.
25 Bundesverfassungsgericht, 90, 286 of July 12, 1994.
26 Ibid.
27 Ibid.
28 Bundesverfassungsgericht, 2 BvQ 18/03 of March 25, 2003, paragraphs (1–41). Available at: http://www.bverfg.de/entscheidungen/qs20030325_2bvq001803.html. Accessed August 9, 2004.
29 Bundesverfassungsgericht, 2 BvE 6/99 of November 22, 2001, paragraphs (1–164).
30 The Bundeswehr contributed an important part of the personnel for NATO's joint AWACS' unit; if German soldiers had been forbidden to join AWACS' missions, there was a serious risk that the planes would have found themselves grounded due to personnel shortages.
31 Gabriel A. Almond and Sidney Verba, *The Civic Culture. Political Attitudes and Democracy in Five Nations* (Princeton: Princeton University Press, 1963).
32 Hanns W. Maull, "Außenpolitische Kultur," *Deutschland-Trendbuch. Fakten und Orientierungen,*" Karl-Rudolf Korte and Werner Weidenfeld, eds, Opladen, 2001, pp. 645–69; quoted here p. 647.
33 Ibid., p. 649.
34 Kerry A. Longhurst, *Strategic Culture. The Key to Understanding German Security Policy?*, PhD dissertation, Birmingham, 2000.
35 Mannheimer Institut für praxisorientierte Sozialforschung (ipos), *Transatlantische Beziehungen. Ergebnisse einer repräsentativen Bevölkerungsumfrage im Auftrag des Bundesverbandes deutscher Banken* (Mannheim: 2003). Available at: http://

www.bdb.de/pic/artikelpic/112003/mT_Transatlant_0903.pdf. Accessed June 25, 2004.

36　Bundesverband Deutscher Banken, *Die Zukunft der Nation: Wer sind wir Deutschen? Was müssen wir sein?*, Berlin, 2002, pp. 4–5. Available at: http://www. bdb.de/pic/artikelpic/032002/9-Forum-2002.pdf. Accessed June 25, 2004.

37　See Gregor Schöllgen, "Die Zukunft der deutschen Außenpolitik liegt in Europa," *Aus Politik und Zeitgeschichte*, 11 (2004): 9–16.

38　Wilfried von Bredow, "Auf leisen Sohlen zur Weltpolitik," *Frankfurter Allgemeine Zeitung*, May 8, 2003.

39　Christian Hacke, *Die Außenpolitik der Bundesrepublik Deutschland. Von Konrad Adenauer bis Gerhard Schröder*, Frankfurt am Main, 2003, p. 436.

40　Emnid opinion poll, October 19, 2001. Available at: www.tus-emnid.com/2004/ 03-presse/ntv.htm. Accessed August 11, 2004.

41　Emnid opinion poll, April 4, 2003. Available at: www.tus-emnid.com/2004/ 03-presse/ntv.htm. Accessed August 11, 2004.

42　Emnid opinion poll, June 20, 2003. Available at: www.tus-emnid.com/2004/ 03-presse/ntv.htm. Accessed August 11, 2004.

43　Gregor Schöllgen, *Der Auftritt* (Berlin: Propyläen, 2003), p. 130.

44　Werner Link, "Kooperative Balancepolitik. Deutsch-französische Zusammenarbeit als Kern europäischer Außen- und Sicherheitspolitik," *Politische Meinung*, 412 (March 2004): 37–42.

45　Christian Hacke, "Deutschland hängt am Rockzipfel der Franzosen," *Hamburger Abendblatt*, September 25, 2003.

46　Werner Link, "Grundlinien der außenpolitischen Orientierung Deutschlands," *Aus Politik und Zeitgeschichte*, 11 (2004): 3–8, quoted here p. 3.

47　Mannheimer Institut für praxisorientierte Sozialforschung (ipos), *Transatlantische Beziehungen. Ergebnisse einer repräsentativen Bevölkerungsumfrage im Auftrag des Bundesverbandes deutscher Banken* (Mannheim: 2003). Available at: http://www. bdb.de/pic/artikelpic/112003/mT_Transatlant_0903.pdf. Accessed June 25, 2004.

48　Ibid.

2
Adapting to Europe? German Foreign Policy, Domestic Constraints, and the Limitations of Europeanization since Unification

Alister Miskimmon and William E. Paterson

Introduction

Germany is not alone in facing major foreign policy challenges that require urgent attention; a plausible argument could be made that incoherence in UK foreign policy is of longer standing and more deeply rooted. However, Germany's position is more precarious than that of other leading European states. Chancellor Gerhard Schröder has been unable to fashion a coherent foreign policy to meet these challenges and to exert German influence on the international stage to make up for the structural advantages enjoyed by the United Kingdom and France of permanent membership on the Security Council and of nuclear power status; neither has he managed to realize his ambition of dealing with other powers at "eye level."[1] In the previous system (during the Cold War and for much of the 1990s), Germany was very good at tuning itself to, or synchronizing its position within, the global and regional order. The assumption contained in this chapter is that Germany is out of step with international developments and that it is no longer able to adequately adjust to the new rhythms of the international order as defined by the United States. In wider terms, this discordance is expressed in the difficulties within the Atlantic alliance and in debates over the future form of European security. Germany is therefore not a singular case, but rather it is exposed to the same challenges as France, the United Kingdom, and the United States. The difference is that the present German government aspires to a greater role for Germany just at the point when its material and ideational resources are shrinking.

Without a clear foreign policy, Germany risks becoming a more passive power in its efforts to determine the new foreign policy system that is emerging, being tossed between the extremes of Atlanticism and Europeanism.[2] Complicating Germany's ability to play a proactive role in foreign policy is the growing impact of a "resource crunch" within the country caused by the continuing impact of unification and a prolonged economic downturn.[3] The resource crunch leaves Germany less equipped to economically deflect the negative consequences of being a leading international actor. Fundamental to our contentions in this chapter is the idea that the German polity has not fully grasped the implications of its country's resource crunch and the knock-on effects on its foreign policy. Germany runs the risk of losing its reputation as a highly effective international actor and being perceived instead as one that has not successfully positioned itself within the emerging multilateral structures of the twenty-first century.

A key theme in Germany's pursuit of a more influential foreign policy role and a classic example of the way the country has attempted to shape its regional milieu[4] is its support for the Common Foreign and Security Policy (CFSP). This chapter will look at whether Europeanisation can provide coherence to German foreign policy and also allow it to escape from the unwelcome dilemmas imposed by the resource crunch. European foreign policy cooperation has been a central pillar of German foreign policy since the inception of European Political Cooperation in 1970. Throughout the 1990s, Germany has played a central role in influencing the development of CFSP.[5] However, developments since the attacks of September 11, 2001 on Washington and New York have witnessed a noticeable decline in Germany's ability to influence foreign policy in the European Union. Domestic and international explanations account for this lack of influence, which we will examine in this chapter.

The Europeanization of German Foreign and Security Policy since unification

The development of EC/EU foreign and security policy has been of key interest to successive German governments since the early failed attempt to create the European Defense Community in the period 1952–54.[6] To all intents and purposes, (West) German foreign and security policy was Europeanized since its very inception and West Germany initially demonstrated the attributes of a "penetrated state."[7] Multilateralism has been the defining characteristic of German foreign and security policy since the beginning of the era of Konrad Adenauer. Germany's semisovereign status and the proximity to a shaming past had led successive governments to adapt a policy of reflexive multilateralism and to define its external goals in terms of shared European, rather than specifically national, interests.[8] This European vocation was flanked by a constitutionally anchored commitment to overcoming German division and a predominant NATO/Atlanticist orientation in security policy.

Unification did not mean a shedding of Germany's European vocation.[9] The impact of Europeanization of German foreign and security policy in the

1990s has witnessed a two-way process of a projection of German preferences on CFSP, mainly in conjunction with France, and of reception in terms
of redefining the role of the Bundeswehr in international military operations
and the character of German foreign and security policy. Germany has exercised what Joseph S. Nye refers to as "soft power" to influence the ideas and
preferences of its EU partners by suggesting the way forward for EU foreign and
security policy cooperation.[10] The overall aim of German foreign and security
policy within the European Union has been to create an "institutional
fit" between European Union and German policy in order to reduce the
adaptational pressures resulting from the development of CFSP.[11]

We thus view Europeanization as a two-way process in which member
states actively participate in setting the constitutive rules and policies of the
European Union and are then affected by the implications of such cooperation and integration.[12] In other words, Europeanization is a process of preference shaping and preference accommodation.[13] This study will balance
both the uploading and downloading aspects of Europeanization.[14]
Uploading is understood as a member state's input into EU-level policy making, whilst downloading is the process through which states adapt on the
domestic level to EU policy developments (see Figure 2.1).

To what extent then has Germany's foreign and security policy adapted to
become Europeanized? The answer is mixed. Adaptation is understood as a
process through which, "actors maintain a balance between international

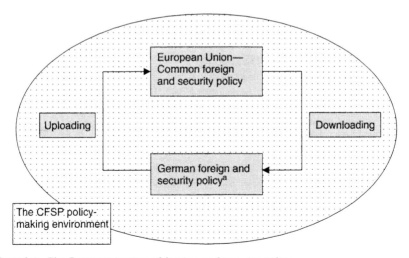

Figure 2.1   The Europeanization of foreign and security policy
[a]Miskimmon and Paterson (see note 11).

needs and external demands."[15] The German Defence Policy Guidelines of 2003 make clear the adaptational pressures facing German foreign and security policy:

> German policy comprises the preventive security action Germany takes within the scope of its foreign and security policy. Armed forces are an integral part of a foreign and security policy that aims at the prevention and containment of crises and conflicts[16] ... Germany's security environment is characterized by changed risks and new opportunities. At present, and in the foreseeable future, there is no conventional threat to the German territory. The Bundeswehr's spectrum of operations has changed fundamentally.[17]

It is also important to note that Europeanization takes place within a wider international context. Foreign policy change is not only the result of European impulses, but also the effect of changes in the international system, as well as domestic reassessments of policy direction. Changes in fundamental structural conditions in the international system, the impact of strategic political leadership within Germany, and finally, the presence of a crisis contribute to forcing policy makers to consider new avenues for foreign and security policy.[18]

Europeanization has been a central pillar in the united Germany's foreign and security policy, but it has not resulted in a dramatic restructuring of foreign and security policy within the country.[19] The 1990's saw a debate over the definition of the nature of European security for the post–Cold War era. This debate focused on the conditions and basis on which Europeanization could, if desired, take place. Germany has had to deal with a highly contentious policy milieu dominated by the existence of competing Europeanizations, or conceptions of how the emerging European security order should be organized.[20] Has Germany then been able to impact upon this debate to shape policies in line with national preferences, or has it been subject to increased adaptational pressures as the European Union's role in international affairs has increased?

Germany's role in the CFSP has been one of uploading and downloading. It therefore is engaged in a process of ensuring that there is a "goodness of fit" between national and European levels and that instances of misfit, that is, where adaptational pressures emerge, are kept to a minimum.[21] Accordingly, Germany was driven for most of the 1990s by a "logic of appropriateness" in CFSP.[22] Even when the CFSP framework was substantially challenged during the Kosovo crisis in terms of the European Union's inability to present a unified position to confront Milosevic,[23] the logic of appropriateness held true in the German case. Germany sought to reassess its role within the CFSP throughout the crisis and suggest a concrete blueprint for the development of EU foreign and security policy in the form of the Stability

Pact for South-Eastern Europe, rather than consider withdrawing support for CFSP.

Assessing German uploading

There are a number of mechanisms contributing to the uploading of German preferences in the Europeanization dynamics within CFSP. These are ideational export, founded on a discursive input into policy developments; institutional export of domestic modes and practices, or well-considered policy blueprints; example setting through the consistent commitment to European solutions to foreign policy challenges and the relative scarcity of overtly national posturing; and finally, the ability to utilize formal structural powers within the CFSP policy process, most notably through the agenda-setting opportunities afforded the council presidency.

Germany's discursive influence has been central to the framing of the realms of the possible in CFSP during the 1990s. Helmut Kohl identified the central problems facing the CFSP in the mid-1990s in the following terms:

> The previous agreements on the Common Foreign and Security Policy are not sufficient for Europe to speak with one voice and act together. We must therefore take the necessary measures within the intergovernmental conference to improve the efficiency, the continuity, the coherence, the solidarity and the transparency of the Common Foreign and Security Policy as part of a total package.[24]

The central themes of efficiency, continuity, coherence, solidarity, and transparency were key during the negotiations of the Amsterdam Treaty, from the convening of the Reflection Group in 1995 to the final conference in the summer of 1997. In addition, Kohl's embedding of the CFSP within the overall aim of achieving a political union to balance Economic and Monetary Union was a defining aspect of German CFSP policy under the coalition government of the Christian Democratic Union (CDU), Christian Social Union (CSU), and the Free Democratic Party (FDP). Kohl consciously "nested" discussions of CFSP within discussions of higher order issues relating to European integration. For Kohl, CFSP did not solely represent a chance to increase German influence in foreign and security policy. Rather, Kohl sought to build on the security that European integration had established for the citizens of Germany and Europe since the Treaties of Rome. Alongside Kohl, Klaus Kinkel's main focus as foreign minister was generating a dynamic among the EU member states for the development of a "[c]ommon foreign and security policy that is worthy of its name."[25]

Kohl and Kinkel also sought to be at the forefront of CFSP institutional developments by continually stressing the rationale for the integration of the European Union/Western European Union (EU/WEU) throughout the 1990s, despite British opposition, in order to facilitate more effective discussions of security and defense policy among EU member states. This German preference has been implemented to all intents and purposes with the signing the Treaty of Nice. This must be seen as a success for German policy. Regarding institutional export as a mechanism of uploading, there is no better example than the case of the Stability Pact for South-Eastern Europe. Schröder and Joschka Fischer were able to export a policy blueprint, worked out at the national level, and receive almost unflinching support from the international community for the model for regional reconstruction contained within the pact. This was facilitated by the effective use Germany made of the agenda-setting powers of the presidency of the WEU/EU and the G-8.[26] But the Franco–German partnership also remained instrumental in maintaining the dynamic toward deepening foreign and security policy cooperation within the European Union throughout the 1990s. Germany played a proactive role in suggesting paths for institutional reform and agreeing to joint positions with France for presenting proposals to their fellow EU member states. This proactive stance on institutional reform at the EU level was not reflected in the domestic reform of foreign and defense policy within Germany, where strategic culture remained resistant to speedy adaptation, thus ensuring the continued importance of German singularities in foreign policy.[27]

The final mechanism of German uploading was that of example setting. Germany remained at the forefront of attempts to deepen cooperation in CFSP, although not always with a great deal of consistency. There remains reticence, however, within the German political system to consider the involvement of the Bundeswehr in crisis management operations, most clearly demonstrated in the Bundestag's central position as the final arbiter of troop deployment. It has been vital, however, for Germany to demonstrate its support for CFSP in material terms in order for both the Kohl and Schröder governments to place Germany at the front of CFSP initiatives. This has been seen most recently in Germany's commitment to the Common European Security and Defense Policy (CESDP) Headline Goal.[28] As pressure grows on improved European capabilities, Germany's ability to play the role of the *Musterknabe*, or model pupil, will be compromised if the resource crunch continues.

Uploading of German preferences has been complicated by a number of limiting conditions affecting German influence in CFSP (see Table 2.1). German foreign policy has demonstrated increasing difficulties in exercising leadership and taking initiatives within the EU context, and growing deficiencies in Germany's ability and willingness to engage in the necessary domestic and international coalition building. A combination of weak leadership and a shrinking foreign policy elite within the Bundestag, due to the domestification of German politics since the achievement of unification, has reduced the impact of German foreign policy within the European Union.[29]

Table 2.1 Mechanisms of policy uploading in CFSP

Uploading mechanism	German actions
Discursive/ideational influence	Centrality of CFSP for Political Union Common European Defense as a means of strengthening the transatlantic community Fusing WEU/EU.
Institutional export *Example setting*	Stability Pact for South-Eastern Europe Commitments to the Capabilities Commitment Conference Mixed results in forging a more effective European voice in international affairs.
Agenda setting	Great success during the European Council/WEU presidencies of 1999 Consistently proactive with France in suggesting institutional reforms.

This is likely to continue.[30] The growing role of the Chancellery in CFSP matters under Schröder has also resulted in muddled discourses emerging from Berlin, with the Foreign Ministry challenging the Chancellery in order to maintain its role as the "sponsoring ministry" of German CFSP policy.[31] Finally, the erosion of material resources in terms of the pressure on the German model and the resultant budgetary squeeze, and the damage caused by German unilateralism over the Iraq war of 2003, have reduced the nonmaterial resources in the form of policy influence that Germany can bring to bear.

Assessing German downloading

Analyzing the downloading aspects of Europeanization highlights the adaptational pressures facing a member state of the European Union. In terms of elites' socialization, there was a consistent commitment from German policy elites to the CFSP process during the 1990s. Like Helmut Kohl and Hans-Dietrich Genscher before them, Schröder and Fischer have sought to reinforce German responsibility for and dependability in developing CFSP with Germany's key partners within the European Union. The most fundamental issue to which German elites have become socialized is that of the need for German involvement in military crisis management. This has been most clearly demonstrated in the military operation in Kosovo in 1999 and subsequently in Afghanistan, and now most recently with the European Union taking over from NATO (North Atlantic Treaty Organization) in Bosnia–Herzegovina.[32]

We suggest that downloading in the case of Germany and the CFSP has focused on what Christoph Knill regards as the "weakest" mechanism of

Europeanization, namely, that of changing the domestic beliefs and expectations of policy elites within Germany.[33] The European Union does not as yet have a concrete institutional model to serve as a focus of adaptation for member states[34] or to replace the cultural and political proximity that national foreign policy institutions provide, even in the case of the post-national German polity. Nor are there sufficient domestic interest groups pressing for a communitarization of German foreign and security policy.[35]

The Defence Ministry has endured the most significant adaptational pressures facing Germany in terms of institutional/bureaucratic reform as a result of increasing the European role in transatlantic burden sharing in crisis management. Whereas European Political Cooperation afforded West Germany a forum in which it could develop its foreign policy without resorting to unilateralism and being exposed to the pressures of doing it alone in international relations, the development of CESDP since 1999 has served as a spotlight on deficiencies in German foreign, security, and defense policy. These pressures developed in conjunction with a domestic reassessment of the role of the Bundeswehr on the international stage.[36] Europeanization has acted as a cover or facilitating milieu for reform of the Bundeswehr by giving successive defense ministers (Volker Rühe, Rudolf Scharping, and now Peter Struck) a template and a raison d'etre for the German armed forces in the new millennium.

The development of CFSP/CESDP has broadened the role of the Defence Ministry in Berlin and Bonn through the inclusion of matters relating to defense. It is becoming less and less the case that CFSP policy within Germany is the exclusive domain of the Foreign Ministry, with pressure coming from the chancellery. However, the Defence Ministry's involvement remains minimal. The inclusion of these matters within the CFSP/CESDP have also raised the profile of the Finance Ministry under the leadership of Hans Eichel. With greater scrutiny and pressure on Rudolf Scharping and Peter Struck, to reform the Bundeswehr to meet the commitments of the Headline Goal and Germany's greater international commitments, there were almost continual struggles between the need for Struck to deliver on these commitments and Eichel's desire to balance the books, especially in light of the tough EMU (Economic and Monetary Union) criteria as outlined in the Stability and Growth Pact. This has led to the huge financial pressures placed on the defense budget by the A440M and Eurofighter projects.

In the area of bureaucratic reorganization, policy making remains firmly embedded within Berlin despite the establishment of EU-level institutions such as the European Union Military Committee, European Union Military Staff, and the Political Security Committee. Much of the coordination work on foreign policy matters is conducted on a bilateral basis between Berlin and Paris or Berlin and London, rather than in Brussels. Germany's permanent representative to the European Union has only a modest input into policy decisions. The role of the Foreign Ministry remains central to CFSP on day-to-day matters, although as the political importance of CFSP/CESDP has risen under the Red–Green government, the chancellery has taken a much greater interest in pursuing policy objectives in this area. Whilst the development of EU military capabilities in the form of the European Rapid Reaction Force would suggest a greater role for the ministry in CFSP affairs, this remains limited. The Defence Ministry remains an institution firmly wedded to the NATO alliance and to transatlantic cooperation and has been cautious over the development of EU capabilities.[37] This cautious attitude to restructuring in terms of the expansion of EU capabilities and in regard to conscription has continued under Scharping and Struck.

Public opinion provides solid support for European initiatives in foreign policy but has been generally reluctant to consider the use of military force compared with other major EU states.[38] In terms of wider foreign policy issues, John S. Lantis finds that "public opinion seems to have lagged behind elite attitudes on German foreign policy restructuring in the 1990s, rather than shaping the parameters of acceptable behaviour."[39] Since the Kosovo War, public opinion has demonstrated remarkable continuity in its support of EU foreign and security cooperation as Table 2.2 shows.

There is clearly strong domestic support for further developing CFSP. Public opinion remains more cautious when it comes to discussions with implications within the European Union.

Germans generally favor greater cooperation in civilian crisis management and diplomatic solutions to foreign policy challenges and are less supportive of German involvement in military crisis management (see Table 2.3). This suggests that public opinion has been resistant to adaptational impulses emanating from Germany's involvement in CFSP. Overall, constitutional and legislative change has been rather limited (cf. the chapter by August Pradetto in this volume). The key event took place in July 1994 with the Constitutional Court's decision on the issue of "out-of-area" deployment of

Table 2.2 German public attitudes toward a European common foreign and security policy. Responses to the *Eurobarometer* survey question, "Some people believe that certain areas of policy should be decided by the [national] government, while other areas of policy should be decided jointly within the EU. Which of the following areas of policy do you think should be decided by the [national] government, and which be decided jointly within the EU ... foreign policy toward countries outside the EU?"[a]

Germany	EU	National governments	Don't know
11/99	75	18	7
5/00	74	19	7
12/00	72	21	7
11/01	75	18	7
5/02	75	17	8
11/02	75	18	7
4/03	75	18	7

Note: [a]Eichenberg (see note 36), 643–4.

the Bundeswehr, which opened up the possibility for Germany to play a larger role in transatlantic burden-sharing. Legislative changes stemming from agreements on CFSP as part of the EU treaties have been insignificant. Finally, and tellingly resource reallocation resulting from commitments to CFSP have been negligible. Germany's defence budget has been greatly reduced, with successive defense ministers being forced to make cuts to the Bundeswehr to find the necessary resources to fund the armed forces' modernization (see Table 2.4). As a result, there has been insufficient

Table 2.3 German public attitudes toward a European security and defense policy. Responses to the *Eurobarometer* survey question, "Some people believe that certain areas of policy should be decided by the [national] government, while other areas of policy should be decided jointly within the EU. Which of the following areas of policy do you think should be decided by the [national] government, and which be decided jointly within the EU ... security and defense?[a]

Germany	EU	National government	Don't know
11/99	57	37	6
5/00	60	35	5
12/00	56	39	5
11/01	58	37	5
5/02	55	40	5
11/02	52	43	5
4/03	60	35	4

Note: [a]Eichenberg (see note 36), 646.

Table 2.4 German defense budgets, 1990–2001[a]

Year	Defense budget (DM millions)
1990	62,914
1991	58,372
1992	56,595
1993	52,291
1994	49,878
1995	47,859
1996	47,807
1997	45,561
1998	45,585
1999	45,282
2000	43,092
2001	44,084

Note: [a]Figures taken from Gunther Hellmann, "Agenda 2020. Krise und Perspektive deutscher Außenpolitik," *Internationale Politik*, no. 9 (2003). Data are calculated at real prices, with 1995 as base year.

investment in the Bundeswehr to build capabilities for Germany's future role in transatlantic burden-sharing. Cuts in the defense budget have gone hand-in-hand with cuts in personnel numbers. Thus, the total strength of the Bundeswehr has fallen from 469,000 in 1990 to about 340,000 in 1995, 321,000 in 2000, and 284,500 in 2004 (see Table 2.5).[40]

Conflicting developments affecting German Europeanization

Whereas the period 1998–2000 represented the highpoint of efforts by the European Union member states to develop CFSP in meaningful operational terms, the period from September 12, 2001 to the present has marked a noticeable retreat from fulfilling the commitments contained within CESDP.[41] Germany has become less adept in pursuing a balanced foreign and security policy on such issues as Iraq, thus complicating its traditional diplomacy of finding a middle way between European and Atlanticist views on the future of European security provisions. Germany's foreign and security policy has become more complicated at the beginning of the twenty-first century, but the Red–Green government has yet to find a solution to the foreign policy challenges facing it.[42]

The Iraq war of 2003 has highlighted the weaknesses not only of European foreign policy, but also of German foreign and security policy, which have serious consequences for the country's traditional role in CFSP. Differences with the United Kingdom over Iraq also threaten to compromise ESDP (European Security and Defense Policy) through German efforts to sideline British involvement.[43] The divisions over Iraq signify a lack of German influence to suggest a credible solution to transatlantic divergences. Germany has been unable to influence President George W. Bush's foreign policy on major issues, resulting in a polarization of transatlantic security between those in favor of the US policy on Iraq and those against.[44] This is particularly serious for Germany's strategic position in debates over European security. As other chapters in this volume illustrate, Germany's ability to influence the development of CFSP and NATO has been grounded on a strategy of not doing anything to jeopardize transatlantic links. Germany has sought a middle way between France's preference for *Europe puissance* and the United Kingdom's avowedly transatlantic calling, despite its occasional flirtation with European initiatives. Schröder has compromised his ability to balance these two positions, thereby weakening his influence in multilateral structures and outlining a more noticeable German position in international affairs. Schröder's position has been weakened in a common European foreign policy environment which has been further complicated by enlargement, with foreign policy divisions in the European Union drawn between "old" and "new" member states over Iraq.[45] Germany's foreign and security

Table 2.5 Mechanisms of policy downloading in CFSP

Downloading mechanism	German adaptation
Elite socialization	Both the CDU/CSU/FDP and the SPD/Alliance '90/Greens have committed to the incremental strengthening of CFSP. Themes of *responsibility* and *dependability* have been hallmarks of the German government's growing role within CFSP. Awareness has increased of the need for greater participation (but only as a last resort) in military crisis management.
Bureaucratic reorganization	Policy-making remains resolutely Berlin-based despite the establishment of new CFSP institutions. The Defense Ministry has only modest input into CFSP/CESDP and plays a conservative role in foreign and security policy due to the ongoing Bundeswehr reform.
Constitutional change/ legislative adaptation	The Federal Constitutional Court's decision of July 12, 1994 remains the landmark decision impacting Germany's deployment of troops in crisis management operations. Legislative changes as a result of implementing treaty commitments as part of CFSP have been modest.
Public opinion adaptation	Public opinion has remained consistently behind Germany's support of the EU's international role. Where public opinion shows signs of national singularities is in its reluctance to consider German participation in military operations as part of CESDP. Public opinion remains a domestic constraint on the scope of Germany's involvement in CFSP.
Resource reallocation	Germany's defense budget has been on a continuous slide throughout the 1990s; therefore, there has not been an increase in or substantial reallocation of resources to build CFSP. The Bundeswehr remains embedded in NATO structures despite small-scale commitments to building European capabilities in the form of the European Rapid Reaction Force.

policy has been highly affected by the preexisting latent transatlantic differences, which have been painfully revealed by the Iraq issue. The war in Iraq also exposed major differences on both sides on the Atlantic concerning how best to tackle international terrorism after the terrorist attacks of September 11, 2001. The cohesive effect of transatlantic sympathy and solidarity with the United States following the attacks soon dissipated when differences emerged over strategy and tactics for combating terrorism. Germany's past success in foreign policy has been in fostering developments within NATO and the European Union that were mutually reinforcing, rather than symbolic of differing trajectories and agendas on both sides of the Atlantic. By explicitly stating German preferences during the run up to the Iraq war, Schröder departed from traditional German practice in foreign policy, thus exposing his country's position to scrutiny.[46]

On top of this, Germany sought to avoid being isolated on Iraq and the debate on European security by pressing ahead with cooperation with France, Luxembourg, and Belgium, signaled by a summit on April 24, 2003. According to this group of four, the breakdown in transatlantic consensus on the major foreign policy issue on the agenda necessitated a new impulse for the creation of a European Security and Defense Union (ESDU) under the European Constitution.[47] The intellectual author of this idea was Eckhard Lübkemeier, formerly with the Friedrich Ebert Foundation and more recently affiliated with the Foreign Ministry and the chancellery.[48] According to the conservative *Frankfurter Allgemeine Zeitung*, the resulting so-called *Pralinengipfel* (chocolate summit) was a diplomatic disaster with the displeasure of other member states reflected by their decision not to attend.[49] Germany's ability to influence the development of CFSP in the 1990s was founded on its ability to find partners to work with (normally France), but without prejudicing Germany's aim of finding agreement within the European Union as a whole. Germany's poor relations with the United Kingdom since the Iraq debacle have made the country more reliant on France, thus demoting Germany to the junior role in the Franco–German tandem.[50]

Conclusion

Europeanization has steadily become more important for German foreign policy since unification. However, Germany's foreign policy has lacked an effective strategy to influence the development of CFSP since the events September 11, 2001. This has serious consequences at a time when the European Union is starting to take seriously its commitments to multilateral burden-sharing. As the case of ESDP demonstrates, the use of force within the EU framework is an area where German policies confront serious domestic economic and political constraints, which have been most clearly demonstrated in the context of reforming the Bundeswehr for international multilateral military service. Germany's normative predisposition to find EU-based solutions to foreign policy challenges clashes with the country's traditional strategic culture dispositions vis-à-vis the use of force and fiscal constraints as EU forces become more widely deployed.

Future foreign policy demands placed upon Germany by its key partners will focus on the need for "improving its military forces for peace enforcement and political stabilisation, to offer diplomatic services in critical situations and to grant financial resources for rebuilding failed states and societies."[51] Europeanization can only partially meet these demands. National responses are required by Germany to address the need for improving military capabilities and allowing a limited return to the "checkbook diplomacy" of the past. Europeanization within the CFSP, therefore, does not allow Germany to evade the pressures of the resource crunch it now feels. For that reason the national economy will remain the priority for Schröder. Herein lies the paradox of German foreign policy today: Germany should find it easier to play a greater role in international affairs since, due to its economic weakness, other states are less concerned than in the past with containing its power. The problem is, however, that this economic weakness makes it difficult for Germany to play the role that other powers are now prepared to accept.

German foreign policy is also characterized by two conflicting visions. First, there is Schröder's vision of a more pragmatic, self-confident nation that seeks to exert international political influence to complement its global economic interests, which has been highlighted by the chancellor's goal of being given a permanent seat on the United Nations Security Council. Schröder also appears to have chosen a European path alongside France on the major foreign policy issues of the day, despite continued German commitment to NATO. Second, there is Fischer's vision of a new transatlantic strategic consensus founded on Germany's traditional strategy of balancing European and transatlantic callings and that of an emerging global diplomacy. Vital for a more effective German foreign policy is a clear signal from Berlin on which of these strategies Germany will pursue. The reelection of George W. Bush arguably leaves a bigger opening for more European cooperation. However, ironically Germany must concentrate more on addressing domestic weaknesses to prove a more credible player on the international stage.

Notes

1 Gunther Hellmann and Reinhard Wolff, "Neuer Spielplan auf der Weltbühne: Deutschlands Auftritt muss abgesagt werden," *Internationale Politik*, 8/2004: 73–80; quoted here p. 73.

2 Hellmann has described this as a German foreign policy tightrope walk. Gunther Hellmann, "Der 'deutsche Weg': eine außenpolitische Gratwanderung," *Internationale Politik*, 9/2002: 1–8.

3 Charlie Jeffery and William E. Paterson, "Germany and European Integration: A Shifting of Tectonic Plates," *West European Politics*, 26 (2003): 59–78.
4 Simon Bulmer, Charlie Jeffery, and William E. Paterson, *Germany's European Diplomacy* (Manchester: Manchester University Press, 2000).
5 Axel Lüdeke, *Europäisierung der deutschen Außen- und Sicherheitspolitik: Konstitutive und operative Europapolitik zwischen Maastricht und Amsterdam* (Opladen: Leske & Budrich, 2002).
6 Helga Haftendorn, *Deutsche Außenpolitik zwischen Selbstbeschränkung und Selbstbehauptung* (Stuttgart/Munich: Deutsche Verlags-Anstalt, 2001), pp. 31–46.
7 Wolfram F. Hanrieder, "Compatibility and Consensus: A Proposal for the Conceptual Linkage of External and Internal Dimensions of Foreign Policy," *Comparative Foreign Policy*, Wolfram F. Hanrieder, ed. (New York: David McKay Company Inc., 1971), pp. 242–65.
8 Simon Bulmer and William E. Paterson, "Germany in the European Union: gentle giant or emergent leader?," *International Affairs*, 72: 1 (1996): 9–32.
9 Thomas Banchoff, *The German Problem Transformed: Institutions, Politics and Foreign Policy, 1945–1995* (Ann Arbor: The University of Michigan Press, 1999).
10 Joseph S. Nye, *Bound to Lead. The Changing Nature of American Power* (New York: Basic Books, 1990).
11 Alister Miskimmon and William E. Paterson, "Foreign and Security Policy: On the cusp between transformation and accommodation," *German, Europe and the Politics of Constraint*, Ken Dyson and Klaus Goetz, eds (Oxford: Proceedings of the British Academy/Oxford University Press, 2003), pp. 325–45.
12 Koenig-Archibugi explains government preferences on institutional change in CFSP by analyzing four central factors: relative power capabilities, foreign policy interests, Europeanized identities, and domestic multilevel governance structures. Mathias Koenig-Archibugi, "Explaining government preferences for institutional change in EU foreign and security policy," *International Organization*, 58: 1 (2004): 137–74. This study factors in these four criteria to its analysis of German participation in the development of CFSP.
13 Patrick Dunleavy, *Democracy, Bureaucracy and Public Choice* (Hemel Hempstead, UK: Harvester Wheatsheaf, 1991). Russell Holden has charted the development of the Labour Party's European policy in these terms. See Russell Holden, *The Making of New Labour's European Policy* (Houndmills, UK: Palgrave, 2002). For an analysis of how member states contribute to the bottom-up aspect of Europeanization, see also Jan Beyers and Jarle Trondal, "How nation-states 'hit' Europe: Ambiguity and Representation in the European Union," *European Integration Online Papers (EIOP)*, 7: 5 (2003). Available at: http://eiop.or.at/eiop/pdf/2003-005.pdf.
14 Elizabeth Bomberg and John Peterson, "Policy Transfer and Europeanization: Passing the Heineken test?," *Queen's Papers on Europeanization*, 2/2000, Belfast. Available at: http://www.qub.ac.uk/ies/onlinepapers/poe2.html.
15 James N. Rosenau, *The Study of Political Adaptation: Essays on the Analysis of World Politics* (London: Frances Pinter, 1981), p. 29.
16 Peter Struck, *Defense Policy Guidelines*, May 21, 2003 (Berlin: Federal Defense Ministry, 2003), paragraph 6.
17 Ibid., paragraph 9.
18 Jakob Gustavsson, "How should we study foreign policy change?," *Cooperation and Conflict*, 34: 1 (1999): 73–95.
19 Hanns W. Maull, Sebastian Harnisch, Constantin Grund, eds, "Deutschland im Abseits? Rot-grüne Außenpolitik 1998–2003" (Baden-Baden: Nomos, 2003);

Hanns W. Maull, " 'Normalisierung' oder Auszehrung? Deutsche Außenpolitik im Wandel," *Aus Politik und Zeitgeschichte*, B 11/2004 (March 8, 2004): 17–23.

20 Ole Waever, "Three competing Europes: German, French, Russian," *International Affairs*, 66: 3 (1990): 477–93.

21 Johan P. Olsen, "The Changing Political Organization of Europe: An Institutional Perspective on the Role of Comprehensive Reform Efforts," *The Yearbook of Comparative Government and Public Administration*, Vol. II, Joachim Jens Hesse and Theo A. J. Toonen, eds (Baden-Baden: Nomos, 1996), pp. 225–50; Johan Olsen, "The Many Faces of Europeanization," *ARENA Working Papers*, WP01/2 (2001). Available at: http://www.arena.uio.no/publications/wp02_2.htm; James G. March and Johan P. Olsen, *Rediscovering Institutions* (New York: Free Press, 1989); James G. March and Johan P. Olsen, "The logic of appropriateness," *ARENA Working Paper*, WP04/09 (2004). Available at: http://www.arena.uio.no/publications/wp04_9.pdf.

22 James G. March and Johan P. Olsen, "The logic of appropriateness," *ARENA Working Paper*, WP04/09 (2004). Available at: http://www.arena.uio.no/ publications/wp04_9.pdf; quoted here p. 1.

23 Joachim Krause, ed., *Kosovo: Humanitäre Intervention und cooperative Sicherheit in Europa* (Opladen: Leske & Budrich, 2000); Peter Rudolf, "Germany and the Kosovo Conflict," *Alliance Politics, Kosovo and NATO's War: Allied force or forced allies*, Pierre Martin and Mark R. Brawley, eds (Houndmills, UK, Palgrave, 2000); 131–43; Marc Weller, "The Rambouillet conference on Kosovo," *International Affairs*, 75: 2 (1999): 211–51.

24 "Deutsche und Franzosen bilden Kern der Europäischen Union," *Frankfurter Allgemeine Zeitung*, October 14, 1993.

25 Klaus Kinkel, "Speech to the Bundestag on the Agenda for the German Council Presidency," Bundestag, Bonn, June 29, 1994, *Drucksache*, 237. Sitzung, 12. Wahlperiode, 20779D.

26 Jonas Tallberg, "The agenda-shaping powers of the EU Council Presidency," *Journal of European Public Policy*, 10: 1 (2003): 1–19.

27 For an excellent examination of the development of German strategic culture see, Kerry Longhurst, *Germany and the Use of Force: The Evolution of German Security Policy 1989–2003* (Manchester: Manchester University Press, 2004).

28 "Germany's contribution to the Headline Goal will comprise some 30,000 soldiers, 90 combat aircraft and 15 ships, from which an initial contingent tailored to the demands of the situation can be composed for an EU-led operation. The maximum size of a German contingent is set at 18,000 personnel. Additional forces will ensure the sustainability of such a contingent." See Bundeswehr homepage. Available at: http://eng.bmvg.de/sicherheit/buendnisse/index.php#6, Accessed July 1, 2005.

29 Hanns W. Maull, "Auf leisen Sohlen aus der Außenpolitik?," *Internationale Politik* 58: 9 (9/2003): 19–30.

30 Hellmann and Wolff, *Internationale Politik* (see note 1).

31 Ibid.

32 For more information of the Bundeswehr deployment as part of the EUFOR Operation Althea, which replaces NATO's SFOR, see the Bundeswehr homepage. Available at: http://www.bundeswehr.de/forces/030728_einsatz_welt.php. Germany is contributing 1100 of the 7000 troops to the mission. Michael Martens, "Aus SFOR wird EUFOR," *Frankfurter Allgemeine Zeitung*, December 2, 2004, and "Bosnien: EU übernimmt Friedenseinsatz von der NATO," *Die Welt*, December 2, 2004.

33 Christoph Knill, *The Europeanization of National Administrations* (Cambridge: Cambridge University Press, 2001.) See also Christoph Knill and Dirk Lehmkuhl, "Difference mechanisms of Europeanization," *European Integration Online Papers*, 3:7 (1999). Available at: http://eiop.or.at/eiop/pdf/1999-007.pdf.

34 Jolyon Howorth, "France," *The European Union and National Defense Policy*, Jolyon Howarth and Anand Menon, eds (London: Routledge, 1997), 23–48; quoted here p. 24.

35 Miskimmon and Paterson, *German, Europe and the Politics of Constraint* (see note 11), p. 343. Smith makes this point in relation to the relative insulation from transnational, sectoral interests of European foreign policy elites on issues relating to CFSP. Michael E. Smith, "Rules, Transgovernmentalism, and the Expansion of European Political Cooperation," *European integration and Supranational governance*, Wayne Sandholtz and Alex Stone Sweet, eds (Oxford: Oxford University Press, 1998), pp. 304–33.

36 Von Weizsäcker Report, "Gemeinsame Sicherheit und Zukunft der Bundeswehr Bericht der Kommission an die Bundesregierung," May 23, 2001.

37 Interview by the author with members of the Defense Ministry Planning Staff, Berlin, June 12, 2001.

38 Richard C. Eichenberg, "The Polls-Trends: Having it Both Ways: European Defense Integration and the Commitment to NATO," *Public Opinion Quarterly*, 67 (2003): 627–59.

39 John S. Lantis, *Strategic Dilemmas and the Evolution of German Foreign Policy since Unification* (London: Praeger, 2002), p. 176.

40 Ibid.

41 Judy Dempsey, "Power to the Capitals," *Financial Times*, October 15, 2001.

42 Christian Hacke, "Die Außenpolitik der Regierung Schröder/Fischer: Zwischenbilanz und Perspektiven," *Aus Politik und Zeitgeschichte*, 48/2002. Available at: http://www.das-parlament.de/2002/48/Beilage/002.html; Gunther Hellmann, "Deutschlands Kraft und Europas Vertrauen oder: Die Selbstbewussten, die Befangenen und die Betroffenen der neuen deutschen Außenpolitik," *Neue deutsche Außen- und Sicherheitspolitik? Eine friedenswissenschaftliche Bilanz zwei Jahre nach dem rot-grünen Regierungswechsel*, Christiane Lammers and Lutz Schrader, eds (Baden-Baden: Nomos, 2001), pp. 42–78.

43 Paul Cornish, ed., *The Conflict in Iraq, 2003* (Houndmills, UK: Palgrave, 2004).

44 Michael Clarke, "The Diplomacy that led to war in Iraq," *The Conflict in Iraq, 2003*, Paul Cornish, ed. (Houndmills, UK: Palgrave, 2004), pp. 27–58.

45 Spanish-sponsored "Group of Eight Letter" supporting America's position on Iraq, Jose Maria Aznar *et al.*, "Letter to The Times," *The Times*, January 30, 2003. Available at: http://www.timesonline.co.uk.

46 Michael Hedstück and Gunther Hellmann, " 'Wir machen einen deutschen Weg': Irak-Abenteuer, der transatlantische Verhältnis und die Risiken der Methode Schröder für die deutsche Außenpolitik," *Brandherd Irak, US-Hegemonieanspruch, die UNO und die Rolle Europas*, Bernd Kubbig, ed. (Frankfurt am Main: Campus, 2003), pp. 224–34.

47 Gemeinsame Erklärung Deutschlands, Frankreichs, Luxemburgs und Belgiens zur Europäischen Sicherheits- und Verteidigungspolitik, April 29, 2003. Available at: http://www.bundesregierung.de/. Accessed July 21, 2003.

48 Interviews by the author with staff members of the German Foreign Ministry, Berlin, July 7, 2003.

49 Horst Bacia, "Unnötige Eile: Das Treffen könnte der gemeinsame europäischen Sicherheitspolitik schaden," *Frankfurter Allgemeine Zeitung*, April 28, 2003. See also Leonard Doyle, "French Call for Military Cooperation divides EU," *The Independent*, April 28, 2003; "Vierergipfel berät über EU-Verteidigungspolitik," *Financial Times Deutschland*, April 29, 2003.

50 Christian Schweiger, "British-German relations in the European Union after the war on Iraq," *German Politics*, 13: 1 (2004): 35–55.

51 Helga Haftendorn and Michael Kolkmann, "Germany in a Strategic Triangle: Berlin, Paris, Washington ... and what about London?," *Cambridge Review of International Affairs*, 17: 3 (2004): 467–80, quoted here p. 477.

Part II

Security Policy Issues: Between NATO and the European Union

3
Germany and the Proliferation of Weapons of Mass Destruction

Harald Müller

Introduction: nature and scope of the problem after the end of the Cold War

The risk of the proliferation of weapons of mass destruction (WMD) was seen as a threat to world stability throughout the Cold War. The emphasis was on nuclear weapons, which were regarded as the most powerful and dangerous threat. Biological weapons, which were not seen as significant before the dawn of bioengineering, began to generate major attention and concern only during the course of the 1980s. Chemical weapons were deemed inhuman and reprehensible, but here again, it took the 1990s and the large-scale use of these weapons by Iraq against Iran and Iraqi Kurds to alert the international community to their inherent dangers.

After the end of the east-west conflict, the nonproliferation of WMD became a high priority almost by default; since the risk of a global military confrontation between the two superpowers and their alliances had melted away, security experts and governments shifted their focus to the next most pressing security problem—that of proliferation. Additional concern arose that several countries beyond the "usual suspects" (Pakistan, India, and Israel) were working to develop WMD. This suspicion was confirmed in spectacular fashion in Iraq when, following the 1991 war, inspectors discovered a broad network of programs for developing an array of WMD and missiles. Briefly thereafter, a similar suspicion regarding North Korea's weapons program was also proved true.

Another serious risk emerged gradually: that of terrorists acquiring and using WMD. In the old days, it was conventional wisdom that terrorist groups would not wish to employ such weapons. "Terrorists want many people watching, not many people dead" was the consensus formula coined by the dean of US terrorist experts, RAND associate Brian Jenkins.[1] Since that time, however, the character of terrorism has fundamentally changed. Already in the mid-1980s, an international expert group combining terrorism specialists, nonproliferation scholars, and nuclear weapons manufacturers concluded that nuclear terrorist incidents could not be excluded. As the 1990s wore on, it became overwhelmingly clear that a new generation of religiously motivated terrorists did indeed view mass murder as both legitimate and strategically instrumental in prevailing in an asymmetric conflict with vastly superior enemies. After the 1993 attack on the World Trade Center, the consensus of terrorism experts shifted to this new assessment, and US policy, began focusing on this new and ominous threat.[2] Alerted by a wave of cases of diversion and illegal trafficking in radioactive and nuclear materials (a few of which involved tiny amounts of weapons-usable material originating primarily from the former Soviet Union), nonproliferation policy began incrementally to expand its scope to address the risk that weapons, technology, or material could spread to nongovernmental actors.[3]

With the new salience of the issue, the evidence of a few, but significant, weapons programs, and the enhanced scope, a debate ensued as to whether existing nonproliferation policy instruments were sufficient for addressing the problem and needed only adaptation and amendment, for example with regard to verification, compliance, and enforcement—a view predominant in Europe—or whether the reliance on multilateral regimes represented an outdated approach needing replacement by new, more unilateral, forceful, and ad-hoc instruments—a view taken by US neoconservatives. German nonproliferation policy evolved in this context.

Germany, the "Trading State": nonproliferation policy before 1989

German nonproliferation policy, notably in the nuclear sector, is set apart from other areas of foreign policy in that only Germany fully achieved the status of a "civilian power" after the end of the Cold War.[4] For the period between the conclusion of the Nuclear Non-Proliferation Policy in 1969 and German unification, the political approach of Germany followed the model of a "trading state"[5]: the emphasis was not on keeping the nuclear option open or even on developing the conditions for a nuclear break-out clandestinely. The same applies for chemical and biological weapons. Germany's renunciation of WMD was sincere. However, while subscribing to the letter of the Non-Proliferation Treaty (NPT), the country's main concern—regardless of who held the reins of government—was to ensure that Germany's industry sustain as little negative impact as possible because of international norms and rules derived from nonproliferation agreements and objectives.

As a consequence of these policies, Germany emerged as the leading supplier of dual-use goods feeding the nuclear, chemical, and biological weapons programs of countries such as Libya, Iraq, and Pakistan. Beginning in 1987, a scandal over this involvement gradually broke, reaching its unfortunate climax when it was revealed by the work of the United Nations Special Commission (UNSCOM) and the International Atomic Energy

Agency (IAEA) in Iraq that the largest number of suppliers for Iraq's WMD programs were German companies.[6]

Germany, the civilian power: the shift at the beginning of the 1990s

The turning point: export controls

In the early 1990s, this attitude underwent a radical change. Germany revamped its export control policies in an impressive manner. Features that, at the time, were only found among the most security-conscious Western states, such as the United States or Canada, became part of the German legal system in rapid succession; these changes included licensing requirements for intangible technology, brokerage and transit trade transactions, and a catch-all clause to submit to license dual-use items not written into export list in cases where the exporter had reasons to suspect that the recipient country intended to procure this item for military purposes. After having been a laggard in international export control negotiations, Germany became a proactive player almost overnight.

The diminished role of the nuclear industry in the industrial strategy of Germany in the 1990s contributed to this change of heart. The failure to build a commercial reprocessing plant in Germany, which was deplored in the 1980s by every pronuclear pundit, was later seen as a blessing that had saved the utility sector a great deal of money. The 1990s also witnessed the inglorious dismantlement of the pilot reprocessing facility at the Karlsruhe Research Center, the conversion of the Kalkar fast breeder reactor containment building to non-nuclear use, and the efforts to rid the country of its weapons-grade plutonium load for the breeder by shipping it to Britain. What could have been a carefully designed network of facilities and materials for retaining a German breakout option was gradually given up. In parallel, the influence of the nuclear industry also declined.

Shifting attitudes on verification

When the so-called Additional Protocol to the NPT verification system was negotiated between 1992 and 1997, the German position was that all parties to the Treaty, the nuclear weapon states included, should be subject to several new rules. Behind this stance were economic and normative concerns. Since the Additional Protocol grants inspectors access to facilities beyond those strictly understood to be "nuclear sites"—namely, facilities where fissile material was available—the scope of companies affected by the new system widened considerably.[7] Germany eventually agreed to a solution that placed some burden on the nuclear weapon states, but visibly less than on non-nuclear weapon states.[8]

Likewise, Germany participated actively in the negotiations leading up to the 1992 Chemical Weapons Convention, notably its verification system, and on a protocol to the Biological Weapons Convention that was designed to add some minimum verification conditions. In both cases, German delegates labored to reconcile the accepted objective of shaping a strong and viable instrument to combat WMD with the legitimate concerns of industry that intellectual property be protected and inspections not unduly interrupt the production process of private companies. To do so, the German government engaged industry in very close consultations, at times including industry representatives in the negotiation delegations, to help develop a verification system compatible with economic needs. The same practice was followed by other Western countries.

Thus, in the first half of the 1990s, a change in priorities regarding nonproliferation occurred: arms control became central and economic interests, while not becoming irrelevant or unimportant in shaping the German position, were recognized and pursued to the extent that they were compatible with this objective. This policy shift did not depend on the relative decline of the importance of the respective industries; while this might have been the case in the nuclear sector, it was clearly not so in the chemical and biological sectors; yet in all three areas, German policies were strikingly similar.

Reorganizing nonproliferation bureaucracy

Concomitant with this policy shift was a redistribution of influence among political actors. Until 1990, Office 431 (later renamed 411)—a part of the economics department within the Foreign Office that deals with civilian nuclear energy issues—was clearly in the lead in the field of nonproliferation policy, while the Department for Disarmament (nuclear nonproliferation and disarmament) took second place. Consequently, it was not one of the offices in the Disarmament Department but Office 431 that represented Germany in the Working Group on Nonproliferation (the predecessor of the Committee on Nonproliferation of Weapons of Mass Destruction (CONOP). In the interagency setting, the influence of the Ministry for Research and Technology (which in the 1960s grew out of the Atomic Ministry) was stronger than that of the Foreign Office, with the Economics Ministry rivaling the latter's position. The Defense Ministry office responsible for arms control (Staff III/5) watched over the compatibility of disarmament and nonproliferation policies with alliance interests in mind.

In the 1990s, two changes took place. Within the Foreign Office, the Department of Disarmament became the lead agency. In the interagency competition, the Foreign Office became dominant. Within the Disarmament Department, the three offices formerly responsible for various aspects of nonproliferation were later condensed into one, Office 240. The role of representing the German position before CONOP also shifted to this office.

Stronger emphasis on nuclear disarmament

The shift in priorities and the integration of the various NPT-related offices into one had an important consequence. Rather than setting economic priorities and only then adding on the other issues, German nuclear nonproliferation policies became more holistic and integrated. Disarmament, previously a side-issue in the shadow of NATO (North Atlantic Treaty Organization) positions, became an important aspect in the German political posture. Before, no initiatives were taken and no tensions risked with nuclear-armed allies on issues related to disarmament; when Germany engaged in political conflict, the dispute was about the civilian side of nuclear energy. Now, Germany dared to challenge, in a measured but distinct way, the nuclear weapon states on their own turf. One spectacular example was the proposal for a nuclear weapons register by then-Foreign Minister Klaus Kinkel in his December 1994 "10-point initiative" on nonproliferation. Kinkel suggested the creation of a binding commitment by nuclear weapon states to give data on their arsenals and material stocks and regularly update them, including any changes that may occur due to armament or disarmament measures. The proposal was strongly rebuffed by the three Western nuclear allies, and was not made again. Nevertheless, it demonstrated a new attitude on the German side.[9]

The preference for regimes and the neglect of enforcement needs: German opposition to "Counterproliferation"

For Germany, relying on international regimes had become the means for achieving the objectives of nonproliferation. The obvious question of "what if"—that is, how to react in the case of a failure of the regimes to prevent members or nonmembers from acquiring the proscribed weapons—was thoroughly avoided. This question was put on the agenda in 1993 when the administration of President Bill Clinton started the Counterproliferation Initiative (CPI), which was aimed at developing ways to address proliferation by military means. Much of what entered CPI were old programs; other elements aimed predominantly at procuring effective defenses against threats by WMD, notably for deployed troops, such as early warning, agent detection, improved protective gear, and mobile tactical antimissile defense. But a last element was the option to attack, possibly preemptively, facilities, storage areas, deployment sites, and troops wherever there was evidence that such weapons might exist.

When the concept was introduced into NATO discussions, Germany balked, as did many of its European partners. The fear was that the traditional regimes were to be replaced, rather than complemented, by new military concepts. Germany was still too deep in its pacifist mood; the first deployments of German soldiers "out of area" had just occurred (in Kampuchea), and law and force were not regarded as mutually reinforcing, but rather as opposites.[10] Together with several other European countries,

Germany prevented the term "counterproliferation" from entering NATO communiqués and succeeded in placing emphasis in these documents on diplomacy and on the support of existing international regimes. Nevertheless, NATO studied the matter thoroughly in a diplomatic and a military high-level working group, and arrived at the conclusion, predictably, that its soldiers should be prepared to act in a WMD environment. A chance was missed to connect and subordinate military force to the greater goal of upholding regimes and to affirm the necessity for a UN Security Council mandate if its forces were ever used in that capacity.

Strengthening multilateral regimes

Germany's opposition to the Counterproliferation Initiative grew out of the concern that the WMD nonproliferation regimes might be weakened. Throughout the 1990s, strengthening these multilateral instruments remained the clear priority of German policy. This goal was pursued with considerable vigor in the context of the European Foreign and Security Policy, where the two committees on disarmament in the United Nations (CODUN—Committees on disarmament in the United Nations) and on the nonproliferation of WMD (CONOP) were the operative bodies to shape and direct joint policies. Both were instrumental in developing and maintaining joint European policies in the negotiations on the Chemical Weapons Convention (CWC) and the Biological and Toxic Weapons Convention (BWC) protocols, and on coordinating European positions in the Organization for the Prohibition of Chemical Weapons (OPCW) once the conventions had come into force.[11]

The most significant effort was devoted to the indefinite extension of the NPT. In this context, Germany succeeded in persuading the other EU members to use the new foreign policy instrument of "Joint Action" as provided by the Maastricht Treaty. That agreement triggered the most powerful diplomatic campaign in EU history so far, including joint demarches by all member states to more than 60 countries and visits of high-ranking delegations by the major members to those countries with which they had privileged relations; Germany, inter alia, visited Teheran to convince the Iranian government, one of the more difficult parties as far as indefinite extension was concerned, to assume a constructive attitude for the conference.

During the conference, the leadership of the German delegation, at several crucial junctures of the negotiations, supplied compromise language to overcome logjams. Outside the presidential negotiation group, Germany was backed into a corner only once, when it had to defend the use of highly enriched uranium for the new research reactor in Garching, a project strongly criticized by other Western delegations and many nongovernmental organizations. It was, in many ways, the last grasp of "Germany, the trading state" in the field of nuclear nonproliferation.[12]

Nonproliferation diplomacy in crucial cases

The 1990s witnessed several crises in proliferation, starting with the perpetual quarrels about Iraqi cooperation with UN inspectors. Germany did not show a high profile on this issue; it supplied UNSCOM with valuable transport equipment, but withdrew it in the second half of the decade due to cost considerations. With respect to North Korea, there were considerable misgivings about the 1994 Framework Agreement between the United States and Pyongyang, as this agreement virtually suspended North Korea's undertakings under the NPT. Germany would eventually give in, since no other deal was in sight, and also entered into a partnership with KEDO, the Korean Energy Development Organization, which handled the supply of fuel and reactors to North Korea, thus supporting US diplomacy in this matter.

German bitterness over the Framework Agreement resulted not the least from deep misgivings about the unequal treatment of the Iranian case by the United States. In the early 1990s, Germany had proposed to Washington to complete the Busheer nuclear reactor; the construction was started by the German company Siemens, but then was suspended when the Iraq–Iran war started and never resumed. The German government suggested that the resumption of construction work should adhere to strict guidelines: renunciation of all sensitive fuel-cycle activities; enhanced access to IAEA inspectors anytime, anywhere, in the sense of what would later become the "Additional Protocol"; and the return of nuclear fuel to the source in order to make reprocessing physically impossible. Washington would have nothing of this. In hindsight, from the perspective of 2004, the German proposal seems impressively enlightened, and the US policy blatantly shortsighted. If the deal would have been struck, the nuclear nonproliferation regime would have been tremendously strengthened, in correspondence with Germany's priority goal in this policy field.

After 1998: Plus ça change?

Disarmament initiatives and regime politics

The Red–Green coalition started with a general expectation that German arms control, disarmament, and nonproliferation policies would gain a new impetus.[13] After all, it was Willy Brandt's government in 1969 that had established this area as part and parcel of the Federal Republic's security policy, and disarmament was one of the pillars of the Green party's identity. Indeed, the administration's beginning appeared to confirm these expectations. Foreign Minister Fischer suggested in the fall of 1999, shortly after taking office, that NATO should renounce the first use of nuclear weapons, since under the prevailing strategic circumstances the doctrine was obsolete and, indeed, an invitation to nuclear proliferation to anybody living in a worse security environment than the members of the Atlantic Alliance.

Fischer's initiative was utterly reasonable, but this does not count as a good argument in the camp of strategists in the nuclear weapon states. As happened to Kinkel in the case of the nuclear arms register, Fischer was promptly reprimanded by leaders in Washington, London, and Paris. While the German proposal was supported openly by Canada (and more subtly by a few other member states), the combined power of NATO's nuclear weapon states sufficed to suppress it. Rather than changing its doctrine, NATO embarked on a review of arms control possibilities as a compromise. The review was duly implemented, but with very meager results. As in the early 1990s, a German initiative was boldly started, but by and large buried due to resistance from nuclear weapon states and their allies.

Another parallel with the previous government was the initiative Germany took to achieve a joint approach to the 2000 NPT Review Conference. This time, the aim was not a EU Common Foreign and Security Policy (CFSP) "Joint Action," but a "Common Position." To achieve this, compromises had to be found for policies that are strongly contested in the European Union, such as nuclear disarmament and the peaceful uses of nuclear energy; in 1995, in contrast, it was much easier to reach agreement on a campaign for the indefinite extension of the NPT, an objective shared by all EU members.

For this reason, the German initiative met considerable skepticism in France and Ireland (and, to a lesser degree, in Sweden and Austria). French leaders worried that they would be obliged to support disarmament proposals that would not be in their country's interest, as an independent nuclear weapon state. Ireland (as well as Sweden and Austria) feared that they could be pressed to renounce their traditional, far-reaching positions on disarmament; for Ireland and Sweden, this was particularly undesirable, as they had already made commitments to their partners in the "New Agenda Coalition," a newly formed pro-disarmament group of seven states (which, in addition to Ireland and Sweden, includes Brazil, Egypt, Mexico, New Zealand, and South Africa), to support a common platform on nuclear disarmament. Austria, the country with the strongest attitude against the peaceful uses of nuclear energy, suspected that it was to be drawn into endorsing pronuclear statements.

However, the German government persevered, and its efforts ultimately bore fruit. A substantial Common Position was agreed upon and jointly pursued during the conference. Inter alia, it contained the notable principles of transparency of nuclear arsenals and the irreversibility of disarmament steps, both important parts of Germany's nonproliferation and disarmament strategy. In addition, the document called for the inclusion of tactical nuclear weapons in the disarmament agenda with the possibility of eventual elimination; here, the Germans succeeded in tackling a problem that the initiative in NATO had failed to address successfully. All three elements of the European document found their way into the conference's Final Declaration, establishing new, politically binding commitments by the NPT's member states.[14]

The end of support for the nuclear industry

During the conference, the German delegation supported suggestions to omit highly enriched uranium in all civilian applications. This contradicted past domestic policy, where the new research reactor at Garching in Bavaria was to be run on high-density, highly enriched uranium fuel to create an optimal neutron flux. The Red–Green government wanted to change this policy against the emphatic opposition of the Bavarian state government. Later, a compromise was reached: the reactor would start up with highly enriched uranium fuel, but then turn to lower enriched uranium grades later.

The controversy signaled the antinuclear policies of the government that embarked on a phase-out policy for nuclear power and reached agreement on long-term plans with the utilities in 2002. These policies led to a step that hurt the otherwise highly appreciated objective of nuclear disarmament and the security of weapons-grade material in Russia. International experts had recommended the transfer of the Hanau MOX fabrication plant to Russia, in the hopes of accelerating the transformation of weapons plutonium to reactor fuel and its degrading and contamination with fissile products by in-reactor burn-up. The move was blocked by the Green coalition partner because of its principled ideological opposition to MOX use and nuclear exports. When the chancellor later promised to the Chinese government to transfer this plant to the China, where it would presumably be used for the growth of the nuclear industry, this was again effectively opposed by the Greens (and also by some antinuclear SPD [Social Democratic Party] deputies). In the new political constellation, the nuclear industry finally lost the clout over German policy that it had held for more than three decades.

Enforcement and the hour of truth: the crisis in Iraq

That the issue of nonproliferation had assumed a serious political character rather than remaining an afterthought in foreign economic policy was impressively confirmed in the Iraqi crisis.[15] After the terrorist attacks of 9/11, Chancellor Schröder called for "unlimited solidarity" with the United States.[16] Germany sent special forces to Afghanistan, military transport units to help with logistics in Central Asia, a naval task force to the Horn of Africa, as well as a Bundeswehr unit specifically equipped to deal with biological and chemical weapons threats to Kuwait for exercises and permanent deployment. This deployment in Kuwait created risks that only became visible as 2002 progressed, as the United States moved closer to going to war against Iraq. Whatever position the German government would take toward such a military operation, the BC defense unit would need to assist allies if Iraq employed chemical weapons and would probably enter into combat, contrary to the political preferences of both the German government and public.[17]

German leaders had not agreed with the approach expressed in US President George Bush's "axis of evil" speech. The lumping together of three very diverse cases appeared unwise from Berlin's perspective. Concerning Iraq, the German threat analysis regarded Saddam Hussein's regime as a political problem and a long-term risk, but not as a current and present danger that required immediate military action. The German position reflected traditional preferences for diplomatic solutions and the exhaustion of all peaceful instruments before military action was considered. Using the United Nations and its multilaterally installed UNMOVIC (United Nations Monitoring, Verification and Inspection Commission) inspection system for resolving the crisis was clearly in line with the traditional German preferences for multilateral diplomacy as the first line of defense in nonproliferation, as reflected in the skepticism toward the US Counterproliferation Initiative of the early 1990s. Public opinion was firmly behind the government's stance before, during, and after the war;[18] and while the opposition criticized Schröder's absolute refusal to give in to military pressure and his confrontational tone toward the US Administration, their candidate Stoiber evaded the issue. His alternative policy was never elaborated; at one point, he even declared that overflight rights would not be granted to the United States if he were elected.[19]

In the end, the German government's position was confirmed by events. UNMOVIC worked successfully and asked for a brief extension of its mandate, only to be overtaken by the hasty opening of the war by the United States and Britain. No WMD were found in Iraq, and much of the intelligence used beforehand to justify the attack proved wrong, one-sided, or even forged in the aftermath. The war engendered the negative consequences that the government had feared and stimulated rather than reduced terrorist incidents.

After the war: political readjustment

The nonproliferation crises at the beginning of the new century pushed the subject of compliance powerfully onto the agenda. The instinctive German rejection of military counterproliferation, including for preemptive purposes in emergencies, had to be reconsidered, and the Iraqi episode brought this fact to the fore, even if, in this case, military counterproliferation was redundant and even detrimental, rather than useful. Nevertheless, it dawned on the German leadership that supporting international law, notably in the field of security policy, meant that one must also consider compliance and enforcement, if legal rules were to be upheld against wrongdoers and rule-breakers. In addition, the subject of preventing terrorists from gaining access to WMD, which had been on the agenda in the context of nuclear smuggling since the early 1990s, gathered new urgency following revelations about Al Qaeda's interest in such weapons and about a nuclear smuggling ring directed by Pakistan's "nuclear godfather," Abdul Kader Khan. This insight led to an adjustment of German policy, which became visible in three political arenas: the provisions set out in the new "European Security Strategy" and its sequel on nonproliferation, the "Proliferation Security Initiative," begun by the US administration; and United Nations Security Council Resolution 1540, dealing with the proliferation of WMD.

The European Security Strategy and its application to the nonproliferation field has often been described as the attempt to come as close to the Bush administration's position as possible. This is a misreading that can only lead to further misunderstandings. The European strategy reflects well the attachment to international law and the United Nations that has increasingly become the distinctive feature of "old Europe," as compared to a US approach dedicated to the pursuit of the "US national interest," which reflects German priorities quite well.[20] It is true that the European Security Strategy and its adaptation to the nonproliferation field contain the possibility of the use of military force, including in a preemptive mode. Nevertheless, in strong contrast to the US stance, in the European strategy military force is explicitly subject to international law and bound to the supreme authority of the UN Security Council as the ultimate guardian of the international regimes to curb the spread of WMD. This approach, the result of long and agonizing debates among the 15 members of the European Union prior to enlargement, reflects the strong German engagement that ultimately prevailed, with French support against the British push for broader support for the use of force. With these new documents, German multilateralism has a sounder basis now, as it can also address the more uncomfortable cases of noncompliance by aggrieved or aggressive regime members in a manner guided by rules rather than by ad-hoc considerations.

The conception of the Proliferation Security Initiative (PSI)[21] is one of the few occasions where the neoconservative pundits in the Bush administration started a line of policy in the nonproliferation field that proved acceptable, after some give and take, to the German position. This initiative tries to fill the gap that opens if export controls fail and a shipment of dangerous materials or technology is underway to an undesirable destination. The past regime had no answer to this challenge. The Bush answer was interception. The answer, notably the German one, was a new question: what is the legal basis for interception? In the course of the deliberations over the Proliferation Security Initiative, it was established that broad interception authority exists if the flag state where the ship is registered, the country where the shipowner resides, or the state in whose territorial waters the intercept happens agree to the action; in addition, flagless ships are legitimate prey for any interceptor. This limits potential interceptions without authority to actions in international waters. Germany and others successfully insisted that PSI can only act on the basis of legal authority contained in national laws and the international law of the sea. Germany joined on this basis, and a successful intercept of a German-owned ship with nuclear-related cargo destined for Libya was made by a joint German–American team in the fall of 2003.

At present, UN resolution 1540 is the most essential instrument the Security Council has ever adopted for dealing with the problem of WMD, notably their possible spread to nongovernmental actors.[22] In essence, the resolution extends obligations contained in the Non-Proliferation Treaty, the Biological Weapons Convention, the Chemical Weapons Convention, and the voluntary, only politically binding "club arrangements" of the Nuclear Suppliers Group (on nuclear weapons) and the Australia Group (on biological and chemical weapons) to all members of the United Nations. The resolution was adopted under the leadership of a German Security Council president, with full German diplomatic involvement. It demonstrated the German desire to fill in its principal policy blind spot of the past, namely the unwillingness to address compliance and enforcement policy, without compromising the basic stance regarding the supreme position of international law and multilateralism.

Enforcement revisited: the case of Iran

The other major enforcement problem developed in 2002, when it was revealed that the Islamic Republic of Iran had been working since 1985 on a clandestine program to close the fuel cycle, including in particular the construction of a centrifuge enrichment facility. That these activities were not reported to the International Atomic Energy Agency and that Iran admitted their existence only after an opposition group had tipped off the CIA and irrefutable evidence was presented to the IAEA enhanced the suspicion that they were not meant for civilian purposes, as Iran was quick to claim, but that they were part of a nuclear weapons program.

Germany had continued to cultivate good relations with Iran after the revolution. This rapport suffered only a short-lived setback after Iranian intelligence operatives killed four Kurdish opposition members in Berlin in 1992, and the Court charged with the subsequent criminal trial indicted several high-placed Iranian officials and finally convicted Iranian Intelligence Minister Ali Fallahian in his absence for instigation of murder. Germany, as well as other EU member states, recalled their ambassadors; but after a period of time, the ambassadors returned, and relations went back to normal. The election of President Mohammad Khatami contributed to this normalization, because it was seen as a turning point and as confirmation of the EU consensus that patience and cooperation would pay off, since Iran would incrementally evolve toward regime change.

In terms of German diplomacy, the compliance crisis could be seen in one of two ways. On the one hand, it challenged the rationale for the European policy of "critical dialogue" with Iran, of which Germany was the strongest champion. On the other hand, it offered the opportunity for this policy to prove its value, and Germany, with its good relations with Iran, had a chance to play a key role in attempting to defuse the crisis. In the summer of 2003, while the United States was consistently pressing for a condemnation of

Teheran in the IAEA Board of Governors and for moving the matter to the UN Security Council, where sanctions could be imposed on Iran, German diplomats were busy talking to Teheran and to the major European allies in order to forge a sensible compromise that would help Teheran to find a face-saving way out of its situation, while upholding the principles of the nonproliferation regime.

These efforts bore fruit: in the fall of 2003, the French, British, and German foreign ministers visited the Iranian capital to extract concessions on the suspension of Iran's sensitive fuel-cycle activities. The meeting was preceded by intense negotiations at the highest levels in which Germany, due to its good relations with Iran's Mullahs, played the leading role. The three-party mission was a highly visible implementation of the new European nonproliferation strategy that emphasizes diplomacy and multi-lateral regimes. The objective was to bring Iran back into full compliance with its NPT undertakings without resorting to threats of sanctions and possibly military action by the Security Council. The Europeans used the prospect of technical support for power reactors in Iran (safety technology), of extended economic relations (an EU–Iran trade agreement), and support for Iran's accession to the WTO (World Trade Organization) as the carrot, and the severing of economic exchange as well as moving the issue before the Security Council as the stick. Again, Germany played a leading role in an initiative that used a new setting.[23]

Unfortunately, the success proved short-lived, and German policy had a role in its failure. For nuclear cooperation, the German company Siemens would have been the appropriate partner as the Busheer reactors, the core of the civilian nuclear program of Iran, were manufactured by Siemens, and the company would have been the best fit to supply any complement to the Russian technology that was meanwhile incorporated into the plant design. Notably, safety technology would have been highly desirable from the Iranian perspective. However, because of the principled refusal of nuclear energy by the Red–Green coalition, granting the necessary licenses was out of the question. This left the United Kingdom in the position of being the only European country willing and ostensibly capable to help, and Foreign Secretary Jack Straw apparently made assurances to that effect to Teheran, only to discover later that the equipment in question was of American origin and could not be transferred without prior consent from the United States. This consent, however, was not forthcoming, since the United States was unwilling to make concessions before Teheran had unequivocally scrapped its broader fuel-cycle activities. As the Europeans did not deliver on their promises, Teheran recanted on its own concessions and withdrew the promise to "suspend" its enrichment and related activities. This triggered a new crisis and a new flurry of diplomatic initiatives. As of the fall of 2004, the issue remains unresolved.[24]

This episode exposes several characteristics of German policies: political aspects are far more in the foreground than economic ones; the preference for cooperative approaches and solutions continues; there is a new willingness to be active and visible in the "high politics" area of nonproliferation, notably the most difficult and sensitive field of compliance politics; in these activities, a multilateral embedding of German policy is seen as desirable. But Germany may now be willing to accept more coercive instruments, if sanctioned by the UN Security Council, when the cooperative approach fails.

Conclusions

In the early 1990s, German nonproliferation policy underwent a clear, substantial change in terms of priorities of goals, preferences of instruments, and bureaucratic setting. All three changes were mutually dependent.

Table 3.1 documents the shift in priorities from economic to security interests that occurred at the beginning of the 1990s. Economic objectives did not disappear, but they deferred to the cooperative security norms to which Germany had subscribed. Nuclear disarmament, formerly of low importance, became a mission actively pursued. Between the second and third phase under review, there is a lot of continuity. Most significantly, the strengthening of the regimes is priority number one in both phases. Change is observable, notably the insertion of the goal of compliance/enforcement with a high priority, and the disappearance of support for the nuclear industry as a goal of German policy, but the change is more incremental and less abrupt than for the previous transition.

In terms of policy instruments, change appears more steady among the three phases. Economic diplomacy disappears between phases one and two, while German initiatives on a national basis enter the spectrum of instruments (see Table 3.2). Between phases two and three, the most remarkable development is the much greater flexibility in the way Germany handles multilateralism, and the increased emphasis on initiatives pursued on a national basis. These aimed uniformly at strengthening the multilateral

Table 3.1 Objectives of German nonproliferation policy, 1969–2004

1969–1989	1990–1998	1998–2004
1. Supporting nuclear industry	Strengthening the regimes	Strengthening the regimes
2. Free trade	Nuclear disarmament	Compliance/ enforcement
3. Alliance policy	Free trade	Nuclear Disarmament
4. Conformity with regime	Alliance policy	Alliance policy rules
5. Nuclear disarmament	Supporting nuclear industry	Free trade

Table 3.2 Instruments of German nonproliferation policy, 1969–2004

1969–1989	1990–1998	1998–2004
1. Economic diplomacy with recipient countries 2. Regime-multilateralism 3. European Political co-operation	European political co-operation Regime-multilateralism own initiatives	Flexible multilateral groupings CFSP/own Initiatives

Table 3.3 Distribution of influence within the German nonproliferation bureaucracy, 1969–2004

1969–1989	1990–1998	1998–2004
1. Research ministry	Foreign office, disarmament department	Foreign office, disarmament department
2. Foreign office, economics department	Foreign office, economics department	Defense Ministry
3. Economics ministry	Research ministry	Foreign office, economics department
4. Defense ministry	Defense ministry	Research ministry
5. Foreign office, disarmament	Economics ministry	Economics ministry

regimes and were addressed to multilateral forums. This indicates a shift in tactics, but not in the substance of policy or its objectives.

Changed priorities are clearly reflected in the regrouping of the bureaucratic structures charged with formulating nonproliferation policy. The decline in influence of the ministries and departments whose missions are predominantly economic, as well as the rise of bureaucratic units focusing on issues of security policy, corresponds with the new priorities (see Table 3.3). Most notably, the uncontested leading role of the Foreign Ministry and its disarmament department reflects the strong orientation toward the strengthening of the regimes. At the same time, the relatively stronger impact of the Defense Ministry reflects the importance of security aspects now seen in nonproliferation.

Throughout the 1990s, German policy was consistent with the criteria for a "civilian power." The basic objective was to achieve security by cooperative means, to broaden and deepen international law and international organization in the security sector, thereby strengthening the regimes that had been constructed to cope with the problem of WMD. Considerations on the use of force were entered with an almost irrational reluctance, and when it eventually happened, these considerations kept the possibility of military action strictly within the frame of the regimes and of international law.

When the Red–Green coalition assumed power, the concept was modified but not changed. The furthest deviation from the high road of multilateralism occurred when two basic tenets of German identity, multilateralism and pacifism, collided—and this amidst an election campaign. The conflict was quickly solved by tipping the balance toward pacifism, but the imbalance was promptly repaired after the crisis (and the elections) ended. By and large, continuity, not revolution, characterized German nonproliferation policy in the last 15 years.

Acknowledgment

Many of the insights discussed in this chapter result from the author's long-term involvement with German and other European governments, since 1985, in his capacity as consultant and advisor, and also as a member of the German delegation to the NPT Review Conferences in 1995 and 2000; some of them cannot be ascribed to particular persons, quotes, and dates for obvious reasons.

Notes

1 Brian Jenkins, *International Terrorism: A New Kind of Warfare* (Santa Monica: Rand Corp., 1974).
2 Bruce Hoffman, *Inside Terrorism* (London: Victor Gollancz, 1998); Walter Laqueur, *Die globale Bedrohung. Neue Gefahren des Terrorismus* (Munich: Propyläen, 2001); on US policy cf. Richard A. Clarke, *Against All Enemies: Inside America's War Against Terror* (New York: Free Press/Simon & Schuster, 2004), Chapters 4–9.
3 Graham T. Allison, Owen R. Coté, Jr., Richard A. Falkenratz, and Steven E. Miller, *Avoiding Nuclear Anarchy. Containing the Threat of Loose Russian Nuclear Weapons and Fissile Materials* (Cambridge, MA: MIT Press, 1996).
4 For a more extensive treatment of the evolution of German nonproliferation policy, cf. Harald Müller, "German National Identity and WMD Nonproliferation," in *The Nonproliferation Review*, 10: 2 (summer 2003): 1–20.
5 Richard Rosecrance, *The Rise of the Trading State. Commerce and Conquest in the Modern World* (New York: Little, 1986).
6 On this phase cf. Harald Müller, "After the Scandals: West German Nonproliferation Policy," PRIF Reports No. 9, February 1990 (Frankfurt, MA.: PRIF, 1990).
7 Apart from uranium enrichment facilities, for example, factories where high-speed centrifuges were produced or even companies that made certain specialized machine tools to shape centrifuge parts could be legally visited by inspectors, if and when they so desired.
8 Susanna van Moyland, "A New Era in Safeguards: Assessing the IAEA Model Protocol," in *Disarmament Diplomacy* 16 (June 1997): 5–11.
9 Katja Frank, Harald Müller, "A Nuclear Weapons Register: Concepts, Issues and Opportunities," in Malcolm Chalmers, Mitsuro Donowaki, Owen Green, eds, *Developing Arms Transparency. The Future of the UN Register* (Bradford, University of Bradford Arms Register Studies No. 7, 1997), pp. 233–52.
10 Harald Müller, "Compliance Politics: A Critical Analysis of Multilateral Arms Control," in *Nonproliferation Review*, 7: 2 (summer 2000): 77–90.

11 Harald Müller, Alexander Kelle, "Germany," in Harald Müller, ed., *European Non-Proliferation Policy 1993–1995* (Brussels: European University Press, 1996), pp. 103–28.

12 Ibid., pp. 123–27.

13 Altogether, one of the best informed observers has credited German nuclear nonproliferation and disarmament policy in the First Committee of the United Nations, the Conference on Disarmament, and the NPT Review Process as "desiring to be more proactive," Rebecca Johnson, "Rogues and Rhetoric: The 2003 NPT PREPCOM Slides backwards," in *Disarmament Diplomacy* (June/July 2003): 3–23, quoted here p. 14.

14 For the EU Common Position, cf. NPT/CONF.2000/19.

15 On this subject, cf. the excellent analysis by Sebastian Harnisch, "German Non-Proliferation Policy and the Iraq Conflict," in *German Politics* 13: 1 (2004): 1–34.

16 *Bulletin der Bundesregierung* 61/1, September 19, 2001.

17 Cf. Michael Hedstück, Gunther Hellmann, "Wir machen einen deutschen Weg," *Irak-Abenteuer, das transatlantische Verhältnis und die Risiken der Methode Schröder für die deutsche Außenpolitik*, Chapter 3. Available at http://www.uni-frankfurt.de/fb03/prof/hellmann/mat/irak.pdf. Accessed December 2, 2002.

18 Polls in 2002 are well captured in Hedstück and Hellmann, *Irak-Abenteuer*, pp. 224–34; the continuity in German public opinion was proven in 2003 polls such as those published in: Dietmar Wittich, *Die Einsamkeit der Supermacht* (Berlin: Rosa-Luxemburg-Stiftung, 2003). Available at: www.emnid.tnsofres.com/presse/ntv/ntv-2003_01_17.html, Accessed December 3, 2002.

19 Cf. Stoibers statement in the *Frankfurter Allgemeine Zeitung*, August 9, 2002, p. 1; SPIEGEL online. Available at http://www.spiegel.de/politik/ausland/0,1518,211356,00.html. Accessed August 28, 2002.

20 Clara Portela, *The Role of the EU in the Non-Proliferation of Nuclear Weapons: The Way to Thessaloniki and Beyond* (Frankfurt, M.: PRIF Report 65, 2003).

21 Proliferation Security Initiative (PSI) Meeting, Paris, September 3–4, Statement of Interdiction Principles, *Disarmament Diplomacy* 74 (December 2003): 63–66.

22 Resolution 1540 (2004), Adapted by the Security Council at its 4956th meeting on April 28, 2004, *Disarmament and Diplomacy* 77 (May/June 2004): 61–63.

23 Rebecca Johnson, "Addressing Iran's Nuclear Programme: The US, IAEA, and European Foreign Ministers," *Disarmament Diplomacy* 74 (December 2003): 51–56.

24 Stephen Pullinger, Dany Shoham, "Libya, Iraq and Iran: Updates and Analysis," *Disarmament Diplomacy* 77 (May/June 2004): 37–55; "Implementation of the NPT Safeguards Agreement in the Islamic Republic of Iran. Resolution adopted by the Board on 18 September 2004," International Atomic Energy Agency, GOV/2004/79.

4
Civilian Power under Stress: Germany, NATO, and the European Security and Defense Policy[1]

Marco Overhaus

Introduction

The notion of "civilian power" has been used to describe the foreign policy consensus that emerged in Germany after the Second World War. After German accession to the North Atlantic Treaty Organization (NATO) in 1955, the firm integration of the country into the Western web of multilateral institutions under American leadership became the core of this consensus. Since then, Germany has—most of the time successfully—sought to balance its membership commitments in NATO and the European Community. In the context of the latter, Germany, along with France, soon assumed a leading role in the political and economic integration process, while also taking into account the interests of the other—especially smaller—member states. In the Atlantic Alliance, it relied on American leadership in the area of "hard power" and military policy.

Recently, observers have come to the conclusion that German foreign policy has lost a good deal of its multilateralist enthusiasm.[2] In the European context, Berlin forfeited much of its credibility as an advocate of deeper integration as it began to put more emphasis on the pursuit of its *national interests*. Major German policy initiatives within NATO have been by and large absent since the middle of the 1990s. Moreover, with the establishment of the European Security and Defense Policy (ESDP) since 1998 and 1999, Berlin's ability and willingness to balance Atlantic and European commitments seems to have waned as well. This led to the impression that Germany had an ambivalent foreign policy or also lacked any meaningful strategy whatsoever.[3] The impression was reinforced during the most recent Iraq crisis, when Germany openly dissociated itself from its longstanding American ally and instead formed a coalition with France, raising fears of a new German "special path."

In this chapter I argue that, since the mid-1990s, Germany's traditional foreign policy orientation as a "civilian power" has come under pressure from two sides. The first is the international framework of the transatlantic relationship, which has changed fundamentally during the last decade and especially since George W. Bush entered the White House in 2001. Specifically, the decline of what G. John Ikenberry and others call "liberal American hegemony" has made it ever more difficult for Germany to reconcile its traditional foreign policy principles with new external circumstances.[4] I consider these new circumstances to be the driving factor behind German policy change and will focus on them accordingly. In the domestic context of German foreign policy making—the second side—two factors in particular have reinforced the pressure on Germany's civilian power orientation. During the run-up to the 2002 German federal elections, foreign and security policy became hijacked by the domestic struggle for the chancellorship. Whether this indicates a more general trend toward the subordination of foreign and security policy to domestic concerns, however, remains to be seen. Moreover, with the election of Chancellor Gerhard Schröder in 1998, a new generation of political leaders came to office who have a more pragmatic, less inhibited foreign policy approach, as well as less emotional affinity toward the United States. This generation is thus less willing to accept compromises for the sake of good relations with Washington per se. Both domestic factors are likely to have aggravated the transatlantic rift over Iraq in 2002 and 2003, yet they did not cause it. Their importance should therefore not be overestimated. Rather, Iraq revealed a structural crisis of the transatlantic relationship.

Declining hegemony, the emergence of ESDP, and the German splits

As the transatlantic crisis reached its climax on the eve of Washington's military intervention in Iraq, policy makers and analysts wondered whether the dispute was just a temporary irritation, principally caused by a specific constellation of governments and personalities, or whether deeper structural changes were at work.[5] Iraq revealed that the post–Second World War "constitutional bargain"[6] no longer functioned: while the Bush administration was more than willing to take the lead in toppling the regime of Saddam Hussein, half of the European governments, as well as a majority of the European populace, were not willing (or only reluctantly so) to follow this lead. At the same, the American decision-making system proved anything but transparent and offered few opportunities to European governments to raise their concerns in Washington.

There are good reasons to assume that the crisis is more structural and long-term than momentary. First, the declining security interdependence between Europe and the United States after the end of the Cold War is likely to have altered strategic calculations on both sides of the Atlantic. David Lake points out that historically, unilateralism has been the dominant strategy of American foreign policy.[7] In the post-Cold War world, with the Soviet threat gone, he sees the interwar battle between unilateralists and internationalists in Washington reemerge, because "there is no 'obvious' foreign policy choice for the United States. [...] Although cooperation remains attractive, unilateralism is now a more viable alternative than at any time since World War II."[8]

Second, the system of benign American hegemony depended on the premise that a transatlantic consensus existed on the basic principles of the European and international order.[9] Yet today, several crucial aspects of this consensus seem to have eroded, most importantly on the use of military force and the role of multilateral institutions. "[D]iverging perspectives of what drives the new age of global politics" did not occur for the first time under George W. Bush's term.[10] Yet, these splits have widened considerably since Bush assumed the presidency.

Finally, the process of "de-coupling" between Europe and America has been reinforced by sociological and demographic changes in the United States and Europe as a new generation of politicians have taken office whose attitudes were not shaped by the immediate post–Second World War environment. These leaders (among them Bill Clinton, George W. Bush, and Gerhard Schröder) generally tend to see transatlantic relations and foreign policy in a more pragmatic, less "emotional" way. In the United States, demographic shifts increasing the Hispanic and Asian segments of the population are likely to influence foreign policy and to divert attention away from Europe and toward the Pacific Rim and Latin America.[11]

As the coordinates of the longstanding constellation that marked the period from 1945 to 1999 began to shift, German traditional foreign policy orientations came under pressure. The German role in building the European Security and Defense Policy has clearly reflected these problems. Although a European security and defense component had been part of the integration process from the beginning (the first, far-reaching attempt failed in 1954 with the European Defense Community), its development in the 1990s was closely linked to the crisis in transatlantic relations emerging with the outbreak of the Yugoslav conflict. The first substantive steps—the upgrading of the Western European Union (WEU), the creation and development of the European Union's Common Foreign and Security Policy with the Maastricht and Amsterdam treaties and the European Security and Defense Identity (ESDI) *within* NATO—were still compatible with the traditional German foreign policy goal of reconciling its transatlantic security integration with its involvement in the European project. When European security and defense cooperation became more concrete and gradually began to detach itself from NATO, however, the German splits became more painful.[12]

The transformation of the relatively loose concept of European defense into a proper policy field with concrete military structures and capabilities began to unfold on the eve of the Kosovo crisis in 1998 and 1999. The emergence of ESDP—with the Franco–British Saint Malo Initiative in December 1998—was related to (though not exclusively caused by) European dissatisfaction with America's political and military leadership during the NATO-led Operation Allied Force in Kosovo.[13] Moreover, Kosovo and the deliberations before the alliance's April 1999 Anniversary Summit in Washington revealed diverging conceptions across the Atlantic over the scope and functions of NATO.

Although in the first phase of the ESDP, Berlin played the role of a bystander more than a protagonist, the German government soon adopted a proactive position when it held the EU presidency in the first half of 1999 to integrate the bilateral Saint Malo initiative into the multilateral European framework. The first institutional steps were taken on the Cologne Summit in June of that same year. Subsequently, Berlin supported the creation of a European Rapid Reaction Force (ERRF) and of permanent political–military structures within ESDP.

During the whole process, European defense policy owed a good deal of its new dynamism to the relationship between Paris and Berlin. Despite the fact that bilateral relations had cooled considerably since the Red–Green coalition took office in 1998, both countries were able to leave their imprints on the ESDP.[14] Unlike France, however, Germany did not conceive of the project as an effort to counterbalance the United States in a multipolar world. Instead, Berlin was strongly interested in reinforcing cooperation between NATO and the European Union. The fact that London was aboard (and that Turkey and Greece were approaching each other) made prospects for more effective cooperation between both organizations look promising. Despite the constructive role the Red–Green coalition played in this phase, the creation of ESDP caused ambivalence in German foreign and security policy, as old principles became less compatible with new circumstances. Most notably, it became increasingly difficult for Berlin to maintain its traditional equidistance toward the United States and France. The somewhat artificial debates on "unnecessary duplications" of military planning and command structures in NATO and ESDP have most clearly reflected the German splits. Since 1998, the Red–Green coalition government has in fact supported the creation of exactly such structures, which already exist in NATO, at least in a similar form (for example, the new EU military staff). Another striking example of German ambivalence was seen in Gerhard Schröder's 1999 speech before the French National Assembly.[15] The chancellor adopted the French idea of *Europe Puissance*, even though it was absolutely clear to German decision makers that the French reading of the term meant a Europe that would act independently from and outside of the framework of the Atlantic alliance.

September 11 and the crisis of NATO

The collapse of the World Trade Center towers on September 11, 2001, and the new calibration of American foreign policy under George W. Bush—which was based, in Ivo Daalder's words, "on the belief that the preponderance of power enables the United States to achieve its goals without relying on others"—had the effect of further worsening the transatlantic rift that had already become visible in the 1990s.[16] As a consequence, the Atlantic Alliance experienced one of the most serious crises in its history.

After 9/11: from transatlantic solidarity ...

After the initial shock of the attacks on the World Trade Center and the Pentagon, Europeans felt a wave of solidarity with the United States. The revival of transatlantic security cooperation became the watchword of the day—at least in European capitals. For the first time ever, NATO member countries activated Article 5 of the Atlantic Treaty[17] on the day after the attacks, which was followed by concrete measures to support Washington. The German government, declaring its "unlimited solidarity" with the United States, was a staunch supporter of these measures. Moreover, in November 2002 Chancellor Gerhard Schröder compelled his razor-thin parliamentary majority to approve German participation, under the American leadership, in Operation Enduring Freedom in Afghanistan, the Persian Gulf, and the Horn of Africa.

Soon after the ousting of the Taliban regime in Afghanistan, Berlin tried to bring NATO into the process of postconflict reconstruction. In particular, the Ministry of Defense promoted such a role. After the International Security Assistance Force (ISAF) had been installed in December 2001, Defense Minister Peter Struck soon demanded logistical and other support from NATO for the ISAF troops.[18] It is notable that, in the case of Afghanistan, Germany had silently dropped its earlier reservations concerning NATO's role in crisis management outside of Europe. As Defense Minister Struck later put it: "The question whether NATO ought to restrict its role to alliance territory became irrelevant on September 11, 2001."[19]

With its support for the Alliance's activation of Article 5 and its remarkable policy change, the German government tried to keep NATO in business and to tie Washington's reaction to the terrorist attacks to a cooperative, multilateral framework. Yet, this strategy did not prove successful. Apart from the modest, largely symbolic measures outlined above, the United States did not fall back on Europe's offer to any significant degree. Yet, the Bush administration had no interest in rendering the alliance irrelevant. Politically, it valued the Europeans' support and the activation of Article 5 as a source of legitimacy for its "international war on terrorism." Yet, Washington was mostly interested in NATO as a military tool. For this reason, Bush administration officials drafted the initiative for a NATO Response Force (NRF) before the November 2002 Prague Summit in order to endow the defense organization with the military capabilities to effectively confront the new security challenges posed by terrorism and the proliferation of weapons of mass destruction. In Berlin, the plan was initially received with some skepticism, but the Schröder government understood that it could not reject the offer without paying a political price within NATO. A rejection would have made the ongoing integration of US security policy into multilateral structures even more problematic.[20]

After the Prague Summit, NATO emerged looking very much as the Bush administration wanted it to look. In terms of the (potentially global) geographical scope of its activities, decisions favored the US perspective. In return, Germany and some of its European partners, for the time being, could block the informal introduction of initiatives permitting a more flexible decision-making process for military deployments, which would have reduced the allies' influence on American policy even further.[21]

... to transatlantic confrontation

Even before the Prague Summit, however, it had become clear that profound transatlantic differences remained. These diverging strategic concerns between the United States and some Western Europe governments fully surfaced during the Iraq crisis in 2002 and 2003.[22]

While much of the confrontation over Iraq was carried out in the United Nations, it was revealing that NATO failed to serve as a transatlantic forum in this critical situation. It only became so in the winter of 2003, when assuming center stage as the Bush administration asked its alliance partners to plan and execute preparatory measures to defend Turkey in the event of an attack from Iraq. When Belgium and France blocked this request in February, the dispute threatened to escalate. Germany behaved in a rather ambivalent way. In effect, it supported the veto politically but refrained from direct intervention itself. Moreover, Berlin supported Washington and Ankara indirectly when it delivered defensive Patriot batteries to Turkey via the Netherlands.[23] A compromise was finally reached in the Defense Planning Committee of the alliance (in which France is not represented). NATO promised to support Turkey with its Airborne Early Warning Aircraft (AWACS), Patriot Air Defenses, as well as protection against biological and chemical weapons.[24] Germany strongly supported the compromise, but at the same time warned that it would have to withdraw German AWACS personnel should Turkey enter the war.[25] For France, Belgium, and Germany, the principal motive for initially blocking defense planning for Turkey was political. The opponents of military intervention in Iraq did not want to anticipate such a move through NATO's activation.[26]

Mending fences after the war

Soon after the war had been "officially" declared over by President Bush, the question emerged as to whether NATO should play a role in the process of Iraq's reconstruction. The issue was placed on NATO's agenda by US Defense Secretary Donald Rumsfeld, but also by the alliance's Secretary General Jaap de Hoop Scheffer and the Polish government, which had taken the lead in a multinational force in southern Iraq. From the beginning, the German government adopted a pragmatic stance on the issue and tried not to aggravate further its relations with Washington. In May 2003 NATO decided the planning of logistical support for the Polish sector in Iraq with German approval.[27] The German government repeatedly and categoricaly ruled out sending German troops to Iraq[28] and declared its skepticism about any NATO involvement, but German officials repeatedly assured Washington that they would not block any such action should a consensus in the alliance evolve.[29] While Berlin rejected any direct military involvement in Iraq, it offered the Bush administration an expansion of its engagement within the ISAF operation in Afghanistan. Beginning in February 2003 Germany and the Netherlands had jointly assumed ISAF leadership, and on April 16, 2003 the NATO Council had agreed to the German request that the alliance take over ISAF command in August 2003. Subsequently, Germany supported the idea of creating additional Provincial Reconstruction Teams (PRTs) under NATO command outside of Kabul in order to stabilize the countryside before the general elections in Afghanistan. The German Bundeswehr assumed responsibility for a PRT in Kunduz. Moreover, Chancellor Schröder offered assistance from the five-nation Eurocorps and the Franco–German Brigade in this effort.[30]

Beyond a more pragmatic stance over Iraq and a supportive role in Afghanistan, Berlin has since then undertaken efforts to restore NATO's role as a consultative body across the Atlantic. On the occasion of the fortieth Security Conference in Munich in 2004, Foreign Minister Fischer presented the idea of a "new transatlantic initiative" on the Middle East,[31] with NATO playing a central role. The idea echoed a similar initiative of the Bush administration which had been announced shortly before. Moreover, Defense Minister Struck presented his idea of a modern-day Harmel report, "a new conceptual document as a foundation for the future of NATO, compiled by European and American experts."[32] Thus far, however, both German initiatives have had only a modest impact on Washington and other NATO allies. During the G-8 Summit on Sea Island and the June 2004 NATO Summit in Istanbul, they did not trigger any new initiatives. The outcome of the Istanbul Summit also reflected the smallest common denominator among member countries concerning NATO's role in Iraq and Afghanistan. While the engagement in Iraq was limited to the training of security forces, the alliance pledged to reinforce its military presence at the Hindukush in the period leading up to the Afghan elections.

The European context: from defense policy to defense union

The more assertive and unilateralist US policy in the wake of September 11, 2001 had two major—and interrelated—effects on the European context. First, it triggered a crisis of multilateralism and political leadership in European foreign policy that became obvious as the Iraq crisis unfolded. Not only did it divide Europe from America, but it also divided Europe itself. While a coalition of countries around Germany and France opposed any military intervention, another group, which included most of the new EU member countries from Central-Eastern Europe (CEE), as well as Britain, Spain, and Italy, expressed their support for the US policy. The intra-European conflict escalated when Germany and France, together with Russia, expressed their opposition in a joint memorandum on February 25, 2003.

The close cooperation among the three countries (and especially between Paris and Berlin) led to resentment in other European capitals. Shortly afterwards, eight countries, mostly from CEE, signed a letter of solidarity with Washington endorsing Bush's tough stance toward Saddam Hussein. This move was clearly in breach of a common declaration that the EU heads of state and government had issued a few days earlier and that struck a much more skeptical note with respect to American policy in Iraq. During the whole crisis, Europe's Common Foreign and Security Policy was virtually blocked. The German government was not wholly innocent in this. Some analysts have rightly criticized that Schröder too easily gambled away Germany's traditional advocacy of the European Union's new and smaller members when he sought the close alliance with France.[33] In a situation where the US policy in Iraq threatened to split Europe in two, Germany's inability to forge comprehensive coalitions and bridge European differences turned out to have grave consequences for European foreign policy.

As a second result of both the new calibration of US foreign policy under the Bush administration and Europe's failure to act in unison, the more traditionally integrationist European countries (most notably Germany, France, and Belgium)[34] began to push for the further development of ESDP. This was reflected both in the work of the European Convention on a draft Constitutional Treaty and in the work of the EU's High Representative, Javier Solana, on a European Security Strategy. In the run-up to the November 2002 NATO summit, Foreign Minister Fischer and his French counterpart, Dominique de Villepin, published a joint initiative for the convention that proposed the creation of a European Defense Union.[35] The central idea behind it was to allow closer cooperation among those European countries that would be both willing and able to push European military and defense policy forward (so-called structured cooperation). The initiative included other elements, as well, such as a mutual defense clause, the formation of a European Armaments Agency, and the closer interlocking of European defense industries. In April 2003 both countries, along with Belgium and Luxemburg, proposed the creation of a European Forces Headquarters in Tervuren (close to Brussels), which met with stiff American and British resistance and was later watered down. Initially, the initiative in security and defense policy failed to muster majority support within the European Union. It was only when the British government relaxed its previous opposition to some central elements of the Franco–German initiative that a compromise on the European Defense Union could be reached in the run-up to the December 2003 European Council. The compromise, which finally became part of the Constitutional Treaty approved by the EU Heads of State and Government in June 2004, included a scaled-down "European headquarters" within the military staff of the European Union. Moreover, the "structured cooperation" was tied to the approval of the Council.[36]

Despite the agreement, the leadership problem in the European Union has not yet been satisfactorily solved. There remains much resentment about a "directorate" or "triumvirate" that other countries fear might dictate the future direction of the European integration process. The phenomenon of a " 're-nationalization' of foreign policy as initiatives and actions return to the big capitals"[37] and the corresponding proliferation of shifting "bilateralisms," "trilateralisms," and other "mini-lateralisms" demonstrates the crisis of multilateralism and political leadership in Europe in the area of security and defense policy. As the stable multilateral order that had been created under the *Pax Americana* after Second World War began to show visible cracks, Europe started to grapple with a post–hegemonic alternative. The phenomenon of "free-floating coalitions"[38] has become a challenge to Germany's traditional focus on multilateralism. In this picture, where "… old complicities and forms of co-operation are more difficult to sustain because they seem less rewarding than short-term coalitions," the recent double-backs in German foreign policy seem to be in accordance with the zeitgeist rather than indications of a German "special path": "To that extent, Germany is going with the flow instead of being the odd man out that some feared after unification."[39]

Conclusion

Recently, and most visibly during the Iraq crisis in 2002 and 2003, German foreign policy has shifted away from some of its traditional postwar features, which have fallen under the category of "civilian power." Although its predominant orientation toward multilateralism has not been questioned in principle, recent German foreign policy, as evidenced in NATO and ESDP, has been marked by ambivalence. During the Iraq crisis, Berlin dismissed its long-standing policy of equidistance between Washington and Paris and clearly sided with France. Moreover, the Schröder government was criticized for having betrayed its role as a champion of smaller member states as well as EU newcomers.

I have argued in this chapter that—while Germany's civilian power orientation came under pressure from two sides—the driving force for policy adaptation has been the changing transatlantic context. The argument is not that American foreign policy—especially under the presidency of George W. Bush—should be blamed for all that went wrong in Iraq and in relations between the United States and its European allies. Rather, the core argument is that long-term, structural factors have caused the decline of the "benign American hegemony", which formed the foundation of the post–Second World War multilateral order. Against this backdrop, Germany has had to adopt its old principles to new circumstances.

The other factor, albeit in a secondary role, has been German domestic politics. Rather than causing the rift between the United States, Germany, and other European countries, domestic politics reinforced the effect of the rift. The 2002 electoral campaign was characterized by the "hijacking" of an important foreign policy issue (the war in Iraq) by domestic concerns (Schröder's quest to become reelected). Whether this represented an exception or a more general shift in German foreign policy remains to be seen. Moreover, the members of the so-called Schröder generation and their pragmatism regarding transatlantic relations are less prepared than their predecessors to make compromises in order to avoid open disputes with Washington. It is remarkable, though, that bureaucratic politics also played a role. While the chancellery and the foreign ministry were more willing to risk a confrontation with Washington, the defense ministry turned out to be a bastion of Germany's traditional transatlanticism.[40]

What are the consequences for German and European foreign and security policy? In the past, German governments have all too often taken American leadership for granted. The Iraq war demonstrated that this policy is no longer tenable. While Washington was willing to lead a more flexible "coalition of the willing" into the war, it was not willing to grant the Europeans a significant voice in its policy-making process. One should not assume that in the future any security cooperation across the Atlantic will perform so miserably as it did in the case of Iraq. Still, Europe has proven unable to provide political and military leadership from within when the situation demanded it. Moreover, Europe and America have to find a new balance between NATO and the European Union. The United States will surely remain an important player in European security for some time to come, but the stability of the past has gone. As one of the major players in Europe, Germany has to find answers to these pressing questions.

Notes

1   For an extended version of this chapter see Marco Overhaus, "In Search of a Post–Hegemonic Order: Germany, NATO and the European Security and Defence Policy," *German Politics*, 13: 4 (2004): 551–68.

2   For a summary of the arguments see Hanns W. Maull, " 'Normalisierung' oder Auszehrung? Deutsche Außenpolitik im Wandel," *Aus Politik und Zeitgeschichte*, B11 (2004): 17–23.

3   Marco Overhaus, "Deutschland und die Europäische Sicherheits- und Verteidigungspolitik 1998–2003: Gewollte Ambivalenz oder fehlende Strategie?," *Deutsche Sicherheitspolitik. Eine Bilanz der Regierung Schröder*, Sebastian Harnisch, Christos Katsioulis and Marco Overhaus, eds (Baden-Baden: Nomos, 2004), 37–58.

4   G. John Ikenberry, "Institutions, Strategic Restraint, and the Persistence of American Postwar Order," *International Security*, 23: 3 (1998/1999): 43–78, quoted here p. 43.

5   For contrasting views see, for instance, Elizabeth Pond, "Das NATO-Trauerspiel," *Blätter für Deutsche und Internationale Politik*, 4 (2003): 433–45, and Stephen F. Szabo, "Germany and the United States After Iraq: From Alliance to Alignment," *International Politics and Society*, 1 (2004): 41–52.

6   According to G. John Ikenberry, a quasi "constitutional bargain" has been at the heart of "benign American hegemony" after the Second World War. This bargain meant that the United States would constrain its own powers through multilateral institutions while granting its European allies a voice in foreign policy making. In return, European allies accepted the American lead, which was most visibly embedded in NATO. Ikenberry, *International Security* (see note 4), p. 46.

7   David A. Lake, *Entangling Relations. American Foreign Policy in its Century* (Princeton: Princeton University Press, 1999).

8   Lake, *Entangling Relations* (see note 7), p. 16.

9   Beate Neuss, " 'Benign Hegemonic Power': A Means of Refashioning Western Europe in the Image of the United States?" *Amerikastudien* (Special Issue), 46: 4 (2001): 495–524, quoted here p. 535.

10 Ivo Daalder, "The End of Atlanticism," *Survival*, 45: 2 (2003): 147–66, quoted here p. 149.

11 Dominique Moisi, "Reinventing the West," *Foreign Affairs*, 82: 6 (2003): 67–73.

12 Franz-Josef Meiers, "Deutschland: Der dreifache Spagat," *Die Europäische Sicherheits- und Verteidigungspolitik. Positionen, Perzeptionen, Probleme, Perspektiven*, Hans-Georg Erhart, ed. (Baden-Baden: Nomos, 2002), 35–48.

13 For more details see Charles A. Kupchan, "Kosovo and the Future Engagement in Europe: Continued Hegemony or Impending Retrenchment?," *Alliance Politics, Kosovo, and NATO's War: Allied Force or Forced Allies?*, Pierre Martin and Mark R. Brawley, eds (New York: Palgrave, 2001), 75–89.

14 Josef Janning, "Bundesrepublik Deutschland," *Jahrbuch der Europäischen Integration 1999/2000*, Werner Weidenfeld and Wolfgang Wessels, eds (Bonn: Europa Union Verlag, 2000), 309–16, quoted here p. 313.

15 Rede von Bundeskanzler Gerhard Schröder vor der französischen Nationalversammlung am 30. November 1999 in Paris, Available at: http://www.bundeskanzler.de

16 Daalder, *Survival* (see note 10), p. 152.

17 Article 5 states that an attack on one NATO ally is considered to be an attack on all allies. It remains a sovereign decision of member states, however, how they contribute to the collective defense.

18 In German military circles, such a move was seen *and welcomed* as a "political springboard" for a permanent NATO engagment at the Hindukush. "Struck will sich NATO-Hilfe in Afghanistan gewiss sein," *Frankfurter Rundschau* (Online Edition), October 12, 2002.

19   "Nicht jedes Land muss alles können—Interview mit Verteidigungsminister Peter
     Struck," *Berliner Zeitung*, November 21, 2002.
20   There were visible intra-governmental differences, however. While Foreign
     Minister Fischer expressed his lukewarm support, the Defense Ministry seemed
     more enthusiastic about the idea. See Joschka Fischer, "Regierungserklärung zum
     NATO-Gipfel   am   21/22.   November   in   Prag,   abgegeben   durch
     Bundesaußenminister Fischer vor dem Deutschen Bundestag," Speech delivered on
     November 14, 2002.
21   Johannes Varwick, "Deutsche Sicherheits- und Verteidigungspolitik in der
     Nordatlantischen   Allianz: Die   Politik   der   rot-grünen   Bundesregierung
     1998–2003," *Deutsche Sicherheitspolitik. Eine Bilanz der Regierung Schröder*, Sebastian
     Harnisch, Christos Katsioulis, and Marco Overhaus, eds (Baden-Baden: Nomos,
     2004), pp. 15–36.
22   The Iraq crisis has triggered considerable debate among pundits and academics
     on the impact of domestic factors on German foreign and security policy, espe-
     cially the subordination of foreign policy to domestic concerns or a general shift
     of the foreign policy outlook of German elites. The focus of this chapter is on the
     changing *external* conditions of German foreign policy making. For a more in-depth
     discussion of the domestic sources of the transatlantic dispute over Iraq see the
     contribution of Rudolf in this volume.
23   "Ein Veto spaltet die NATO," *die tageszeitung*, February 11, 2003.
24   "Nato beendet ihre Blockade," *Frankfurter Allgemeine Zeitung* (Online Edition),
     February 17, 2003.
25   "Deutschland droht mit Abzug der AWACS-Besatzungen," *Frankfurter Allgemeine
     Zeitung* (Online edition), March 22, 2003.
26   For Germany, legal reasons related to the provisions of the Basic Law played a role
     as well.
27   Varwick, *Deutsche Sicherheitspolitik* (see note 20).
28   Chancellor Schröder instead offered to train Iraqi security forces in Germany and
     to dispatch "flying hospitals" (in the form of the MEDEVAC Airbus) to the
     country.
29   Joschka Fischer, "Rede von Bundesaußenminister Joschka Fischer auf der 40.
     Konferenz für Sicherheitspolitik in München," delivered on February 7, 2004.
     Again, it is interesting to note that the Defense Ministry had a more "Atlantic"
     outlook than the Chancellery and the Foreign Ministry. In August 2003, Defense
     Minister Struck declared in public that he would support a direct involvement of
     NATO in Iraq. He even did not exclude the participation of German troops.
     However, he had to back away from his remarks the next day, "Struck befürwortet
     NATO-Einsatz im Irak," *Frankfurter Allgemeine Zeitung* (Online edition), August 10,
     2003.
30   "Deutschland will Irak-Einsatz der NATO nicht blockieren," *Frankfurter Allgemeine
     Zeitung* (Online edition), February 7, 2004.
31   Fischer, "Rede von Bundesaußenminister Joschka Fischer auf der 40. Konferenz
     für Sicherheitspolitik in München" (see note 29).
32   Peter Struck, " 'Future of NATO'—Speech delivered by the Federal Minister of
     Defense, Dr. Peter Struck, at the 40th Munich Conference on Security Policy on
     7 February 2004."
33   See, for instance, Christoph Bertram, "Deutschland: nicht normal, sondern zentral.
     Von der Notwendigkeit einer deutschen Führungsrolle in der Außenpolitik
     Europas," contribution to the radio series "Für eine bessere Außenpolitik" of the

Deutschlandfunk, broadcast on August 8, 2004. The full transcript is available at http://www.deutsche-aussenpolitik.de/resources/dossiers/bertram.pdf,   Accessed September 10, 2004.

34   France has always been more intergovernmentalist than integrationist, but at the same time it has strongly promoted what has been called "Europe Puissance."

35   Joschka Fischer and Dominique de Villepin, "Gemeinsame deutsch-französische Vorschläge für den Europäischen Konvent zum Bereich Europäische Sicherheits- und Verteidigungspolitik," November 22, 2002. Available at: http://register.consilium.eu.int/pdf/de/03/cv00/cv00489de03.pdf, Accessed on March 21, 2005.

36   Charles Grant, "EU Defence Takes Step Forward," *Center for European Reform Briefing Note* (December 2003), and "Einigung über Europas Verteidigungspolitik," *Süddeutsche Zeitung*, November 29, 2003.

37   In the words of Tomas Valasek, the director of the Brussels-based Centre for Defense Information, "Big Three Shift Seen to Weaken German Position," *Financial Times* (online edition), February 17, 2004.

38   Anne-Marie Le Gloannec, "The Unilateralist Temptation: Germany's Foreign Policy after the Cold War," *International Politics and Society*, 1 (2004): 27–39, quoted here p. 36.

39   Le Gloannec, *International Politics and Society* (see note 38), p. 37.

40   See Notes 18, 20.

5

Normalization in Security Policy? Deployments of Bundeswehr Forces Abroad in the Era Schröder, 1998–2004

Martin Wagener

Today, Germany is using military means to achieve its foreign and security policy goals much more intensively than in the early 1990s. Whereas the government of Helmut Kohl stationed, at the most, 2800 soldiers abroad, this number occasionally rose to more than 10,000 during the tenure of Chancellor Gerhard Schröder. Under the Social Democratic–Green coalition, for the first time in German postwar history, the Bundeswehr participated in combat missions. In 1999, the German Air Force bombed Serb positions in the war over Kosovo, and in 2002–2003, the Special Forces Command (*Kommando Spezialkräfte*, KSK) took part in ground operations in Afghanistan.

How should these developments be interpreted? Do they indicate a normalization in German foreign and security policy? What does "normal" mean at all in this context? The most popular German dictionary, the *Duden*, equates the term "normal" with "ordinary," "common," or "average."[1] Accordingly, a "normal" power should behave as do most other states. A more precise measurement of what constitutes a "normal" military engagement stems from the perspective of a strong middle power with considerable territorial, economic, and demographical potential: while Germany cannot be on an even standing with the United States or Russia, it is among the three leading powers of Europe (together with France and the United Kingdom). Thus, Berlin can be fairly characterized as a "normal" power if it utilizes its resources for—and demonstrates a determination to participate in—military operations under the auspices of the United Nations, North Atlantic Treaty Organization (NATO) or the European Union on even terms with Paris and London.

This chapter will assess how far the process of normalization of German security policy has progressed by examining the way in which military actions abroad have been performed. This will be done by taking two perspectives: first, the military actions under the Social Democratic–Green government will be examined quantitatively; then, qualitative indicators of normalization should be applied—namely, principles of deployment, capability profile, and the readiness to engage in combat operations and take on military command responsibilities. Finally, the limits of the process of normalization will be explored.

Military operations abroad under the Social Democratic–Green Government

In September 2004 just over 7000 German soldiers were engaged in Bosnia–Herzegovina, Kosovo, Georgia, the Mediterranean Sea, Ethiopia, Eritrea, the Horn of Africa, Djibouti, Afghanistan, and Uzbekistan.[2] Previously, Chancellor Schröder had approved additional Bundeswehr deployments in, among other places, East Timor, Uganda, Kenya, Kuwait, Macedonia, and the Strait of Gibraltar. With the exceptions of the missions in Bosnia–Herzegovina and Georgia, all operations abroad were initiated by the Social Democratic–Green government.[3]

The Balkans

The Social Democratic–Green government continued with German participation in the international protection mission in Bosnia–Herzegovina. On December 20, 1996, the Stabilization Force had succeeded the Implementation Force and taken over the further implementation of the Dayton Peace Accord of December 14, 1995. Its aim was to ensure the viability of the Bosnian state made up of the Muslim-Croat Federation and the Serb Republic around the undivided capital of Sarajevo. Whereas this operation initially involved up to 30,000 troops, among them 3000 Bundeswehr members, by June 2004 its size had decreased to 7000 troops, with the German contingent down to about 1000. The Bundestag approved the Stabilization Force follow-up operation on June 19, 1998 without any temporal restriction but required a mandate of the UN Security Council for Bundeswehr participation. The European Union intends to take over the command of the international forces at the end of 2004. Since January 2003 Brussels has participated, within the framework of the European Security and Defense Policy, in conjunction with the EU Police Mission in Bosnia–Herzegovina, which included, as of June 2004, 552 members, among them 73 officials from the German police force.[4]

Shortly after its inauguration, the federal government extended its engagement in the Balkans by approving the participation of German aircraft in the war against Yugoslavia, despite the lack of a UN Security Council resolution. The aim of this engagement was to prevent genocide against the Albanian population in Kosovo and a humanitarian crisis from the resulting refugee flow. In Operation Allied Force, which lasted from March 24, to June 10, 1999, 14 Electronic Combat and Reconnaissance (ECR) and Reconnaissance (RECCE) Tornados of the Bundeswehr took part, performing nearly 500 sorties. After the discontinuation of combat actions, the Kosovo Force (KFOR) and the United Nations Interim Administration Mission in Kosovo assumed responsibility for the area disputed by the Serbs and Albanians. Originally, the international protection force had included approximately 50,000 soldiers, out of whom roughly 5800 were Bundeswehr troops. After the serious upheavals in Kosovo in March 2004 KFOR, which consisted of only 18,500 troops at the time, was reinforced. In September the strength of the German contingent was 3240. On May 27, 2004, the Bundestag extended the mandate for this mission for another year.

From August to September 2001 the Bundeswehr took part in Operation Essential Harvest in Macedonia, after being requested to do so by the government in Skopje, which feared an escalation of the violent clashes between the Albanian and Macedonian populations. The 3500 soldiers of the international task force making up this operation collected weapons surrendered by resistance fighters; up to 500 Bundeswehr members participated in this mission. This disarmament operation was followed by operations Amber Fox and Allied Harmony, designed to support and protect international observers and thus the implementation of the Ohrid accord of August 13, 2001 (a peace treaty concluded between representatives of the Slavo-Macedonian majority and the ethnic Albanian minority). On March 31, 2003, the European Union for the first time assumed responsibility for a military operation that had been conferred on it by NATO (Operation Concordia). The Bundeswehr engagement ended with the mission's termination on December 15, 2003. At this time, only 40 German soldiers remained on duty, out of a total of roughly 350. On the same day, Brussels continued its engagement through the civilian mission Proxima, with a nominal presence of 200 police officers.

The struggle against international terrorism

On November 16, 2001, the Bundestag approved the participation of up to 3900 German troops in Operation Enduring Freedom.[5] Among the measures taken against international terrorism, the deployment of German Navy units to control the maritime area around the Horn of Africa and prevent possible movements of terrorists between the Arabian peninsula and the African coast is one of the most extensive. Maritime patrol aircraft, which had been sent to Mombasa, Kenya, and later to Djibouti, supported the deployed frigates. The Bundestag extended the mandate for another year on November 14, 2003 and took the previously assigned Nuclear, Biological, and Chemical (NBC) defense forces out of the contingent. Furthermore, the German Navy supports the struggle against international terrorism through its engagement in the ongoing Operation Active Endeavor, which began on

October 26, 2001. Its purpose is the surveillance of the Mediterranean Sea and the protection of naval travel in this area against attacks by Al Qaeda and similar groups. This endeavor was complemented on March 10, 2003 by Operation Strait of Gibraltar, which sought to better control-access to the western Mediterranean. From October 2003 to June 2004 Germany participated in this mission. In September 2004 the Bundeswehr still had roughly 290 troops deployed at the Horn of Africa and 200 in the Mediterranean. At times, up to 1500 soldiers were allocated to Operation Enduring Freedom.

Meanwhile, two additional, widely noticed military operations have been completed: from February 10, 2002 to July 4, 2003, a small NBC defense contingent was stationed in Kuwait. Officially, the Bundeswehr's task was to support the emirate in case of a terrorist attack with weapons of mass destruction. Additionally, roughly 100 members of the KSK, which was founded in 1996, were deployed to combat dispersed Taliban and Al Qaeda forces in Afghanistan from January 2002 to September 2003. Further missions that were less noticed by the public can also be regarded as a contribution to the struggle against international terrorism. In Operation Eagle Assist, seven aircrafts of the NATO Airborne Early Warning and Control Force were transferred from Geilenkirchen to the United States. Roughly 50 German soldiers participated in this operation until its completion on May 16, 2002. Furthermore, three Transall C-160 aircraft conducted transport flights between Ramstein and Inçirlik from November 26, 2001 to January 10, 2002. These operations as well as the protection of American institutions in Germany through Bundeswehr soldiers were primarily designed to relieve the United States forces.

In Afghanistan, Operation Enduring Freedom was complemented by the International Security Assistance Force (ISAF). On December 22, 2001, the Bundestag approved the participation of the Bundeswehr in order to secure the work of the transition government under the leadership of Hamid Karzai. Germany has participated in the international protection force since January 2002. During the presidential elections in Afghanistan in October 2004, NATO expanded the ISAF contingent to 10,000 troops. With more than 2100 soldiers, Germany provided the backbone of this force. Since the beginning of the mission, logistic support and supplies have come primarily via Termez in Uzbekistan, where an air transport base with roughly 300 Bundeswehr soldiers was established. In October 2003 the German parliament had decided to send a Provincial Reconstruction Team with a maximum strength of 450 soldiers to the northern Afghan city of Kunduz, where it replaced the US contingent. In July 2004 the Bundeswehr began implementation of a second Provincial Reconstruction Team in Feyzabad, which was officially put into action on September 1, 2004. In total, up to 2250 German troops can be deployed in the Hindukush region as specified by the Bundestag. On September 30, 2004, the Bundestag extended the engagement of the Bundeswehr through October 13, 2005.

Germany's small-scale missions

Since August 1993 the United Nations has sought to monitor the security zone installed between Georgia and Abkhazia. A further aim of the UN Observer Mission in Georgia is to help facilitate the return of refugees. The German contingent, deployed since 1994, represents 16 (as of September 23, 2004) out of 129 total uniformed personnel (as of July 31, 2004), a number making it the largest contribution. Among other tasks, the German contingent is responsible for the provision of medical care. On July 29, 2004, the UN Security Council extended the mandate of UN Observer Mission in Georgia to January 31, 2005.

From October 1999 to February 2000 the Bundeswehr participated with 70 troops in the International Force in East Timor, whose task was to evacuate injured and ill persons from the former Indonesian island. A similar function was performed in November 2000, when a number of injured Palestinians were flown out of Gaza in a military aircraft. Beyond that, the Bundeswehr has taken part in several short missions in Africa. In March 2000 just over 100 soldiers were deployed in Mozambique to help those affected by the flood disaster. From June 12, to September 1, 2003, the European Union conducted Operation Artemis in Congo. The mission consisted of 1850 soldiers which were led by France. The aim of Operation Artemis was to terminate the violent clashes between the Hema and Lendu populations that had broken out in the city of Bunia in the spring of 2003. Germany provided 35 soldiers for air transport operations between France and Uganda and two liaison officers for the operation headquarters in Paris. On January 28, 2004, the cabinet agreed to assign two officers to the United Nations Mission in Ethiopia and Eritrea, a mission that was designed to monitor the border between the two countries and whose overall size, as of July 2004, was 3875.

As a result of the decision of the NATO summit in Istanbul in June 2004, Germany will participate in training Iraqi soldiers. For this mission, the federal government intends to send Bundeswehr forces to the United Arab Emirates, where German police officers have already been training their Iraqi colleagues since March 2004.

The normalization of Germany's military engagements

This overview shows that Germany has contributed to international military missions much more intensively during the chancellorship of Gerhard Schröder than in the Helmut Kohl era. The country has become one of the most important providers of troops for international operations. Besides this purely quantitative argument, the normalization of Germany's deployment of military forces can be identified most of all by using four qualitative indicators—namely, the principles of deployment, the capability profile, the readiness to engage in combat operations, and not least the preparedness to take on military command responsibilities.

Principles of deployment

In the Defense Policy Guidelines (DPG), published on May 21, 2003, Defense Minister Peter Struck explained in detail how his famous statement that Germany is also defended in the Hindukush should be interpreted. Section 9 of the document contains one of the central passages: "At present, and in the foreseeable future, there is no conventional threat to the German territory. The Bundeswehr's spectrum of operations has changed fundamentally."[6] In contrast with the DPG of November 26, 1992 and the Defense White Paper of April 5, 1994, these new guidelines proceed from a newly defined concept of defense. Thus, German security is henceforth to be provided independently of its former close territorial definition, that is, the defense of the country itself and of the NATO alliance. Defense "can no longer be narrowed down to geographical boundaries, but contributes to safeguarding our security wherever it is in jeopardy."[7] Theoretically, this implies that the Bundeswehr could be deployed anywhere, against anyone.

The 2003 guidelines outline four fundamental challenges facing German security: (1) international terrorism, which is at the center of all considerations; (2) the proliferation of weapons of mass destruction and ballistic missiles; (3) regional crises and conflicts within and outside Europe; and (4) information warfare. With regard to these scenarios and Germany's greater responsibility in world politics, three types of Bundeswehr deployments can be identified. First, troop missions serve international peace and security; second, they work to improve living conditions in conflict areas; and third—and this lies at the core of the military strategy as envisaged by the 2003 DPG—they keep crises and their effects at a distance. This applies to the Balkans (in terms of preventing refugee flows) and for the Hindukush (in terms of neutralizing terrorist operations control and training centers). According to the government, Germany today can no longer be merely a consumer but also be a producer of security.[8] The DPG stress that the Bundeswehr is to be deployed exclusively in multinational frameworks, except for evacuation and relief operations.

This aspect of German security engagements indicates normalization, inasmuch as limitations with both historic and substantive justifications have been waived for good. Theoretically at least, Germany is now prepared to pursue its interests through military means, as would any other middle power. The emphasis on multilateral action indicates that the Federal Republic does not intend to act unilaterally but rather to pursue military deployment strictly in line with what is agreed upon within NATO and the European Union.

Capability profile

The German forces have become an "army in action." The Bundeswehr had originally been established to ward off invasion from the east; now, it must be prepared to cope with a wide variety of new threats. Therefore, German forces not only need to master the logic of Clausewitzian trinitary but also that of asymmetric warfare. Ideally, they bring their capacities to bear through network centric warfare, thereby fulfilling missions of evacuation and rescue, peace-keeping, conflict management, and peace-making.

Currently, the Bundeswehr is principally able to participate in all missions involving multinational forces. However, it does not have the equipment to bring itself fully to bear in all operations.[9] For instance, it cannot perform independent reconnaissance missions without entering the operational areas with fighter aircraft (RECCE-Tornados, Breguet Atlantic) or drones (CL 289, LUNA X-2000, ALADIN, KZO). In several areas, especially communications, the German forces depend on civilian service facilities. Serious shortcomings also exist with regard to air transport: the Transall C-160 planes are suitable only for short distances. In order to transport large equipment to Kabul, the German forces had to rent Antonow and Iljuschin strategic transport aircraft, which, for example, can take in Sikorsky CH-53 transport helicopters. Already today, it is capable of performing limited out-of-area national rescue operations autonomously. However, the challenges (such as telecommunications, logistics, and intelligence) become greater the further the location of the operation and the longer the mission.

Thus, the Bundeswehr's capability profile does not yet fully meet the challenges of ongoing operations abroad. This is so for two reasons: first, the German forces are still in a stage of reconstruction and thus not ready to become an intervention army. This means that the greatest part of the Bundeswehr's equipment is still devised for scenarios of territorial defense. Second, with a view to the procurement of new equipment, too much has been invested in projects with no direct impact on the daily work of German soldiers deployed abroad. Most of all, this applies to cost-intensive projects of the Air Force. For instance, €15.42 billion have been allotted for the procurement of 180 Eurofighter planes alone, thereby tying up money needed for investment until the year 2015.

Should the Bundeswehr be successfully modernized, this would have several effects on the performance of operations abroad. By optimizing interoperability, German forces would be better suited to cooperate in multinational frameworks. In several sectors, reforms could also enhance national options of military action. Among other things, this could be achieved through the procurement of A-400M transport aircraft, which would be available beginning in 2010, as well as the modification of four Airbus A-310 to Multi-Role Tanker Transporters, the first of which was introduced to the press in December 2003. Furthermore, beginning in 2007, Germany will probably have its first national strategic reconnaissance system, SAR-Lupe, which is an all-weather radar satellite system. These measures would ameliorate the security of the troops, as well as provide better protection of the bases in areas of operation, to which the Medium Extended Air Defense System (MEADS) could also contribute. The development of the new Puma infantry fighting vehicle, which will be operational in 2006, also will serve this purpose. Finally, another result of the Bundeswehr's modernization would be the extension of its operational efficiency. Toward this end, highly effective and precision-guided long-distance weapons (RBS 15 Mk 3/200 km, Taurus/350 km) are being procured. This could enable the Bundeswehr to intervene earlier in future operations of a predominantly peace-making character.

The modernization of the Bundeswehr means that the forces would be able to participate not only in observer and peace-keeping missions but also to a higher degree in combat operations. In effect, the Bundeswehr would be able to contribute to all military duties in the areas of operation on equal terms. This is one of the most important aspects of normalization because armed forces lose credibility if they are deployable only in already pacified areas.

Readiness to engage in combat operations

In principle, the Schröder government has stuck to the position that military measures are to be seen as acts of deterrence, but in so doing, the government has relied on offensive armed operations to a much higher degree than its predecessor.[10] True, the first combat operation of the German Air Force since Second World War took place during the Kohl era. NATO's Operation Deliberate Force (air attacks on Serb positions in Bosnia–Herzegovina that commenced on August 30, 1995) was accompanied by ECR and RECCE Tornados of the Bundeswehr. These forces participated in conducting reconnaissance but not in actions against ground targets. However, the decisive step toward normalization was taken in 1999 with the deployment of ECR Tornados to attack ground targets during Operation Allied Force in Kosovo: the German Air Force participated in eliminating the air defense of the enemy, firing 236 High-Speed Anti-Radiation Missiles in total.

Perhaps one of the most important organizational steps to enable combat operations abroad was the April 2001 establishment of the Special Operations Division (*Division Spezielle Operationen*, DSO). This division has a projected strength of 7300 troops, including the two airborne brigades of the army and the KSK, which consists of approximately 800 soldiers (of whom 300 can be deployed in command units).[11] The DSO's commander-in-chief, Major General Rainer Glatz, distinguishes between four operative tasks— namely, armed repatriations, operations against irregular forces, fast initial and concluding operations, and in-depth operations. Among these are not only the operations against terrorists in the Hindukush region but also apprehensions of war criminals in the Balkans. DSO vanguard troops are available within twenty-four hours and additional forces within three to four days. This division is especially suited for pursuing national interests because it exists, as Glatz puts it, "without restriction by multinational obligations."[12] The KSK mission to Afghanistan was the first occasion in history when Bundeswehr ground forces were sent into a combat area.

On August 9, 2004, Defense Minister Struck issued the latest reform of the Bundeswehr.[13] In doing so, the Schröder government has structurally secured the concentration of the German forces in intervention scenarios. In this context, the DPG 2003 states in Section 10 that the "Bundeswehr focuses on operations in the context of conflict prevention and crisis management as well as in support of allies, also beyond NATO territory."[14] The German army will now be divided into forces for intervention (35,000 troops), stabilization (70,000), and support (147,500). Previously, Struck had stated in relation to imposing an upper limit on the number of German soldiers to be sent abroad: "The Bundeswehr must have the ability to send up to 35,000 troops to every thinkable place on the Earth, be it for peace missions or, if necessary, for combat operations as well. The forces must be able to hold out for one year and, besides that, perform smaller operations."[15] The Federal Ministry of Defense has stated the following distribution: 18,000 troops for a first contingent of the European Rapid Reaction Force, 5000 for the NATO Response Force, 1000 for the United Nations Standby Arrangements System, and 1000 for national rescue and evacuation operations.

Assuming military command responsibilities

During the Kohl era, German officers had never assumed responsibility for any supreme command or any multinational contingent. On a lower level, however, they did assume responsibilities. For instance, German medical officers had commanded a medical unit deployed to support the United Nations Transitional Authority in Cambodia from May 1992 until November 1993. But it was only at the beginning of the KFOR mission in June 1999 that Germany assumed more visible and elevated responsibilities in NATO or UN missions. Thus, for the first time the Bundeswehr in a peace-keeping operation was allotted its own sector in southern Kosovo, with its headquarters in Prizren. From October 8, 1999 until April 18, 2000, German General Klaus Reinhardt served as supreme commander of the KFOR multilateral forces, thus becoming the first Bundeswehr general to hold an out-of-area NATO command. From October 3, 2003 until August 31, 2004, a second German general, Holger Kammerhoff, was awarded the post as supreme commander of KFOR. Currently, leadership of the Multinational Brigade South-West in Prizren alternates annually between Italy and Germany. In Macedonia, the Bundeswehr led the Task Force Fox, which includes approximately 1000 troops, from December 13, 2001 to June 26, 2002 (and itself contributed a temporary contingent of 600 soldiers).

Further leadership tasks have been carried out by the Bundeswehr in Operation Enduring Freedom and in Afghanistan. In 2002 (from May 4 to October 30) and 2003 (May 31 to September 29), the German Navy held the supreme command over multinational naval forces at the Horn of Africa. On September 25, 2003, it assumed command of the NATO Standing Naval Force Mediterranean. Additionally, on March 19, 2002, the Bundeswehr took over tactical leadership of the Kabul Multinational Brigade, passing it on to Canada on July 17, 2003. A further leadership task arose through the combined German-Dutch Command of the Afghanistan Protection Force, which was performed by the ISAF Operations Coordination Center from February 10, until August 11, 2003. Thereafter, this mission had been led directly by NATO, and in August 2004, leadership passed over to the Eurokorps.

Perspectives of normalization

The future of armed forces deployment will depend on two factors: (1) the amount of financial resources available for security policy, and (2) the direction envisioned by the Berlin Republic, according to its self-image. These factors will determine the role Germany plays in the context of multilateral operations.

The defense budget

By its own fault, the Social Democratic–Green government finds itself in a dilemma that is proving difficult to resolve. On the one hand, it demands that the Bundeswehr manages an increasing number of operations abroad; but on the other hand, it is prepared to allocate the necessary resources only to a limited extent. The government decreased its defense budget from an original €24.39 billion to €24.04 billion for 2005. However, two other factors will further decrease this nominal amount. First, inflation will reduce the amount of resources available each year. Thus, calculated on the basis of an inflation rate of 1.5 percent for 2003, the Defense Ministry's financial power is diminished by nearly €366 million. This amount could rise up to €1.5 billion by 2006 and will climb even higher should the inflation rate grow. Second, pay rises for staff tie further resources without adding any value to the efficiency of the forces. Additional, incalculable costs can arise in the context of operations abroad. These costs have already risen from €186.2 million in the last year of Helmut Kohl's chancellorship to more than €1.56 billion in 2002.

Compared with Paris and London, Berlin commits far fewer resources to equip its armed forces. Thus, German defense spending in 2002 equaled roughly 1.5 percent of the gross domestic product (GDP), whereas the French army was allotted 2.5 percent and the British forces 2.4 percent, with the average among NATO nations at 2.6 percent.[16] The GDP indicator shows that Germany would have to raise its defense budget considerably in order to reach this level. The investment rate also indicates a backlog in this context. According to Ministry of Defense figures, the rate was 24.9 percent in 2003, though in its May 2000 report on Bundeswehr reform, the Weizsäcker Commission indicated that an investment rate of 30 percent was needed for a modernization of the forces.[17] Thus, Berlin expends far fewer financial resources for investment than Paris or London: in its 2001 defense budget,

France allotted 35.43 percent (US$8.595 billion) for research and development, and procurement. In Britain, this portion was 38.59 percent (US$12.583 billion), whereas Germany invested only 23.2 percent (US$4.675 billion) in this sector.[18]

These examples show that successful reform of the Bundeswehr will ultimately depend on a substantial rise in the defense budget and a singular payment in order to get investment going. However, the current situation does not allow for this scenario: a short-term increase of the defense budget by incurring further national debts seems unlikely due to the restrictive budgetary policy of the Federal Ministry of Finance, the obligations stemming from the EU Stability Pact concerning budgetary policy, and new debts for 2003 already amounting to €38.6 billion.

In this situation, Defense Minister Struck has no other option than to secure military efficiency on a low level by reducing staff and operating expenses. Toward this end, he announced on October 2, 2003 a further reduction of Bundeswehr personnel. In 2010, military staff is to be reduced by 250,000 soldiers (as opposed to the Scharping's reform target of 285,000) and civilian staff to 75,000 employees (as opposed to 80,000 to 90,000 under Scharping's plan). Operating expenses have been reduced by sorting out the redundant military equipment and cutting down on the number of pieces with regard to new procurements. Thus, the number of A-400M transport aircraft ultimately ordered was 60 rather than 73. Against this background, fulfilling existing contractual obligations in order to avoid damage lawsuits leads to a degeneration of the true purpose of the armed forces, namely, to serve interests and to master challenges.

Self-image

Berlin shares with its partners not just financial risks but also the risk of loss of life among its troops. From 1993 to the spring of 2004, 59 Bundeswehr soldiers were killed.[19] However, Germany is still in an ongoing process of normalization. This gives rise to the question of what Germany's role in global security will be in the future. For instance, which yardstick should serve as the measurement for "normality" with regard to German troop deployment and equipment needs? From the perspective of the current (and most likely the following government), "normality" will not include the possession of nuclear weapons, aircraft carrier groups, or overseas bases. In contrast, it is probably within the scope of possibility that the German Navy stationed at the Horn of Africa will be awarded more competences as a next step toward normalization. Currently, its boarding teams can only be deployed if the naval vessel to be searched agrees. Normalization with regard to sending German forces abroad, viewed from a European perspective, will primarily proceed in this area for the time being. The issue at stake is an operatively consequent deployment of present resources—that is to say that a complete equalization of France and Britain in terms of military might is not yet at issue.

In the Schröder era, the will to emancipate itself with regard to security policy forms a part of the German self-image. This does not imply an unwillingness to cooperate or to pursue individual courses of action. However, even at the beginning of its tenure, the Social Democratic–Green government has indicated that it will place higher priority on Germany's national interests when taking action.[20] But it remains unclear what is precisely understood by that—and on the basis of which strategic rationale troop deployments are decided. Germany continues to lack a national security strategy, which would be one of the most desirable elements to result from normalization. A systematic approach is not likely to emerge from the new Defense White Paper, whose publication has been announced for 2005, because it will probably take stock rather than change direction. Thus, the missions of German forces abroad frequently lack an understandable justification.[21] For example, it is unclear why Germany offered immediate support to Operation Artemis in the Congo in 2003, but hesitated to send military forces to the Sudanese region of Darfur in 2004. Shifting political moods will therefore continue to prove decisive for assessments of a certain conflict's relevance to German security.

It is questionable whether a change of government in 2006 will alter this situation. Neither the Christian Democratic Union (CDU) nor the Christian Social Union (CSU) presented their own concept on German national interests in foreign policy or clear guidelines for deployment. Thus far, policy statements, such as that of the CDU party executive from April 28, 2003, are too general to be useful.[22] In 2004, both parties sharply criticized the Bundeswehr mission in Kunduz, though all problems were well known when the CDU and CSU agreed to send German soldiers to Northern Afghanistan in October 2003. This does not indicate a superior strategic logic in the oppositional camp. Statements of the Liberal Democratic Party concerning the long-term aims of the Bundeswehr missions in the Balkans and Afghanistan reveal a better understanding of German national interests. But these comments are not based on an overarching policy concept, either.

For the German political elite, common practice remains to speak of national interests in a general manner while avoiding precise definitions. Struck openly admits to this: "Our national interests, our security interests, how far and how precisely one may define them, will not definitely and automatically determine in the future as in the past how Germany should engage itself, in which concrete operation the Bundeswehr should participate."[23] Thus, a good deal of troop deployment occurs out of a nebulous concept of responsibility or, respectively, out of the aim to please international partners or domestic political factions. Even though it is not part of the country's traditional security policy to think in strategic categories, Germany will not be able to evade doing so on its way to becoming a normal power.

Acknowledgment

The author would like to thank Henning Boekle, Vladimir Handl, Karl-Heinz Kamp, Maxim Lefebvre, Hanns W. Maull, and the participants of the conference "German Foreign Policy in the 1990s and Beyond," Brühl, July 14–17, 2004, for helpful suggestions and comments.

Notes

1 *Der Duden, Die deutsche Rechtschreibung*, Band 1, Twentieth revised edition (Leipzig/Mannheim/Wien/Zürich, 1991), p. 510.
2 Cf. Bundesministerium der Verteidigung, "Auslandseinsätze—aktuelle Zahlen der im Ausland eingesetzten deutschen Soldaten," Bundeswehr webpage. Available at: http://www.bundeswehr.de/forces/print/einsatzzahlen.php, 30.09.2004. Accessed September 23, 2004.
3 Cf. Bundesministerium der Verteidigung, *Einsätze der Bundeswehr im Ausland* (Bonn: BMVg, 2000). Bundesministerium der Verteidigung, *Einsätze der Bundeswehr im Ausland* (Berlin: BMVg, 2002). Peter Goebel, ed., *Von Kambodscha bis Kosovo. Auslandseinsätze der Bundeswehr seit Ende des Kalten Krieges*, Verlag Report (Bonn/Frankfurt am Main, 2000). Martin Wagener, "Auf dem Weg zu einer 'normalen' Macht? Die Entsendung deutscher Streitkräfte in der Ära Schröder," *Deutsche Sicherheitspolitik. Eine Bilanz der Regierung Schröder*, Sebastian Harnisch, Christos Katsioulis, and Marco Overhaus, eds (Baden-Baden: Nomos, 2004), pp. 89–118.
4 Cf. Zentrum für Internationale Friedenseinsätze, "EU-Missionen," ZIF website. Available at: http://www.zif-berlin.org/de/Einsatzmoeglichkeiten/EU-Missionen. html. Accessed June 1, 2004.
5 Cf. Bundesregierung, *Unterrichtung des Deutschen Bundestages zum Einsatz bewaffneter deutscher Streitkräfte bei der Unterstützung der gemeinsamen Reaktion auf terroristische Angriffe gegen die USA*, May 8, 2002, BT-Drs. 14/8990.
6 Federal Ministry of Defense, *Defense Policy Guidelines*, May 21, 2003, p. 4.
7 Federal Ministry of Defense, *Defense Policy Guidelines* (see note 6), p. 3.
8 Cf. Bundesministerium der Verteidigung, *Bundeswehr 2002. Sachstand und Perspektiven*, April 8, 2002, p. 13.
9 Cf. "Das Bundesamt für Wehrtechnik und Beschaffung und seine Projekte," *Soldat und Technik*, 12 (2003): 6–66.
10 Cf. Hanns W. Maull, "Germany and the Use of Force: Still a 'Civilian Power'?," *Survival*, 42: 2 (2000): 56–80.
11 Cf. Wolfgang Büscher, "Einfach Elite," *Die Welt*, May 27, 2004.
12 Rainer Glatz, "Die Division Spezielle Operationen," *Soldat und Technik*, 10 (2003): 27–33; quoted here p. 28.
13 Cf. Bundesministerium der Verteidigung, *Grundzüge der Konzeption der Bundeswehr*, August 10, 2004.
14 Federal Ministry of Defense, *Defense Policy Guidelines* (see note 6), p. 4.
15 Interview with Peter Struck, "Jedes Land entscheidet souverän," *Der Spiegel*, December 1, 2003.
16 Cf. International Institute for Strategic Studies, *The Military Balance 2002/2003* (London: 2003), p. 335.
17 Cf. Bundesministerium der Verteidigung, "Einzelplan 14/2004 im Vergleich zum Haushalt 2003 (in EU millions)," FMD website. Available at: http://www.bmvg.de/

ministerium/haushalt/ministerium_haushalt2002.php (June 21, 2004), Accessed November 13, 2003.

Report of the commission "Gemeinsame Sicherheit und Zukunft der Bundeswehr," May 23, 2000, Berlin, p. 136.

18 Cf. International Institute for Strategic Studies, *Strategic Survey 2000/2001* (London, 2001), p. 35.

19 Cf. Einsatzführungskommando der Bundeswehr, Letter to author, May 17, 2004.

20 Cf. Gregor Schöllgen, *Der Auftritt. Deutschlands Rückkehr auf die Weltbühne* (Munich: Ullstein, 2003).

21 Cf. Martin Wagener, "In der Sinnkrise: 'Operation Tantalus.' Der Terror-Bekämpfung mangelt es an einer konsequenten Außen- und Innenpolitik," *Das Parlament*, September 27, 2004.

22 Cf. Christlich Demokratische Union, "Die außenpolitischen Interessen Deutschlands: Stabilität durch Partnerschaft und Vertrauen (Beschluß des Bundesvorstandes)," April 28, 2003.

23 Peter Struck, "Abschließende Stellungnahme auf der Konferenz 'Impulse 21 Berliner Forum Sicherheitspolitik,'" FMD website. Available at: http://www.bmvg.de/archiv/reden/minister/030624_abschlussrede_impulse_21.php. Accessed June 24, 2003.

Part III

Bilateralism and Multilateralism: European and Transatlantic Dimensions

6
Germany's New European Policy: Weaker, Leaner, Meaner

Sebastian Harnisch and Siegfried Schieder

Introduction

When Gerhard Schröder and Joschka Fischer came into office, they claimed that Germany would continue its traditional pro-European course. The new government vowed in its coalition platform to further deepen and widen the European Union (EU). Sounding a note consistent with the German all-partisan pro-European consensus, and even before assuming his ministerial post, the Green party's foremost foreign policy pundit, Joschka Fischer, called for a revival of the debate on the *finalité européene*.

Early in the term, the Schröder–Fischer government successfully managed the German EU presidency to solve a major institutional crisis caused by the resignation of the Santer Commission. In addition, the Schröder team steered the European Union through the Kosovo conflict and a protracted budget stalemate. After serious rifts, Berlin eventually secured a working consensus with France on institutional and budgetary issues at the European Council in October 2002. Then in June 2004, after the divisive Summit Meeting in Brussels (December 2003), the Intergovernmental Conference (IGC) on the European draft constitution came to a close, agreeing (among other things) the dual majority voting system (i.e. 55 percent of the members of the Council, comprises at least 65 percent of the population of the Union) in the Council of Ministers, which Berlin has always advocated for.

Therefore, the message of the first six years in office seems clear: the Schröder–Fischer government has not only maintained the pro-integrationist tradition but has also continued to work closely with Germany's longtime European ally, France. Furthermore, it would appear that the first Red–Green government, after 16 years in opposition, overcame the long shadow of Helmut Kohl's impressive European record by successfully pushing its own ambitious reform agenda for the European Union.

And yet, as we argue in this chapter, a closer look at the Schröder government's European track record reveals that the case for policy continuity is not convincing and, in some respects, is even misleading. Indeed, we posit that Germany's European policy has changed considerably, both in terms of process and substance. First, we hold that changes in Germany's European policy process in the 1990s have resulted in a shift of formal competences and informal policy influence in the executive as well as between the executive and other actors, especially the German *Länder*. Through Article 23 of the Basic Law, and subsequent legislation in particular, the *Länder* (and the *Bundestag* to a lesser degree) have increasingly been able to make their voices heard in European affairs. In addition, the ever deeper and wider European integration of the 1990s has shaped the expectations of increasing numbers of domestic political actors and ministries, thereby politicizing a growing number of European policies. As a consequence, we identify a growing *domestication of Germany's European policy* through normative and procedural restrictions that have substantially altered the Executive's European course.[1]

Second, we posit that, while a pro-integrationist stance remains the norm across the political spectrum in Germany, one finds strong indications that the German notions of Europe's role have undergone a marked change in the last decade. On the one hand, *Länder* governments, most prominently Bavaria, Baden-Württemberg, and North Rhine-Westphalia, and the Federal Constitutional Court (FCC) have tried to establish clear and identifiable limits on the European integration process. On the other hand, the politicization of Europe in Germany has led to a marked differentiation of party positions on the present and future state of the European Union. Accordingly, in the Schröder government two distinct concepts have struggled for policy primacy: Chancellor Schröder's "contingent Europeanism," as presented in the Social Democratic Party's (SPD) Leitantrag of 2001, and Joschka Fischer's ambitious concept of a "federation of nation states," as presented in his now famous May 2000 speech at Humboldt University.[2] Moreover, bipartisanship in European affairs came under considerable pressure at the end of the 1990s, as the incoming Red–Green coalition pushed for serious EU accession talks with Turkey, while the oppositional Christian Democratic Union (CDU) hardened their resistance to Turkish membership.

Third, we argue that the above-mentioned changes in Germany's polity and politics met with structural constraints of postunification Germany, resulting in a series of European policy changes. Most prominently, Germany's failure to revive economic activity and growth in the former German Democratic Republic (GDR) and to reform the West German *Sozialstaatsmodell* has severely limited the government's fiscal resources for implementing new policies (or sustaining existing ones). In addition, Germany's traditional societal pro-integrationist consensus has also softened considerably. As a consequence, Germany's European track record at the beginning of the twenty-first century is marked by protectionist impulses, non-compliance in major European policy projects, such as the EU Stability and Growth Pact, and a stiffened opposition to the European Commission's efforts to enforce EU legislation. In terms of strategy, one now sees a "contingent German Europeanism" that combines pro-integrationist positions—for example, in foreign, security, and defense affairs—with a demand for clearer delineation of competences between the European Union, Germany at the federal level, and the *Länder*. The effect of this "contingent German Europeanism" under the Schröder–Fischer government has thus far been twofold: on the one hand, the Red–Green coalition has been the main protagonist for constitutional reform in the European Union, beginning with the EU Charta on Fundamental Rights, Joschka Fischer's speeches on the *finalité européene*, and the insistence on a "post-Nice-Process." On the other hand, Germany's commitment to the European Union as a legal entity with binding obligations and as a redistributive social entity with (growing) financial obligations has become more circumspect. In short, Germany's European policy has become weaker, leaner, and meaner.

Germany's Polity and the Changing Nature of its European Policy Process

In the Federal Republic's early days, the constitutional framers equipped the guilt-stricken German polity with an unprecedented constitutional framework for checking executive power and enabling international (and European) cooperation.[3] A strong basic rights catalogue and an empowered FCC, as well as the parliamentarian and federal system, provided for internal reassurances against executive usurpation of competences. Externally, the preamble, Article 24, and a host of other constitutional norms foresaw a polity without armed forces that would integrate itself into a system of collective security as well as European institutions. In the 1950s, German policy makers ceded newly regained sovereignty to the European Community for Coal and Steel (ECSC) and the European Economic Community (EEC), thereby providing for additional external safeguards against any new German adventurism.

The domestication of the executive in European affairs

Article 24, the key constitutional clause legitimizing Germany's pro-integrationist policies, came under scrutiny for the first time in the 1970s. The FCC held that, after two decades of pro-European rulings, German constitutional law would not automatically defer to European Treaty Law in cases were the two collided. In the so-called *Solange* ruling, the Court argued that Article 24 did not authorize the transfer of German sovereign rights to the European level but rather opened the country's constitutional realm for the direct implementation of European law (opening theory). With regard to basic rights, the FCC made clear that it would retain its control responsibilities as long as (*solange*) European Institutions—and the European

Court of Justice (ECJ) in particular—could not provide an equivalent standard of basic rights safeguards.[4]

In the 1970s, the *Länder* also became increasingly concerned about the growing impact of European legislation, and tried to gain compensation for this loss in policy competences. However, the resulting changes in the policy process—the 1979 *Länderbeteiligungsverfahren* (State Participation procedure) and the 1986 *Bundesratsverfahren* (State Chamber Procedure)—did not satisfy the *Länder*. Consequently, in 1992 the *Länder* successfully threatened to veto the constitutional revision brought about by unification and to refuse ratification of the Maastricht Treaty. They thus managed to extract an amendment to the Basic Law in Article 23, the so-called *Europa-Artikel*, which provided them (and the *Bundestag*) with veto power (provided they can muster a two-thirds majority) over transfers of sovereignty. Article 23 now ensures *Länder* participation and grants veto competences where state interests are involved; it also allows *Länder* representatives, under certain circumstances, to negotiate on behalf of the federation in EU institutions. Moreover, Article 23 contains several guiding principles for Germany's integration policy, the so-called *Struktursicherungsklauseln*. These oblige the executive to respect the Basic Law's core principles (fundamental rights, democracy, rule of law, federalism, social security, subsidiarity) when engaging in European affairs. In effect, the *Struktursicherungsklauseln* ensure that, if German sovereignty is transferred, it will be transferred only when the receiving institutions resemble Germany's constitutional order to a substantial degree.

In a similar vein, Germany's FCC, in its controversial 1993 Maastricht Ruling, not only established a high degree of control for itself vis-à-vis the executive and EU institutions (especially the ECJ), but it also created a set of normative criteria that any additional transfer of competences would have to meet. Thus, the Court held that any further transfer would have to leave substantial functions and competences for the German parliament. In this way, the FCC also established concrete legal limits for Germany's integration policy while leaving considerable leverage for itself, since the Court itself would define just how much competence and how many functions would be substantial enough.[5]

Shifting powers in the executive: coordinating more players less successfully

The revision of the Basic Law not only resulted in increased power for the *Länder* and the FCC vis-à-vis the executive, but it also introduced new policy institutions both in the legislative and executive branches. While the *Bundestag* and the *Bundesrat* established or empowered their respective European Committees in accordance with the new constitutional provisions (Articles 23 and 45), institutional change in the executive was less formal but more widespread. First, many ministries set up their own European policy sections in the 1990s, as integration began to affect an increasing number of policy fields. Second, in the aftermath of the Maastricht Treaty negotiations, the Foreign Office created a new European Division (*Grundsatzabteilung Europa*) that rivals the traditional coordinating role of the Federal Ministry of Economics and Technology. The Economics Ministry lost this coordinating role to the Finance Ministry in 1998, when Oskar Lafontaine successfully brokered a bigger role for his ministry in European affairs. In 2002, Foreign Minister Fischer successfully rejected Chancellor Schröder's initiative to create a European Ministry attached to the Chancellery and managed to secure overall responsibility for the secretariat of the committee of all ministries' European state secretaries.[6]

German society's traditional pro-integrationist consensus has also softened considerably over the last several years. First, the general willingness of the German population to integrate into the European Union declined from over 80 percent in the early 1990s to 40 percent in the decade's final years.[7] Second, while a majority of the German populace in 2003 still favored a closer political union, less than 40 percent felt that EU membership held more benefits than non-membership.[8] A clear downward trend can also be identified with regard to voter turnout in European elections (1989: 59.3 percent; 1994: 57.5 percent; 1999: 45.2 percent; 2004: 43 percent). Third, however, a closer look reveals that, while the general pro-integrationist stance softened, strong support still exists for closer integration in Germany in some policy areas, especially in foreign and security affairs.[9]

In sum, these changes in Germany's polity and European policy process resulted in a two-pronged development: on the one hand, Germany's pro-integrationist executive European policy was domesticated, adding normative constraints and new actors to the process; on the other hand, these structural changes resulted in a contingent pro-integrationist European track record that combined pro-integrationist approaches in some policy areas (e.g., common foreign and security policy) with much more narrowly defined positions in others (e.g., the EU budget and subsidies).

Germany's contingent Europeanism and the constitutionalization of Europe

The Schröder–Fischer government started its European policy in a challenging international setting. During the second half of 1998, the Kosovo conflict escalated, and soon after the federal election the Red–Green coalition had to make a decision on German participation in military action to quell Serbian aggression against ethnic Albanians. In the first half of 1999, Germany took over the EU presidency and the West European Union (WEU) chairmanship. In addition, Germany hosted the G-8 Summit in May, which focused on coalition-building (including with Russia) in efforts to end the war through a UN Security Council Resolution.

Further worsening matters, the Red–Green coalition entered this environment with vague, often diverging ideas about the European Union. During his time in opposition, Joschka Fischer, as the Green party's eminent foreign policy personality, had pleaded for a continuation of the pro-integrationist, reflexive multilateralism and cautious foreign policy of the "old Federal Republic."[10] The SPD lacked a coherent European strategy other than demanding a "Social Europe" to counterbalance a neoliberal "Europe of enterprises." As prime minister of Lower Saxony, Chancellor Schröder himself had criticized the European Union for being too centralized and explicitly dismissed the Euro as "stillborn."[11] Yet the Schröder government ultimately continued its predecessor's application of financial incentives to achieve overall political goals in the Union.

Germany's new contingent Europeanism is most visible in the differentiated German push for a constitutionalization of the European Union, a trend that was already discernible under the Kohl government. In the 1996 Amsterdam Treaty negotiations, the conservative–liberal coalition had proposed a further deepening of the competences of the commission and the European Parliament and stronger integration in the Common Foreign and Security Policy. But under pressure from the *Länder*, the Kohl government had also insisted on unanimity for EU decisions on Justice and Home Affairs and the preservation of Germany's public law institutions (most notably regional savings banks, public broadcasting services, and utilities). As a response to the Maastricht Ruling of the FCC, the Kohl government also began to call for a catalogue of fundamental rights to be integrated into all EU treaties.

In the first years of the Schröder–Fischer government, the drive toward constitutionalization accelerated. First, at the Cologne Summit Meeting in June 1999, Germany introduced an initiative for a convention on the EU Charta of Fundamental Rights; second, the German EU presidency followed up on the French–British initiative in St. Malo calling for deeper integration in foreign, security, and defense policies by securing the nomination of Javier Solana as the Union's high representative. Third, in his Humboldt University speech in May 2000[12] Joschka Fischer advanced the idea of a new constitutional debate. Fischer envisioned the European Union as a "federation of nation-states," thus distancing himself from the traditional German concept of a "European federal state." In sum, the Humboldt speech balanced a strong push for further integration with a clear commitment to the nation-state as a building block and source of democratic legitimacy for the European Union.

Fourth, one of Germany's major successes at the December 2000 EU Summit in Nice was the initiation of the "post-Nice process," which led to the European constitutional convention in 2002/03. In the run-up to that summit, the German *Länder* had pressed Chancellor Schröder (by threatening to veto the ratification of the Nice Treaty) to insist on an additional IGC, which would focus on a clear delineation of competences of the European Union vis-à-vis the member states and *Länder*. Formally, the constitutional process can be traced back to a German–Italian initiative in Nice. But in substance the convention resulted from the insistence of the *Länder* governments, the FCC requirements for a clearer delineation of European fundamental rights and democratic legitimization, and the strong leadership of Foreign Minister Fischer in shaping a pragmatic debate on the *finalité européene*.

Because of policy disagreements among the *Länder*, however, they managed to exert less influence on the draft constitution than on the initiation of the convention itself. Thus, the *Länder* failed to establish a binding catalogue of competences and a renationalization of specific policy areas (for example, regional and structural policies), although they did achieve arrangements close to their positions in two areas: first, they succeeded in shaping the three different competence categories for EU legislation, thereby clarifying the delineation somewhat; second, the *Länder* introduced an elaborate early warning process to ensure that the subsidiarity of member states' parliaments was respected by the Union.[13]

Despite the leadership on the *finalité*, the German government initially maintained a low profile at the convention. This changed only after the coalition won the October 2002 federal elections,[14] when Foreign Minister Fischer took over as the government's representative in the convention. In several joint Franco–German proposals, the Red–Green government followed up on the traditional pro-integrationist course, introducing a new dynamic to the process of constitutionalization. A Franco–German proposal on November 22, 2002 called for a "European Security and Defense Union" and a reform of the European Union's foreign policy.[15] A few days later, on November 28, 2002, the Franco–German duo launched another joint initiative on combating terror and crime. The Fischer-de Villepin paper of January 16, 2003 on deeper institutional integration represented the culmination of the cooperation between Berlin and Paris.[16]

The timing of these Franco–German initiatives was carefully chosen. They closely coincided with the celebrations marking the fortieth anniversary of the Elysée Treaty. Thus, the aim was to strengthen Germany's special relationship with Paris after the debacle of the Nice summit. Moreover, the proposals also coincided with the preparatory phase of the discussions on institutional reform in the convention's plenary session. Finally, the renewal of the Franco–German relationship concurred with the German–French opposition to the US policy on Iraq. These joint proposals represented a compromise between the traditionally divergent German and French approaches to integration. In reaching the compromise, Germany accepted the long-term presidency, which would improve continuity in the council's work. France, for its part, accepted that the commission president should be elected by the European Parliament.[17]

While the German–French proposal offered a compromise for the convention, it was viewed by many smaller countries as a "hegemonic compromise"
that reflected the interests of the Union's larger countries while neglecting those of the smaller ones.[18] Similarly, Germany faced outright opposition
in the Council of Ministers during the IGC to the introduction of the dual
majority voting system. Some member states suspected a German scheme to
expand its influence in the EU Council of Ministers. Poland, above all, feared
a Franco–German directoire, which Polish Prime Minister Leszek Miller
judged could only be blocked by a policy of denial.[19]

The December 2003 Brussels summit failed because Germany and other
supporters of the dual majority system insisted upon an improvement of
their relative voting power, while opponents, most notably Poland and
Spain, rejected any revision of the Nice status quo.[20] Finally, in June 2004, at
a special session of the European Council, a compromise was reached. In this
compromise Germany not only lost some of its voting power but also much
of its reputation of a facilitator of European integration.[21] Germany's failure
to push its own candidate, Guy Verhofstadt, for the commission presidency
can also be interpreted as a sign of the country's waning capacity for
leadership in the European Union.

The domestication of EU enlargement

Eastern enlargement had been a priority in the foreign and security policy of
all German governments since unification. Domestically, eastern enlargement remained uncontroversial up to the late 1990s. Borne by a broad
German consensus between parties and in society, both the Kohl government and the present Red–Green government have played a key role in
determining the direction of the process of EU enlargement. Other member
states—France, in particular—expressed skepticism over this process because
they viewed eastern enlargement as a "German project." Only in December
1993 at the Copenhagen summit did Germany secure the necessary support
among its EU partners for eastern expansion; its principle ally had been the
commission.

Why did Berlin push so hard for expansion?[22] First, Germany had a
particularly keen interest in a durable stabilization of its neighboring postcommunist countries. Second, enlargement was seen as a powerful means of
pacifying the European periphery and securing democratic transformations.
Third, Germany's proactive enlargement policy was also driven by tangible
economic interests; German industry associations, in particular, were
anxious to open up new markets. German foreign trade statistics illustrate
that the country has indeed benefited substantially from this policy: its
external trade with the central and eastern European countries has long
shown disproportionate growth and has of 2003 reached a share of about

12 percent.[23] Finally, Germany also advocated eastward enlargement out of historical responsibility and gratitude to those neighboring countries that played an active role in Germany's reunification. During the 1990s, Berlin found support for its pro-enlargement position among countries with a similar geographical situation—notably Scandinavia and Austria, but also the United Kingdom and Denmark, which have viewed enlargement as a means to prevent deeper integration.

In principle, the Red–Green government continued the dual strategy of "deepening" and "widening" used by the Kohl government. While the Social Democrats saw enlargement as a historical continuation of Germany's *Ostpolitik*, an element constitutive of the SPD's political identity, the Green party backed the project as part of its pan-European peace policy.[24]

In practice, however, the Red–Green pro-enlargement policy was dotted with qualifications. Thus, the government wanted a clear-cut reduction of Germany's fiscal contributions to the EU budget; this initiative failed at the March 1999 Berlin Summit because of the resistance of those states, France and Spain in particular, that feared losses as a result of a reallocation of EU resources (Common agricultural policy [CAP], structural, and regional funds) in favor of the central and eastern European countries. Although the German government achieved its primary objective of eastward enlargement by adopting the Agenda 2000, the hoped-for fiscal relief failed to materialize. The only core German demand to be fully realized was a freeze on the upper limit for a given country's contribution to EU budget at 1.27 percent of the Union's gross national product.[25]

Since 1998, societal consensus on EU enlargement has also softened considerably. While more than half (54 percent) of German respondents polled in November 2002 still voiced support for EU enlargement, by November 2003 this share had fallen to 41 percent. West Germans took a particularly critical view of EU enlargement; the rate at which they supported this policy ran seven percentage points behind that of eastern Germans. With the exception of France, western Germany recorded the lowest level of support among member states.[26]

Growing budget gaps, declining public support, and also increasing labor union demands for protection of Germany's high wages continued to weigh heavily on EU enlargement policy. In the fall of 2000, the German government sought to allay labor union fears by demanding protracted transitional periods (of five to seven years) for the free movement of labor.[27] Moreover, Berlin once again came out in favor of a limit on expenditures for the Common agricultural policy. Prior to the December 2002 enlargement summit in Copenhagen, Chancellor Schröder declared in a signed article in the *Frankfurter Allgemeine Zeitung* that, in the German view, a continuation of the old CAP was out of the question: "Germany's financial breaking point has been reached."[28]

But the EU Commission and the candidate countries insisted that accession states had a right to direct Common agricultural policy support. This meant that a reduction in direct support payments (phasing out) had become a sine qua non for support of the new member countries after 2004 (phasing in) of support payments for new EU members. While Schröder reached a compromise with French President Jacques Chirac prior to the Brussels EU summit, the preliminary Franco–German agreement ran up against resistance among the other partner countries. Thus, at the December 2002 Copenhagen summit, three issues remained controversial: (1) the level of direct payments to farmers, (2) budget equalization payments, and (3) the overall resources to be provided for the new member states. In hindsight, the German–French compromise appeared to be astonishingly simple: for 2004 to 2006, a gross funding framework of €40.4 billion per annum was envisaged for agricultural expenditures, a figure that would be increased annually by 1.5 percent to compensate for inflation.[29] The resulting increase of about €600 million per annum would benefit farmers in the new member countries. The agricultural expenditures of the old EU member states would thus have to be lowered, though lesser than the Red–Green government had been demanding. For Poland, a special arrangement was agreed upon that helped both sides to save face: of the €8.6 billion earmarked for Poland in the funding framework for 2007 to 2013, one billion was transferred to the budget aid for the years 2005 and 2006 for the structural fund (which supports infrastructure projects in disadvantaged regions).

In sum, our analysis suggests that the Red–Green government had to straddle a growing gap between its political support for enlargement and the limited resources available for the process, as well as between the political exigencies of enlargement and Germany's commitment to deepening the European Union. Thus, the Schröder team tried to link the financial aspects of enlargement with the reform of the existing EU transfer system. When this failed, Berlin's insistence on reducing German net contributions eroded its traditional role as a facilitator of European compromise and an advocate of the accession countries. Continuing fiscal constraints and Germany's waning competitiveness in an enlarged Europe are bound to trigger additional domestic skepticism over enlargement. Germany's traditional civilian power role will thus be compromised by Berlin's new "contingent Europeanism."

Conclusion

Over the last six years, Germany's European policy has witnessed a marked shift from a generally pro-integrationist philosophy to a contingent Europeanism that combines a push for a deeper Europe in a few policy areas with a strong call for a clearer delineation of competences in other policy areas. Clashes with the European Commission on competition and subsidy policy, conflict with smaller member states over net transfers and voting rights, as well as a closer cooperation among the "big three," suggest that Germany has shed at least part of its old role as the "good European."

The evidence, however, does not support the claim made by some analysts that this new policy trajectory reflects the growing strength of postunification Germany. Rather, we hold that the Red–Green government has tried to keep central elements of its traditional civilian power role, but has found it harder to sustain them, given domestic change and international environments.

Thus, Germany's traditional role has been weakened both internally and externally. Domestically, more players with increasingly divergent views on the European Union now interact in the policy process. Interest groups and the public at large have become more politicized by the deepening of the integration process, resulting in more frequent calls for protection, exemptions, or better participation. Institutional players such as the *Länder* or the FCC are trying to preserve their power and constitutional competences. As a consequence, Germany's traditional *Leitbild* of "Europe as a federal state" has tilted toward that of a "*Staatenverbund*,"[30] or confederation or a "federation of nation states".[31]

Since the Red–Green government has been in power, these structural changes in the policy process have been amplified by the decrease of traditional German power resources: money and integrationist spirit. This not only led to several conflicts with the commission and other European partners, most notably on the Stability and Growth Pact, on public law banks, on reforming Common agricultural policy and structural policies, but it has also eroded Germany's traditional role as a facilitator of compromise between large and small member states that smoothed frictions by offering financial incentives.

Consequently, Germany's traditional European role has also been weakened externally. While effective French–German cooperation in European integration has gained in importance, this cooperation at times has also hampered Berlin's ability to provide leadership in the European Union. Two recent examples stand out: first, when France insisted on blocking reform of the CAP and Germany proved unable to consolidate its budgetary deficit, the Red–Green government not only violated the Stability and Growth Pact but also strained its relationship with the incoming member states by calling for a cap on EU transfer payments. Second, the more domesticated Germany's European policy has become, the more it has tilted toward France's intergovernmental concept of Europe. The price has been steep: the smaller and new European member states have become increasingly irritated with Franco–German leadership. Should the Constitutional Treaty ever be ratified by all member states, both politics and economics would continue to limit Germany's former pro-integrationist policy in every field.

Notes

1 Sebastian Harnisch, Internationale Politik und Verfassung. Die Domestizierung exekutiver Außen- und Europapolitik in der Bundesrepublik Deutschland, (Baden-Baden: Nomos, 2006).
2 Charlie Jeffery and William Paterson, "Germany and European Integration: A Shifting of Tectonic Plates," *West European Politics*, 26: 4 (2003): 59–75.
3 Cited from the chapter by August Pradetto in this volume.
4 Peter-Christian Müller-Graff and Anja Reichel, "Die Europäische Integration aus der Sicht der Rechtsprechung nationaler Verfassungsgerichte," *Europapolitische Grundverständnisse im Wandel. Analysen und Konsequenzen für die politische Bildung*, Mathias Jopp, Andreas Maurer, and Heinrich Schneider, eds (Bonn: Europa Union Verlag, 1998), 365–418.
5 Stefan Hobe, "The German State in Europe after the Maastricht Decision of the German Constitutional Court," *German Yearbook of International Law*, 37 (1994): 113–34.
6 Simon Bulmer, Andreas Maurer, and William Paterson, "The European Policy-Making Machinery in the Berlin Republic: Hindrance or Handmaiden," *New Europe, New Germany, Old Foreign Policy? German Foreign Policy since Unification*, Special Issue of *German Politics* 10/1, Douglas Webber, ed. (London: Frank Cass, 2001), 177–206; see also Franz C. Mayer, "Nationale Regierungsstrukturen und Europäische Integration. Verfassungsrechtliche Vorgaben für den institutionellen Rahmen der Europapolitik auf nationaler und europäischer Ebene," *Europäische Grundrechte Zeitschrift*, 29: 5–8 (2002): 111–24.
7 Karl-Rudolf Korte and Andreas Maurer, "Innenpolitische Grundlagen der deutschen Europapolitik: Konturen der Kontinuität und des Wandels," *Eine neue deutsche Europapolitik? Rahmenbedingungen—Problemfelder—Optionen*, Heinrich Schneider, Mathias Jopp, and Uwe Schmalz, eds (Bonn: Europa Union Verlag, 2001), 195–230; quoted here pp. 205–09.
8 Eurobarometer, National Report: Germany, 60/1 (autumn 2003). Available at: http://europa.eu.int/comm/public_opinion/archives/eb/eb60/eb60.1_germany.pdf. Accessed September 15, 2004.
9 Ibid.
10 Joschka Fischer, *Risiko Deutschland. Krise und Zukunft der deutschen Politik* (Cologne: Kiepenheuer & Witsch Verlag, 1994).
11 Sebastian Harnisch and Siegfried Schieder, "Europa bauen—Deutschland bewahren: Rot-grüne Europapolitik," *Deutschland im Abseits? Rot-Grüne Außenpolitik 1998–2003*, Hanns W. Maull, Sebastian Harnisch, and Constantin Grund, eds (Baden-Baden: Nomos, 2003), pp. 65–78; quoted here p. 67.
12 Joschka Fischer, "Quo-vadis Euopa? Vom Staatenbund zur Föderation—Gedanken über die Finalität der europäischen Integration, Rede an der Humboldt-Universität zu Berlin," May 12, 2000. Available at: http://www.whi-berlin.de/fischer.htm. Accessed September 15, 2004. See also Joschka Fischer, "Rede vor dem Europäischen Parlament, January 12, 1999. Available at: http://omk/ omnsapir/so/debats?FILE=99-01-12&LANGUE=DE&LEVEL=DOC& GCSELECTCHAP=1&GCSELECTPERS=2. Accessed September 15, 2004.
13 Andreas Maurer and Daniela Kietz, *Die neuen Rechte der nationalen Parlamente. Umsetzungsprobleme und Empfehlungen* (Stiftung Wissenschaft und Politik: Berlin, 2004).

14 Barbara Lippert, "European Politics of the Red-Green Government: Deepening and Widening Continued," *Germany on the Road to 'Normalcy': Politics and Policies of the Red-Government (1998–2002)*, Werner Reutter, ed. (London: Palgrave, 2004), pp. 235–52; quoted here p. 245.

15 See the chapter in this volume by Marco Overhaus.

16 Dominique De Villepin and Joschka Fischer, "Contribution submitted by Mr Dominique de Villepin and Mr Joschka Fischer, members of the Convention, CONV 489/03," January 16, 2003. Available at: http://register.consilium.eu.int/pdf/en/03/cv00/cv00489en03.pdf. Accessed September 15, 2004.

17 Paul Magnette and Kalypso Nicolaïdis, "The European Convention: Bargaining in the Shadow of Rhetoric," *West European Politics*, 27: 3 (2004): 381–404; quoted here p. 392; see also Ulrike Guérot *et al.*, "British, French and German views on the European Convention," *EPIN Working Paper*, 7 (2003). Available at: http://www.epin.org/pdf/FDUK_Guerot_Hughes_Lefebvre.pdf. Accessed September 15, 2004.

18 Ibid., p. 3; see also Paul Magnette and Kalypso Nicolaïdis, "Large and Small Member States in the European Union: Reinventing the Balance," Groupement d Études et de Recherches Notre Europe, Research and European Issues May 25, 2003. Available at: http://www.notre-europe.asso.fr. Accessed September 15, 2004.

19 Kai-Olaf Lang and Andreas Maurer, "Polens Gewicht und die doppelte Mehrheit. Vor dem Endspiel der Regierungskonferenz," *SWP-Aktuell*, 51 (2003). Available at: http://www.swp-berlin.org/common/get_document.php?id=570. Accessed September 15, 2004.

20 Andreas Maurer and Simon Schunz, *Auf dem Weg zum Verfassungsvertrag. Der Entwurf einer Europäischen Verfassung auf der Regierungskonferenz* (Berlin: Stiftung Wissenschaft und Politik, 2003). Available at: http://www.swp-berlin.org/common/get_document.php?id=575. Accessed September 15, 2004.

21 The new mode of voting provides for a dual majority of 55 percent of member states and 65 percent of the EU population, with a majority requiring the consent of at least 15 of the 25 member states. This veto minority was agreed on for four member states.

22 Barbara Lippert, "Die EU-Erweiterungspolitik nach 1989—Konzeptionen und Parxis der Regierungen Kohl und Schröder," *Eine neue deutsche Europapolitik? Rahmenbedingungen—Problemfelder—Optionen*, Heinrich Schneider, Mathias Jopp, and Uwe Schmalz, eds (Bonn: Europa Union Verlag, 2002), pp. 349–92, quoted here p. 351ff.

23 "Bundesministerium der Finanzen, Ökonomische Auswirkungen der EU-Erweiterung auf den Standort Deutschland, Arbeitspapier vom 5. Dezember 2003," Berlin. Available at: http://www.bundesfinanzministerium.de/Anlage24450/Auswirkung-Erweiterung.pdf. Accessed September 15, 2004.

24 Lippert, *Eine neue deutsche Europapolitik?* (see note 22), p. 380.

25 Ibid., p. 383.

26 Eurobarometer, National Report: Germany, 60/1 (see note 8), p. 13ff.

27 Deutscher Bundestag, Plenarprotokoll, December 19, 2002.

28 Gerhard Schröder, "Neue Direktbeihilfen für Deutschland zu teuer," *Frankfurter Allgemeine Sonntagszeitung*, June 16, 2002.

29 Henning Tewes, "Rot-Grün und die Osterweiterung der Europäischen Union," *Deutschland im Abseits? Rot-Grüne Außenpolitik 1998–2003*, Hanns W. Maull,

Sebastian Harnisch, and Constantin Grund, eds (Baden-Baden: Nomos, 2003), pp. 79–90; quoted here p. 85.

30 Decision of the Federal Constitutional Court, October 12, 1993, BVerfGE 89, pp. 155–213.

31 Fischer, "Quo-vadis Euopa? Vom Staatenbund zur Föderation—Gedanken über die Finalität der europäischen Integration, Rede an der Humboldt-Universität zu Berlin" (see note 12).

7
The Franco–German Relationship, 1998–2005

Hans Stark

Introduction

Franco–German cooperation has always been a history of progress and setbacks, stagnation and revival. The Chirac–Schröder era is no exception to this rule, quite the opposite. Following the days of the Nice Summit in 2000, many were under the impression that the Franco–German couple was breathing its last breath, and to some European observers, the deterioration of Franco–German relations recalled, even more seriously, the crisis of confidence of the period 1969–74.[1]

Kohl's legacy

When the right-of-center German Christian Democratic Union (CDU) lost power in 1998, it appeared that Jacques Chirac did not lament the defeat of his German counterpart. The French president had never managed to develop the same tight, confidence-based relationship with Chancellor Helmut Kohl that his predecessor, François Mitterrand, had, or a friendship comparable to that between Helmut Schmidt and Valéry Giscard d'Estaing. But things were almost the same on the other side of the Rhine, where Kohl first backed Jacques Delors, before supporting the candidacy of Édouard Balladur during the French presidential election campaign in 1995. However, beyond personal discrepancies, it was more fundamental questions that sparked dispute between France and Germany. What was seen in Paris as the increasingly neoliberal monetary, economic, and financial policies of the Kohl government annoyed both the Gaullists and the Socialist officials who had taken office in 1997 with the aim of managing the European currency. The misunderstandings that were at the heart of the discussion were related to the German demand to tighten the Maastricht convergence criteria using the growth and stability pact, whereas France wished to introduce the growth criteria as a means of handling the Euro.

During the European Council of Amsterdam of June 1997, Kohl refused to extend qualified majority voting in most crucial areas, thus giving the impression that Germany's long-standing federalist vision of European construction would be replaced by a more intergovernmental and rather British approach—a point of view that was openly confirmed by some high-ranking German officials. Since that time, French politicians were convinced that Germany had renounced its earlier ideal of deepening the European institutions in order to speed up the enlargement process for Eastern European countries.

Splits also appeared from 1995 to 1998 in the field of security policy. Resumption of nuclear tests in Mururoa and the reactions it sparked abroad, the end of mandatory military service in France and its maintenance in Germany, the non-return of Paris into the NATO (North Atlantic Treaty Organization) integrated military system and the weak impact of the "common strategic concept" of Nuremberg added to the quarrelsome atmosphere of Franco–German relations.

Many reasons can be put forward to explain the growing deterioration of the Franco–German relationship during the 1990s. First of all, France, very suspicious of the potential political and economic power of a united Germany, did not accept the idea of a privileged bilateral partnership in which Germany would assume the leadership role. Germany's emergence as a full-fledged political actor on the European, or even on the worldwide stage gave rise to very hostile reactions in France. One has to remember that the cohabitation between socialists and conservatives from 1993 to 1995 and from 1997 onward greatly hampered the running of foreign policy, as did the fratricidal struggle between the neo-Gaullists Chirac and Balladur between 1993 and 1995. The opposition between French federalists and euroskeptics, spawned by the referendum on the Maastricht Treaty, further impeded Franco–German relations. Opposition not only considerably restrained France's European policy but it also changed the country's policy toward Germany.

But Germany was also partly to blame for the deterioration of Franco–German relations. The country's so-called *sowohl als auch* strategy imposed a policy of equidistance between Washington and Paris. Furthermore, the motivations behind Germany's commitments in central and eastern Germany—whether concerning the reconciliation with Poland, the partnership with Russia, or the pro-Croatian actions in the beginning of the Yugoslavian crisis—were not properly explained to the French, who remained wary about the prospect of German domination in Eastern Europe. Finally, the German ambiguities regarding the Monetary Union gave rise to constant questioning in France about the sincerity of German European policy. In short, far from forming a tightly aligned driving force in Europe, which would have presupposed unwavering mutual confidence and similar views on the core issues, the positions of France and Germany were all too often divergent, and sometimes even diametrically opposed at the end of Kohl's long rule.

The first revival of the Franco–German motor

When the German Social Democratic Party (SPD) and the Green Party came to power in the aftermath of the September 27, 1998 general election, French Socialist representatives viewed the accession of their German counterparts, at least at first, as a godsend. The coalition of the Social Democrats and the Green Party also planned far-reaching actions to lay the groundwork for broader cooperation with France. But this postelectoral commitment on the traditional cornerstone alliance was not a self-fulfilling prophecy as shown by candidate Schröder's proposition to transform the Franco–German couple into a trilateral Franco–German–British relationship.

However, the idea of Germany's Red–Green coalition to extend cooperation to Britain failed from the very beginning. In fact, Germany's position rapidly moved closer to France's in terms of European construction: according to the coalition treaty, internal reforms ("deepening") would be necessary before the eastern enlargement of the European Union (EU). Germany thus rejoined the positions of France, Belgium, and Italy, all of whom favored deepening the political dimension of the European Union. Like the French government, the Red–Green coalition considered that negotiations on the Agenda 2000 should have been completed before the negotiations on enlargement and that the next step of the European integration should be implementing institutional reforms left uncompleted since Amsterdam. Even though France and Germany shared a common view on the medium- and long-term development of the European Union, they had different opinions regarding current problems of European construction. Whereas the main objectives of the Agenda 2000 legislative package were to design a new financial framework for the period 2000–06 with a view toward eastern enlargement and to reform certain community policies (in particular the Common Agricultural Policy, or CAP, and the Structural and Cohesion Funds) in order to control the costs of EU enlargement, the German government tried to link the question of net contribution to the EU financial package with the outcome of the negotiations.

Crumbling under the pressure of the Christian Democrats and public opinion, the new government tried to diminish German contribution from the very beginning. During the seventy-second Franco–German summit, which took place in Potsdam from November 30, to December 1, 1998, with the aim to renew bilateral relations, financial problems came to be at the center of the debate. To diminish CAP expenditure, the German government advocated a cofinancing strategy involving direct aids from the European budget and public expenditure out of the hands of national treasuries. But a majority of European member states was hostile to this solution. For France, such a strategy would mean abandoning the European Union's own resource-ceiling principle, to implement a system of national contributions and to give up the whole CAP. During the 1999 European Summit in Berlin, Chirac openly criticized German reform proposals and Chancellor Gerhard Schröder. This event triggered a crisis of confidence between France and Germany that would last for more than three years. Many reasons help explain this state of affairs. In Germany, the government moved from Bonn to Berlin, and power passed to a generation of politicians who had not experienced the Second World War. This new generation is less tainted by the shock and shame of defeat and has ventured into a process of normalization, seeking to redefine the country's place in Europe and the world. Along with the generational shift, the right- and center-left wing German parties started to cast doubt on the German model of social market economics. The resignation of Oskar Lafontaine, chairman of the SPD and finance minister of the Schröder government highlighted this profound change in Germany's political development, which would have been unimaginable in France. This shift partly explains why British Prime Minister Tony Blair and Schröder inched closer after Lafontaine's departure. A few days before the European elections of June 1999, the two heads of government published a common economic paper with a clear neoliberal orientation, worsening the Franco–German relations even further.

One important reason for discord between Paris and Berlin was thus an ideological battle between the three leading European socialist parties about how to best conduct economic policy in times of globalization. The French prime minister considered the German "New Center" policies and the British "Third Way" as disloyal to the French Socialist Party.

But France was far from rejecting the possibility of broader cooperation between the three European heavyweights, as the Franco–British declaration of Saint-Malo, which formed the basis for launching a European Common Security and Defense Policy, demonstrated. When Blair came to power, he put an end to the British tradition of obstructionism. At the December 4, 1998 Saint-Malo Summit, drawing the lessons from the wars in Kosovo and Bosnia, the heads of state and government of France and the United Kingdom agreed in a joint declaration that "The Union must have the capacity for autonomous action, backed up by credible military forces, the means to decide to use them, and a readiness to do so, in order to respond to international crises."

The German government had no choice but to join this initiative. Anything else would have marginalized the German government on the European stage and provoked a deterioration of Franco–German relations. On the other hand, the Saint-Malo Treaty allowed Germany to fully participate in the European defense decision-making process, along with its French and German partners. In addition, it created new opportunities to foster Franco–German relations, which had greatly suffered from the diverging ideological positions and economic policy views expressed by French Prime Minister Lionel Jospin and Schröder. But the state of Franco–German relations also followed the rules of domestic politics. Schröder needed a success on the international scene to improve his image in the face of domestic problems that his coalition was facing at the time.

The bilateral declaration adopted during the meeting of the Franco–German Council on Security and Defense of May 29, 1999 in Toulouse retook the essential proposals of the Franco–British Saint-Malo[2] declaration. Toulouse thus transformed the dual (Franco–British and Franco–German) partnership into a triangular discussion between Paris, London, and Berlin regarding European defense. Germany ended up gaining the presidency of the European Union and the Western European Union (WEU) by launching the Common European Security and Defense Policy (CESDP) at the European Council of Cologne on June 3, 1999, transferring many of the functions of the WEU to the European Union.

Nice and beyond

At first sight, intergovernmental conferences (IGC) represent a perfect springboard for the Franco–German "couple," allowing the two to exercise leadership in the European arena through bilateral initiatives. Yet, the 2000 IGC and its break—the Nice Summit—is a big exception to this rule. Nice has come to symbolize the split between Berlin and Paris. Far from crowning the common positions from the four bilateral summits preceding the Nice European Council, the two announced that they "agreed on agreeing on everything," a formula that made clear the existence of persistent disagreements.

The meetings in Rambouillet and Mainz, which according to participants were conducted in a "very good atmosphere," thus obviously hid a seriously damaged bilateral relationship. At the Mainz Summit of June 9, 2000, the French and German leaders appeared to agree to equitably take into account the demographic factor in the context of the reweighting of votes in the council, one of the four leftovers of the Amsterdam Treaty. But the agreement did, in reality, hide the persistence of a several years-old disagreement between France and Germany. Whereas France wished to reestablish balance at the expense of small countries, Germany wanted rebalancing for all EU member states and rejected the standpoint from which equality between France and Germany in the council is a definite fundamental principle and, especially, one that was acknowledged by the Federal Republic of Germany at the moment of creation of the European Economic Community.

This last issue triggered the third Franco–German crisis in three years, following the confrontation between Chirac and Kohl in May 1998 regarding the designation of the president of the European Central Bank, and the clash between Chirac and Schröder in March 1999 over CAP reform and the adoption of the Agenda 2000. France reckoned that the federal government was taking advantage of the reweighting quarrel in seeking to monopolize the leading position of the European Union and to "translate into political terms the demographic and economic primacy it had obtained through reunification."[3] France found itself trapped in an extremely uncomfortable situation in Nice: the country was forced to ask certain countries, notably Belgium and Portugal, to make concessions for the very same demographic reasons that France itself refused to admit to Germany. Paris tried to justify this situation by presenting equality between France and Germany as a fundamental principle of reconciliation between the two countries.

But the German position was just as incoherent. Germany, with its more than 80 million inhabitants and as the largest net contributor to the European budget by far, under the old weighting system would have had ten votes in the council, whereas 19 other smaller countries could have 57 combined votes in an European Union enlarged to 27 countries. Schröder considered this option unacceptable. Yet the demographic gap between France and Germany has always existed. What is more, the 1992 Edinburgh European Council had already taken into account the increase in this gap after the reunification and decided to raise by 18 the number of German members of parliament. Last, demographic differences do not constitute an abnormality in a federal political system such as the one Germany preferred. Schröder was never disturbed by the fact that Lower Saxony, his old fief, has just as many votes in the Bundesrat as North Rhine–Westphalia, a region with a population almost three times larger, for that matter.

This Gordian knot could finally be cut, but at the price of a decision-making system so complicated that its principal authors, Germany and France, hastened a revision of the mechanism in the context of the European Constitutional Convention. But it would be simplistic to ascribe the relative failure of the Nice summit only to Franco–German divergences. These were to be put in a general context that was prevailed since the ratification of the Maastricht Treaty, marked by the aspiration of each of the member states to defend national interests above all and to keep, if possible, a veto power on sensitive issues. The absence of bilateral initiatives, as well as disagreements between Berlin and Paris at the Nice summit nevertheless had paralyzing effects and increased leeway for those who opposed further integration of European institutions and policies.

Hence, it is not surprising that the Nice agreement, revealing a ten-year-old Franco–German malaise, provoked caustic comments on both sides of the Rhine. Not everyone went as far as to call Nice a "diplomatic Suez," but the feeling that "Europe is no longer a French garden" was nevertheless fairly widespread in France. For the French, Nice marked the end of the intellectual hegemony it had previously exerted on the issue of European integration. This observation keeps recurring in Germany as well, where France's difficulty to adapt to the new European order has constantly been underlined for several years. If the Germans accuse the French of being nostalgic, they don't understand that for the French, Schröder's Germany reflects, wrongly or rightly, the image of a country different from the one they had known before 1998—a country accused of desolidarization from France. The Nice Summit thus left deep scars in France, from which it illustrated a new German attitude, and in the Federal Republic, which saw it as the refusal of the French to accept post–Cold War realities.

Nice thus confirmed the limits of the Franco–German revival announced by the French socialists and the German Social Democrats. In France, politicians and numerous "experts" remained suspicious about the geopolitical intentions of the Germans. To them, the chancellor's wish for normalization reflected a quest for power. But those suspicions had no real foundation: the much-degraded budgetary situation in Germany and the "pacific" reflexes and traditions of the Red–Green coalition deputies were solid safeguards against any potential "power" policy. Also, Schröder's request for a rebalancing of votes in favor of Germany did not reflect a hegemonic attitude toward France, but rather a wish to avenge the defeat he suffered at the Berlin Summit in 1999.

After Nice, Paris and Berlin maintained their rather diametrically opposed positions concerning the future of European integration. This divergence in part reflected France's antifederalist instincts, as the country was still traumatized by the Maastricht experience. In the wake of the 2002 presidential election, Chirac and Jospin felt they had to take into account the euroskeptics within their parties. But the Germans did not attach sufficient importance to a permanent dialogue with France on European issues. German Foreign Minister Joschka Fischer's speech at Humboldt University in May 2000[4] was very ambitious, but it went against the well-established rule which holds that propositions aiming to deepen the European construction should systematically come from joint Franco–German initiatives. The dialogue of the deaf over institutional issues between the main French and German actors and the non-respect of this fundamental rule were at the origin of the deterioration of Franco–German relations between 1999 and 2000.

The Blaesheim process

Nice presented France and Germany with a relatively simple choice: declare separation or prepare the ground for proper revival. The second option was chosen. During the Blaesheim meeting of January 31, 2001, Chancellor Schröder and President Chirac assigned the German and French ministers of foreign affairs to deal with "forms and details" of a reopening of the Franco–German dialogue, to prepare the future deepening of the European Union. In early 2001, both sides firmly determined to conclude the Nice chapter and restore a privileged cooperation within the European Union. This very ambitious objective was to be obtained through two distinct processes. The first one, the so-called Blaesheim Process" aimed at revitalizing the Franco–German dialogue through regular meetings between the French president and the German chancellor every six to eight weeks, as well as meetings between the ministers of foreign affairs of the two countries nearly once a month. In theory, this initiative was to lead to a better understanding of the interests and positions of the "other." The second element to bring Paris and Berlin closer to one another was that of the "2004 process," initiated by the federal government in Nice with the intention to work out a European constitution. During the bilateral Nantes Summit of November 23, 2001, Germany and France clearly declared, for the first time, their support for a European constitution.

Retaining the lessons learned at the Nice Summit, Berlin shifted back to an integrationist, rather than an intergovernmental policy approach. From January 2001 onward, three major interventions punctuated this pro-European awakening of German leaders: that of Fischer at Humboldt University in Berlin on May 12, 2000; the speech made by the federal president at the time, Johannes Rau, in front of the European Parliament in Strasbourg on April 4, 2001;[5] and finally, the European project of Gerhard Schröder, published in Berlin on April 30, 2001, for the congress of the SPD in Nuremburg in November 2001. In this vision for the future of the Union, Schröder demanded an "amelioration of the transparency of decision schemes at European level, in turning the commission into a strong executive, by strengthening the rights of the European Parliament through extended co-decision and by giving it full budgetary authority, and by turning the council into a European Chamber of States".[6] At the institutional level, the document stressed the need to clarify the distribution of competences between the Union, the member states, and the regions. Hence—and this is probably the most contradictory point in the chancellor's European project—Schröder pleaded in favor of a "Europeanization" of foreign and security policies, as well as of a transformation of the commission into a "strong European executive." But he also argued that some community policies (the document notably mentions agriculture and regional policies) should, at least partially, return to the member states, implementing the principle of subsidiarity. These proposals forced the other member states, and particularly France, to clarify their positions on European integration. Although it is hard to imagine a Europe of 1925 or 1930 to function in any other way than within a decentralized, federal framework, France interpreted the German propositions first and foremost as designed to impose German federalism on Europe as a whole.

The official reactions in Paris regarding the German propositions were thus mainly negative—the exception being within the profederalist sphere in France. Fischer's speech was judged premature as it risked disrupting the IGC 2000 Agenda, which the French government didn't intend to change; that of Johannes Rau did not provoke much reaction, probably because it was issued by an institution—the German Federal Presidency—that the French tend to ignore. The proposals of the chancellor were the ones that provoked the most passionate criticism in France. Thus the French minister of foreign affairs at the time, Hubert Védrine, bluntly criticized Schröder's propositions in a meeting with members of the Bundestag on May 10, 2001. Védrine opposed the transformation of the Council of Ministers into a Chamber of States, and particularly denounced the fact that the SPD project would result in a disruption of the European institutional balance to the detriment of the council and the member states. French commentators also pointed to the fact that Schröder's project wanted to turn the commission into the future European government, while at the same time depriving it from the management of some of the most important issues in European politics—agriculture and regional policies—which Berlin wished to "renationalize." The official response of the French prime minister at the time, Lionel Jospin, was perceived by Berlin as a rejection of the German federal project. In his speech delivered on May 28, 2001, the former French prime minister did indeed confirm that one couldn't bring forward institutional architecture without having reflected beforehand on the political profile one wished to give Europe. Jospin wanted to build Europe without dismantling France. But, following the example of German leaders, the former prime minister was in favor of a European constitution, of a clarification of competences of the Union and the states, respectively, and of a European defense policy.

Jospin's intervention had the virtue of reestablishing the Franco–German dialogue on Europe. But, for the former French prime minister, the main issue was not the institutional architecture but the project itself—that is to say the future of community policies. Thus, divergences persisted between France and Germany, for it was crucial for Germany to have the CAP reformed before the Eastern European countries became full members. Germany thus revived the cofinancing idea that caused confrontation between Chirac and Schröder in February 1999 by suggesting a progressive reduction of direct support which, according to Berlin, was to be partly financed by member states.

France remained profoundly hostile to this idea. In his speech in Strasburg on March 6, 2002, Jacques Chirac insisted that the CAP should keep evolving to advance rural development and the quality of products. Chirac's speech nevertheless attested to a significant evolution of French positions favoring a more-integrated Europe. Paris no longer rejected out of hand the German supranational approach as before. The debate on Europe between Paris and Berlin was thus relaunched in 2001 and 2002, although the electoral campaigns of 2002 in France and Germany once more accentuated divergences concerning the reform of the institutions and the financing of community policies.

The second revival ... and its limits

These divergences were surmounted after the end of the electoral campaigns in France and Germany. From the autumn of 2002, the revival of the Franco–German cooperation was spectacular, starting off in October with an unexpected compromise on the CAP. The ceiling agreed on CAP spending, a common policy that has been a primary interest of the French, was possible thanks to substantial concessions from the Germans, who renounced their project of partial renationalization of the CAP.

The agreement came against the background of rapidly deteriorating German–US relations, provoked by the SPD electoral campaign, which made a strengthening of the ties with Paris necessary from a German point of view. The Élysée palace, which had supported the candidacy of right-wing politician Edmund Stoiber for the post of chancellor, was all the more favorable to this development as Franco–British relations had deteriorated since the British government had started to support the American idea of a new war against Iraq.

The Franco–German revival then focused on elaborating common positions within the Convention on the Future of Europe. A whole series of joint propositions was launched by the two countries in a fairly short period of time: propositions on European security and defense policy (November 22, 2002), in the field of justice and interior affairs (November 28, 2002), on the contribution on economic governance (December 22, 2002), and on the institutional architecture of the European Union (January 16, 2003). These propositions translated the desire of the two countries to renew the "European driving force" tradition that had characterized their European policies in the past. It also reflected the ambition of the two governments to assume a leadership role in the greater Europe, where the balance between small and large countries was yet to be defined. This reasoning explains a certain disinterest shown on both sides of the Rhine in the reactions of smaller member countries.

The common position of the two countries on the Iraq crisis paved the way for the Franco–German unity of January 2003. This event was bolstered further by growing instability in Iraq, by the difficulties of the United States in reestablishing order and promoting a democratic transition in the country, and especially by the total absence of evidence for the supposed possession of weapons of mass destruction or any link between the regime of Saddam Hussein with Al Qaeda. Paris and Berlin now feel vindicated in their view that conditions legitimizing military action against Baghdad were lacking.

The price to pay for the Franco–German revival was heavy, however—on the European as well as on the transatlantic level. The way in which France and Germany handled the Iraqi crisis within the United Nations created a deep gap of incomprehension between France and Germany on the one hand, and Britain, Spain, Italy, and the countries of Central Europe on the other. By giving the impression that they wanted to create an informal European directory around the Franco–German couple, the two countries marginalized themselves: France's political influence in southern Europe greatly diminished to the advantage of Italy and Spain (at least until the terrorist attacks of March 11, 2004, and the change in government in Madrid), whereas Poland, and no longer Germany, henceforth became the defender of transatlantic interests of central European countries. The Franco–German blockage in the United Nations and NATO also strengthened the unilateralist current within the Bush administration. Nothing illustrates the risk of French and German marginalization within the Europe of 1925 better than the call for solidarity with the United States contained in the "Letter of Eight," published on January 30, 2003. Orchestrated by Washington in order to play the card of the divided Europe, this initiative brought into light both the incapacity of the Union to adopt a common position vis-à-vis the United States, and the rejection incited by the way in which Paris and Berlin had relaunched their bilateral relationship.

In the past, the Franco–German "motor" had elaborated joint initiatives from national interests that were originally diametrically opposed. In fact, French and German positions often diverged so far from each other that they reflected more or less those among all other partners. Today, the situation is different. The Franco–German horizon has become too narrow to represent the whole spectrum of interests of a Europe of 1925. In the larger Union, the French and German positions have become almost identical when compared to those of the new member states. And a majority of the European countries are now reluctant to accept any form of "directory," especially one formed by the Franco–German tandem. Gone are the times when France and Germany spoke "in the name of Europe." If our two countries do not open up to third countries—big and small—they risk becoming marginalized in a new kind of German *Sonderweg*.

Conclusion

In October 2002 after four long years punctuated by crises of confidence, failing revivals, and political confrontations, Jacques Chirac and Gerhard Schröder eventually decided to breathe life into the Franco–German friendship and to renew a relationship dating back to Charles de Gaulle and Konrad Adenauer, and buttressed during the Valéry Giscard d'Estaing–Helmut Schmidt and François Mitterrand–Helmut Kohl eras. Both Chirac and Schröder remained in power after the 2002 elections. On both sides of the Rhine, everybody knew that at least four more years of collaboration now lay ahead. Continuing the quarrels of the past would probably have cast doubt over the reconciliation of the two countries, which is seen as one of the main pillars of the postwar order. For French and German officials, that was a price too high to pay.

Yet , the spectacular revival of the Franco–German relationship did not result so much from a political strategy cleverly orchestrated by Berlin and Paris—although the "Blaesheim Process" has started to bear fruit—but from the consequence of a whole series of events and coincidences that happened in parallel, independent from one another. With the end of cohabitation in June 2002, Chirac had a real room for maneuver on foreign policy for the first time since 1997. This new political constellation, accentuated by the replacement of the euroskeptic Hubert Védrine by the very active Dominique de Villepin at the head of the French Foreign Office, also laid the foundation of a new policy toward Germany.

Chirac immediately ensured the leadership of the Franco–German duo. While France had long suffered from an inferiority complex vis-à-vis Germany, it is at present well aware of the economic difficulties and the inexorable population decline in Germany. With a gross national product per capita higher than that of Germany and a population growth that will allow the country to outgrow its eastern neighbor in terms of inhabitants by 2050, France no longer approaches Germany from a subordinate position. This change also explains why the rapprochement was largely the result of the work of the French president and his minister of foreign affairs, rather than by their German counterparts. This observation may surprise all, but the French, who generally tend to overestimate the potential power of their partner from the other side of the Rhine, attach greater importance to Franco–German relations than do the Germans, and who are traditionally more inclined to underestimate the means and capacities of their western neighbor.

However, the Franco–German rapprochement that has come about since October 2002 has also largely been due to the deterioration of transatlantic relations. The increasingly pro-American orientation of the Blair government following September 11 was an obstacle to the establishment of any alternative alliance with Britain, and the deterioration of German–American and Franco–American relations in the wake of the Iraq war reduced the diplomatic options available to both Chirac and Schröder. This situation explains the very close dialogue between the two countries in the UN Security Council at the beginning of 2003. The deterioration of Germany's relations with the United States, as well as with Washington's main European allies, confronted Germany with a risk of being marginalized for the first time since 1949. It was therefore strategically important for Germany to strengthen the Franco–German coordination.

However, the renewal of Franco–German ties does not mean that the positions of the two countries will easily generate a majority within the European Union. Indeed, Paris and Berlin are aware of the urgency of an opening of the Franco–German "couple" to European countries other than Belgium and Luxemburg. Thus, in May 2004, French politicians, including Nicolas Sarkozy[7] and Michel Barnier[8], openly pleaded in favor of a European leadership of the six large countries of the European Union. Germany is not opposed to this idea, but it cannot disregard the fact that several of its neighbors are among the smaller countries of the European Union. A European leadership assumed by the big countries would add to the frustration of the small countries within the European Union and make political relations with neighbors extremely difficult for Germany. The debate is far from closed, and it reveals the continuing fragility of ties between France and Germany. As Védrine said on numerous occasions, "the Franco–German relation is indispensable but insufficient."

Notes

1 Thierry de Montbrial, "France-Allemagne: une vision partagée?" *Le Figaro*, January 31, 2001.
2 According to the declaration, it would be "important to achieve full and rapid implementation of the Amsterdam provisions on CFSP [and to give] the European Council the responsibility to decide on the progressive framing of a common defence policy in the framework of CFSP." The Union would have the capacity for autonomous action in order to cope with international crises, thanks to a 50,000-troop-strong European Rapid Reaction Force. At the November 15, 1999, Brussels meeting of both foreign and defense ministers, French and German officials declared that the Rapid Reaction Force should back up the existing military forces (Eurocorps, Eurofor, Euromarfor) and become operational by 2002.
3 Thierry de Montbrial, "France-Allemagne: quelle vision partagée?" *Le Figaro*, June 31, 2001.
4 "Joschka Fischer voit à long terme une fédération européenne", *Agence Europe*, May 13, 2000, p. 3.
5 "Johannes Rau plaide pour une constitution européenne", *Agence Europe*, April 5, 2001, p. 3.
6 "Schröder propose une relance de l'UE aux antipodes des thèses françaises", *Le Monde*, May 3, 2001.
7 "Nicolas Sarkozy trouve insuffisant le moteur franco-allemand", *Le Monde*, June 24, 2004.
8 "Barnier insiste sur la dimension politique à donner à l'UE", *Agence Europe*, April 3, 2004, p. 3.

8
Parting Ways: The German–American Relationship after Iraq

Stephen F. Szabo

Personal or structural?

The US–German relationship was an especially close one during the Cold War, culminating in President George H.W. Bush's call in 1989 for Germany to join America as a partner in leadership. The rapid deterioration that occurred because of differences over the Iraq war has lead many on both sides of the Atlantic to attribute the conflict to the leaders involved. Both the German leadership and the public believe that George W. Bush and his group of radicals are to blame for this friction and that, once he is gone, things will return to some semblance of normalcy. On the American side, there is also a sense that a change in leadership will heal the wounds. Many conservatives share the view of two of the most vocal American neoconservatives, Richard Perle and David Frum, who wrote, "We are optimistic that once Chancellor Schröder leaves the scene, Germany will revert to its accustomed friendliness."[1] During the 2004 presidential campaign, Democrats argued that a John Kerry administration would have facilitated the return to a more alliance-oriented foreign policy and a rapprochement with Germany.[2]

Now that the Bush administration has been confirmed for a new four-year term, however, German and American leaders will have to face the fact that the fundamentals shaping the German–American relationship have shifted and that the old "partners in leadership" concept is gone for good.

Theoretical approaches to understanding German policy

There are fundamentally two ways of regarding what drives the US–German (and broader transatlantic) relationship. The first, realism or neorealism, focuses on the strategic relationship as a function of the structure of the international system. The second, which includes liberal-institutional and constructivist approaches, considers the impact of norms and institutions and stresses the domestic factor in the shaping of foreign policy.[3]

The so-called German problem was the central strategic and political question that confronted twentieth-century Europe. The strategic problem concerned the role of German power within the broader European system of balances and the inability of the major European powers to balance and contain the rising power of unified Germany. Two non-European powers, the United States and the Soviet Union, had to enter the European system in order to create equilibrium, one that remained stable during more than 40 years of the Cold War.[4] This problem of power was linked to Germany's late unification and geographical setting in the heart of Europe.[5]

German unification in 1990 reopened fears of a return of the German problem as a geopolitical challenge resulting from both a new imbalance within the European system and from the assertiveness of a newly sovereign Germany led by a new postwar generation less constrained both by the Nazi legacy and the transatlantic community. However, the decade that followed unification did not confirm these fears. Unified Germany, under the firmly Europeanist leadership of Helmut Kohl, did not seem to follow the expectations of realists who believed that a more fluid international context, combined with an increase in national power, would result in a more nationalist Germany. While Germany began to enhance its military role, it did so within a multilateral context and generally continued the "civilian power" paradigm.[6] The academic consensus on the German problem at the end of the century was that it had been transformed. Constructivist and neoliberal paradigms seemed to carry the day over realism. These approaches reflect the importance of the internal dimension of the German problem, especially the failure of democracy. As Heinrich August Winkler concluded in his study of Germany's path to westernization, "It was not the solution of the question of national unity which stands at the beginning of the road to catastrophe, but the failure to settle the question of freedom."[7] This internal problem has been solved. Germany is a mature and stable democracy. Those favoring this approach would argue that the new German and European political cultures have created a new postmodern approach to international relations in which realism has been superceded by a civilian power approach.

The 1990s, however, represented an interregnum between two eras, which opened with German unification in 1990 and closed on September 11, 2001. The end of the Cold War and the unification of Germany marked a new era and a more fluid international environment. Added to this was the major external shock provided by the 9/11 attacks.[8] In short, both the realist and the neoliberal approaches were at least partially right. The new fluidity in the structure of international power has interacted with the domestic context of foreign policy, opening new options and perspectives for domestic foreign-policy makers at a time when the domestic environment has undergone a transformation in both countries.

In addition, the personalities of the leaders also mattered in the evolution of the transatlantic relationship. When the political environment is flexible and unrestricted, personality and leadership style have a greater impact. Although German–American relations saw great clashes of personalities during the Cold War, such as those between John F. Kennedy and Konrad Adenauer or Helmut Schmidt and Jimmy Carter, the impact of these struggles was constrained by the rigidity of the bipolar international system and the limits on Germany's room for maneuver. The crisis over Iraq was the first time that a German chancellor opposed an American president on a matter of vital interest to the United States. Without the strategic cohesion of the Cold War, politics and personality were given great leeway to effect policy outcomes.

The new American strategic debate: hegemonists and realists

The new international fluidity is most important in regard to the declining US–European security relationship in an enlarged Europe. In the period immediately following the end of the Cold War, the United States stood alone as the most powerful state in the international system.[9] American policy makers were less constrained by the concerns of other nations and thus had more freedom to take action than at any time in US history. The real constraints came from within, from the Republican majority in the Congress, especially the House of Representatives, whose views reflected a widespread public disinterest in foreign policy. As Stephen Walt and others pointed out at the time, "the United States enjoys enormous influence but has little idea what to do with its power or even how much effort it should expend."[10] In the absence of a unifying geopolitical threat, domestic interest groups with narrow, often extreme goals had more influence on policy as power began to shift from the executive branch to the legislature, with the waning of the national security role of the president.

In addition, the end of the Cold War weakened the strategic glue that held the United States and Europe together in the face of the Soviet threat. This was especially dramatic in the case of Germany, which was now fully sovereign and no longer faced a direct military threat on its border from 400,000 Warsaw Pact forces. Similarly, Germany and Europe were no longer the key frontier of its global conflict with the Soviet Union for the United States. NATO (North Atlantic Treaty Organization) now had to find a new mission, and the United States a new rationale for its continued presence in Europe.

US policy makers faced a choice between a hegemonist, "smothering" strategy and a realist balancing approach. The hegemonist strategy was favored by conservative Republican nationalists who believed that, because the United States was the most powerful nation, it could do what it wanted in areas of vital interests. Allies had little to contribute in terms of military power and only ended up getting in the way. Strong American leadership would result in the allies following their cues. As John Ikenberry describes this school of thought, "order is created by a hegemonic state that uses power capabilities to organize relations among states." He differentiates between a strong version of hegemonic order, which is "built around direct and coercive domination of weaker and secondary states by the hegemon, ... and ... more benevolent and less coercive (forms of hegemony, S.S.), organized around more reciprocal, consensual and institutionalized relations."[11] The more coercive approach is one of an informal imperial order; the latter, which Ikenberry labels liberal hegemony, implies a strategy based on bandwagoning rather than balancing, a "smothering strategy" designed to prevent the rise of any peer competitor,[12] which rejects an alternative approach that would encourage multiple centers of power to share in global governance.

This approach contrasts fundamentally with that of balance-of-power realists, who believe that order in the international system is created not by the dominance of a hegemonic state but by balance. Realists hold a balance-of-power view of world politics in which the international system is based on the struggle for power among states. Their view of the national interest is one of limits, constraints, and the non-ideological use of American power. Realists are pessimistic about the ability of human nature to change and worry about the overextension of American power and commitments in utopian crusades led by people who have no direct experience in war or with the limits of power. While their primary concern is with the national interest, they are multilateral in the sense that they see the need for alliances and a broader international framework as the best way to exercise American power because it minimizes the dangers of overextension and of countervailing coalitions being formed against it.[13]

Before the storm: George H.W. Bush and Bill Clinton

Traditional realism had dominated Republican foreign policy since the era of Dwight D. Eisenhower. It reached its high point during the Nixon administration and was the dominant perspective in the first Bush administration, during which the key leaders were James Baker, Colin Powell, Lawrence Eagleburger, and Brent Scowcroft. However, even in the administration of the senior Bush, a more assertive nationalist or "unipolarist" view was present, represented by the views of his defense secretary, Richard Cheney, and his deputy, Paul Wolfowitz.[14]

Both hegemonists and realists regarded the newly unified Germany with caution. The first Bush administration supported German unification within NATO to insure that the country remained within a multilateral framework and did not return to a more militaristic posture. Bush, Scowcroft, and Baker were all concerned that a sovereign and independent Germany would lose interest in having an American troop presence, thus undermining the US position in Europe and bringing new instability to the region.[15] There was concern that a unified Germany, without the need for an American security umbrella, could become a challenger to America's position in Europe. The Defense Planning Guidance, which was drafted by Cheney's Department of Defense and was a precursor to the National Security Strategy of the second Bush administration, advocated that the United States deter any peer competitor from emerging to challenge its power, and "this language seemed to apply to Japan and Germany or a united Europe, as well as China and Russia."[16]

The Clinton administration represented, in Ikenberry's terminology, the "liberal hegemonist" approach. It saw itself as the "indispensable nation," without which little of global consequence could be accomplished. Yet the administration believed in "effective multilateralism," through which it would shape broad coalitions to deal with foreign policy challenges. With his emphasis on economics and globalization as the key forces in post–Cold War American policy, Clinton was primarily concerned with strengthening the US economy and lessening the demands of defense in favor of investments that would enhance American competitiveness. In this light Germany and Japan were seen as global economic competitors, both of which benefited from the diversion of American resources to defense.[17] Clinton's focus in his first election campaign and first term was predominantly domestic. He wanted to avoid the distractions of foreign military engagements and to limit the use of American military power. His administration, therefore, stressed a multilateral approach and international agencies and institutions, including the United Nations, as a way of sharing the burden of global leadership. It was also initially open to a more independent European security identity for the same reasons. At the same time, there was a strong strain of liberal interventionism, which would engage military forces to defend human rights and to prevent humanitarian catastrophes, as well as to promote democracy. As the Balkans became an unavoidable crisis, Clinton committed American forces but only in a multilateral context and without risking ground wars or high casualties. The rationale for the war was at least humanitarian rather than solely strategic.

Germany's importance as a partner was then based upon both its role in the international economy and its willingness to deploy peacekeeping forces and reduce the burden on the US military. It proved to be an important partner in the Clinton strategy of "democratic enlargement" when it supported the enlargement of both NATO and the European Union into East-Central Europe.[18] This close partnership continued during the first two years of the Red–Green government in the war in Kosovo and in the commitment, at least verbal and symbolic, by the Clinton administration to the Kyoto Protocol and the International Criminal Court and Nuclear Test Ban treaties, knowing that the Republican-dominated Congress would block their enactment.

The Bush revolution

The administration of George W. Bush represents the ascendancy of the imperial hegemony approach. Bush's key foreign policy appointments included three strains or schools of conservative foreign policy: the traditional realists, the neoconservatives (or democratic imperialists), and the nationalist conservatives or (assertive nationalists).[19] In the current administration, unlike that of the senior President Bush, the realists were marginalized around an ineffective secretary of state and his department. Policy making shifted to the vice president's office and to the civilians in the Pentagon, resulting in a coalition of neoconservatives and aggressive nationalists.

The neocons, with their belief in the power of ideas and the universality of American values, were part of a longer tradition of American exceptionalism.[20] They regarded American power as a force for good and believed that its preeminence should be used aggressively to shape a new world order based on the ideals of free market economies and democracy.[21] While both traditional realists and conservative nationalists were pessimistic about America's ability to change the world and feared an overextension of American power and commitments, the neocons were optimists, hyper-Wilsonian in their belief that the world could be democratized and hence pacified.

By themselves, these urban neocons would not have prevailed. What was decisive was their alliance with a broader "Jacksonian" school of nationalist conservatives from the south and the west, a school of thought that was represented by George W. Bush, Dick Cheney, and Donald Rumsfeld. This group is strongly nativist, nationalist, and religious in the Christian right sense.[22] These conservatives are concerned about limits on US sovereignty and are deeply pessimistic about the world and the threat it poses to American security and values. Unlike the neocons, this group does not want to remake the world but simply to protect America.[23]

These "assertive nationalists" were primarily from the "red states" of the south and Midwest, which is the base of Jacksonian America. This tradition, which has deep historical roots in those parts of America, is associated with middle- and working-class white Protestants; it emphasizes a version of realism that, while skeptical of humanitarian interventions and global institutions, places great weight on "honor, concern for reputation, and faith in military institutions."[24] The latter view was reinforced by a Congress, especially the Republican-dominated House of Representatives, that was parochial and distrustful of the world and hostile to multilateralism.

In their analysis of the current Bush administration, Ivo Daalder and James Lindsay outline the logic behind Bush's hegemonist foreign policy. This logic is based on the following five key propositions:

- the world is a dangerous place;
- self-interested nation-states are the key actors in world politics;
- military power is the key factor in international relations, and power includes will;
- multilateral agreements and institutions are neither essential nor conducive to American interests;
- the United States is a unique great power that stands for good and threatens only those who opposed the spread of liberty and free markets.[25]

Kulturkampf: The clash in strategic cultures

This approach resulted in a *Kulturkampf* or clash of strategic cultures with that of the *Zivilmacht Deutschland*. The Bush revolution posed a frontal challenge to the German consensus. Perhaps the most concise formulation offered to explain the contemporary German strategic culture is that of a civilian power, or *Zivilmacht*, developed by Hanns W. Maull.[26] This approach emphasizes Germany as a civilian rather than a military power, projecting its influence and seeing its interests in a multilateral rather than national framework. It seeks influence through cultural and economic means rather than the use of force, although force is not ruled out as a last resort. This paradigm is the product of history, political culture, and the new geopolitics of Europe.

As Klaus Larres observed, this strategic culture clashed with that of the Bush administration and produced misunderstandings on at least three major dimensions: multilateralism, nationalism, and the use of force in international relations.[27] Any German leadership, whether Social Democratic or Christian Democratic, would be very uneasy about the serious consideration of the use of military force. NATO was based on the integration of German forces into a multilateral system limited to defending NATO territory. During the Cold War, force was regarded as a deterrent, although this doctrine was modified with the détente component of the Harmel formula adopted by NATO in 1967.[28] The result was what the former Christian Democratic Defense Minister Volker Ruehe once called a "culture of reticence."

With the end of the Cold War, the definition of the legitimate use of force was gradually expanded, both by the Kohl government and the Red–Green coalition, to include use of force outside of NATO territory, so long as a multilateral basis existed for legitimization and deployment. The Balkan wars created a new justification for military action based upon humanitarian values, in this case to prevent "ethnic cleansing." The growing Europeanization of Europe also provided another rationale—namely, the need for Germany to contribute to a credible European Security and Defense Policy. The German public has accepted these modifications to a strategic culture, which moved from one of "a culture of reticence" to one of limited, multilateral engagement. That a Red–Green government could deploy German forces in Kosovo, Macedonia, and Afghanistan was a remarkable achievement, although one that was not more than provisionally accepted within its activist core. The limits on the use of force by a German government were quite explicit. Force can only be used as a last resort and defensively, not preemptively. Force must be used for humanitarian purposes and not simply for national or economic interests. Finally, the use of force must have a broader multilateral framework, preferably with a mandate either from the United Nations or NATO.[29]

The unilateralism of the Bush administration and its emphasis upon an early and robust use of force went against the fundamentals of German political and strategic culture. Thus, the strategic cultures of Germany and the United States diverged in fundamental ways.[30] The escalating rhetoric of a potential war with Iraq, combined with the German election campaign, further divided the two countries.[31] The prominence of the role of neoconservatives in the administration and their alliance with the Christian right had created a climate of strong skepticism about and hostility toward Europe. Richard Perle, the chairperson of Rumsfeld's Defense Policy Board, typifies this attitude of neocons who never tire of lecturing the Europeans for "lacking a moral compass" and of asserting that "Germany has subsided into a moral numbing pacifism."[32]

The dispute escalated the aversion held not only by the neocons but also by the nationalist conservatives to "old Europe." In this view, old Europe, led by France and Germany in an alliance with Russia, sought to dominate the new Europe of the former Warsaw Pact states of East-Central Europe and to create a new counterbalance to American power and purpose. According to this narrative, old Europe was using the European Union and the United Nations to thwart American efforts to deal with the "axis of evil" much as they had accommodated the Soviet Union during the détente era. The new Europeans, being less removed from the experience of living under totalitarianism, were more willing to challenge it than the more complacent and self-satisfied old Europeans.[33] The reaction in Europe and Germany to the rise of this group has been, unsurprisingly, critical. Helmut Schmidt, the former Social Democratic chancellor, wrote that this "nationalist-egocentric influence of imperialistic minded intellectuals on US strategy is greater than at any time since the Second World War," and that this unilateralist school will be in the ascendancy for at least a decade.[34]

Additionally, there was the contrast in personality and generational experiences of the American and German leaderships. Bush and Schröder could not have differed more in terms of social and political background and experience. Bush was the scion of a wealthy and politically influential family who benefited throughout his life from family connections. He rose to the top almost without any effort. Schröder, in contrast, never knew his father, who was killed in the Second World War. His mother was a house cleaner, and he made it to the top through fierce personal determination, intelligence, and superb tactical skills. Bush was transformed, in his thirties, from an alcoholic and purposeless man into someone with the conviction of an evangelical Christian and reformed alcoholic. He believed that the tragedy of 9/11 gave his presidency and life a mission and purpose.

Schröder was thoroughly secular, without any apparent set of political convictions, a pure *Macher*. He viewed politics and political alliances as matters of interest, not of personal trust. Bush, in contrast, placed great emphasis on personal loyalty and trust; thus, when he believed that

Schröder had reneged on an assurance that he would not to make Iraq an issue during the German election campaign, he never forgave the chancellor.

Neither leader came to office with deep interest or experience in foreign policy, and both were to a great extent provincials. Neither had much interest in or understanding of the other, and neither wanted to admit that they had made a mistake or to be seen as conceding to the other in what became a struggle of wills. Neither had many friends or contacts in the other's country, and there was no one on either side who could pick up the telephone or fly over to find a compromise based on mutual trust. Their attitudes set the tone for their governments and made it very difficult for their advisers.[35] Yet the personality clash should be seen as a catalyst for deeper-seated changes that had been underway since the fall of the Berlin Wall and were accelerated by the personal chemistry of the two leaders.

How solid are the foundations? The factors underpinning the relationship

In spite of the major changes in the relationship, there are a number of factors that could act as buffers or stabilizers on the tendencies unleashed by the international and domestic situations. These include the economic relationship, the community of values, a new common threat, and the lack of alternative allies.

The economic relationship

The economic relationship between the two countries, which is dense and important, remained stable throughout the crisis.[36] While the Franco–American dispute had serious economic effects on the French, this was not the case in the German–American flare-up. One saw little evidence of boycotts on either side. The economic interdependence is simply too great to be jeopardized by the fallout from a political crisis. On the other hand, the economic relationship did little to prevent the crisis, although key business leaders lobbied their respective governments to damp down the conflict. The conclusion is that the economic relationship will not replace the strategic one as the new transatlantic cement. The logic of private-sector interests is quite different from that of strategic interests.

The community of values

Many would argue that a broad overlapping of values exists between the United States and Germany that will sustain the weakening of the strategic relationship. In fact the political and strategic conflict over Iraq both reflected and accelerated a growing value gap between Germans and Americans. The use of the term "American conditions," by Schröder and a wide range of political and even business leaders in Germany, reflects a distancing from the US social and economic model and a preference for a "social market" economy. German conceptions of democracy are also more closely linked to a positive idea of freedom in which the state helps provide equality in living conditions, compared to the "negative" American idea of freedom with its emphasis upon equality of opportunity and a diminished role for the state. The discussion over economic reform has become more heated in Germany since the 2002 election and became the central issue in the 2005 election; if Germany continues along a path of economic liberalization, this difference might ease. However, resistance could lead to a wider transatlantic rift over economic and social models.

Demographic factors might also lead to a further clash. Projections suggest that a growing and relatively youthful America will face an aging and more conservative Germany and Europe. As a survey in the *Economist* noted, "by the middle of this century America's population could be 440 m–550 m, larger than the EU's even after enlargement, and nearly half China's rather than a quarter ... America will be noticeably younger then and ethnically more varied."[37] The median age in America today is roughly the same as that in Europe (thirty-six, compared to Europe's thirty-eight); but by mid-century, while the median age in the United States will remain at around thirty-six, it will increase to fifty-three in Europe. The contrast between demographic dynamism and ethnic diversity could create real risks for a value gap in the transatlantic relationship. Already by 2015 the German government will be preoccupied with managing the demands of an aging population while trying to modernize an economy that relies too heavily on the manufacturing sector.

There could also be a clash between the US and German concepts of identity and citizenship if Americans decide to apply their model to Germany and Europe. These societies have different social and cultural identities, and they need a sense of cultural and social cohesion, especially as Europe experiences integration and globalization. During the 2002 campaign, Edmund Stoiber's spokesperson, Michael Glos, stated that the Christian Democrats rejected the ideal of a multicultural society. On the German side, the danger exists that, in reaction to the multicultural model, Germans may revert to old prejudices about America being a polyglot society without a soul or identity. Clearly this dynamic could generate new transatlantic tensions or, alternatively, could facilitate a transatlantic learning process.

Most importantly, Germany and the European Union have developed an approach to world order that differs fundamentally from that of the Bush administration. Although many argue that democracies are the best safeguard against war, and that democracies do not fight other democracies, the Iraq case proved that democracies can fight wars without the broader support of international institutions and law, and may even flaunt the rules and norms of the international system. It also demonstrated that democracies can have ugly disputes with other democracies and that a perception of strategic interests or domestic political imperatives trump the comity of democratic states.

In search of common interests

For the first time in 50 years, the resilience of the transatlantic relationship as a pillar of German foreign policy is now in question. Yet the fallout from the Bush administration's intractability on the issue of Iraq has resulted in a major reassessment of the viability of the Bush revolution as the best approach for America's post-9/11 strategy. The costs of the postconflict situation and the United States' isolation, along with the substantial loss of American legitimacy after the Abu Ghraib prison scandal, have led to a renewed understanding of the importance of coalitions and "soft power." Furthermore the American strategic culture is going through a *Kulturkampf* of its own. The polarization between "red" and "blue" America extends to foreign policy as well. A Pew Research Center survey conducted in November of 2003 found that the gap between Republicans and Democrats on the issue of the use of military power "has never been wider," as were the gaps on a number of national security dimensions.[38] While Bush was reelected by a thin margin in 2004, his foreign policy revolution, especially its consequences in Iraq, remains questioned by a majority of the American public. Bush won on leadership qualities, values, and countering terrorism, but not on his policies in Iraq or on his broader foreign policy.

The German–American relationship was fundamentally changed over the Iraq war. It will not return to a status quo ante even if the Democrats occupy the White House and the Christian Democrats the Chancellery. The long-term strategic trends are unlikely to see a return of the centrality the relationship held in the Cold War. Alliances do not necessarily survive victories, as all alliances must be based on strategic relationships. Thus the German–American alliance is over, a victim of its own success.

Some have argued that terrorism could replace the specter of the Soviet Union as a unifying threat. Yet, it is highly unlikely that a broad "war on terrorism" will ever provide the new strategic glue to repair the alliance because terrorism represents a tactic rather than an identifiable enemy. The American public remains traumatized by the memory of 9/11 and feels the threat more existentially than does Europe. Germans take the internal terrorist threat seriously but see counterterrorism as largely police and intelligence work rather than as a new strategic challenge for NATO.

Additionally, the inclusion of the Middle East in an attempt to build a new strategic consensus also stretches the alliance both outside the area of greatest common interest—Europe—to a region in which US–European differences have always been great. The speech of Foreign Minister Fischer to the 2004 Wehrkunde meeting, in which he proposed a new initiative by NATO to promote the transformation of the region, indicates that German leaders understand that the status quo has been deeply shaken in the Middle East and that the growing instability in the region is not in their interest, but the advocated approach relies more on the European Union and development assistance than on NATO and the military.[39] Schröder and his successor Angela Merkel, continue to rule out a military role for Germany in Iraq. In fact, the reelection of George W. Bush has reduced pressure on the Red–Green government to do more in Iraq.

The gap between American military capabilities and those of Europe will not diminish, and the unilateralist option remains for a continental superpower, an option that does not exist for medium-sized and integrated states such as Germany. Both the responsibilities and the hubris of great power will continue to influence American leaders. This does not mean that the relationship will necessarily become an adversarial one, although it could. The future relationship will be based on strategic interests and on alignments made up of ad hoc coalitions of interest as well as areas of divergence. The Iraq case not only drove Washington and Berlin apart, but it also brought them together on new agreements in other areas. The challenge posed by terrorism has been taken seriously by both nations, and the level of police, immigration, and intelligence cooperation has been by all accounts excellent. The United States emerged from the Iraq experience understanding that both hard power and unilateralism have real limits and that a war on terrorism must be multilateral and include state and society building as well as the military dimension. Germans have also gained a better appreciation for the dangers posed by the new form of terrorism represented by Al Qaeda and its spin-offs; they understand the dangers posed by the proliferation of weapons of mass destruction and the nexus with terrorism. The German government has acknowledged the need for a military element to any nonproliferation strategy, has extended its military role in Afghanistan, and has pushed for a broader mandate for the NATO command force there, a force co-led for a time by the Germans. However, American credibility has been severely damaged in Germany and in Europe, and it will take years if not decades to repair. The United States no longer represents a shining city on a hill, and many young Germans have come of age with an image of a dangerous and brutal America rather than an America that defends freedom. The next time a US government claims that it and the West face a serious and immediate threat, the claim will evoke greater skepticism than at any time since the end of Second World War.

Given all the changes both domestically and internationally, there will be some parting of ways between Washington and Berlin. If there is to be a new partnership, it will have to be one more of equals, of real partners, and this will require great adjustments on both sides of the Atlantic and a deeper degree of European foreign and defense policy integration. Germany without Europe cannot be an effective partner for the American superpower. In Washington, there will need to be a rejection of neoconservatism and a return to either a realist or liberal hegemonist approach. At the same time, the serious possibility of a deepening, permanent rift and a relationship based on rivalry—in short, a split in the West—is greater than at any time in the postwar period. Leadership in both Washington and Berlin will be crucial in determining whether the transatlantic relationship will be present at the rebirth or the destruction of what has proved to be the guarantor of European stability for over half a century.

Notes

1   David Frum and Richard Perle, *An End to Evil: How to Win the War on Terror* (New York: Random House, 2003), p. 248.
2   Samuel R. Berger, "Foreign Policy for a Democratic President," *Foreign Affairs*, 83: 3 (May/June 2004): 47–63.
3   For an extensive review of the recent literature on the topic, see James Sperling, "The Foreign Policy of the Berlin Republic: The Very Model of a Post-Modern Major Power?," *German Politics*, 13: 1 (2004): 1–34.
4   The classic formulation of this interpretation remains that of A.W. DePorte, *Europe Between the Superpowers: The Enduring Balance* (New Haven: Yale University Press, 1979).
5   See David Calleo, *The German Problem Reconsidered* (Cambridge: Cambridge University Press, 1978).
6   See Sebastian Harnisch and Hanns W. Maull, eds, *Germany as a Civilian Power? The foreign policy of the Berlin Republic* (Manchester: Manchester University Press, 2001); Hanns W. Maull, "Zivilmacht Bundesrepublik Deutschland," *Europa Archiv*, 47: 10 (1992): 269–78; and Hanns W. Maull, "Germany and Japan: The New Civilian Powers," *Foreign Affairs*, 69 (winter 1990/91): 91–106.
7   Heinrich August Winkler, *Der lange Weg nach Westen: vom Dritten Reich bis zur Wiedervereinigung*, vol. *II* (Munich: Beck Verlag, 2000), p. 655.
8   For more on this linkage model, see Jeffrey S. Lantis, *Strategic Dilemmas and the Evolution of German Foreign Policy since Unification* (Westport, CT: Praeger, 2002), pp. 5–9.
9   Stephen M. Walt, "Two Cheers for Clinton's Foreign Policy," *Foreign Affairs*, 79 (March/April 2000): 64.
10 Walt, *Foreign Affairs* (see note 9), p. 65.
11 John Ikenberry, ed., *America Unrivaled: The Future of the Balance of Power* (Ithaca, NY: Cornell University Press, 2002), p. 9.
12 Ted Galen Carpenter, *Peace and Freedom: Foreign Policy for a Constitutional Republic* (Washington: The Cato Institute, 2002), cited in Quentin Peel, "Caught in the Web of Nation Building," *Financial Times*, October 16, 2002, p. 15. For a broad survey of the intellectual origins of the Bush strategy, see Frances Fitzgerald, "George Bush and the World," *The New York Review of Books*, September 26, 2002, pp. 80–86.
13 As John Ikenberry describes realism, "This is the most elegant and time-honored theory of international order: order is the result of balancing by states under conditions of anarchy to counter opposing power concentrations or threats. In this view, American preponderance is unsustainable: it poses a basic threat to other states and balancing reactions are inevitable." Ikenberry, *America Unrivaled* (see note 11), p. 3.
14 See James Mann, *The Rise of the Vulcans: The History of Bush's War Cabinet* (New York: Viking, 2004).
15 Horst Teltschik, in his memoir of the diplomacy of German unification, reported a conversation that occurred on May 17, 1990 between President Bush and

Chancellor Kohl in Washington in which Bush indicated his concerns for both German and American domestic support for a continued US troop presence. Horst Teltschik, *329 Tage: Innenausichten der Einigung* (Berlin: Siedler, 1991), p. 222.

16 Mann, *The Rise of the Vulcans* (see note 14), p. 210.

17 See George Szamuely, "Clinton's Clumsy Encounter with the World," *Orbis*, 38 (summer 1994): 373–95, an early conservative assessment of Clinton's foreign policy.

18 For a full account of the German role in NATO enlargement see Ronald D. Asmus, *Opening NATO's Door: How the Alliance Remade Itself for a New Era* (New York: Columbia University Press, 2002); see especially pp. 29–34.

19 These classifications are modifications of those offered by Fidler and Baker, "America's Democratic imperialists," p. 11. The terms "democratic imperialists" and "assertive nationalists" originate with Ivo Daalder of the Brookings Institution and Charles Kupchan of Georgetown University, both of whom are cited by Fidler and Baker. They are more fully elaborated in Ivo H. Daalder and James M. Lindsay, *America Unbound: The Bush Revolution in Foreign Policy* (Washington: The Brookings Institution Press, 2003), especially Chapters 1 and 3.

20 The term was originally coined by de Tocqueville. See a recent discussion of its expression in post-9/11 America in John Parker, "A Nation Apart: A Survey of America," *The Economist*, November 8, 2003. See also Daalder and Lindsay, *America Unbound* (see note 19), pp. 6 and 45.

21 Peter Steinfels, *The Neoconservatives: The Men Who Are Changing America's Politics* (New York: Simon and Schuster, 1979), p. 50.

22 Stephen Fidler and Gerald Baker, "America's democratic imperialists," *Financial Times*, March 6, 2003, p. 11; and Mann, *The Rise of the Vulcans* (see note 14), pp. 177–97.

23 See Thomas E. Ricks, "Holding Their Ground," *The Washington Post*, December 23, 2003, pp. C 1–2.

24 Walter Russell Mead, "The Jacksonian Tradition and American Foreign Policy," *The National Interest* (winter 1999/2000): 17. See also Daalder and Lindsay, *America Unbound* (see note 19), Chapters 1 and 3.

25 Daalder and Lindsay, *America Unbound* (see note 19), pp. 41–45.

26 See Harnisch and Maull, *Germany as a Civilian Power?* (see note 6); and Maull, *Europa Archiv* and *Foreign Affairs* (both works cited in note 6).

27 Klaus Larres, "Mutual Incomprehension: US–German Value Gaps Beyond Iraq," *The Washington Quarterly*, 26:2 (spring 2003): 23–42.

28 Walt, *Foreign Affairs* (see note 9), p. 68.

29 For a concise formulation of these restraints see Anja Dalgaard-Nielsen, "Gulf War: The German Resistance," *Survival*, 45: 1 (spring 2003): 99–116.

30 Gunther Hellman, "Deutschland in Europa: eine symbiotische Beziehung," *Aus Politik und Zeitgeschichte* 48 (2002): 26. "The two most important members of NATO were in central questions of international politics, from climate change, through the International Criminal Court and to policy toward Iraq, were marching more decisively than ever in different directions."

31 While 76 percent of the German public found German–American relations to be "good" or "very good" at the end of the 2002 campaign, 46 percent opposed the participation of German troops in a war against Iraq, even with a UN mandate, while 50 percent supported participation with a UN mandate. Only one month after the election, those numbers shifted slightly more in favor of participation with a UN mandate. Confidence in the SPD's handling of relations with the

United States dropped from 41 percent in September to 34 percent in October, but with only 27 percent expressing confidence in the CDU's policy toward the United States. Forschungsgruppe Wahlen e.V.Mannheim, *Bundestagswahl: Eine Analyse der Wahl vom 22. September 2002*, Bericht Nr. 108, pp. 48–49; the month after the election figures from the FGW can be found in the "Der Kanzler verliert seinen Vertrauensbonus," *Süddeutsche Zeitung*, 19/20 (October 2002): 7.

32   Edward Pilkington and Ewen MacAskill, "Europe lacks moral fibre says US hawk," *The Guardian*, November 13, 2002.

33   For a litany of neocon concerns about Europe see "Continental Drift," *The American Enterprise* (December 2002), pp. 24–41. Charles Krauthammer, "Don't Go Back to the U.N.," *The Washington Post*, March 21, 2003, p. A 37; also "The French Challenge," *The Washington Post*, February 21, 2003, p. A 27.

34   Helmut Schmidt, "Europa braucht keinen Vormund," *Die Zeit*, August 5, 2002.

35   For more on this clash of personalities, see Stephen F. Szabo, *Parting Ways: The Crisis in German-American Relations* (Washington: The Brookings Institution Press, 2004).

36   US investment in Germany in 2001 totaled $65 billion, while German investment in the United States was $137 billion; 734,800 Americans were employed by German firms in the United States, while 652,600 Germans were employed by American firms in Germany; German exports to the United States in 2002 totaled over $62 billion (23 percent of non-EU German trade), while the United States exported $337.5 billion to Germany (about 16 percent of non-EU German imports). See Daniel S. Hamilton and Joseph P. Quinlan, *Partners in Prosperity: The Changing Geography of the Transatlantic Economy* (Washington: The Center for Transatlantic Relations, Johns Hopkins University, SAIS, 2004), pp. 108–11.

37   John Parker, "A Nation Apart: A Survey of America," *The Economist*, November 8, 2003, p. 7.

38   The Pew Research Center for the People and the Press, "The 2004 Political Landscape: Evenly Divided and Increasingly Polarized," November 5, 2003, pp. 27–38. For the debate on the future of the Bush revolution see Francis Fukuyama, "The Neoconservative Moment," *The National Interest* (summer 2004): 57–68; and G. John Ikenberry, "The End of the Neo-conservative Moment," *Survival*, 46 (spring 2004): 7–22.

39   Speech by Joschka Fischer, Federal Minister for Foreign Affairs, at the Fortieth Annual Munich Conference on Security Policy, Munich, February 7, 2004. Available at: http://www.ausaertiges-amt.de.

9
The Transatlantic Relationship: A View from Germany

Peter Rudolf

Introduction

As the German–American clash over Iraq was unfolding, such an astute observer as Henry Kissinger interpreted the way in which German Chancellor Gerhard Schröder handled the topic of Iraq in the German election campaign as the harbinger of a profound change in German foreign policy. In his view, the electoral benefits derived from Schröder's strategy indicated that a kind of anti-Americanism may have become "a permanent temptation of German politics." For Kissinger, the issue of Iraq was merely a "pretext for a reorientation of German foreign policy in a more national direction." The new "German way"—in whose name Germany allegedly sought confrontation with the United States without consulting other European states—represented, he argued, a challenge not only to the United States but also to Europe.[1]

More than a decade after the disappearance of the common threat of Soviet communism, and after the departure of old political elites that were shaped by the experiences of the Second World War and the Cold War, does the special German–American relationship finally belong to history? Is it accurate to argue that German foreign policy is moving in the direction of unilateralism and nationalism? Twelve years after unification, was Germany finally fulfilling the expectations of those US security-policy experts who could not imagine that Germany's leaders had internalized constraints on the use of power and come to understand national interests in a multilateral sense?[2]

From a specific (American) realist view of international relations, it had been expected that, after the end of the Cold War, Germany would turn toward a nationalistic foreign-policy stance that increasingly emphasizes and asserts its own interests. Whoever shares this view could easily interpret the confrontation over Iraq as an indication of such a development. From this perspective, it made sense to elevate German Foreign Minister Joschka Fischer's response to US Defense Secretary Donald Rumsfeld making the case for war at the 2003 Munich Conference on Security Policy—"Excuse me, but I'm not convinced"—to something very fundamental: a "declaration of independence from the United States, the end point of a half-century of nearly automatic compliance with the American wish."[3]

One might speculate about whether Rumsfeld would share this view of a "Golden era" in German–American relations. He will remember another crisis, 30 years ago, in October 1973 during the Yom Kippur War when he was US ambassador to NATO (North American Treaty Organization). At that time, the German government—first confidently, then, after the US administration had raised the alert level of American military forces without consulting the allies, publicly—demanded that the United States stop delivering weapons from and over West German territory to Israel. Most other NATO members, among them Britain and France, had already denied the United States the right to fly over their territory. In the 1973 confrontation, France and Britain led the opposition. Therefore, it was indeed something new that Germany, together with France, took the lead in opposing the United States on a security-policy issue that the administration considered vital.[4] But despite all diplomatic maneuvering and the denial of international legitimacy to the war, the Schröder government did nothing to restrain the United States from using the military infrastructure in Germany.

Thus, one should be cautious of attempts to revive the "myth" of German assertiveness. This myth was originally created in the aftermath of Germany's unilateral recognition of Croatia and Slovenia, presumably the first time that Germany openly defied the United States and its West European partners by coming up with an ill-conceived and clumsy policy. In reality, however, the announcement of recognition was more a sign of helplessness than assertiveness, more a symbolic act to defuse domestic pressure than the beginning of a new geopolitical venture.[5]

Looking at Germany's role in transatlantic relations and the Iraq crisis, I can detect neither a dramatic break in the premises and approaches guiding German policy in dealing with the United States nor a departure from the fundamental norms shaping German national interests. German policy toward the United States can be interpreted as an adjustment process to strategic changes in US grand strategy that, in effect, amounted to a rather consistent new paradigm of hegemonic unilateralism: the preservation of unipolarity, that is the maintenance of military supremacy regardless of potential threats and adversaries; a heightened perception of intolerable threats, which has led to the rejection of containment as *the* fundamental concept of security policy with respect to the new threats; the attempted legitimization of preventive war against states that support terrorism in whatever form and the emphasis on strategic independence (which, of course, does not rule out instrumental multilateralism).[6] Those changes accentuated structural problems in the transatlantic relationship: the deeply rooted difference in the perception of security threats and the response to them and, more fundamental, those diverging perspectives on world order that have led to conflicts over the role of international institutions.[7]

As a result, the transatlantic framework as one of the two pillars of German foreign policy has been eroding at a time when normative world order conflicts have become sharper in the German–American relationship as a result of the "war on terror."[8] The changing strategic setting made it more difficult for Germany to balance its basic orientation as a civilian power with the imperative of preserving the transatlantic link.

The strategic and normative changes emanating from the United States have had a couple of consequences: first, with the strategic change in US foreign policy, one of the main settings of German multilateralism has been eroding. With the geostrategic paradigm shift—the focus on the Middle East and the challenge of terrorism and rogue states—NATO is no longer what it used to be: "a unique institutional framework for the Europeans to affect American policies" with consultation norms and joint decision-making procedures as the underpinnings of Europe's influence on the United States.[9] Second, the traditional premise of German foreign policy in the transatlantic setting, gaining influence by cooperation, has been put into serious doubt. Even the most imaginative counterfactual speculation cannot make plausible how Germany could have influenced the Bush administration in its steadfast move toward regime change by force. Third, the vexing issue of when to use force has become dominant with the Bush administration's push for a normative change with respect to the purposes for which legitimate wars can be waged. Fourth, as a consequence, Germany gave up its so-called *sowohl als auch* ("as well as") policy of avoiding to choose between France and the United States and sided with France against the United States (after the French saved Germany from being left alone).

German Amerikapolitik: old premises, new problems

German diplomatic vocabulary seems to lack the word *Amerikapolitik*; instead, we speak about transatlantic relations. Relations with the United States are so interwoven with a variety of institutional settings, and so many international issues and interactions are so dense and complex that it is hard to isolate a policy toward the United States from the wider context of transatlantic relations. Yet, for analytical clarity, it is useful to distinguish a spectrum of approaches on dealing with the United States as the preponderant power.[10] Those approaches range from dissociating to associating strategies, from "balancing" on one side of the spectrum to "bandwagoning" on the other.

At the level of the fundamental foreign-policy orientation, "hard" balancing in the traditional sense of building up Europe as a countervailing power dissociated from the United States is certainly not the approach guiding German foreign policy. There may be issues, especially in the economic field, where Europe effectively acts as a counterweight within a highly symmetrical relationship, able to restrain American options through the threat of economic retaliation. In the security field, where power is highly asymmetrical, the development of a European Security and Defense Policy (ESDP) is often perceived as an attempt at restraining the United States by building up a counterweight. But from the mainstream German position, ESDP, which is a natural outgrowth of the European unification process, is an effort to lessen dependence in security matters on the United States and to gain more leverage vis-à-vis the United States. And it is a hedge against security risks and the renationalization of security policies should the transatlantic link weaken or dissolve.

Thus far, Europeanization follows the logic of Germany's basic strategy of "self-containment"[11] through integration into Western institutions. The balancing act has been to reconcile the Europeanization of security policy with US insistence on the institutional primacy of NATO. Some sort of the highly feared "European Caucus" in NATO would change the structure of transatlantic interactions—from hegemonic leadership relying upon the traditional "multiple bilateralism"[12] to a new form of cooperation based upon greater equity. This scenario might lead to a "redistribution of power in the alliance."[13]

Some in the German foreign-policy community may be tempted to use a widening Atlantic in order to promote a common European identity. But from the prevailing perspective, Europe cannot be developed into a strong effective international actor against the United States. There are too many European nations that prefer bandwagoning with the distant hegemon to bandwagoning with the most powerful European nations. The Iraq crisis in transatlantic relations, the political debates in Germany, and self-critical commentaries have tended to obscure the tenets of basic consensus within the political class in Germany. The transatlantic relationship is still seen as a basic framework of Germany foreign policy. The Christian Democratic Union (CDU)/Christian Social Union (CSU) might be more emphatic in stressing common values, interests, and a common destiny.[14] Others, including the chancellor and the foreign minister might prefer a more businesslike focus on common interests. According to Schröder, NATO epitomizes the transatlantic core of German foreign policy; it remains the "most important pillar of our common security" and the "most important forum for transatlantic dialogue and transatlantic cooperation."[15]

The defense-policy guidelines from May 2003 reaffirm the traditional premise of German security policy: "The transatlantic partnership remains the foundation of our security. Also in the future, there will be no security in and for Europe without the United States."[16] It is a rather astonishing feature of the German foreign-policy debate that one geopolitical core aspect of this premise is so infrequently debated: the assumption that United States still remains necessary as a European power in order to allay fears of an overly powerful Germany. As German Foreign Minister Joschka Fischer put it, "Without transatlantic relations in Europe, including the Europe of today, Germany would immediately assume a role for which we should definitely not strive. This would put too much strain on us. The US provides not only a global balance; it also provides a balance in Europe up to this very day."[17] This subtle reassuring role accorded to the United States is still an aspect of German thinking on foreign policy, though only a minority in the broader German elite would subscribe to this view.[18]

German foreign policy follows an approach in dealing with the United States that lies between "hard balancing" and "full bandwagoning" in the traditional sense. In the spirit of its own self-constraint, Germany is interested in the continuation of functioning transatlantic relations as a basic framework for German foreign policy. However, in order for Europe to assert itself in cases where European and American strategies diverge, it is deemed necessary to steer transatlantic relations in the direction of a cooperative balance. If Germany rejected the new American security agenda, the United States could lose interest in the alliance, and the chance to influence the United States could be even smaller than it is now. If Germany fully aligned itself with the American agenda encapsulated in the Bush doctrine, in which the "new" NATO and its centerpiece—the multinational NATO Response Force proposed by the United States—play a role, Germany would risk costly involvement in policies over which it has little to no influence.

German policy so far can be interpreted as an attempt at adapting to the new American agenda while at the same time staking out its own positions and avoiding too close an alignment with the United States in the Middle East. The Iraq conflict, in which Germany and France pursued a policy of "soft balancing," as Robert Pape calls it, of trying to restrain American power through the United Nations or, at least, of denying legitimacy to the war, has overshadowed the fact that Germany adjusted to the American war on terror in a way most analysts would not have dared to predict. It was a Social Democratic chancellor leading a Red–Green coalition government who went to great political risks to get a mandate to send German troops to Afghanistan as part of Operation Enduring Freedom. And it was a Social Democratic defense minister who in December 2002 declared: "Our security is also defended on the Hindukush."[19] And it was a Green foreign minister who eased the pragmatic rapprochement with the United States by declaring the "destructive Jihad terrorism and its totalitarian ideology" to be the greatest threat to regional and global security at the beginning of the twenty-first century and by proposing a new transatlantic initiative for the Near and Middle East.[20] The challenge for German and European foreign policy is to incorporate the new agenda, which is focused so much on the nexus of terrorism and weapons of mass destruction, without succumbing to the naive illusions and imperial temptations originally associated with this agenda.

Changes in German public opinion

Public opinion in a liberal democracy such as Germany places constraints on and creates incentives for foreign-policy making and serves as a framework for discussions and decision-making processes among the political elite.[21] As will be shown, changes in public opinion create incentives for keeping some distance from the United States and for pursuing a "Europe first" option. But NATO as the traditional transatlantic link remains part of Germany's foreign policy identity. Well before the Iraq crisis, one could recognize a shift toward a more skeptical view of the international role played by the United States. The extent of American power, and particularly its unilateral deployment in the pursuit of narrow national interests, appears to be the most important factor contributing to a less positive view of the United States' international role in German public opinion.[22]

The Iraq confrontation led to further changes in German public opinion toward the United States. The number of people holding the view that a strong US leadership role in world affairs is desirable declined to 45 percent in June 2003, from 68 percent the year before.[23] Asked whether the European Union or the United States were more important to German vital interests, 81 percent chose the European Union in June 2003, up from 55 percent in 2002—a fact interpreted by American analysts as meaning, "Germany, the long-time ally, now expresses an unambiguous preference for Europe over the United States."[24] Compared with France, the United States is no longer seen as Germany's most important partner.[25] The preference for France is part of a wider "Europe first" orientation, having emerged as a reaction to a high level of frustration with US foreign policy.[26] In June 2003, 70 percent of Germans (up from 48 percent the year before) wanted the European Union to become a "superpower."[27] A growing number prefers a more independent European course in diplomatic and security affairs, compared to those who believe that the United States and the European Union should remain as close as they had been. The preference for a more independent course rose from 51 percent in April 2002 to 63 percent in February 2004.[28] According to another poll taken in 2003, 81 percent supported the view that a common European stand is more important for German foreign policy than close relations with the United States.[29]

Interestingly, the more skeptical view of the United States and the preference for Europe over the United States has not negatively affected NATO's image. Asked whether NATO was needed in the future, 85 percent agreed, with only a minor difference between West Germans (86 percent) and East Germans (80 percent). Only a small minority of 11 percent judged NATO to be unimportant in the future. And the opinion that NATO will remain necessary is even higher among younger than older Germans.[30] Thus, it is not surprising that the "Europe first" orientation does not translate into a preference for building up a European military organization. Two-thirds (68 percent) prefer the European Union to include NATO in its security policy. This preference cuts across party lines, age, and education level.[31]

How can one make sense of this more negative view of US foreign policy and at the same time the unfaltering preference for NATO? Obviously NATO is less seen as an instrument of US foreign policy than as part Germany's foreign policy identity.[32] The fact that NATO was not the premier location where the transatlantic dispute was being played out seems to have insulated NATO from the more negative perception of the US international role. If NATO had played a role in the war, one could have expected a deteriorating view of the organization. This expectation certainly holds true for the German "East" where, as the Kosovo war made plain,[33] one has to reckon with lingering uneasiness about NATO missions going beyond collective self-defense.

The clash over Iraq and its meaning

The "war against terror" and the war against Iraq have raised the most trouble-some question for German foreign policy and, as a result, for German–American relations: how does one justify the exercise of military force? In the wake of 9/11, there was widespread support for "Operation Enduring Freedom"—except in the left fringe of the German political and intellectual elite. Three-fifths of the German public supported the war against the Taliban and Al Qaeda in Afghanistan, and approximately one-third did not. The intervention could be justified as a legitimate form of self-defense, even though the way in which the war was conducted aroused concern.

Germany parted ways with the United States only when the Bush administration, driven by the quest for absolute security, unilaterally extended the scope of the "war on terrorism," merging different risks and threats into a "monolithic threat" and waging the war in a state-centered way directed against "rogue states" with weapons of mass destruction.[34] In the Iraq case, the German–American confrontation had two dimensions: the normative, world-order conflict over whether preventive war should be accepted as legitimate, and the political clash over the negative, counterproductive regional results of waging war against Iraq in the midst of an unfinished campaign against Islamic terrorism.

If one takes a sober look at the problems and dilemmas that US policy toward Iraq has raised, the position of the German federal government appears by no means to be as unreasonable as many critics believe, despite all electoral tactics and all the loud noise that surrounded the election campaign. Most accounts of the Iraq confrontation in German–American relations suffer from one or all of the following three errors: first, they assume a policy driven by primarily domestic considerations without any strategic rationale. The fact that the policy had domestic functions does not imply that this policy cannot at its core be rational in terms of balancing foreign-policy interests. Second, standard accounts neglect the basic insight that policies generally have to be evaluated in terms of alternative policies. A policy may be far from optimal, but compared with alternative policies it may be the least bad one, given the international and domestic context. Third, some of the more polemical accounts ignore the common sense wisdom that the deterioration of a relationship is mostly the outcome of interaction.[35]

Political positions that are adopted with electoral results and the political survival of the Red–Green coalition in mind are not necessarily devoid of strategic rationality.[36] If Berlin had adopted the US line on Iraq, how could it then have credibly rejected future American demands to participate? This decision would have meant supporting a policy considered wrong and overly risky even if it were ultimately sanctioned by the UN Security Council under US pressure. The doubts, criticisms, and questions expressed by the German government were of the kind that were repeatedly articulated in the American debate as well: doubts concerning the allegedly growing threat posed by Iraq, doubts concerning the United States' willingness to be involved in the long term in the construction of a new order in Iraq and the Middle East after a military intervention had ended, and doubts concerning the wisdom of a policy that—in the midst of a war against Islamist terrorism—sought to open up a new conflict before progress had been made toward achieving peace in the Middle East.[37] Yet it was an unusual provocation when Schröder, in an interview with the *New York Times*, publicly expressed such fundamental doubts about the wisdom of US policy and reproached the Bush administration for changing its policy in favor of regime change in Iraq without consulting its allies.[38]

Those who argue that an ill-conceived policy driven by domestic imperatives reduced Germany's influence on US policy to a minimum must be able to present a plausible argument as to how a different approach would have enabled Germany to effectively influence an American president who had decided to overthrow the regime of Saddam Hussein. There was no prospect of a common European position from the outset due to London's adoption of Washington's stance. Thus, how could Germany have acted as broker? The measuring stick used by critics of German policy in the Iraq crisis is Germany's role in the good old days when US foreign policy was Europe-centered and NATO played an important role in finding common ground, despite recurring strategic disagreements.[39] This perspective ignores the structural changes in the transatlantic relationship and the mindset of an administration that had no intention of letting its vision become watered down by consultations and that believed that in the end other states would simply jump on the bandwagon.[40]

German behavior during the Iraq crisis is often interpreted as a renunciation of multilateral norms, as a departure from principled multilateralism.[41] Philip Gordon and Jeremy Shapiro, two American analysts who blame both sides for setting in motion the vicious circle leading to transatlantic crisis, argue that "Germany was the first to depart from alliance norms," explaining it solely to be the domestic calculus of Chancellor Schröder:

> His declared refusal to support the use of force against Iraq even if autho-
> rized by the UN Security Council was, simply put, irresponsible. It went
> against everything German foreign policy has stood for since the found-
> ing of the Federal Republic. Germany's decision to stand with France
> in blocking NATO's preparation for the possible defense of Turkey in
> the context of an Iraq war was also difficult to defend. Whatever the
> American motives in calling for a NATO role in planning for the defense
> of Turkey, Germany's decision to refuse that role was deeply damaging to
> the notion of NATO as a defense alliance on which its members
> could rely.[42]

Was the German government's sweeping rejection of even a UN-sanctioned military intervention, as German journalist Stefan Kornelius was one of the first to state, really a "dramatic change in German foreign policy away from multilateralism and international organizations."[43] The reason that this issue was not debated very much might have been, as he argued, that no one took such a foreign-policy shift seriously. But the fundamental question has rarely been raised: should Germany support a policy that is viewed as strate-gically wrong and morally dubious simply for the sake of a multilaterally ori-ented foreign policy? The fact that the limits of multilateralism in security policy were so little debated shows how ingrained this mindset still is.

One can very much dispute whether, from a foreign-policy point of view, it was tactically smart and politically wise to make this "no participation" pledge directed toward the German electorate. But to interpret this position as a "great power gesture" ("*Großmachtgebärde*") and a "clear break" with the tradition of the Federal Republic misses a crucial point:[44] never before had a German government faced the question of whether to actively take part in a war deemed wrong and not in Germany's vital interests just for the sake of demonstrating its multilateral orientation. One has to keep in mind that it was all too clear that the question was not to enforce UN resolutions by force, but to overthrow a regime and to occupy a country. The often-criticized statement that such a question of war and peace had to be decided in Berlin is so self-evident that it is takes a highly idealistic, even apolitical notion of multilateralism to find fault with this simple truth.

What about the criticism that Germany damaged NATO as a defense alliance? One cannot claim that, in substance, Germany violated allied norms. There was no indication that Germany would not assist Turkey if it needed help. It was the United States, not Turkey, who pushed the issue within NATO, demanding a German contribution (among them Patriot missiles and participation in AWAC [Airborne Warning and Control] missions), thereby instrumentally using this organization to create a dilemma for the German government: either accepting that war was coming or exposing itself to the accusation of lacking solidarity.[45] Pushing NATO to get involved in Turkey's defense was a trap set by the Bush administration.[46] As a senior German official put it: "We promised to supply the Patriots to Turkey bilaterally and asked the United States please do not force us to be an obstruction within NATO. But the Bush administration was determined to make life difficult for Schroeder by having Germany vote yes to the deployment, thus undermining the chancellor's own position against the Iraq war. That was a really nasty bit of political game-playing, and we viewed [it] as bullying, pure and simple."[47] One wonders whether the US administration was aware of the fact that a request that included the participation of German military personnel would have necessitated a vote in the German Bundestag, exposing the government to great political risks.[48] When Turkey requested support, Germany, concerned about the damage to the alliance, decided to go along with a scaled-backed version of the proposal now being handled in NATO's Defense Planning Committee (of which France is not a member).

How much fundamental foreign policy change?

In my view, those observers who warn about a "German way"—an expression, by the way, that Schröder claims not to have used with respect to foreign policy—have read too much into the Iraq crisis. Thus, I would dispute the claim that the German position not to support military measures against Iraq even if mandated by the UN Security Council can be interpreted as a "clear turning away" (*"eindeutige Abkehr"*) from the role conception of a civilian power, as Hanns Maull has put it. Maull added one important differentiating observation: the approach of the Red–Green government resonated so much with the German public because of the deep roots of the resentments against the use of military force typical of the civilian power conception.[49]

This observation leads to the more general question of how to "measure" basic foreign-policy change. A policy position may be inconsistent with "core components"[50] of Germany's traditional national role conception: the general strategic preference for embedding German foreign policy into multilateral frameworks; second, the milieu goal of a civilized international order; and third, at the level of foreign-policy instruments, a preference for nonmilitary means and strong aversion against the use of military force. Even if this were the case (and I have offered a more benign evaluation of German behavior in the Iraq crisis), one would have to tackle the basic analytical question: under which conditions would it be possible to make the general inference that core components of Germany's foreign-policy identity no longer shape foreign-policy interests? Policy positions at odds with one of the core components may well be explained by situational pressures and the need to balance tensions emerging among these core components. Neither the foreign-policy discourse in Germany with respect to the transatlantic relationship nor actual policies in the wake of the Iraq crisis indicate a profound change in the orientation of German foreign policy.[51] But we can expect the strains of further adjustment and nonadjustment to a changing transatlantic framework.

Notes

1 Henry A. Kissinger, "German–US Relations Thrown into Crisis," *Korea Times*, October 23, 2002.

2 On these basic elements of German political-military culture, see Thomas U. Berger, *Cultures of Antimilitarism: National Security in Germany and Japan* (Baltimore: Johns Hopkins University Press, 1998) and Gebhard Schweigler, *West German Foreign Policy: The Domestic Setting* (New York: Praeger, 1984).

3 Richard Bernstein, "The German Question," *The New York Times Magazine*, February 5, 2004.

4 See Rajan Menon, "The End of Alliances," *World Policy Journal*, 20: 2 (summer 2003): 1–20.

5 See Peter Viggo Jakobsen, "Myth-making and Germany's Unilateral Recognition of Croatia and Slovenia," *European Security*, 4: 3 (autumn 1995): 400–16.

6 Speaking of a new paradigm does not imply that elements do not have old roots or have not been part of US foreign policy. But taken together and in contrast to US foreign policy in the second half of the twentieth century, we certainly can talk about a new paradigm. In more detail, see G. John Ikenberry, "America's Imperial Ambition," *Foreign Affairs*, 81: 5 (September/October 2002): 44–60; Robert Jervis, "Understanding the Bush Doctrine," *Political Science Quarterly*, 118: 3 (fall 2003): 365–88; David C. Hendrickson, "Toward Universal Empire: The Dangerous Quest for Absolute Security," *World Policy Journal*, 19: 3 (fall 2002): 1–10; Ken Jowitt, "Rage, Hubris, and Regime Change," *Policy Review*, 118 (April/May 2003): 33ff; Edward Rhodes, "The Imperial Logic of Bush's Liberal Agenda," *Survival*, 45: 1 (Spring 2003): 131–54; John Lewis Gaddis, *Surprise, Security, and the American Experience* (Cambridge: Harvard University Press, 2004).

7 For a variety of perspectives on the problems and developments in transatlantic and German–American relations, see Philip H. Gordon and Jeremy Shapiro, *Allies at War: America, Europe, and the Crisis over Iraq* (New York: McGraw-Hill, 2004); Helga Haftendorn, "A Poisoned Relationship? Die transatlantischen Beziehungen nach den Terrorangriffen des 11. September 2001," Weltmacht vor neuer Bedrohung. Die Bush-Administration und die US-Außenpolitik nach dem Angriff *auf Amerika*, Werner Kremp and Jürgen Wilzewski, eds (Trier: Wissenschaftlicher Verlag Trier, 2003), pp. 249–75; Markus Kaim, "Friendship under strain or fundamental alienation? German–US relations after the Iraq war," *International Journal*, 59: 1 (winter 2003/04): 1–17; Joachim Krause, *Die transatlantischen Beziehungen seit dem Ende des Kalten Krieges* (Kiel: Institut für Sicherheitspolitik an der Christian-Albrechts-Universität zu Kiel, 2003); Gert Krell, "Arroganz der Macht, Arroganz der Ohnmacht. Die Weltordnungspolitik der USA und die transatlantischen Beziehungen," *Aus Politik und Zeitgeschichte*, B 31–32/2003 (July 28, 2003): 23–30; Harald Müller, "Das transatlantische Risiko—Deutungen des amerikanisch-europäischen Weltordnungskonflikts," in *Aus Politik und Zeitgeschichte*, B 3–4/2004

148   *Peter Rudolf*

(January 19, 2004): 7–17; Gustav Lindstrom, ed., *Shift or Rift? Assessing US–EU relations after Iraq* (Paris: European Union Institute for Security Studies, 2003); John Peterson and Mark A. Pollack, eds, *Europe, America, Bush: Transatlantic Relations in the Twenty-First Century* (New York: Routledge, 2003); Thomas Risse, "Die neue Weltordnung: US–amerikanische Hypermacht—europäische Ohnmacht," *WeltTrends*, 39 (summer 2003): 110–19; Peter Rudolf, "Die USA und die transatlantischen Beziehungen nach dem 11. September 2001," in *Aus Politik und Zeitgeschichte*, B 25/2002 (June 21, 2002): 7–13: Stephen F. Szabo, *Parting Ways: The Crisis in German–American Relations* (Washington: Brookings Institution Press, 2004).

8   See Gunther Hellmann, "Der 'deutsche Weg.' Eine außenpolitische Gratwanderung," *Internationale Politik* (September 2002): 1–8.

9   Thomas Risse-Kappen, *Cooperation Among Democracies: The European Influence on U.S. Foreign Policy* (Princeton: Princeton University Press, 1995), p. 225.

10 On general strategies for dealing with American preponderance, see United States Central Intelligence Agency, National Intelligence Council, G. John Ikenberry, *Strategic Reactions to American Preeminence: Great Power Politics in the Age of Unipolarity* (July 28, 2003). Available at: http://www.cia.gov/nic/confreports_stratreact.html. Accessed January 9, 2005.

11 For this characterization of German foreign policy, see Wolfram F. Hanrieder, *Germany, America, Europe: Forty Years of German Foreign Policy* (New Haven: Yale University Press, 1989).

12 Michael Brenner and Phil Williams, *Europa und die Vereinigten Staaten. Amerikanische Sicherheitspolitik in den neunziger Jahren* (Sankt Augustin: Forschungsinstitut der Konrad-Adenauer-Stiftung, 1992); quoted here p. 13.

13 Ernst-Otto Czempiel, "Nicht von gleich zu gleich? Die USA und die Europäische Union," in *Europa oder Amerika?* (Stuttgart: Klett-Cotta, 2000), pp. 901–15; quoted here p. 910.

14 See the foreign-policy guidelines passed by the CDU Vorstand on April 28, 2003, in *Frankfurter Allgemeine Zeitung*, May 6, 2003.

15 Gerhard Schröder, "Grundsätze und Instrumente deutscher Sicherheitspolitik," Speech, Berlin, March 19, 2004; in addition, see Joschka Fischer, "Europe and the Future of Transatlantic Relations," Speech, Princeton University, Princeton, NJ, November 19, 2003.

16 Bundesministerium der Verteidigung, *Verteidigungspolitische Richtlinien für den Geschäftbereich des Bundesministers der Verteidigung* (Berlin: May 2003), p. 22, Translation by the author.

17 Joschka Fischer before the German parliament during a debate on transatlantic relations, June 27, 2002. Available at: www.auswaertiges-amt.de. Accessed January 9, 2005. Translation by the author. See, for example, the speech by defense minister Peter Struck before the German parliament on December 20, 2002. Available at: http://www.bmvg.de/archiv/reden/minister/021220_isaf_mandat.php

18 According to a survey in late 1995 on the foreign-policy views of the German elite, only 29 percent held this view. See *Das Meinungsbild der Elite in Deutschland zur Außen- und Sicherheitspolitik. Eine Studie von Infratest Burke Berlin im Auftrag des Liberalen Institutes der Friedrich-Naumann-Stiftung in Kooperation mit der RAND Corporation* (Berlin: March 1996).

19 See, for example, the speech by defense minister Peter Struck before the German parliament on December 20, 2002, at: http://www.bmvg.de/archiv/reden/minister/021220_isaf_mandat.php

The Transatlantic Relationship: A View from Germany 149

20 Joschka Fischer, Speech on the fourtieth Munich Conference on Security Policy, Munich, February 7, 2004. While bandwagoning in general with the new American agenda, mainly supporting the goal of a long-term transformation of the Middle East, German foreign policy has tried to put a clear European stamp on the emerging transatlantic debate over the Greater Middle East, mainly by insisting that the Israeli–Palestinian conflict has to be addressed head on.

21 On the role of public opinion in liberal democracies and on the German case, see Thomas Risse-Kappen, "Public Opinion, Domestic Structure, and Foreign Policy in Liberal Democracies," *World Politics*, 43 (July 1991): 479–512; Frank Brettschneider, "Massenmedien, öffentliche Meinung und Außenpolitik," *Deutschlands neue Außenpolitik, Band 4: Institutionen und Ressourcen*, Wolf Dieter Eberwein and Karl Kaiser, eds (Munich: Oldenburg Verlag, 1998), pp. 215–26; Christian Holst, "Einstellungen der Bevölkerung und der Eliten: Vom alten zum neuen außenpolitischen Konsens?" *Deutschlands neue Außenpolitik*, Wolf-Dieter Eberwein and Karl Kaiser, eds (Munich: Oldenbourg Verlag, 1998), pp. 227–38.

22 In 2002, nearly two-thirds of Germans shared the opinion that the United States is pursuing only its own interests when it intervenes in the world's crisis regions. Less than ten years ago, in 1993, only 58 percent expressed this opinion. An even more significant indicator of changing attitudes toward the international role of the United States is the declining number of Germans who view the United States as the guarantor of peace and security throughout the world. In 2002, only 48 percent shared this view, compared to 62 percent in 1993. In 1993, when Germans were asked whether the United States played a dominating role in German-American relations or whether Germany had become an equal partner, opinions were still very mixed. Less than ten years later, the German public appears to have shed all illusions: Seventy-three percent ascribe a dominating role to the United States, while 26 percent still consider Germany an equal partner. Nevertheless, a more skeptical view of the United States should not be equated with increasing anti-Americanism. The number of persons holding self-declared anti-American attitudes remains relatively constant at one-fourth of the population. See the public opinion data in *Der Spiegel*, May 18, 2002, pp. 26–31.

23 *Transatlantic Trends 2003*, p. 8. Available at: http://www.transatlantictrends.org/Apps/GMF/TTweb.nsf?OpenDatabase. Accessed January 9, 2005.

24 *Transatlantic Trends 2003* (see note 23), figure on p. 9, quoted here p. 3.

25 In September 2003 49 percent of Germans considered France to be more important, 46 percent, the United States. The majority of the German public seems to have lost confidence in the United States as the most reliable partner (in comparison with France and Britain). Whereas in 1996 almost two-thirds of the German public considered the United States to be the most reliable partner in a crisis, it is France that has now almost reached the level of confidence (56 percent) the United States once enjoyed. *Transatlantische Beziehungen*, Ergebnisse einer repräsentativen Bevölkerungsumfrage im Auftrag des Bundesverbandes deutscher Banken (Mannheim: Institut für Praxisorientierte Sozialforschung, November 2003), p. 6. Available at: http://www.kas.de/upload/dokumente/trans_portal/Umfrage_Nov03.pdf. Accessed January 9, 2005.

26 Eighty-two percent believe that the United States only pursues its own interests without regard for the interests of European allies. See *Transatlantische Beziehungen* (see note 24), p. 9.

27 *Transatlantic Trends 2003* (see note 23), p. 10.

28   The Pew Research Center for the People and the Press, *Mistrust of America in Europe Ever Higher, Muslim Anger Persists* (Washington: March 2004), p. 28.
29   *Transatlantische Beziehungen* (see note 23), p. 5.
30   *Transatlantische Beziehungen* (see note 23), p. 12.
31   *Transatlantische Beziehungen* (see note 24), p. 13.
32   In general on this issue, see Mary N. Hampton, "NATO, Germany, and the United States: Creating Positive Identity in Trans-Atlantia," *Security Studies*, 8: 2/3 (winter 1998/99): 235–69.
33   See Renate Köcher, "Das Kosovo spaltet Deutschland in Ost und West," *Frankfurter Allgemeine Zeitung*, June 16, 1999.
34   See Jeffrey Record, *Bounding the Global War on Terrorism* (Carlisle: Strategic Studies Institute, US Army War College, December 2003), quoted here p. v.
35   For the view that the fault for the "breakdown" ("Zerrüttung") of German–American relations lies with the Red–Green coalition, see Nikolas Busse, "Die Entfremdung vom wichtigsten Verbündeten. Rot-Grün und Amerika," *Deutschland im Abseits? Rot-Grüne Außenpolitik 1998–2003*, Hanns W. Maull, Sebastian Harnisch, Constantin Grund, eds (Baden-Baden: Nomos, 2003), pp. 19–32.
36   For an elaborate explanation focusing on the "domestic political consideration of preserving the Red–Green government in the face of considerable opposition within the coalition government to foreign military interventions in general and early military action against Iraq in particular" see Sebastian Harnisch, "Bound to Fail?—Germany's Policy in the Iraq Crisis 2001–2003," paper presented at the Twenty-seventh Annual conference of the German Studies Association, New Orleans, LA, September 2003, pp. 18–21, quoted here p. 4.
37   See, for example, the interview with Foreign Minister Joschka Fischer in *Frankfurter Rundschau*, August 7, 2002.
38   *The New York Times*, September 5, 2002.
39   This is obviously the yardstick of Christian Hacke, "Deutschland, Europa und der Irakkonflikt," *Aus Politik und Zeitgeschichte*, B24-25/2003 (June 10, 2003): 8–16.
40   The fact that such a tested, proven relationship as the German–American one could be thrown into crisis shows how troublesome and divisive conflicting strategic and normative perspectives can become if heated by mutual frustrations and animosities at the highest level (see Stephen F. Szabo, "Germany and the United States after Iraq: From Alliance to Alignment," *Internationale Politik und Gesellschaft*, 1/2004: 41–52). The political leaders on both sides believed the other had broken promises. According to senior US administration officials, Schröder had allegedly indicated at a meeting with President George W. Bush in January 2002 "that he 'understood' that Bush might have to go to war in Iraq, and he advised Bush only to do so quickly and decisively." Again in Berlin in May 2002, US officials say, Schröder pledged not to run his election campaign against a possible US war in Iraq. When Schröder ended up doing so, Bush—who aides say "believes the character of a person is known by whether he keeps his word"—felt betrayed and did not hesitate in private conversations to call Schröder a "liar" (Gordon and Shapiro, *Allies at War* (see note 7), pp. 102–03, based upon interviews with "senior administration officials" conducted in October 2003). According to a "senior German official" interviewed by Philip Gordon and Jeremy Shapiro, Schröder denied misleading Bush. Schröder himself could claim to have been misled by Bush, who, in May 2002 in Berlin, had promised consultation on the issue of going to war against Iraq (Gordon and Shapiro, *Allies at War* (see note 7), p. 103). Bush's assurance during this trip to Europe in May 2002, when he

met Schröder and then Chirac ("I have no war plans on my desk"), was at best misleading, given the fact that war planning was well underway, according to Bob Woodward, *Plan of Attack* (New York: Simon & Schuster 2004), p. 129.

41 For example, Johannes Varvick, "Die NATO-Politik der rot-grünen Bundesregierung 1998–2003," *Zeitschrift für Politikwissenschaft*, 14: 1 (2004): 1, 93–121.

42 Gordon and Shapiro, *Allies at War* (see note 7), pp. 175–76.

43 Stefan Kornelius, "Der Rosenkrieg," *Süddeutsche Zeitung*, November 2, 2002.

44 Gunther Hellmann, "Von Gipfelstürmern and Gratwanderern: 'Deutsche Wege' in der Außenpolitik," *Aus Politik und Zeitgeschichte*, B 11/2002 (March 8, 2004): 32–9, quoted here p. 37.

45 For an account, see Gordon and Shapiro, *Allies at War* (see note 7), pp. 136–41, who ignore the domestic problems for the German government related to the decision.

46 Gordon and Shapiro, *Allies at War* (see note 7), p. 141.

47 James Kitfield, "Damage Control," *National Journal*, July 19, 2003.

48 Steven Erlanger, "German Leader's Warning: War Plan Is a Huge Mistake", The New York Times, September 5, 2002. Harnisch, "Bound to Fail?—Germany's Policy in the Iraq Crisis 2001–2003" (see note 36), pp. 20–1, emphasizes this domestic factor.

49 Hanns W. Maull, "Editorial: Deutschland auf Abwegen?" *Deutschland im Abseits? Rot-grüne Außenpolitik 1998–2003*, Hanns W. Maull, Sebastian Harnisch, and Constantin Grund, eds (Baden Baden: Nomos-Verlag, 2003), pp. 7–17; quoted here p. 16.

50 On these "core components," see Ulrich Klotz, *National Role Conceptions and Foreign Policies: France and Germany Compared* (Cambridge: Minda de Gunzburg Center for European Studies, Working Paper, 2002).

51 For a similar view, see Thomas Risse, "Kontinuität durch Wandel: Eine 'neue' deutsche Außenpolitik?," *Aus Politik und Zeitgeschichte*, B11/2004 (March 8, 2004): 24–31.

10
Pan-European Stability: Still a Key Task?

Günter Joetze

Europe in transition: stability and change, illusions and problems, deficits and strategies

In the Cold War era of unstable equilibrium, maintained by a balance of nuclear deterrence, all conflicts risked to escalate into armed superpower conflicts. In this situation stability was the key consideration; all governments had to act extremely carefully. After the end of the east-west conflict, the new mood of political leaders from Vancouver to Vladivostok was best expressed in a phrase in the Charter of Paris: "The strength of the will of the peoples and the power of the ideas of the Helsinki Final Act have opened a new era of democracy, peace and unity in Europe." In the mood of the day, all problems seemed surmountable. German diplomacy had been both an important catalyst in bringing about change of historic proportions, and its principal beneficiary.

This new mood of a pan-European departure lasted until the 1992 meeting of the Helsinki Conference on Security and Cooperation in Europe (CSCE). Tellingly, the subtitle of its final document reads "The Challenges of Change." Change had begun to produce new problems—but the sense of promise in this new era still prevailed. The first decisions of the newly established CSCE Council of Ministers (on Yugoslavia in June 1991 in Berlin and on Nagorno Karabakh in March 1992 in Helsinki) documented a belief in peaceful conflict resolution by advice and mediation. This belief was not so naive as it may appear today, since diplomatic means did indeed diffuse some of the security risks that began to (re-)appear. In this category belong Russian revisionist tendencies relating to the Crimea and Eastern Ukraine and Hungarian irredentism in Slovakia, Transsylvania, and Wojvodina. For the problems in Yugoslavia and in the Caucasus, however, the CSCE instruments of the time proved insufficient.

Internal stability was lacking throughout Central and Eastern Europe and the former Soviet Union. Administrative, financial, and legal structures were totally inadequate after the collapse of the Communist party systems. Mass unemployment and, worse, a lost sense of identity gave rise to demagoguery. Irresponsible nationalists in Russia and elsewhere advocated solving ethnic conflicts by force. In hindsight, it is surprising how few violent conflicts resulted from this volatile atmosphere.

The challenges of change

Some say the main merit of the 1975 Helsinki Final Act was a solemn confirmation of the political status quo in Europe. This implied the partition of Germany, which the Germans had to accept in the name of stability. The official German policy responded with various methods of peaceful change, Egon Bahr's "change through rapprochement" being the most prominent. German diplomacy distinguished between "stable" and "dynamic" principles of the Helsinki Final Act; human rights, peaceful change of borders, and the right to self-determination were included among the dynamic principles, while the inviolability of borders formed the cornerstone of stability. Foreign Minister Hans-Dietrich Genscher's rush to recognize the independence of Slovenia and Croatia, resented by many, was justified by him in terms of self-determination: how could Germany deny other people what it had claimed for itself? Yet this created a dilemma: how could this right be reconciled with the existing territorial status quo, whose maintenance was generally considered important by governments for very practical reasons? Thus, the Balladur Commission, instituted by the European Union to adjudicate on the conflicts of dissolution in Yugoslavia, found in 1991 that the central government of Yugoslavia had ceased to function, but it restricted the right of secession to the federal republics (i.e., it denied this right to Serbia's autonomous provinces, such as Kosovo).

There were extremely good reasons for refraining from a change of borders, which are summarized by the cliché of the "Pandora's box." From a postnationalist viewpoint, which prevails in Germany, nationalist aspirations find little understanding. Yet there are numerous cases in which a peaceful separation has enhanced stability: the Czech and Slovak republics, the beginning of normalization between Croatia, Serbia, and Slovenia, and between the two big Slavic states, Russia and Ukraine, in a slow consolidation of relations. On the other hand, the breaking up of Iraq would present immeasurable risks.

Next is the problem of standards, for both interstate relations and intrastate governance. The UN Charter and the CSCE Charter of Paris provide them in abundance. The European Union is a peace-creating construction based on standards. But it is unique in that it has been able, so far, to enforce its standards on member states. The only convincing reason for humanitarian intervention against Serbia because of Kosovo was that these were integral parts of Europe where particular standards of political civilization had to prevail. This avoids a criticism of double standards. The events in Beslan (a town in Europe) put this question on the pan-European agenda. Is the reconstruction of a strong Russian state a central prerequisite of stability in Eurasia (as the Russian elite claims)? Does it therefore take precedence over the enforcement of democratic standards? Or is democratic modernity needed to give the new Russian edifice the necessary flexibility, in the name of stability?

Strategy and instruments

Western and German strategic thought has evolved dramatically since 1990. In a first, optimistic phase, the approach was based on the logic of collective security via the CSCE by standard-setting and mutual conviction. This was successful as long as the leaders concerned were eager to belong to a Western-oriented community of states. This was the case early in the presidency of Boris Yeltsin, roughly until 1994. The lasting result of this strategy has been to defuse Russia's conflicts with the Baltic states and the Ukraine, and secure a Russian troop withdrawal from the Baltic states as a result of moral pressure by the West.

In 1994, after President Bill Clinton's decision to favor Poland's admission to NATO (North Atlantic Treaty Organization), the West shifted to a strategy of power projection by its own institutions, NATO first and later the European Union. Admission to NATO was seen by virtually all post-Soviet, post-Warsaw Pact, and post-Yugoslav states as a remedy for all their security fears and as a status symbol. Therefore, the hope for admission was and remains a powerful means of influencing behavior. The biggest country in Europe, Russia, has no prospect for NATO or EU membership. Its hope for inclusion in a strategic framework were disappointed with the beginning of CSCE and the emasculation of the NATO–Russia Council.[1]

Stability projection into Central and Eastern Europe

All post-Warsaw Pact states had weak administrative, fiscal, and juridical structures. They had no democratic systems. The Baltic states, in particular, had been completely Sovietized. In some cases, prewar antagonisms reappeared. All new governments deeply distrusted regional cooperation since it had been imposed on them by their Soviet overlords as a tool of domination and exploitation. The Vishegrad group formed by the Central European republics represents an exception, but it was never more than a loose political consultation grouping. Yet all these governments were unanimous in aspiring to membership in the key Western organizations, NATO and the European Union. Volker Rühe, then German defense minister, was a strong proponent of NATO enlargement. His main argument was defensive: Germany should change from a position in the front line of confrontation into one in the alliance's center, "surrounded by friends." He launched the political debate within NATO, but President Clinton set the train in motion when, mainly for domestic reasons, he declared in Warsaw in June 1994 that Poland's accession to NATO was not a question of "if" but of "when."

NATO enlargement began a gradual shift in Western strategy from the promotion of pan-European stability by "soft" means (collective security) to stability projection by the two powerful Western institutions, NATO and European Union, by accepting new members, or by sponsoring regional cooperation (Partnership for Peace for NATO, TACIS [Technical Assistance to the Commonwealth of Independent States] or the first Stability Pact, proposed by then French Prime Minister George Balladur and concluded in 1995).

NATO membership obliged new member countries to participate in various NATO modernization programs, to make military reform and NATO "interoperability" a priority. The core ratio of European integration was regional stability from the outset. While it was fundamentally security-oriented, the way to achieve stability was through a gradual process of integration, starting with economics. The European Communities represented a political framework in which unequal power potentials were controlled and diffused.[2] All German chancellors were unanimous in advocating the extension of these stabilizing functions to Central and Eastern Europe. The *acquis communautaire* demands economic and social reforms that hurt large segments of the population in the new member states, in particular Polish farmers. This may appear to them as an *octroi* by an anonymous foreign power and a limit to the newly recovered freedom of the nation-state. Responsible politicians in the new member countries realize that EU negotiators demanded well-considered concessions, but irresponsible demagogues or ideologues may use them for their own aims. Yet in reality, the expectation of access had a positive effect on the transformation in countries belonging to the first wave of new EU members.[3] After entry, they will compete with old members for financial resources from the European common agricultural policy, as well as from the European Union's regional and structural funds, although these funds will certainly not be increased in proportion to the needs of new members.

Problems in postwar Yugoslavia and the effects on Southeastern Europe

In August 1992 the European Union initiated its conference on Yugoslavia in cooperation with the United Nations. It was to be "the hour of Europe." In its first venture into security policy, the European Union sent an unarmed observer force to the front line in Croatia. European politicians were confident of settling the conflict without the United States, which meant without military force. They believed in the instruments of crisis settlement of the day: mediation, armistices, observers, and lightly armed, neutral peacekeeping forces to watch borderlines. At that time, a few fighter aircraft could have silenced the Serbian artillery positions on the hills above Dubrovnik and Sarajevo, as they were dislocated openly with no surface-to-air capabilities. But the time was not ripe. If today there is too much eagerness to use force to settle political problems, at that time there was too little.

During 1994, when the mood turned to military action, NATO air forces, mostly American and British airplanes, attacked Serbian positions to enforce constraint. In April 1994 a contact group was established between France, Germany, the United Kingdom, the United States, and Russia. Russia was needed because of its influence on the Serbian leadership and military. This group advised on pending decisions of the UN Security Council or the NATO Council. The Contact Group served Germany as a platform to regain influence on the settlement of the Bosnian, and later Kosovar, crisis. In 1995 at the Dayton Conference, which nominally worked under the auspices of the Contact Group, the German delegation was the only non-US participant to make a substantive contribution by mediating an agreement between Bosnians and Croats on the reinforcement of their federation.

The beginnings of the Kosovo crisis

After Serbian special police launched their first major suppressive operations in February and March of 1998, the Kosovo problem quickly became an international problem. A first Security Council Resolution (No. 1160) imposed an arms embargo on Serbia, with little effect. Thus, the use of force soon became the central issue. Russia was opposed to it from the beginning. In Washington, the Pentagon saw no strategic interest in Balkan stability and was entangled in public and congressional outcries over two less than brilliant military air interventions (Infinite Reach in August and Desert Fox in December 1998).

At their NATO meeting in June 1998, European defense ministers extracted from their US colleague the grudging concession of contingency planning for a military intervention. Surprisingly, German Foreign Minister Klaus Kinkel was among the earliest advocates of military force (23 July), of course arguing for it under a UN Security Council mandate and NATO command. In September when the number of Albanian refugees rose to 265,000 because of renewed Serbian repression, the Security Council issued Resolution 1199, which had exceptionally strong wording but no mandate for military intervention. US Special Envoy Richard Holbrooke was sent to Belgrade in October to seek a settlement with the blessing of the Contact Group. As a means of pressure he procured the famous "activation warning" (ACTORD—Activation Orders) of NATO, an authorization of military action under certain conditions. Now that Kinkel's own wishes were to be realized, he hesitated and had to be pushed from many sides.

In order to approve ACTORD, the old Bundestag, already in summer recess, had to be recalled on October 16. The Red–Green coalition agreement had envisaged military enforcement action only under a UN mandate. But Gerhard Schröder told Joschka Fischer that there could be no coalition without agreeing to ACTORD. He did not want to enter the international scene by confirming the reservations that most allied governments had about his coalition. In his first visit to Washington on October 9, he first communicated to Clinton the old German stance that he would not block NATO's decision on ACTORD but would also not commit Germany's troops. But when Washington insisted on full German participation he quickly gave in.[4] Thus, the first foreign policy act of the new coalition was to prepare for Germany's first military action after 1945 without clear legal basis. That decision was of course made easier by the hope that Slobodan Milosevic would give in to the threat (as he had done before) or that at least the Serbian resistance would not last long (it never had before). The motives of the new team were best expressed by future Defense Minister Rudolf Scharping: "We want to give a signal to our friends abroad; we will continue to be a reliable and steadfast partner."

Last chance for the Organization for Security and Cooperation in Europe

In US planning, Holbrooke's agreement, expected to last only over the winter, was intended to avoid a humanitarian catastrophe. Holbrooke negotiated what he could obtain: a hybrid solution that did not oblige the Albanian side and did not provide for a "robust" (i.e. NATO) peace force. Instead, a Kosovo "verification mission" (KVM) of about 2000 unarmed persons was to be organized by the Organization for Security and Cooperation in Europe (OSCE). Bonn did little to gain influence in KVM, partly out of skepticism and partly for lack of staff. It let the United States and Britain run the show. Its director, William Walker, a former US ambassador to Central America, used it openly as a tool of the State Department's policy. Later, German critics would maintain that the United States and Britain did not even want KVM to work in order to prove that military force had been inevitable all along. Washington's "principals" were divided over the issue of military force, with only Secretary of State Madeleine Albright advocating it. She tried to build public pressure by increasing awareness of Serbian atrocities, which Walker's KVM helped to amplify.

The attempt to avoid military action

The term "NATO action" is ambivalent. What Madeleine Albright had in mind was a short bombing campaign by NATO under US leadership with a Serbian surrender and an international administration of Kosovo as its result. What the European allies, and certainly Germany, wanted was a "robust" NATO-controlled peacekeeping force for the province, preferably as a result of an agreement with Belgrade and peacefully achieved under the threat of ACTORD. After the public outcry over the mass killings at Racak (January 15–16, 1999), the Contact Group settled on a conference where Serbs and Albanians would agree on an international status of the province including an "international military presence." The latter element was essential in the eyes of all German diplomats with experience dealing with Yugoslavia.

The Western members of the Contact Group (with Russian toleration) imposed conditions on Serbia that were later characterized as a "Diktat." Its harshest parts, those on the civilian and military international "presences" in Kosovo, were revealed to them only in the last moment—after Washington was ready to agree to a NATO-led military presence, following the acquittal of President Clinton in his impeachment proceedings.

Was there ever a chance of success for such a "take it or leave it" approach? A high-ranking Serbian officer said at the time that the country had to be defeated in war to accept the imposed terms. The head of the German delegation expressed his doubts from the outset. Foreign Minister Fischer spoke of a "small window of success," but for him as for other political leaders in Western Europe, even the remotest chance of success had to be explored before agreeing to military action. By refusing to negotiate, Belgrade saved Western unity. Whereas at Dayton the US delegation had spared no effort to steer the conference to an agreement, at Rambouillet the United States was seen by many as working toward a collapse of the negotiations, which would be followed by military enforcement in Serbia.

Russia and the Kosovo conflict

Throughout the Kosovo crisis, Russia was guided by two conflicting aims: to play a role in the unfolding conflict and to support Serbia. Until very late in the game, Russian leaders sincerely believed that NATO was only bluffing. Thus, when NATO took action, official disappointment and public fury were intense. Demonstrative countermeasures were taken, such as the dispatch of an electronic intelligence vessel to the Montenegrin coast to monitor NATO naval movements. But when nationalists drafted volunteers to help their Slavic brothers, parallel initiatives mushroomed in Muslim republics. From then on, Yeltsin had only one objective: to put a speedy end to the conflict, which would allow him to leave office with peace reigning inside and around the country. He appointed Viktor Chernomyrdin, his former prime minister and still a confidant, as chief negotiator to Milosevic—no doubt with the appropriate instructions to help Yeltsin achieve his primary objective. Nationalistic elements in the Russian General Staff and Foreign Ministry actively supported Serbia and openly sabotaged Chernomyrdin's negotiations.

The Kosovo affair mirrored Russia's international situation at the time: its intentions disregarded, its advice neglected, it solemnly declared positions turned around. As for the new German chancellor, his initial efforts to avoid military involvement enjoyed broad public support. Schröder made it his first priority to show solidarity with Germany's allies. When the Russian prime minister at the time, Jewgeni Primakov, visited Bonn in late March to report on his meeting with Milosevic, Schröder almost brusquely told him that the offer he brought did not meet NATO's minimum demands.

Fischer and his team spared no effort to "get Russia on board", as he put it, Wolfgang Ischinger traveled three times to Moscow in March and April for conversations with Russian Foreign Minister Igor Ivanov. At the same time, political director Günther Pleuger cleverly exploited the preparations of the Cologne G-8 summit meeting in June in order to obtain Russian support for the West's minimum demands on Serbia in the summit declaration. German diplomats performed brilliantly as soon as ending the war had become the objective. But they were careful to work along western guidelines, which they helped to define. The environment was one of cooperative self-assertion in a functioning multilateral framework, Germany's preferred working condition for decades. When contingency plans for the use of ground troops began to be discussed in the sixth week of the bombing campaign, Schröder clearly objected. Whether this related to German military participation or German authorization of a NATO decision (the latter was demanded by the Greens at their party congress) remained mercifully unclear. Through his sudden surrender at the beginning of June, Milosevic prevented a split between Germany and its Anglo-Saxon allies. Yet, deeply rooted differences over the use of force had become visible; later, these same differences, this time over Iraq, would cause much bitterness.

Post-Kosovo events in the Balkan area

The end of the Kosovo crisis saw Fischer at the zenith of his reputation and influence, both of which he used to devise and implement a scheme of cooperative reconstruction for the Balkans. Launching the Stability Pact for South Eastern Europe was no easy task, however; some successor republics of the former Yugoslavia suspected attempts to reintroduce neo-Yugoslav structures, the European Union claimed sole responsibility for the economic aspects of reconstruction, and the United States and Russia had a final round of symbolic wrestling over the way of referring to NATO.[5] The central element in cooperating was the prospect of EU membership.

In October 2000 when Serbians elected a new president, Vojislav Kostunica, German diplomats were eager to have the country readmitted to the United Nations and the OSCE. The wave of benevolence for Serbia after Milosevic's downfall may be one of the reasons for the uprising of the Kosovars and the Ushtria Çlirimtare e Kosovës (UCK) leadership in southern Serbia and western Macedonia. Under American influence, the search for weapons by the NATO-led security force, KFOR (Kosovo Force), had been half-hearted. Nor were there border controls between Kosovo and western Macedonia. After the crisis broke out, a series of Western interventions from all sides, but mainly from NATO Secretary General George Robertson and EU Representative Javier Solana, helped to convince the Slavo-Macedonian majority to form a government inclined to compromise, then forced the two parties together in August 2001 at Lake Ohrid to conclude an armistice and a political settlement. Both sides wanted a modestly sized NATO contingent as a stabilizing force because of their mutual distrust. The NATO soldiers had partially disarmed Albanian insurgents (largely as a symbolic act) and later protected the unarmed OSCE observers who oversaw the agreement's implementation. Today the European Union has assumed control of the force, and to the surprise of all those involved, the agreement has lasted for three years. The most likely reasons for this surprising success are the great subtlety of the Slavo-Macedonian politicians in dealing with their Albanian minority, which was never suppressed in the way Milosevic treated the Kosovars, and the West's financial assistance, including the first stability and association agreement with one of the Balkan countries.

The European Union is well suited for tasks of this kind, and Germany has a key interest in solidifying its international position by scoring successes in this field. But central to Balkan stability is a complex issue (on which EU members will never agree) that entails great risks, including that of international terrorism: the future status of Kosovo. The uprising of March 2004, with KFOR unprepared once again, shed a cruel light on this festering problem. It looks as if the Kosovars cannot much longer be restrained by the mantra "standards before status." On the contrary, if the status issue is not resolved soon, a danger exists of large-scale underground partisan guerilla resistance by the clandestine successor organizations of the UCK (which are intact, dispose of weapons in abundance, and have combat experience from their war against Serbian forces). Since the Kosovars are Muslims, they may, with or against their will, be supported by branches of the international Jihad terrorist movement. The "war against terrorism" will then have a new front; it would be extremely difficult for Western governments to retreat, but it would be equally difficult for a German government and parliament to have German regular troops engaged in active counterinsurgency.

Stability in and from Russia

In the later years of the Yeltsin presidency, Russia did not matter much in the Western strategic calculus. The country still had its nuclear arsenal, but analysts were confident that deterrence would continue to work. More importantly, there was a risk of proliferation from poorly controlled Russian nuclear storage sites, which was indicative of a much greater problem: the decay of Moscow's central authority. Yet both Washington and Bonn found it politic to compensate for the *de facto* neglect of Russia's concerns by expressions and symbolic acts of high regard for Yeltsin in person.

The Kosovo affair mirrored this facade: whereas Russia's positions had been coolly disregarded, the G-7 at their Cologne summit accepted Yeltsin as a peer to form the "G-8" session, but of course without a real say in its decisions on economic matters. Today Russia is a promoter of external stability, but it also poses a risk because of its own internal problems.

Germany and Vladimir Putin's Russia

Missile defense was one of the first areas of interest of the incoming Bush administration. In early 2001, Washington was preparing to renounce the Anti-Ballistic Missile (ABM) Treaty with the former Soviet Union, as well as the multilateral Nuclear Test Ban Treaty (NTBT). Throughout much of 2001, Germany criticized these intentions, defending the ABM Treaty as a "cornerstone of the international architecture of arms control" (Scharping) and citing the need to maintain NATO cohesion by avoiding "zones of different security" (with European allies not protected by a new system). In February 2001, however, Chancellor Schröder decided that the issue did not warrant a confrontation with the United States.[6] Germany was equally cautious in other arms-control issues that the new US administration blocked or watered down, notably the reformed Treaty on Conventional Forces in Europe (CFE).[7] Today, the strategic equation for Russia has profoundly changed: the country has lost most of its interest in the former multilateral security framework, and the technical preparations for a strategic missile shield for North America have met with tremendous difficulties. Thus, the issues themselves may be obsolete. But the lack of European, in particular German, support is still remembered in Moscow strategic circles.

Putin placed the second NATO enlargement in a wider perspective. "If we improve the quality of Russia's relations with NATO the question of NATO enlargement loses its importance," he declared in November 2001. In a wave of recognition for Russia's support in the Afghan war, Prime Minister Tony Blair proposed "a new and broader base" for NATO–Russian relations. But experts in Brussels and in allied capitals soon took control of his initiative and, with active participation from Berlin, cut it down to size. At their December 2001 meeting, NATO foreign ministers stressed the organization's "right to autonomous decisions and actions at 19 [member countries, i.e., without Russia's consent]". In the NATO jargon of the day, a "firewall" between the organization and the NATO–Russian Council was established. In Russia's perception, the country was denied equal rights in the European security system. Putin resents this to this day.[8]

From September 2002 to January 2003 German experts predicted that Russia would acquiesce in an American war against Iraq. Putin surprised many when he joined Schröder in an improvised visit to see Jacques Chirac in Paris, where the three publicly opposed the US intentions. But he had observed how the United States rapidly lost influence in the Arab and Islamic worlds; he wanted to avoid similar developments among Russia's Muslim population. In a decisive phone call in the first week of February 2003, George W. Bush hinted that the strategic relationship between the two countries would be in peril if Putin refused to support him. The latter replied dryly that avoiding war in Iraq was also of strategic importance. It would be a wild exaggeration to characterize as permanent this cooperation between the three major continental European countries in the UN Security Council;

in actuality, it is far from an "axis." It is customary in conference diplomacy to consult for a common purpose on an ad hoc basis. What was new for Germany was to do so against the intentions of the United States and, to make things worse in the eyes of some, to do so together with the successor state of the Soviet Union. Schröder's good personal relations with the Russian president facilitated the chancellor's efforts to end the isolation of Germany. But the more power Russia accumulates—as it presently does—the more its leaders will resent being called for cooperation in times of need but will be treated with disrespect and criticized unjustly (in their perspective) in the meantime.

Russia: a cold place again?

The list of criticisms of Putin's Russia is long: state intervention in the economy in a quest for power and wealth by its representatives, rather than the rule of law, characterize the relationship between politics and the economy, as the Yukos case and the treatment of the company's founder, Fjodor Khodorkovsky, has shown. Thus, Russia no longer can be considered a real market economy, and this has begun to show in the decline of inward investment and a renewed capital flight out of Russia. Nor is the country on the way toward becoming a democracy. At best, it is a democracy with defects, such as a dearth of independent media and an abundance of security risks facing independent journalists, the serious institutional weaknesses of its parliamentary system, and major human rights deficits, in particular in the context of the war in Chechnya and the brutal suppression of terrorist activities.

Seen from the perspective of the Berlin Foreign Office, quotidian diplomatic activities have been largely communalized; they are handled by the European Union. The major issues in relations between Russia and EU authorities are the extension of the existing EU-Russian Partnership and Association Agreement (PAA) to the new EU members (almost all former Soviet satellites), the mention of Russian minorities in Estonia and Latvia in these proceedings, the status of Kaliningrad, and Russia's accession to the Kyoto Protocol (completed in late 2004). A new contested issue could arise from the European neighborhood policy. According to a European strategy paper presently under discussion, this policy would apply to Eastern Europe, Southern Mediterranean countries, and the Southern Caucasus republics (at the particular request of Germany). From a European viewpoint, there is an obvious interest in extending stability throughout an enlarged European Union, to mitigate poverty and prevent new ideological borders from arising. Yet Russia considers the countries to the west and south of its borders as its own "near abroad."

In contrast to his foreign minister, Chancellor Schröder is extraordinarily visible in German–Russian relations. He surprised many by declaring that the problems arising from the Yukos case and the war in Chechnya were purely domestic matters involving Russia about which Germany had to refrain from giving advice.[9] In a common declaration issued on September 10, 2004, both leaders agreed on intensified cooperation in security matters, including the establishment of a "senior working group for security policy." During the first Chechen war in 1993, Russia requested and received international help from the CSCE institutions in Vienna. A face-saving method must be found to repeat this experience in whatever institutional framework is available. The CSCE would still have the advantage of Russian participation on an equal basis.

Germany and the European Union cannot remain indifferent to the civilizational climate of its biggest neighbor. Assuming that Russia's economic growth continues, there are two scenarios for its future: first, an autocratic Russia that invests its new riches in military capacities through arms programs and power projection; or, second, a democratic Russia that invests in living standards and social justice for its huge population. The real development will, of course, lie somewhere in between these two models. It is an overriding German (and a common European) interest to help it more closely approximate to the second model. But an indirect approach to the strategic aim of avoiding a cultural barrier is necessary. Most Russians resent foreign advice as arrogant and inapplicable to their country's situation. Democratic progress in Russia will not be promoted by critical rhetoric alone. It needs continuous and comprehensive cooperation. The European Union has defined a valid concept for this in its "four spaces" of European–Russian relations. It must not single out the most sensitive one ("freedom, security and law") but press for constant and patient engagement in all four fields.[10]

Conclusion

The changes of 1989 to 1991 did not signal the "end of history" but certainly the end of the "primacy of foreign policy." In parliaments, for instance, the ranks of heavyweight foreign policy specialists grew thinner. For Germany, as for many other Western countries, domestic reform became the priority of the day. In what remains of its foreign policy, acting in concert continues to be the supreme maxim of German diplomacy. Yet there is less unity in world affairs than during the era of the previous government. Chancellor Kohl could draw on a tight network of personal relations with the American, Russian, and French presidents. In the European Union, Germany was influential as France's preferred partner, and at the same time as the patron saint of the smaller member states. Kohl could rely on solid transatlantic relations, managed by a benign hegemon. A network of informal and restricted circles—the Balkan Contact Group, the Quad (the four larger NATO states), or Quint (with Italy added), or the G-7—provided a system of continuous consultation on all affairs of German interest. These were mainly situated in the CSCE area, in which Europe was a pacified world province with minor disturbances at its fringes; entanglement in extra-European conflicts was avoided to the extent it was possible. The Bundeswehr was rarely used for peacekeeping; peace enforcement was taboo.

Schröder and Fischer tried their best to remain in this comfortable environment, but one element after another eroded it: the security presence in Serbia, the military presence in Kosovo, Macedonia, and Afghanistan, North America's change of orientation, Germany's confrontation with it, the fact that NATO is no longer the only organization capable of action (as it was five years ago), and the distrust, and constitutional and distribution struggles facing the European Union. Although in the first year of the new US administration, Schröder and Fischer spared few efforts to placate the hegemon to keep him benign, important changes nevertheless soon became manifest. First, the Balkan problems lost their prominence after 9/11 in Western policy. By virtue of its "defining power," one of the main attributes of a superpower, the United States has given absolute priority to the greater Middle East and its problems. All European governments, but primarily Germany as the central country, must be blamed for neglecting the Balkan security problem, which became evident during the Kosovo riots in March 2004. Yet preventive diplomacy, the German government's preferred alternative to preventive intervention, would require a serious discussion of Kosovo's future status.

Second, Russia has "a strategic partnership" with the European Union, and the EU strategy papers are full of declarations that Russia is part of Europe. Nevertheless, there is a clear tendency to keep Russia at a distance, and the country's political class, including its liberal elements, consider this unfair. The events at Beslan have highlighted this: when Putin, in order to show strength, announced preemptive strikes against terrorist camps abroad, Foreign Minister Fischer and his political associate Norbert Nachtwei admonished Putin to act according to the rules of international law. No such declaration was ever made by any German politician concerning the US war against Iraq. There are excellent reasons for such restraint. But why not observe restraint vis-à-vis Russia? The European Union has developed good methods for dealing with Russia with its "four spaces" approach. But a decisive German impetus to give life to this policy would be needed. Here, German diplomacy uses one of its standard excuses: that the matter is communalized and thus lies in the hands of the EU authorities.

Third, like the majority of the German public, the generation to which the present foreign minister belongs has reservations about the nation-state. This may be natural for Germans, but it presents a serious impediment to effective foreign policy. The majority of the country's partners in NATO and the European Union, and certainly all nations of the Balkans, accept the nation-state as the basic entity of international life, and in most cases citizens cherish the ideals of their own nation-state. Of course, the nation-state has lost its position as the focal point of power in the international system, but German public opinion and political theory tend to exaggerate the importance of non-state actors. In practical politics, the state—meaning the nation-state—is still the decisive player. It is of little use for policy planners, in particular in the Balkans, to lose sight of this.

Chancellor Schröder has continually set the foreign policy signposts: the participation in the action against Serbia from the beginning, the nomination of President Martti Ahtisaari as the European Union's envoy, the decision to commit German troops to the NATO action Essential Harvest in Macedonia, the cooperation with the presidents of France and Russia during the Iraq crisis. With regard to Russia, he quickly and decisively declared that its problems were domestic problems and that Germany should not interfere or even offer advice. In other foreign policy areas, too, it was the chancellor who determined the course of German foreign policy. Thus, he and his administration handled much of the micromanagement of the Iraq crisis from January to March 2003 and negotiated the attempts to establish a common European military command (after the Tervuren summit in April 2003). By contrast, Foreign Minister Fischer is at his best when it comes to ambitious schemes of international cooperation. When the time is right for it, as it was after the Kosovo crisis for the Balkans, German diplomacy can perform brilliantly in such fields.

Notes

1 Günter Joetze, Auf der Suche nach einem strategischen Rahmen, in Olga Alexandrova *et al.*, eds, *Russland und der post-sowjetische Raum* (Baden-Baden: Nomos 2003), pp. 479–497.

2 Johannes Varwick, "EU-Erweiterung: Stabilitätsexport oder Instabilitätsimport," *Aus Politik und Zeitgeschichte*, B1–2 (2002): 23–31, quoted here p. 25.

3 Jan Delhey, "Die Entwicklung der Lebensqualität nach dem EU-Beitritt," *Aus Politik und Zeitgeschichte*, B1 bis 2 (2002): 31–38, quoted here p. 38.

4 Günther Joetze, *Der letzte Krieg in Europa? Das Kosovo und die deutsche Politik* (Stuttgart und München: DVA 2001), p. 37.

5 For details, see ibid., p. 173ff.

6 Hannes Adomeit, "Putin und die Raketenabwehr" (Berlin: SWP 2001) p. 33. Available at: http://www.swp-berlin.org/produkte/swp_studie.php?id=1766& PHPSESSID=7833fa9d970a29e8f0809a803cebc8ce. Accessed January 17, 2005.

7 A detailed and eloquent account of the damage done is given by Harald Müller, "Antwort auf Colin Powell", *Internationale Politik*, 59:3 (March 2004): 77–84.

8 He said so to a group of 40 German opinion leaders who participated in a discussion in Moscow in early September 2004, as reported by the FAZ on September 9, 2004.

9 In the Yukos affair, the United States do have concrete interests at stake because Khodorkovsky tried to open the Russian energy market to American companies, to the displeasure of the Kremlin. When Russia's authorities prepared the dismemberment of Yukos, there were serious warnings from Washington about the consequences for the price of oil.

10 The other three "spaces" are: a common European economic space, a space of research and education including cultural aspects, and a space of international security. In this field cooperation is generally considered excellent.

Part IV
Foreign Economic Policies

11

German Energy and Security Policy: Technical versus Political Modes of Intervention

Friedemann Müller

Energy policy is relevant to our security. The health of national economies as well as the world economy is closely correlated with a stable flow of energy, mainly in the form of oil. Substitutes to energy imports or short-term saving potentials are essentially unavailable. The industrialized countries of the West depend heavily on energy imports. However, in comparison to other functional areas of foreign policy such as trade, development, or classical security policy, energy security has rarely received the political attention it deserves.

Besides the multilateral Organization for Economic Cooperation and Development (OECD)-based oil stocks and joint crisis-response mechanism of the International Energy Agency (IEA), energy security policy is highly dependent on local contexts. In the United States, where the secretary of energy has traditionally held significant powers, this context generally has helped foster a coherent energy security policy. In August 2003 after the Iraq war but well ahead of the dramatic oil price increases of 2004, the Department of Energy released a "Strategic Plan."[1] This plan is based on the understanding that "the Department of Energy is principally a national security agency and all of its missions flow from this core mission to support national security."[2] The "Energy Strategic Goal" is defined as "[protecting] our national and economic security by promoting a diverse supply of reliable, affordable, and environmentally sound energy."[3]

In Europe, such a tradition is missing. The European Union (EU) Commission has a commissioner for energy who is also responsible for trans-portation—an area that is not normally thought of in security terms. In Germany, questions of energy security are dealt with at the deputy level in the Federal Ministry of Economics and Labour (BMWA). A reason for this low profile of energy security in German politics might lie in massive economic, partially monopolistic, interests that do not care to be politicized.

The structural logic of the world energy market

In 1973, 13 years after its establishment, the Organization of the Petroleum Exporting Countries (OPEC) revealed its power for the first time by announcing, in the context of the Yom Kippur War, continuous monthly production reductions. In addition, OPEC singled out specific countries such as the Netherlands for a complete embargo of oil deliveries. This announcement initiated the deepest crisis of the world economy since Second World War. Growth rates went down and unemployment rates went up, and it took several years to overcome this shock.

A major reaction on the side of the OECD was the establishment of a crisis-management mechanism. The IEA was founded in 1974 to focus on two main tasks: to ensure that its member countries built up oil stocks for a minimum 90 days of average consumption and monitor the implementation of this policy, and to develop an efficient distribution mechanism that would allow a balanced oil delivery to member countries particularly affected by a supply boycott. The IEA membership is restricted to OECD countries. Initially, France was the only OECD country that did not become a member of this (Paris-based) institution. Today, France is an IEA member, and not all new OECD members fulfill the strict requirements (mostly of stock building) to be admitted.

The IEA oil security system includes:[4]

- maintenance of national oil stocks
- operation and coordination of effective national emergency organizations
- a system of reallocation of available supplies in an emergency.

Whereas the world reserve stocks are estimated at approximately 5 billion barrels (bb), the IEA stocks amount to 3.8 bb (111 days of net imports into IEA countries), of which the crisis stocks are 3.2 bb. A little more than one-third is stored in government stocks; the remaining part is held by the oil industry.

In case of an emergency, the maximum drawdown profile (the monthly declining pattern of output from emergency stores) offers about 12.9 million barrels per day (mbd) for the first month, 9.4 mbd in the second, down to 0.8 mbd in the seventh month. This strategy assumes that, after the first shock, alternatives from other energy sources or saving measures will be found gradually or that the cause of the supply deficiency can be neutralized.

The most extreme shortfall of world oil supply during the past 50 years happened in late 1978 and early 1979 during the Iranian Revolution, with a supply loss of 5.6 mbd over a period of six months. This loss could easily be compensated by the current IEA stocks. The most serious action the IEA has ever taken was at the time of the outbreak of the Gulf War in 1991, when the

IEA activated its Contingency Plan to make 2.5 mbd available to the market. The IEA's potential seems impressive. It is impressive, indeed, if any oil crisis similar to what happened since the first oil crises in the 1970s takes place. It is also extremely helpful in a more serious case such as a revolution in Saudi Arabia, because it, at least, offers time to develop a strategy while an emergency supply can still be guaranteed. Besides the fact that the IEA responsibility is limited to oil (not including natural gas, which is steadily gaining market shares in the energy mix of IEA countries' consumption), it will, however, not provide an adequate instrument to influence markets and global economic developments in a time of crisis. If the stocks are used to cap extreme price rises, industry will reduce its own efforts in this direction; and because speculation is aware of the limits on oil amounts that can be thrown onto the market, the anticipation of these limits will affect the world's stock markets and growth expectations. So, while the IEA has developed into an indispensable multilateral institution, its crisis-management mandate covers only a (small) part of what would be needed for a comprehensive energy security policy.

For historical reasons, the IEA only deals with oil and not with natural gas. In 1974, when the IEA was established, natural gas imports played a minor role in OECD's energy consumption. Although natural gas, at that time almost exclusively domestically produced, had a share in energy consumption of 31 percent in North America in the 1970s, in OECD Europe it was only 7 percent at that time. Today, natural gas is second (22 percent share) behind oil, with its 41 percent share in OECD's energy mix, and the gap between the two is narrowing.[5]

Why the oil market is not competitive—and is becoming less so

The most desirable constellation for a secure energy supply is a functioning competitive market on the supply side. This, however, is not the case. First, in every country of the world, the energy sector is more organized under state intervention and monopolistic structures than most other sectors of the economy. Especially those energy sectors with a fixed pipeline or electricity grid are frequently treated as "natural monopolies." Even when privatized, companies are commonly influenced by a public heavyweight shareholder represented by government officials. Therefore, on the consumer side, energy companies operate in an environment of far-reaching state regulations, and this situation leads usually to trade-offs and mutual dependencies between the company and state authorities in a way that significantly reduces competition. On the producer side, monopoly structures are even more strict. In most relevant energy-producing countries (OPEC and Caspian states), oil and natural gas production are run by state-owned companies.

Second, what no state committed to a market economy would accept domestically has been a globally accepted matter of fact for decades: OPEC is a formal cartel that not only provoked the 1973 oil crisis but very openly and successfully drives the world market price for oil up far above the marginal costs and thus runs a business that undermines free competition among producers. Without any average production cost increase, the oil price, averaging $17 per barrel during the 1990s, increased and remained within the OPEC price corridor of $22 to $28 between 2000 and the end of 2002. Since January 2003, when the impending Iraq war drove the oil price up, it generally moved between $30 and $35 per barrel. Assuming that marginal costs are in the range of $17 per barrel (the real figure is probably lower), this means that, for all producers, at least half of their oil income is pure profit. For those who produce at much lower costs, as the gulf states do, the profit share is even higher.

Third, the transport infrastructure, not only with natural gas and electricity but also with oil, is more rigid than the existing spot market and the flexibility of tanker transportation suggest. While the oil spot markets, mainly in Rotterdam, are large enough to determine the oil price and its flexibility worldwide, the overwhelming share of international oil trade travels along rather fixed routes. The following figures help illustrate this: 81 percent of Russian oil exports flow to Europe, 80 percent of Latin American and 99 percent of Canadian oil exports go to the United States, and 68 percent of North African oil is delivered to Europe. Sixty-three percent of the oil of the largest exporting region, the Persian Gulf, goes to South and East Asia.[6] Only West Africa still has no clear preference, though the United States gets more than a third of the region's total exports and is doing much to expand their position as the main customer. One important reason for preferential producer-consumer relationships might be the desire to minimize transportation costs. Exactly for that reason, however, the often-invoked argument that the functioning spot markets and the flexibility of tanker movements could divert the flow of oil immediately to where it is needed most in case of a crisis is not true, because total tanker capacities have also adjusted to the minimization of transportation costs. They could not transport West African oil to Japan if gulf oil would, for some reason, not get to East Asia because the required additional tanker capacity to cover the longer journey would not be available.

In the case of natural gas, the trade and transportation structure is extremely rigid: 81 percent of natural gas flowing to Europe from outside comes by pipeline (100 percent in Germany's case).[7] The spot market is tiny and far from able to determine the international price level. This structure provides a framework for a bilateral monopoly between the world's largest natural gas exporter, Russia, from where all natural gas comes by pipeline, and by far the world's largest natural gas import market, Europe. A similar constellation exists between Europe and its second-largest natural gas supplier, Algeria, which delivers 95 percent of its exports to Europe, 57 percent of it by pipeline. Bilateral monopolies represent an especially fragile constellation if non-economic interests become involved.

Although today's oil production is fairly broadly distributed, it will change, given a much more concentrated reserve structure. OECD countries, for instance, provided 28 percent of world oil production in 2000, while disposing no more than only 6.8 percent of (conventional) world oil reserves. This means that existing reserves will be exhausted relatively quickly. The IEA estimates that the OECD share in world oil production will be reduced to 11 percent in 2030.[8] On the other hand, the six OPEC states[9] in the Persian Gulf producing 26 percent of the world's oil in 2000, less than the OECD countries, will have to contribute 43 percent to world supply in 2030.

The Reserve/Production (R/P) ratio in Table 11.1 expresses rather clearly why a further concentration of world oil supply to the gulf is inevitable. Other suppliers such as Russia, Africa, or the non-gulf OPEC countries will, at best, maintain their market share. OECD production will decline in absolute terms and even more in world market shares.

Besides the major increase of Middle East market shares, only the Caspian region will more than double its share on a low level according to the IEA estimates (Table 11.2). That means the West will have to compete with China, India, and other emerging markets for an increasingly concentrated supply of oil coming from extremely fragile regions (the Persian Gulf, Caspian Sea). Table 11.3 expresses the drastic increase in oil demand in East and South Asia (including China and India). Although their imports in 1990 were still negligible, the regions will by far surpass the large demand of North America and Europe within the next decades.

Table 11.1 Distribution of world oil reserves

	Reserves (billion barrels)	Share of world reserves (%)	Reserves/production* (years)
Middle East	727	63	88
Latin America	118	10	31
Africa	102	9	33
Russia	69	6	22
Asia/Pacific	48	4	17
United States/Canada	48	4	13
Europe	20	2	8
Caspian region	17	1	26
World	1148	100	41
OPEC	882	77	80

Note: *Production in 2003.

Source: BJ Statical Review of World Energy, June 2004.

Table 11.2   Major oil producers in 2000 and 2030 (million barrels per day)

	2000		2030	
	Production	Share in world production (%)	Production	Share in world production (%)
OECD	21.2	28	12.8	11
Russia	6.5	9	9.5	8
Caspian region	1.6	2	5.4	4.5
Africa (non-OPEC)	2.8	4	4.4	4
Guif OPEC	21.0	28	51.4	43
Other OPEC*	7.7	10	12.4	10
Others	14.2	19	24.1	20
Of which				
unconvention oil	1.1	1	9.9	8
World	75.0	100	120.0	100

Note: *Including Nigeria, Algeria, Libra.
Source: International Energy Agency, World Energy Outlook 2002: Paris (September 21, 2002), p. 96.

Table 11.3   Major oil import regions (million barrels per day)

	2000	2030
OECD Europe	7.4	13.9
United States/Canada	10.1	20.2
OECD Pacific	7.6	10.0
East and South Asia	6.0	25.7

Source: International Energy Agency, World Energy Outlook 2002, Paris (September 21, 2002), pp. 92, 96.

The role of natural gas

A somewhat different constellation is given on the international natural gas market. Here, we have a massive concentration of reserves in two neighboring regions, the Middle East and Russia. If we add the Caspian area, we have 72 percent of world oil reserves concentrated in this "strategic ellipse"[10] (Table 11.4).

Natural gas transportation is more expensive than oil transportation per energy unit, and it requires a more sophisticated transportation structure than oil. The long-distance transportation either happens by pipeline or by Liquefied Natural Gas (LNG) tanker, technically a much more ambitious option, due to the necessary liquefaction and regasification process. Even in this case, however, national distribution requires a widespread pipeline

Table 11.4 Concentration of natural gas reserves, 2030

	Reserves (trillion m³)	Share in world reserves (%)	R/P* (years)
Middle East	71.7	41	>200
Russia	47.0	27	81
Asia/Pacific	13.5	8	43
Africa	13.8	8	98
Latin America	7.6	4	49
United States/Canada	6.9	4	9
Caspian Region	8.0	5	63
Europe	7.3	4	23
World	175.8	100	67

Note: *Reserves divided by 2003 production.

Source: BP Statistical Review of World Energy, June 2004.

network to even small consumers in private households. Due to these infrastructure requirements (even Germany does not have a single port where LNG tankers can be unloaded), only a limited number of states and regions in the world are involved in natural gas trade and, due to the high transportation costs and the pipeline structure as the still-dominant transportation system, there is no significant world market for natural gas; only regional markets. Sixty percent of the worldwide natural gas trade is taking place between the neighbors Canada and the United States, and Russia plus Algeria and Europe on the other.[11]

As the IEA predicts, today's demand structure will principally remain constant for decades to come (Table 11.5). Europe will keep its position as the largest import market. North America, currently the largest consumer but, if Canada and the United States are considered as a single entity, mainly a closed market, will, however, become a major importer. OECD Pacific (Japan, South Korea, Australia, and New Zealand) will be number three on the demand side followed by China. On the supply side, Russia will lose its almost monopolistic position, and Africa and the Middle East will take major market shares.

The given structure of natural gas trade precludes a competitive market even more than in the case of oil. Most natural gas is traded within the framework of long-term (twenty years or even longer) bilateral contracts that do not give the consumer the choice of selecting between different suppliers. The spot market is so tiny that this market's price has no influence on the amount of natural gas consumption; and the flexibility provided by LNG is not really relevant for the security of supply, because the combined capacities in the world could not even come close to substituting the transportation capacity of Russian pipelines to Europe.

Table 11.5   Major natural gas import and export regions, 2000–2030 (billion cubic meter)

	Import (+)/Export (−)	
	2000	2030
OECD Europe	186	625
OECD North America	5	345
OECD Pacific	83	121
China	0	47
Transition countries	−112	−227
Middle East	−69	−365
Africa	−10	−299
Latin America	−23	−103
other Asia	−60	−94

Source: International Energy Agency, World Energy Outlook 2002, Paris (September 21, 2002), pp. 110, 117.

In sum, what probably is the most sensitive segment in international trade, given its enormous importance for the viability of practically all economic sectors worldwide, is that we have a high degree of monopolization and state control at all levels on the demand side, and even higher levels on the supply side. This scenario makes supply security fragile because, in contrast to a competitive market, the supplier (or those who have the power to influence the supply) can exploit the dependency of the consumers on energy imports for political reasons. Those reasons need not necessarily follow state interests; they could also reflect calculations of terrorism or organized crime.

German and EU energy security policy

Germany's oil stock management and its emergency response is embedded into the IEA and EU system. These two systems are almost congruent. Whereas the IEA chooses as a basis of the ninety-day stock requirement the net oil imports of each of its member countries, the European Union applies domestic consumption for three categories of products (gasolines, middle distillates, and heavy fuel oil) as the basis for a 90 days stock requirement.

The competence on German energy policy lies in the hands of the Federal Ministry for Economics and Labour (BMWA). This applies also for foreign energy policy, particularly the representation of the Federal Government with the commission in Brussels.

Germany's corporatist energy policy bias

The logic of this mandate is evident, as it gives the legal competence to where the professional competence is accumulated. Nevertheless, this competence seems to be biased in three ways.

First, the main constituency of the BMWA energy policy is the energy industry, much more than the energy consumers. As explained earlier, the energy transmission and distribution system, which used to be a state monopoly, is now mainly privatized but still interwoven with genuine state functions (infrastructure, environment, regulations of monopolistic structures, etc.). This situation constantly requires compromises between business interests and government obligations, and thus it produces a corporatist structure different from a competitive market where the state sets rules as the arbiter. The close links between energy companies and BMWA also lead to a conservative policy of the BMWA toward the European Commission. Companies with a more or less guaranteed market share usually are not interested in a government-regulated competitive structure. The resistance of energy companies to EU energy market liberalization efforts therefore received more sympathy from the BMWA than consumer interests and influenced the BMWA position in Brussels negotiations.

The second bias is the lack of expertise in international (political) relations. The international oil and natural gas structure is far from following the rules of a competitive market. The functioning of the OPEC cartel has proven to be dependent on the degree to which alternative sources of supply were available—as was the case from the mid-1980s to the mid-1990s, when the North Sea and Alaskan production peaked. Table 11.1 demonstrates why these times are over if no substitute to oil is promoted. Since March 1999 the cartel is functioning again: if the members observe the quantity restrictions, they all can earn more money with less production. Given the physical concentration of sources of supply, the functioning of the cartel for the past five years, and the (unexpected) global demand growth due to high import growth rates in China and India, the whole demand and supply structure became highly sensitive and attractive to those who want to strike against the world economy and particularly against the West.

In the case of natural gas, the link between foreign economic relations and foreign policy is even more obvious. The major supplier of the German and European markets from outside Europe is Russia. The gas deals of the 1970, which laid the ground to the pipeline infrastructure in the early 1980s, could never have been signed without political support and blessings—the geographic distance to the reserves of west Siberia is larger and the production costs are higher than the distance to the Middle East natural gas fields and the production costs there. The idea behind the political support of the infrastructure link to Siberia was certainly not security of supply—the Reagan administration tried to hinder the deal in the early 1980s in order to prevent the resulting dependency risk—but detente policy. The structure brought into being during those years still determines the natural gas import structure today, although the political environment and energy security interests have changed significantly.

The third bias is the high degree of independence of energy policy from climate policy commitments. It is obvious that, if the international commitments regarding climate policy such as Article 2 of the United Nations Framework Convention on Climate Change (Rio, 1992) or the Kyoto Protocol of 1997 are taken seriously, a much stronger effort needs to be made to reduce the fossil fuel share in the energy mix. There is no indication that this scenario would take place even if the goal of a 20 percent share of renewables in electricity production in the year 2020 would be met.[12] On the contrary, an increase of fossil energy consumption is to be expected given the reduced contribution of nuclear energy, which is to be phased out. As the conflict between the BMWA and the Ministry of the Environment on the distribution of emission rights within the EU emission trading scheme made clear, the BMWA reflexively defends the interests of its constituency, the energy industry, under almost any circumstances, but it feels little commitment to a comprehensive energy policy like the US Energy Strategy that includes the parameters of a sustainable climate policy.[13]

The three biases lead to a rather defensive policy with respect to such European energy issues as the liberalization of energy markets and the build-up of a regional infrastructure. Yet, though the need for a consistent and comprehensive European energy policy is obvious, in the negotiations on an energy chapter for the European constitution, the BMWA did not recommend the inclusion of such a chapter. The architecture of the constitution made such a chapter inevitable (Article I-13 deals with divided competences, to which energy belongs in paragraph i; in article III-157 (1), goals such as a functioning domestic market and security of supply are listed). The compromise formula that was eventually produced will probably not be sufficient to promote the kind of European energy policy competences that could create a coherent European energy policy with adequate treatment of energy security and climate policy issues in a comprehensive approach.

Implications for German energy security policy

German energy policy follows the "magic triangle" of supply security, competitiveness (Wirtschaftlichkeit), and environmental sustainability.[14,15] Deficiencies with respect to one of the three goals can be explained by constraints resulting from the pursuit of the other two, equally important goals.[16]

Security can generally be perceived as insurance that costs a premium. The same applies for environmental standards. Costs, however, have a negative impact on competitiveness. Energy security can and often is understood in a rather technical (non-political) sense. The best example is the probability of blackouts in the electricity sector. Here, it is obvious that the suppliers of electricity have to go through an optimization process between risk minimization, by providing excess capacities, and cost effectiveness. Private suppliers have a different optimization calculation than consumers, because the suppliers do not have to pay for all costs of the blackout, but transfer most of them to the consumer. Therefore, in order to protect the consumers, state regulation should balance consumer interests with the competitiveness of the suppliers, forcing the supplier to provide excess capacities.

A similar measure is a state regulation with regard to storing energy. This situation applies most of all to oil, which, as a liquid can be better stored than natural gas or electricity. Again, this is a technical regulation, usually put into place on a national level. The oil crisis of 1973–1974 linked for the first time energy security and international politics in OECD countries through the establishment of the International Energy Agency as a coordinator of national oil stocks. The minimum stock of 90 days of average national consumption establishes a regime of joint responsibility to be applied if individual member countries are singled out for supply embargoes. The IEA leaves the organization of the stocks to the national governments but monitors the observation of standards.

This national oil stock-building in agreement with IEA standards represents the core of German energy security policy. Three other components also deserve to be mentioned.

- Besides oil, natural gas storage capacities are built up without a multilateral commitment.
- The subsidization of domestic coal production has been justified by all post–Second World War German governments, not only in terms of protecting a coal working force but also as preventing the share of domestic primary energy in energy consumption, particularly for producing electricity, from declining to practically zero.
- The federal government encourages so-called interruptible contracts between national suppliers and industrial consumers, particularly in the natural gas field but also in the electricity sector. These contracts stipulate that the supply of natural gas can be stopped by the supplier on short notice for a limited time, during which the industrial consumer must be prepared either to change to another energy source (on the basis of its own stocks) or halt energy (electricity) consumption altogether.

The federal government also correctly lists the support of renewable energies and of energy efficiency as measures to improve energy security of supply in its annual economic report.[17] These measures, however, are mainly taken for other reasons (climate policy, technology policy) and they only mitigate but do not change the trend that the import share in the domestic energy consumption is steadily growing. The gradual phasing-out of nuclear energy, however, is mentioned nowhere as contributing to a deterioration of energy security.

Summarizing how the BMWA defines energy security policy, the annual report contains a set of measures that are related to influencing the domestic energy mix, to storage of oil and natural gas, and to support energy efficiency improvements with the effect of reducing consumption and thus import dependence. A diversification of imports is hardly mentioned and totally left to private companies. What is completely missing in the BMWA concept is any foreign-policy consideration regarding the reliability of supply.

With regard to this deficit, the BMWA response is threefold. First, the BMWA argues that the history of three decades since the first oil crisis has shown that, despite price developments that were considered crises in 1980, 2000, and again since 2003, the best instrument to overcome extreme price rises is the market, a solution that has always worked so far. Second, even during the Cold War the supply of natural gas has worked without any problems apart from purely technical, easily manageable ones. The necessity for suppliers to earn money to balance their investment is equal to the dependence of the consumer. This interdependence has proven to be stable. Third, there is nobody who can take the supply risk into consideration better than the companies that import oil and natural gas.

Perspectives from Brussels: the commission and energy security

On November 30, 2000, the European Commission published a green paper titled "Towards a European strategy for the security of energy supply."[18] Its intention was to give an impetus to a necessary discussion. The key issues addressed in the paper are:

- Due to declining domestic production (oil, natural gas, nuclear), dependence on external sources of energy is constantly and dramatically increasing, from approximately 50 percent in the year 2000 to 70 percent in 2030.
- Without an active energy policy, the share of fossil energy (79 percent in 2000) will increase to 86 percent in 2030. It will thus be impossible to meet the Kyoto targets.
- Diversification of supply will become more difficult and, particularly in the case of natural gas, is dramatically low. The European Union's dependence on Russia has increased with the enlargement, and it will increase further.

This green paper was written before September 11, 2001. The regional congruence of the home base of international terrorism and the largest energy supply area add to the urgency of the problem. Neither the green paper nor the "war on terror" have changed the BMWA position, however. The ministry didn't pick up either the issue of political insecurities on the supply side or the steady shift from an equal share of EU domestic and imported energy to a 30 percent (EU domestic) and a 70 percent (imported) share in the energy consumption of the enlarged European

Union. Comments on the green paper concentrated on the commission's desire to enhance its competences, which, member countries' governments and industries argue, will only lead to more bureaucracy instead of giving room to efficient market forces. A serious discussion on the problem of a dramatically rising dependence under conditions of a less reliable supply side hardly took place in Berlin.

Conclusion: where do we go from here?

This paper has shown that energy policy in Germany is mainly understood as a sectoral problem that can be dealt with on a technocratic level. This understanding might have been sufficient from the mid-1980s through the 1990s, when there was a competitive market for energy supplies from abroad, international terrorism was not yet an issue, and climate policy was still in the making. Now, energy policies need to take into consideration the political nature of contemporary global challenges in this policy area: security of supply and climate policy, both in their global dimension.

Energy security forces us to develop specific foreign-policy measures toward regions where resources are concentrated, most of all the Persian Gulf region, Russia and the Caspian region, and also toward the main consumers. Climate policy is linked to questions of energy security by international commitments asking for a long-term strategy for the decarbonization of energy consumption and its emissions. A technical understanding of energy security is not sufficient anymore. The debate needs to be politicized.

These issues overburden the instruments available to just one ministry. It requires cooperation with the Federal Foreign Office (AA) and the Ministry of the Environment. It also needs a firm commitment of the Chancellery and not just a referee function in case of a dispute between the different ministries, as happened in drafting the German allocation plan for the EU carbon dioxide-emission trading scheme in March 2004.

The AA, however, is not equipped to provide the necessary input. Due to the fact that the competence for international energy policy lies with the BMWA, the AA hierarchy provides only a mirror desk (Spiegel-Referat), a counterpart, to the BMWA energy division within its economics department. This desk is not powerful enough to develop an independent AA strategy unless massive support is given from the upper levels of the hierarchy. This support, however, is not given, especially because of a lack of priority given to this topic in the foreign-policy structure.

The BMU (Federal Ministry of Environment) leads the negotiations at the annual Conference of Parties within the United Nations Framework Convention on Climate Change, a process that led to the Kyoto Protocol. Its mandate, however, is very narrowly defined with respect to international commitments, particularly with respect to energy issues. The result is that the climate negotiations cannot be brought forward by compromising on other issues and, whenever, energy issues are touched, such as the establishment of a national allocation plan for an emission trading scheme, the BMWA has to agree.

It is evident that energy security and climate control are overlapping policy issues, with the thrust of both working in the same direction. Oil and natural gas will increasingly have to be imported and will thus produce dependencies, whereas non-fossil fuels (renewables and technologies such as hydrogen) usually can be produced domestically. The US Department of Energy's "Strategic Plan" of September 30, 2003 strongly stresses this link.[19] The subtitle of this plan is "Protecting National, Energy, and Economic Security with Advanced Science and Technology and Ensuring Environmental Cleanup." Even if some doubt that the strategy will be implemented according to a schedule that helps both energy security and the climate, the difference to the German policy process is that such a strategic plan would and could not be developed in Germany. Extrapolating from the officially voiced intentions of the German energy strategy, an increase of fossil fuels in the energy mix until 2020 and beyond is inevitable. This increase will harm energy security and climate policy at the same time.

The policy for improving energy efficiency has been rather successful during the past three decades. Forecasts published by respected institutions in 1976 and 1977 predicted a doubling of European Community energy consumption between 1975 and 2000.[20] The reality is that the increase of energy consumption in this time frame was less than 40 percent and, in the case of Germany, close to zero. No progress, however, has been made with regard to energy security through foreign-policy instruments. In a book published in 1978, five years after the first oil crisis and ten years before the first public recognition of the climate change problem, Hanns Maull wrote:

> The two central problems in the energy field the international system will have to deal with in the years and decades ahead present themselves on the one hand as the transition from petroleum and natural gas to a system in which other sources ... will increasingly take over the role of oil and gas; on the other hand as a radical transformation process in the energy system's international control and steerage mechanisms.[21]

Twenty-six years later, it is time to deal with these central problems.

Notes

1   See the Department of Energy Strategic Plan, "Protecting National, Energy, and Economic Security with Advanced Science and Technology and Ensuring Environmental Cleanup," Draft, Washington, August 6, 2003.
2   Department of Energy Strategic Plan, "Protecting National, Energy, and Economic Security with Advanced Science and Technology and Ensuring Environmental Cleanup" (see note 1), p. 1.

3   Department of Energy Strategic Plan, "Protecting National, Energy, and Economic Security with Advanced Science and Technology and Ensuring Environmental Cleanup" (see note 1), p. 3.

4   The following data are based on the Fact Sheet: IEA Stocks and Emergency Response (2004). Available at http:www.iea.org/Textbase/papers/2004/factsheetcover.pdf. Accessed January 3, 2005.

5   International Energy Agency, World Energy Outlook 2002, Paris, September 21, 2002, pp. 414, 418, 430. Available at: http://www.worldenergyoutlook.org/weo/pubs/weo2002/weo2002.asp. Accessed January 3, 2005.

6   BP Statistical Review of World Energy, June 2004, p. 18. Available at: http://www.bp.com/subsection.do?categoryId=95&contentId=2006480. Accessed January 3, 2005.

7   BP Statistical Review of World Energy (see note 6), p. 28.

8   These estimates are limited to the production of "conventional oil." The largest reserves of unconventional oil (particularly oil sand) are located in Canada. If these oil reserves will be made available for production, to a large extent, the reduction of OECD market share will be less dramatic, but still significant. International Energy Agency, World Energy Outlook 2002 (see note 5), p. 96.

9   Saudi Arabia, Iran, Iraq, Kuwait, United Arab Emirates, Oman.

10 Geoffrey Kemp and Robert E. Harkavy, *Strategic Geography and the Changing Middle East* (Washington, DC: Brookings Institution Press, 1997).

11 BP Statistical Review of World Energy, June 2004 (see note 6).

12 Doubts are justified that this will happen, because national goals sometimes disappear from the agenda, like the goal to which all Kohl and Schröder governments committed themselves from 1988 to 2003, that of a 25 percent carbon dioxide reduction by 2005. The government finally buried the goal on October 28, 2003. Antwort der Bundesregierung auf die Kleine Anfrage der Abgeordneten Dr. Peter Paziorek, Karl-Josef Laumann, Dagmar Wörll weiterer Abgeordneter und der Fraktion der CDU/CSU. Bundestagsdrucksache 15/1851, October 28, 2003. Available at: http://dip.bundestag.de/btd/15/018/1501851.pdf. Accessed January 8, 2005.

13 A thorough overview of what comprehensive measures should be taken is given by a report presented by the Scientific Board of the Federal Government on Global Environmental Change. WBGU, Über Kioto hinausdenken—Klimaschutzstrategien für das 21. Jahrhundert, Sondergutachten, Berlin, 2003.

14 "Competitiveness, supply security and environmental sustainability: Within this triangle, energy policy is made, for which, within the federal government, the Ministry for Economics and Labour is responsible," Federal Ministry for Economics and Labour (BMWA), Energiedaten 2003: Zahlen und Fakten zur nationalen und internationalen Entwicklung, Berlin, 2004, Available at: http://www.bmwa.bund.de/Navigation/Technologie-und-Energie/energiepolitik.html. Accessed January 8, 2005.

15 Deutsches Nationales Komitee de Weltenergierates DNK, Energie für Deutschland, Düsseldorf (2001). Available at: http://www.worldenergy.org/wec-geis/global/downloads/edc/EFD2004.pdf. Accessed January 8, 2005.

16 Federal Ministry for Economics and Labour (BMWA), Jahreswirtschaftsbericht 2004, Vol. 58. Available at: http://www.bmwa.bund.de/Redaktion/Inhalte/Pdf/jahreswirtschaftsbericht-2004,property=pdf.pdf. Accessed January 8, 2005.

17 Federal Ministry of Economics and Labour (BMWA), Jahreswirtschaftsbericht 2004 (see note 16), pp. 60–61.

18   Green Paper: Toward a European strategy for the security of energy supply (June 26, 2002). Available at: http://europa.eu.int/eur-lex/en/com/gpr/2000/ act769en01/com2000_0769en01-01.pdf. Accessed January 8, 2005.
19   The Department of Energy, Strategic Plan, Protecting National, Energy, and Economic Security with Advanced Science and Technology and Ensuring Environmental Cleanup, September 30, 2003. Available at: http:// strategicplan. doe.gov. Accessed January 8, 2005.
20   Hanns Maull, "World energy problems: the search for new forms of international corporation," *Oil Shock: Five Years Later*, Manfred Tietzel, ed. (Bonn: Friedrich-Ebert-Stiftung, 1978), p. 216.
21   Maull, *Oil Shock* (see note 20), pp. 213–38; quoted here p. 213.

12
German Trade Policy: The Decline of Liberal Leadership

Andreas Falke

Introduction

Germany remains one of the leading global trading powers, but some ominous signs appear on the horizon. The share of German high-tech products in total exports has been declining, German services exports are not growing at the same rate as some of the country's competitors, and its sectors of industrial strength, such as electrical engineering, machinery, and automobiles, increasingly rely on outsourcing production to Eastern Europe to remain competitive.

Nevertheless, Germany remains one of the two largest trading nations in the world, with the United States, but ahead of Japan. In 2003, Germany's merchandise trade balance approached nearly 100 billion dollars.[1] Given the country's present economic woes, the trading side should not present any problems. It appears, at least, that German trade policy makers have been making the right choices that have so far eluded their colleagues working on the domestic side.

The European and global setting

Trade policy is an established European Community (EC) competence, with institutionalized European Union (EU) decision-making processes. However, EU trade policy develops closely with member state governments, whose preferences set the agenda. The European Union also depends on member state approval for the results of international negotiations. Trade policy making in the European Union thus has a strong intergovernmental basis,[2] and studying member state trade preferences therefore makes sense. As trade policy has undergone a dramatic transformation under globalization, older characterizations such as those between liberal northern countries and a southern protectionist camp led by France have lost their meaning. Border measures, including tariffs and quotas, have declined in importance, whereas issues such as the liberalization of services and the protection of intellectual property rights increasingly affect domestic regulatory frame-works and thus politicize trade policy by involving well-organized domestic actors. With the introduction of trade-related issues such as labor standards and the environment, the intersection of domestic and international policy approaches has pushed traditional market-access concerns even further into the background. Some scholars, such as William Dymond and Michael Hart, have argued that trade policy has entered a postmodern phase, in which market-access considerations are eclipsed by positive rule-making as a con-tribution to a comprehensive framework for global governance.[3]

This view implies that governments are not only obliged to remove border trade barriers and discrimination but to adopt specific policies and regula-tions that may only be indirectly relevant to market access and that encroach on national regulatory regimes and institutions. In the run-up to the 1999 WTO (World Trade Organization) ministerial in Seattle, trade and investment, trade and competition, trade and environment, and trade and labor standards were all added as possible new areas of rule-making within the WTO context. Today, the most urgent—imminent in terms of the current negotiations—of these are the so-called Singapore issues, which include investment, competition policy, government procurement and trade facilitation. Pushed to its extremes, such an agenda implies an overarching framework of global rules covering major areas of domestic regulation and asserted with the force of trade sanctions under the WTO dispute settlement mechanism. If fully implemented, such a framework would come close to the realization of a regime of global economic governance. Although market access may be facilitated by positive rule-making, it is by no means its prin-cipal goal. Rather, the goal is the consistency and coherence of international legal structures and their implementation. In the case of environmental and labor standards, their application may even make market access more diffi-cult, if market access depends on implementing such standards. Trade-policy measures would thus be transformed into a lever for reaching goals of other emerging international regimes.

The central thesis of this essay is that Germany's capacity and willingness to stake out a distinctive trade policy profile has noticeably declined. Germany has thus lost its capacity to be a potent voice for a liberal, market-access based trade policy. Six factors account for this development:

- The priority German politicians have accorded to pursuing European integration above national trade preferences.
- The "French connection": the tendency to support France's more restric-tive trade-policy positions to prop up the general political relationship between France and Germany, which has served as the engine of European integration.
- The loss of monetary policy sovereignty as a lever to influence reluctant liberalizers in the European Union, particularly France.

- The dramatic decline of the standing of the Economics Ministry within the interagency power structure, coupled with weak trade-policy leadership at the ministry and the German economic policy elite in general.
- The impact of the globalization debate, which, with the Greens and the left wing of the Social Democrats serving as conduits, has given new actors a voice that use trade policy as a means to pursue goals other than market opening, and which has swayed the unions to take more protectionist positions.
- The rhetorical persistence of the free-trade consensus, which, in light of continuing export success, has led to policy complacency.

The domestic setting

The free-trade tradition: seeking market access in a multilateral framework

Although Germany was never an absolute free trader in the postwar period, granting protection to agriculture and some industrial sectors, and later readily acquiescing to protectionist measures on the EC level, trade liberalization and the push for open markets was at the center of German trade policy. The high point of that tradition was certainly Germany's initiatives of unilateral liberalization in the 1950s prior to joining the GATT (General Agreement on Tariffs and Trade) and the European Economic Community (EEC) under the leadership of Economics Minister Ludwig Erhard.[4] The export capacity of Germany's industrial sectors and a structural undervaluation of the deutsche Mark sustained this tradition. Yet, openness in industrial markets was not matched in services, public utilities, and government procurement, where Germany remained as defensive as most other industrialized countries.

At the same time, Germany acted as the guardian of the multilateral trading order of the GATT/WTO system. Upholding the multilateral trading order is fundamental to German trade policy. Supporting the multilateral trading system helped to secure the basis of Germany's enormous postwar export success.[5] For this reason, Germany rejected any form of unilateralism, such as the US-301 or Super-301 instruments or similar instruments of the European Union.

In theory and rhetoric, Germany continues to support the expansion of a rules-based trading system, and it welcomes strategies geared toward greater juridification of trade relations. For these reasons, Germany emphatically endorsed the establishment of the dispute settlement mechanism in the WTO. This development represents a depoliticization of trade policy, implying that political conflicts will increasingly be transferred to independent legal bodies, instead of settling them on an ad hoc political basis. Germany thus tends to show a preference for global governance rules, even if they compromise market-access concerns. Establishing a framework simply for the sake of having rules is at times a greater priority for German policy makers than advocating specific market-access opportunities. This phenomenon was evident in the period following the Uruguay Round, when Germany was content with regimes for financial services and telecommunications that were much less ambitious then the plans of some non-EU actors.

Institutional factors

In institutional terms, the principal responsibility for trade policy lies with the Economics Ministry, a situation that has not changed since the 2002 merger with the Labor Ministry creating the Federal Ministry for Economics and Labor.[6] The labor side accepted the lead of the economics side. Dominated by the Free Democrats, the most liberal German party, from 1969 to 1998, the Economics Ministry has been the bastion of free-trade liberalism until it fell into decline in the early 1990s.[7] For a long time, its major competitor was the Agricultural Ministry, a protectionist stronghold. The other ministry that inevitably plays a role is the Foreign Ministry, the lead agency for EU affairs, which is also the principal supporter of an abstract rule-making approach.

Since the mid-1990s, other ministries, such as those of the environment and foreign aid, have increasingly claimed a stake in trade policy, challenging the Economics Ministry. The chancellor's office rarely serves as a coordinating body, as its institutional capacity in trade policy is weak and it has few mechanisms for adjudicating intraministerial conflicts. The only exception is when a principal policy objective of the chancellor, such as EU strategy or relations with France, comes into play.

On the private-sector side, the Federation of German Industry (BDI), an umbrella association of industrial (and, increasingly, service-sector) associations, is the major actor in trade policy, eclipsing others such as the Association of Chambers of Commerce (DIHK), the Federation of German Retail and Wholesale Trade (BGA), and the Trade Association of German Retailers (AVE), partly because it represents most directly German producer interests (including the country's major corporate players), partly because it can bring more staff resources and expertise into play. Despite the export strength of the German industrial sector, BDI cannot unequivocally be described as a force of trade liberalization. Here, the historically dominant position of heavy industry such as steel and coal, both dependent on subsidies and protection, weighs in. BDI has also long been unable to foster agricultural liberalization, with such important members as the food processors and those members of the chemical industry representing fertilizer production often siding with the closely linked farming sector.[8] As an association of associations, BDI often functions as a filter for market-access concerns of individual member associations, as well as companies.[9] BDI's relationship with politics is shaped by the fading heritage of corporatist structures, which led to a dense network of cooperation between private- and public-sector actors. The emphasis in corporatist networks is the regulation of the domestic economy, a priority that is to be guarded against possible disruptions from second-tier issues such as trade. The maintenance of corporatist structures has led to a deference to governmental actors that, with the transfer of regulatory responsibility to the European Union in such areas as corporate governance, energy deregulation, competition, and environmental policy, also characterizes BDI's relations with Brussels.

BDI's trade strategy is frequently motivated by a search for convergence with dominant trends in Brussels, and by abstract conceptual principles that are inspired less by commercial interests than by internal bureaucratic policy making.[10] All these factors lessen BDI's capacity to be an independent, proactive advocate on trade policy. Although it steadfastly adheres to the free-trade doctrine, it rarely functions as a specific agenda-setter and tends to ratify the positions formulated by public bureaucracies. The BDI case actually proves that if there is such thing as "agency capture" (i.e., the manipulation of decision-makers by vested interests), the reverse exists, too: "association capture" by public-policy makers. Other business-sector groupings carry too little weight to have an impact on trade policy.

The Uruguay Round: paradigm change in German trade strategy

Until the early 1990s, German trade policy makers made good on Germany's claim to be a force of trade liberalization within the EU/EC system, despite the fact that Germany was in a minority position virtually from the inception of the EEC and had to act under the foreign-policy imperative to maintain good relations with France. Yet it insisted on an independent role using the intergovernmental mechanism of the 113/133 committee to shape EC/EU trade policy. In the seventies, Germany's liberal approach was facilitated by its dominant position in monetary policy and in the G-7 process, which was used to push for trade liberalization and persuade such protectionist G-7 EC member states as France and Italy to support the initiation and conclusion of trade negotiations.[11] In the 1980s, under the leadership of the liberal economics minister, Otto Lambsdorff, his state secretaries Dieter von Würzen and Lorenz Schomerus crafted the "northern strategy" of seeking a trade policy alliance with liberal-minded northern states such as the Netherlands, the United Kingdom, and Denmark. In the Uruguay Round, however, the German "northern strategy" was of little avail. German agriculture resisted liberalization until the McSharry reforms of the Common Agricultural Policy introduced set-asides and direct payments to farmers in 1992. It was therefore easy for Chancellor Helmut Kohl to throw his weight behind France (and Ireland), who wanted to block any agreement on liberalizing farm trade at the infamous Brussels ministerial of 1990, which culminated in Brazil and Argentina's walking-out. Although Kohl's position was initially dictated by the need to protect the domestic farm sector, with the impending shift to direct payments, it increasingly shifted to protecting France, his closest ally in pushing his European agenda. Kohl thus backed away from the Blair House agreement, the compromise brokered by the commission with the United States to overcome the impasse on agriculture in the Uruguay Round. After the German Agricultural Ministry had accepted the compromise and the German government had gone on record to oppose any reopening of the hard-won agreement, Kohl supported the French request for modification, thereby making France's hard line viable.[12]

The Uruguay Round was paradigm-setting for German trade policy making in the EU/EC system. It firmly established the "French connection" as the overriding factor, effectively scrapping the "northern strategy." The implication is that political relations with France regarding matters of European integration would override any specific German trade-policy interests. This pattern has been repeating ever since, from the German shift on banana policy to the discussions on the Agenda 2000 and the agricultural aspects of the financing of Eastern enlargement, to the beginning of the Doha Round. It clearly reflects a strategic foreign-policy decision that places European integration above trade policy, but it also compromises any attempts to formulate an independent trade policy and to act as an agenda-setter in the EU trade-policy system. Trade policy is the first and foremost victim of Germany's integrationist aspirations.

German trade policy and the Red–Green coalition government: the impact of the globalization debate

Until the election of the Red–Green coalition in 1998, the globalization debate had little impact on German trade policy. The Economics Ministry managed to hold off the agenda the new trade issues pushed by the antiglobalization movement, that is trade and labor standards and trade and environmental standards. In this respect, Germany was a laggard compared to other countries of the Organisation for Economic Co-operation and Development, such as the United States and Canada, where the impact of the nongovernmental organization (NGO)-based antiglobalization movement was already felt in the early 1990s.[13] On development issues, the attitude was that improved market access in multilateral negotiations, as well as the expansion of preferential tariff treatment, would automatically contribute to development.

This atmosphere all changed with the advent of the Red–Green coalition government. The Greens (and, to a certain extent, the left-wing of the Social Democratic Party) were instrumental in including antiglobalization NGOs into the official policy discourse and the channels of informal policy input, such as hearings and consultation. The most important consequence of this development was that other ministries, particularly the environment, labour, and aid and development ministries gained influence in the trade-policy process. With the Agricultural Ministry being transformed into a Ministry for Consumer Affairs and Agriculture under Renate Künast, a more trade-restrictive agenda on environmental and food-safety standards gained prominence at the expense of producer interests. One of the principal reasons for this trend was institutional: the decline of the influence of the Economics Ministry on trade policy. This was only the latest phase in a secular decline of a cabinet powerhouse of the 1950s and 1960s, which began in the early 1970s with the loss of the monetary and credit division to the Finance Ministry. In 1998, then Finance Minister Oskar Lafontaine also took the Economic Policy Division and the European Affairs Division to the Finance Ministry. The loss of the European Affairs Division was a serious blow to the policy-making capacities of the Economics Ministry for trade policy and its general standing in EU policy coordination, as regulatory policy increasingly intersected with trade policy. Weak political leadership exacerbated the weakened institutional status of the Economics Ministry. Chancellor Gerhard Schröder appointed an unknown second-tier energy manager, Werner Müller, to the post of economics minister in the first Red–Green government. He focused exclusively on the exit from atomic energy and paid scant attention to foreign economic policy. The Foreign Economic Policy Division was isolated and reduced even further in status by the retirement of the highly respected state secretary for international economics, Lorenz Schomerus. The void that the Economics Ministry left behind was largely filled by the environmental and aid and development ministries under Heidi Wieczorek-Zeul and Jürgen Trittin, who, with the full backing of their caucuses, began to dominate the trade-policy discourse in the run-up to the Doha WTO ministerial. The rhetoric of German trade policy shifted from market access-based liberalization to bending trade objectives to developmental, environmental, and labor concerns.

Since the collapse of the 1999 WTO ministerial in Seattle, Trittin's and Wieczorek-Zeul's activism has also resonated more strongly with parliament, where antiglobalization themes received a friendly reception in the Red and Green caucuses, leading to the establishment of a parliamentary commission on globalization (*Enquete Kommission Globalisierung*).[14] The commission, which was dominated by the left wings of both coalition parties, issued a report highly critical of traditional trade liberalization and led to a parliamentary resolution demanding the inclusion of labor and environmental standards in future multilateral trade agreements and the protection of educational, health, and audio-visual services offer as a precondition for beginning negotiations in the Doha Round. As the EU Commission had already shelved the idea of negotiating labor standards as unrealistic, the German government with difficulty resisted the demands for negotiating on labor standards coming from the majority caucuses. But it was forthcoming on environmental goals and a restrictive services offer.

Current multilateral WTO negotiations (Doha Round)

In 1999, during the run-up to the current multilateral trade round, now dubbed the Doha Development Round, the European Union developed a highly ambitious multifaceted agenda. It included the following issue areas:[15]

- Market access for industrial goods
- Negotiations on agriculture (built-in agenda)
- Liberalization of services
- Investment
- Competition
- Public procurement
- Trade facilitation
- Electronic commerce
- Reform of trade-remedy procedures (antidumping)
- Technical barriers to trade
- Environment and trade (including the precautionary principle)
- Social/labour standards and trade
- Reform of trade-related intellectual property rights (TRIPS) (with particular emphasis to the concerns of developing countries)
- An accelerated phase-out of the multifiber agreement.

On the surface, this approach appeared very much like a laundry list, but in its ambitious range, the program mirrored the shift of EU trade policy from a market-access driven agenda to a postmodern approach that has comprehensive rule-making at its center.[16] Central to the European Union's agenda were the Singapore issues, particularly rule-making on competition policy and investment, which would require extensive rule-making and intrusive adjustments of policy regimes presenting a serious challenge for developing countries. On a more critical note, however, the inclusion of these issues could also be viewed as a stalling tactic that the European Union might use to avoid greater concessions on agriculture. The European Union saw the Singapore issues, particularly investment and competition, as something it was entitled to get in exchange for what it would offer elsewhere, including agriculture. With the inclusion of the new issues, rule-making could be expanded to a global governance agenda harnessing globalization, thus responding to the antiglobalization agenda of civil society forces. Market-access concerns would be pushed back even further.

Theoretically, the comprehensiveness of the agenda also afforded the European Union with an opportunity for multiple trade-offs with its WTO partners. But this did not mean that the agenda was acceptable to the European Union's trading partners in its entirety, especially the developing countries, who had little interest in accepting costly new commitments that would overburden their domestic policy regimes. Thus, in the real world of negotiations, the non-market-access concerns of the commission were successively peeled away from its global government agenda. In the run-up to the Doha ministerial, the commission dropped the demand for the inclusion of labor and social standards. At Doha, it had to accept a drastically watered-down negotiating mandate on trade and environment, which only called for a possible reconciliation of conflicting demands of international trade agreements with international environmental agreements. Particularly, it failed to establish its cherished "precautionary principle" as a basis for trade measures. At Cancún, the commission had to give up competition and investment as a possible negotiation topic. Under the pressure from developing countries and some developed countries such as the United States, Canada, and Australia, the global governance agenda was stripped of all global governance elements. There was simply no global demand for global governance. At the expense of its own pharmaceutical industry, the European Union managed to craft a compromise on the relaxation of patent protection in developing countries, but it failed to win any concessions in return. The reason that the global governance agenda had so little resonance was that its central tenets, that is the new trade-related issues such as social standards, environment, competition, and investment, met with stiff resistance from developing countries, the principal beneficiaries of the new round. Despite all the rhetoric extolling global governance, the real lesson of Cancún was that market access was still king, and that agriculture remained the major stumbling block.[17]

Of course, Germany alone cannot be blamed for the failed negotiating strategy of the commission. But if the lead member state for market access-based liberalization drops out, the liberalizing thrust of EU trade policy as a whole will be weakened. Thus, Germany's departure from its traditional market access-based approach did facilitate the commission's global governance approach to trade. In the run-up to the Doha meeting, for instance, Germany's reticence and uncritical acceptance of the development rhetoric, which was very much a product of the position of the Aid and Development Ministry, contributed to the lack of emphasis on market opening in advanced developing countries (Brazil, India) and encouraged the recalcitrance of these countries to offer any concessions on market access. It also led to concessions on intellectual property rights for pharmaceuticals to third-country providers without receiving reciprocal concessions from them. Germany actually sacrificed the interests of its pharmaceutical industry for a failed commission strategy that sought to buy off developing countries' demands on agricultural market liberalization for giving up patent protection on pharmaceuticals. Germany also supported the commission's global governance agenda, centered on negotiating rules on investment and competition, although the market-access potential of such rules was minimal, and their viability in light of opposition from developing countries small. Here, the German tendency to support a system of rules for the sake of rules was evident, and the political and market-access based implications were never fully articulated. The same may be said about pushing environmental standards, in particular the precautionary principle pursued by the commission, which eventually fell by the wayside because of opposition by developing countries and developed countries such as the United States and Australia.

The consequences of decline

The paradigm of market access-based multilateral liberalization thus has been significantly watered down, and the profile of German trade strategy has lost all its characteristic liberal thrust. Although liberal trade ideology and rhetoric are still dominant in the abstract, its recurrent ritualistic chant rather glosses over the fact that German trade policy has become a shopping bag of conflicting demands, ranging from market opening to consumer protection to animal welfare. Germany will support a lot of things, but it will leave to others or to events what outcome will prevail. This "hodge-podge" approach to trade policy makes Germany a congenial partner for the commission.

All factors identified here, such as the priority of European integration, the "French connection," the decline of the Economics Ministry, the loss of an independent monetary policy as a lever over trade issues, and the pressures of the antiglobalization movement have lowered Germany's profile in trade policy. The question is, does it matter? The answer must be affirmative. Although there is certainly a need to discuss cross-cutting issues such as trade, labor, and environmental standards and to coordinate conflicting objectives between different policy fields, trade policy at its core remains centered on market-access issues.[18] The inability to set priorities accordingly has robbed Germany of a trade-policy profile of its own and thus of its traditional role as a promoter of trade liberalization in the policy concert of EU member states. This situation has created a void that is filled by member states such as France and its southern allies, who are more reluctant about liberalization, and by commission bureaucrats who are prone to advocate abstract concepts of global governance.

The result of Germany's lack of a trade-policy focus is an excessive deference to Brussels, a surprising fact, considering its size and its substantial trading and market-opening interests and its traditional role as a trade liberalizer. This is also in marked contrast to other member states such as France, Britain, and even small countries such as the Netherlands and Sweden. Deference to Brussels is most evident in the lack of a proactive agenda and the reluctance to forge an alliance with like-minded states to influence commission agenda-setting. As long as there are no major foreign-policy issues with a French interest at stake, Germany is the perfectly docile member state. That has consequences. The commission can count on Germany as a reliable a priori supporter for whatever compromise package the commission devises. The absence of German profile thus corresponds to the lowest-common-denominator strategies that inevitably dominate Brussels policy making.

Germany's deference, however, may be a double-edged sword for the commission. It undoubtedly does come in handy when the commission pursues a hybrid strategy that utilizes market-opening as only one element in a global governance strategy. But, because such a strategy is not necessarily viable, as the Cancún ministerial has shown, the commission may want to have a Germany that plays its more traditional role as an advocate of pure trade liberalization. This is particularly true if it needs counterweights to the more protectionist forces in the European Union, especially on agriculture, such as France. The lesson here is that German deference to Brussels disturbs the equilibrium in EU trade policymaking. When the linchpin of the liberal camp drops out, the options available to EU policy makers are diminished. EU trade policy will not only be less liberal, it will be less constructive in terms of forging bargains that are viable in the world trading system.

The future of German trade policy: the return of market access-based liberalization?

Arguably, the demise of German trade policy was as much the result of political personnel as of the political context of trade policy making. With Wolfgang Clement's appointment as "Super" minister for economics and labor affairs, international economic issues seem to have received new attention from the top of the ministry. As a governor of North Rhine-Westphalia, Clement had taken an active interest in relations with the neighboring Netherlands and had learned firsthand what globalization meant for the businesses of his state. Clement's concerns thus focused on the competitiveness of the German businesses, rather than on issues of global governance. On the state secretary level, Alfred Tacke, a close associate of Chancellor Schröder, was appointed in 2000 as "sherpa" for G-7 and G-8 summits, representing the first step in restoring the standing of the Economics Ministry. Under Clement, Tacke also assumed responsibility for trade policy. In addition, the Greens had a liberalizing impact on agricultural policy: by shifting subsidies from increasing production to supporting quality agricultural production ("decoupling"), German agricultural policy became less protectionist. The conflicts between the Economics Ministry and Agricultural Ministry now seem to be history. Both Tacke and Clement took an active interest in the discussion in the run-up to the Cancún ministerial. Although they did not explicitly disavow global governance issues, they were most interested in helping to achieve a constructive outcome of the Cancún meeting. Unlike his predecessor, Müller, Clement (and Tacke) actively concerned themselves with the crucial issues on the trade agenda and attended the Cancún meeting. Renate Künast also took a constructive approach to the WTO negotiations. Prior to the Cancún meeting, Clement tried to block, albeit unsuccessfully, Heidi Wieczorek-Zeul's participation in the meeting, because her relentless beating of the drum for development issues (particularly her plans for a "cotton-day rally") was seen as counterproductive to reaching a consensus at Cancún. This was the first indication that the timid stance of the ministry toward non-trade interests would change. But even more crucial was that the behavior of civil society groups at the tumultuous and chaotic meeting served as a wake-up call for Clement and Tacke. They came away with the impression that many NGOs played a rather destructive role, particularly in manipulating the strategies of some developing countries, and that the organizations' main objective was to deal a lethal blow to the negotiations. According to sources close to the minister, Clement was planning to depart Cancún even before the Mexican foreign minister, Luis Ernesto Derbez, declared the meeting deadlocked.

Although the media heralded the Cancún meeting as the beginning of a new era, the Cancún meeting may have signified a turning point in the influence of the civil society sector. For senior German policy makers, NGOs had their day in court in Cancún, and the groups were found wanting in terms of making a contribution. After all the mist had cleared away, it became clear to German policy makers that at the core of the Doha Development Round were still difficult market-access issues of both developed and developing countries, particularly in agriculture. This attitude was fully shared by private-sector actors such as BDI. There are indications that this development is pushing German policy makers to their more traditional role as guardians of market access in multilateral negotiations. At Cancún, Germany quietly pushed for the removal of investment and competition as negotiating items. And it also signaled that it could live with the termination of agricultural export subsidies, thus departing from solidarity with France and leaving behind the old vestiges of German agricultural protectionism.

In sum, German trade policy under the Red–Green government was characterized by neglect for trade issues in general, the continued weakness of the Economics Ministry, and the impact of the antiglobalization forces in the Green party and the left-wing of the Social Democratic Party. This situation allowed once-marginal actors, such as the Development Ministry and the Environmental Ministry, to play lead roles. Germany also remained passive vis-à-vis the EU Commission and accommodating toward France. While Germany's trade performance continued to show its traditional strength, the victim of neglect was Germany's liberal policy leadership in the European Union, a process that had already begun under the Kohl government.

German behavior at Cancún and the appointment of Wolfgang Clement as economics minister may signal a revival of its traditional leadership role. However, this revival is not due to a strategic decision based on a strong consensus, but it is very much dependent on personalities. The departure of State Secretary Tacke, one of the promoters of a revival, to the private sector in September 2004, weakened the personnel and institutional constellation that has been behind the revival. The future course of German trade policy making thus remains uncertain.

Acknowledgment

This chapter is based on extensive interviews with trade officials from Germany and elsewhere and representatives of business associations and nongovernmental organizations. The chapter extends the arguments of a previous paper, German Trade Policy: An Oxymoron? which will be published in Wyn Grant and Dominic Kelly, eds, *The Politics of International Trade in the 21st Century: Actors, Issues, and Regional Dynamics* (New York: Palgrave Macmillan, 2005).

Notes

1 Bundesministerium für Wirtschaft und Arbeit, *Handelsstatisken Außenwirtschaf 2003t*. Available at: http://www.bmwi.de/textonly/Homepage/Politikfelder/Au%DFenwirtscha

2 Sophie Meunier, "Trade Policy and Political Legitimacy in the European Union," *Comparative European Politics*, 1: 1 (2003): 67–90.

3 William A. Dymond and Michael M. Hart "Post-Modern Trade Policy," *Journal of World Trade*, 34: 3 (2000): 21–38.

4 Alan S. Milward, with the assistance of George Brennan and Federico Romero, *The European Rescue of the Nation-State* (Berkeley: University of California Press, 1992), pp. 144–47.

5 See Knut Kirste, Internationale Wirtschafts- und Handelsbeziehungen Japans, der USA und der Bundesrepublik Deutschland. DFG-Projekt "Zivilmächte," Fallstudie, University of Trier. Available at: http://www.deutsche-aussenpolitik.de/resources/conferences/wirt.pdf. Accessed December 12, 2004.

6 Throughout this chapter, we will refer to the ministry as simply the Economics Ministry.

7 Thomas R. Howell, "Germany," *Conflict Among Nations: Trade Policies in the 1990s*, Thomas R. Howell *et al.*, eds (Boulder: Westview Press, 1992), p. 154.

8 Howell, *Conflict Among Nations* (see note 7), p. 188.

9 The best example of this relationship was the lack of support that BDI gave the German pharmaceutical sector in protecting patent rights under the renegotiating of the TRIPS agreement in the current Doha round.

10 The best example of this behavior is the support that BDI has given to pursuing issues of competition and investment in the Doha round of trade negotiations, although their market access potential was not well articulated and was likely to provoke resistance from developing countries. See A. Böhmer and G. Glania, The Doha Development Round: Reintegrating Business Interests into the Agenda—WTO Negotiations from a German Industry Perspective," *Beiträge zum Transnationalen Wirtschaftsrecht*, No. 15, 2003. Available at: www.telc.uni-halle.de

11 Robert D. Putnam and C. Randall Henning, "The Bonn Summit of 1978: A Case Study in Coordination," *Can Nations Agree? Issues in International Economic Cooperation*, Richard N. Cooper *et al.*, eds (Washington, DC: Brookings Institution Press, 1989), pp. 12–118.

12 See Florian Lütticken, "Deutsche und Spanische Außenhandelspolitik im Rahmen der Uruguay-Runde des GATT," MA thesis, University of Trier, p. 7.

13 I. M. Destler and Peter J. Balint, *The New Politics of American Trade: Trade, Labor, and the Environment* (Washington, DC: Institute for International Economics, 1999).

14 See H. Höhn, ed., "Globalisierung der Weltwirtschaft—Herausforderungen und Antworten. Eine Dokumentation in Auszuegen aus dem Schlussbericht der Enquete-Kommission des Deutschen Bundestages," *Aus Politik und Zeitgeschichte*, B05/2003: 35–46.

15 Andreas Falke, "New Thinking? Außenhandelspolitik der USA im Licht der neuen Bedrohung," *Weltmacht vor neuer Bedrohung. Die Bush Administration und die US-Außenpolitik nach dem Angriff auf Amerika*, Werner Kremp and Jürgen Wilzewski, eds (Trier: Wissenschaftlicher Verlag, 2003), pp. 157–84; and "EU–US Trade Relations in the Doha Development Round: Market Access versus a post-Modern Trade Policy agenda," *European Foreign Affairs Review*, 10: 5 (fall 2005): 339–57.

16 See Klaus. Günter Deutsch, "The EU: Contending for Leadership," *The World Trade Organisation Millennium Round: Freer Trade in the Twenty-First Century*, Klaus Günter Deutsch and Bernhard Speyer, eds (London: Routledge, 2001), pp. 35–47.

17 Jagdish N. Bhagwati, "Don't Cry for Cancún," *Foreign Affairs*, 83: 1 (January/February 2004).

18 For a strong theoretical argument along these lines, see Kent Jones, "The WTO core agreement, non-trade issues and institutional integrity," *World Trade Review*, 1: 3 (2003): 257–76.

13
Germany and the International Financial Order
Reinhard Wolf

Introduction

In the wake of the Mexican crisis of 1995, the G-7 countries and the International Monetary Fund (IMF) first initiated policy debates on rebuilding the world's financial architecture. While these deliberations were still going on, a sequence of even graver and more surprising currency crashes underlined the need for reforming both national and global capital markets. Southeast Asian economies, which had recently been praised for both high growth rates and sound fundamentals, suddenly experienced rapid capital outflows that resulted in massive depreciations. Now, it was not only emerging markets in distant continents that would be affected, nor only international investors who had been willing to place risky financial bets; rather, the sequence of crises now started to threaten the very hub of global finance in New York. Heavy involvement of US banks in South Korea and the near collapse of the US hedge fund LTCM during the Russian crises of 1998 proved that nobody was immune against the risk of malign contagion.

As one of the three largest economies with one of the most important international currencies, Germany had to play an important role in the ensuing reform process. For Berlin, a prominent say in this policy debate seemed even more logical when the specific nature of the issue area was taken into account. After all, force is completely dysfunctional in the current world of international finance, and unilateral initiatives hardly look more promising given the integrated nature of globalized capital markets. Heavy-handed measures in traditional realpolitik style were out of the question. Instead, the situation called for persuasion and compromise in multilateral settings. Thus, reorganization of global financial governance appeared almost an ideal opportunity for the successful application of the very procedures and norms that defined the Federal Republic's foreign policy identity.

As the following pages will show, however, German authorities failed to capitalize on this opportunity by exerting a distinct influence on the reforms

of the global monetary order(s). During the final days of the Kohl administration, the Federal Republic displayed little initiative and largely engaged in
defensive reactions against apparent Anglo-Saxon generosity concerning
IMF bail outs and debt relief for poor countries. The incoming Gerhard
Schröder administration initially changed that pattern by surprising its
international partners with three major initiatives. Two of them indicated a
new self-confidence, if not even the assertiveness some pundits had
predicted in the wake of unification. Yet, when Berlin's proposals for
enhanced monetary cooperation and a new IMF chief were thwarted, the
administration quickly retreated to a more conventional posture. Due to
these failures, and following the discontinuation of the Deutsche Mark,
Germany's influence further receded. At the time of this writing, the Federal
Republic no longer plays the prominent role in managing the global
monetary architecture it did during the final decades of the last century.

New ambitions

Within 13 months after its inauguration, the Schröder administration
embarked on three new initiatives. The incoming treasury secretary (and
chairman of the Social Democratic Party, or SPD), Oskar Lafontaine, resur-
rected the idea of target zones for the world's major currencies; the chancellor
himself used the German G-7 presidency to announce an upgraded plan for
the debt-relief initiative for the heavily indebted poor countries (HIPC); and
the new coalition government, above all Schröder himself, tried to capitalize
on the departure of the IMF's managing director, Michel Camdessus, by
pushing a German national on the top position in the world of global
finance. Although Germany's HIPC proposal was highly appreciated for its
greater generosity, Schröder's unprecedented assertiveness in getting a
German placed at the head of a first-rate international organization almost
ended with the same kind of embarrassing climb-down that Lafontaine's
reform initiative brought about.

Initially, Lafontaine and his advisors Heiner Flassbeck and Wolfgang Filc
aimed at applying the model of the European exchange rate mechanism
(ERM) to global cooperation. Even before taking office, the incoming
treasury secretary started to voice his ideas about establishing similar target
zones for the euro, the US dollar and the yen. According to this proposal,
financial leaders were to agree on relative exchange rates that reflected
economic fundamentals, such as differences in inflation and interest rates.
Exchange rates would have been permitted to float around the approved
target rates within agreed currency bands. Once they threatened to leave
these zones, it would be left to central banks and finance ministers to reign
in markets. By hints about possible market interventions, actual interventions
(that is, buying depreciating currencies), and by adjusting interest rates,
speculative attacks should have been either deterred or defeated.[1]

The whole idea was stillborn. Brandished as an exercise in diplomatic "hara-kiri,"[2] the initiative testified above all to Lafontaine's characteristic overconfidence in his political and economic competences. To be sure, the new finance minister could claim some support for his proposal among both his colleagues and professional economists. French and Japanese officials had hinted their approval for closer coordination of macroeconomic policies while renowned figures in the world of international finance, such as the former chairman of the US Federal Reserve, Paul Volcker, and John Williamson of the Institute of International Economics, had put forward similar, if not even more ambitious, proposals for target zones.

However, as soon as it had been voiced, the target zone proposal met unqualified resistance from almost all relevant quarters: from US decision makers, German bankers, the Bundesbank, the European Central Bank (ECB), and the international financial press.[3] Even within the office of the German chancellor, doubts were expressed as to the practicality of Lafontaine's ideas.[4] US Treasury Secretary Robert Rubin made it clear that, during an economic downturn, US authorities would hardly raise interest rates just to keep the dollar within a proscribed exchange rate band.[5] ECB board member Sirka Hämäläinen publicly labeled the target zone initiative "a very dangerous idea" which would imply "enormous adjustment costs" for the involved currency areas.[6] The German council of economic advisors (*Sachverständigenrat*) opined that Lafontaine's plans "should be laid to rest as soon as possible."[7] In arguing that currency interventions would compromise central banks' autonomy in combating inflation, the advisors clearly echoed the concerns of the Bundesbank leadership. Given the fact that, at the very time of his target zone initiative, Lafontaine also pressured the Bundesbank to lower interest rates, it should not have come as a surprise that Bundesbank opposition was firm and unanimous. But when even French Treasury Secretary Dominique Strauss-Kahn publicly started to question the efficacy of target zones, Lafontaine found himself strangely isolated at the first G-7 meeting he was supposed to chair.[8] Soon afterward, Lafontaine left the treasury and stepped down as party chairman. His successor, Hans Eichel, and his new team quickly reverted to more traditional policies.[9]

Lafontaine's sudden departure, however, did not put an end to the Schröder government's energetic efforts to leave its mark on the evolving architecture of international finance. Less than a year later, the chancellor himself led another campaign, this time to install a German on the commanding post of global economic governance. In this instance, the driving force behind the administration's zeal was not an idiosyncratic diagnosis for the world's susceptibility for currency crises but a mere quest for greater international status. When Camdessus stepped down as managing director, the IMF's top position had been occupied by a French national for 32 of the last 37 years. For a new chancellor who had voiced his disinclination early on to accept traditional German self-constraints, this vacancy presented a tempting opportunity to display his ability to promote his country's interests and prestige. Because the IMF's top position traditionally goes to European, Schröder and his team apparently assumed that preempting other European candidacies would suffice to ensure the eventual acceptance of Berlin's leader of choice, Caio Koch-Weser, a state secretary in the treasury. Thus, instead of embarking on a careful behind-the-scenes campaign for building a global consensus, the administration publicly announced the name of its candidate before the Clinton administration and major European governments had signaled their support for Koch-Weser. While fellow EU members reluctantly toed into line and officially backed the German nominee, the US government bluntly questioned the competence of Schröder's candidate.[10] After an unprecedented standoff in the IMF's executive board, Berlin had to withdraw Koch-Weser and resort to nominating the only available German with a chance of US approval. Eventually, the Red–Green government succeeded in getting a German accepted as managing director. However, it was a victory of sorts: after all, the appointed person, Horst Köhler, was a card-carrying member of the Christian Democratic Union who had long served Schröder's conservative predecessor, Kohl, as the "Sherpa" for the G-7 meetings.[11] The Schröder administration thus barely avoided yet another humiliating climbdown. Köhler's eventual appointment could hardly be regarded as proof of Berlin's acceptance as an international heavyweight that had successfully shed the inhibitions of a burdened past.

It was only in the field of debt relief where the Schröder administration's break with its predecessor's policies registered international success. The outgoing Kohl administration had shown little enthusiasm for far-reaching cancellation of debt owed by the HIPCs. Specifically, it had prevented the IMF from selling part of its gold reserves to finance its contribution to the HIPC initiative.[12] The Schröder government reversed this hesitant course in the run-up to the Cologne G-7 summit. It agreed to the use of the IMF's reserves and also proposed both to widen the criteria for eligible debtor states and to speed up the process for the countries included. Moreover, to ease the financial strains of the indebted poor countries, Berlin was also willing to offer a greater national contribution. It cancelled all debts owed by HIPC countries that had resulted from German development loans, stepped up its contribution to relief funds of IMF and the World Bank, and forgave a larger share of loans in the Paris club of sovereign creditors.[13] In the final result, adoption of the Cologne Debt Initiative by the other G-7 countries could be seen as one of those few instances where Germany, albeit in concert with others, successfully acted as an international leader.[14]

Back to "Normal"

With Lafontaine and his team gone, German officials once again argued for cautious adjustments of the global financial architecture.[15] The official treasury position soon fell back in line with the "ordoliberal" outlook that had always guided the Bundesbank's policy.[16] According to this view, free capital markets are a cure rather than a disease. As Lafontaine's successor, Hans Eichel put it: "Participation in international trade and capital movements offers all countries great opportunities for increased growth and employment."[17] Safeguarding this potential, a treasury spokesperson described it as "the primary goal of German economic and financial politics."[18] Of course, treasury and Bundesbank officials admitted that liberalized capital markets entailed some risks of severe financial crises. Yet, according to their analysis, crashes experienced by emerging markets could hardly be considered an inevitable consequence of global financial integration. Although aggravated by irrational herding behavior of investors, the recent crises, it was claimed, primarily resulted from fundamentals caused by inappropriate national policies: "Crises prevention is primarily the responsibility of individual countries. As a matter of fact, crises stem from deficiencies in national economic policies."[19] Such an outlook clearly implied that reforms of the international financial architecture should focus on improving rather than restraining the market mechanism.[20]

Due to this renewed trust in financial markets, the treasury and Bundesbank stressed above all the importance of proper reforms in emerging markets. To this end, both institutions called for the consequent implementation of standards, codes, and core principles that G-7 and IMF members had agreed or reinforced in the wake of the preceding financial crises.

Apart from reemphasizing the importance of sound macroeconomic policies, these regulations primarily focused on improving the stability and transparency of national financial sectors for all kinds of products and transactions. By carefully observing such codices, emerging markets were expected to reduce their vulnerability to sudden financial flows so they could be fully reintegrated into global capital markets.[21] Hence, proper "sequencing" of domestic reforms and capital account liberalization was considered key to successful growth policies.[22]

As a consequence, German officials saw the proper role of international financial institutions (IFIs), such as the IMF, chiefly as mechanisms for encouraging and improving the observance of these regulations. By offering its advice to national authorities, issuing "Reports on the Observation of Standards and Codes" (ROSC) and by analyzing the resilience of national capital markets with its new "Financial Sector Assessment Program" (FSAP), the IMF was meant to be refocused from crisis management to the prevention of future crises.[23] This emphasis on international supervision also motivated German support for establishing a new overarching coordination body—the Financial Stability Forum (FSF). When British Chancellor of the Exchequer Gordon Brown had proposed the creation of an institution to supervise global financial regulations, both the Bundesbank and the Kohl government had been first opposed to setting up yet another IFI. To mitigate such concerns, the G-7 settled on a compromise, according to which the outgoing Bundesbank president, Hans Tietmeyer was charged with reviewing the global interplay and effectiveness of financial regulations.[24] On the basis of his assessment Tietmeyer suggested setting up a new forum that would assemble representatives from the G-10 central banks, the global IFIs, and the most important international regulators. By replacing numerous ad hoc bodies with regular discussions among all major regulating actors, the FSF was expected to substantially improve the coordination and implementation of relevant codices.[25] Hence, it fitted well with the German priority on crisis prevention through domestic reforms reinforced by enhanced international surveillance. German authorities, the treasury in particular, actively pursued this approach by deftly promoting a broad agreement on standards and codes that served the interests of both private and public actors.

Crisis management, on the other hand, was accorded a far lower priority by German authorities. Bundesbank and treasury officials were particularly anxious to prevent additional rescue operations on the scale of the Mexican bailout of 1995. At the height of this crisis, US authorities cajoled the IMF leadership into assembling a huge loan that enabled Mexico to avoid defaulting on billions of so-called teso bonos, or bonds denominated in pesos but pegged to the US dollar, owned primarily by American investors.[26] According to Tietmeyer, the "world's most influential decrier of moral hazard,"[27] massive bailouts suffered from the typical problem of all interventionist policies: they induced private investors to anticipate the same kind of intervention in similar circumstances. In the case of big IMF loans, interventionist policies entailed the risk that investors started to assume that the IMF would always provide enough money to repay foreign investors. With their risks covered by public money, the latter would become too willing to heavily invest in high-risk markets.[28]

In the wake of yet more large rescue packages for the crisis-stricken Asian and Russian economies, German authorities were determined to constrain both future IMF largesse and US discretion. To this end, they insisted on clear rules that would involve the private sector in any rescue packages, while clearly limiting the IMF's financial contribution. The fund's loans should play merely a "catalytic" role for mobilizing private money. By insisting on general ceilings for official contributions, Bundesbank and treasury representatives hoped to achieve two purposes at the same time: on one hand, agreements on binding rules that limited the IFIs' share to a certain percentage of the affected country's quota would have curbed US leeway for cajoling the IFIs into large packages tailored to Wall Street's needs; on the other, such general regulations would have amounted to an advance notification to private investors that they could not escape paying their full share if they wanted to avoid their debtor's default.[29]

Consequently, the Germans favored a "rule-based approach"[30] to strengthen the "objectivity and political independence"[31] of IMF lending policies. They criticized the notion that the IMF might be turned into an international "lender of last resort" with no effective upper ceiling for official rescue packages.[32] To forestall such "mission creep," German authorities voiced their opposition to increasing the fund's resources: "The IMF possesses adequate liquidity. Providing the IMF with overabundant resources might give rise to the expectation of large-scale financing packages and thus run counter to our efforts to involve the private sector."[33] For similar reasons, Germany also rejected the US proposal to create a large new fund facility for protecting healthy economies from the risk of crisis contagion, the so-called contingent credit line.[34] Even after the United States succeeded in getting its proposal accepted by the G-7 and the IMF's board, the German finance minister continued to advocate the early abolishment of the contingent credit line[35] until the United States eventually gave in.[36]

Instead of offering additional public resources to crisis-stricken countries and their creditors, Berlin and Frankfurt supported legal reforms that aimed at promoting private-sector involvement. Specifically, the German representatives backed an increasing use of collective action clauses that facilitated bond-holders' decision making in the face of imminent government default.

More controversially, German authorities also welcomed proposals for establishing a Sovereign Debt Restructuring Mechanism to avoid the costs of chaotic government default. Modeled after national insolvency procedures, this mechanism is supposed to ensure an efficient and balanced handling of severe debt crises. On activation, outflow of capital (including official debt service) would be halted so that an impartial debt administrator could help to negotiate an orderly restructuring agreement. As its proponents argue, such a standstill followed by negotiations should prevent the costs of financial panics and ensure an equitable involvement of all types of creditors. The latter aspect made it particular attractive for German authorities.[37] Backing by European authorities, however, did not suffice to overcome opposition from private banks, potential debtors, and the US administration.[38]

Germany was more successful in its efforts to impede international money laundering and in its defense of the professed interests of smaller firms during the negotiations for the second Basel accord concerning capital adequacy standards for international banks. In order to contain systemic risks in the banking sector, Basel I obliged the international banks to hedge their risks by withholding reserve capital amounting to 8 percent of each loan. The planned reform of Basel I aimed at enhancing the effectiveness and fairness of this global standard. To that end, banks shall be enabled to adjust their level of reserves to the individual credit worthiness of their various debtors. However, adoption of the original proposals might have increased interest rates for the great number of smaller German firms, as most of them lacked a debtor rating by an external rating agency. Confronted with this problem, Schröder (in quite characteristic fashion) immediately reacted with a public announcement to veto a Basel II accord.[39] In the end, the accord was adjusted to the demands of small firms, primarily by having small loans included in the banks' retail portfolios, which are considered to bear a lower standard credit risk.[40] With regard to the international crusade against money laundering, Germany partly acted as a frontrunner by introducing more stringent regulations, which were later adopted by other members of the G-7 Financial Action Task Force. Moreover, Berlin was instrumental in getting other states to accept more effective measures against offshore finance centers.[41]

In both cases, German negotiating efforts were enhanced by significant shifts in the US stance. In the final phase of the Basel negotiations, many US banks suddenly voiced significant concerns that partly echoed those of their German counterparts.[42] In the case of moves against money laundering in offshore finance centers, US willingness to act was greatly enhanced by the increased urgency that September 11 stimulated in the fight against international terrorism.

Overall, German authorities clearly faced an increasingly dominant United States that paid less and less respect to Berlin's preferences. With regard to regulations for private financial markets, German influence had always been eclipsed by American and British decision makers representing much deeper markets. Concerning official coordination within the most prominent IFIs, Germany's loss in standing is of more recent origin. Whereas in the preceding decades the Germans used to be undisputed number two in global monetary and currency affairs, as the century came to a close they were declining to an average G-7 member.[43] This loss of influence was due to a number of reasons, among them political mistakes, but also institutional and personnel changes for which Berlin could hardly be blamed. To be sure, Lafontaine's ill-fated target zone initiative and Berlin's awkward push for a German IMF head certainly did not improve the international prestige of the Red–Green government,[44] and, in the sensitive field of international finance, this loss of professional reputation did not count for little. Moreover, it was reinforced by the exit of Bundesbank President Hans Tietmeyer, who had managed to win the great respect and confidence of his international colleagues, above all among top officials in Washington.[45] However, the prime factor compromising German influence is to be seen in the introduction of the euro. The replacement of the deutsche Mark, and by implication, of the deutsche Mark zone, transformed the position of Bundesbank president from a key global decision maker to a board member of the ECB. In this particular case, European integration clearly brought about a net decline of German influence.

In light of Germany's declining role, it was hardly surprising that Berlin was reluctant to see its influence further restrained by quota changes at the expense of the European IMF members. Despite all the rhetorical support for an increased voice for developing countries, German officials unequivocally hold on to the principle that quotas should reflect a country's relative economic weight. Thus, while they favored more basic votes for Third World states (which would have slightly increased their power relative to the industrial countries), they unambiguously rejected proposals to consolidate Euro country quotas to a single quota for the Economic and Monetary Union.[46] At the time of this writing, an integrated European representation is still seen as a project for the more distant future.[47]

Financing development

In the field of multilateral financing of development, German authorities adopted the prevailing view that the division of labor between the IMF and the World Bank should be improved. In practical terms this arrangement meant that, from the German point of view, social-policy issues and efforts to reduce poverty should be largely left to the World Bank.[48] Nevertheless, German representatives declined US proposals to focus the IMF exclusively on containing regional or global currency crises. Instead, they insisted that the fund should remain active in all of its member states, not just by supervising policies and giving advice but also by offering financial resources to countries in need. In this respect, Berlin clearly rejected the recommendations of the Meltzer Commission, which practically called for a leaner fund and for an end to IMF loans to the poorest countries. German authorities, on the contrary, stressed the importance of strong IFIs[49] and continued to insist on maintaining the IMF's Poverty Reduction and Growth Facility for the benefit of the poorest member states.[50] However, Berlin partly shared the concerns of those politicians and experts who criticized both the IMF and the World Bank for micromanaging development processes by attaching too detailed and intrusive conditions to the loans they offered to countries in need. From the German point of view, such remote control impeded country ownership of the programmes that the IFIs proposed. Therefore, Berlin echoed demands that conditionality should be streamlined and focused.[51]

Concerning additional funds for debt relief and development, Berlin favored some kind of new international tax. Due to its ongoing budgetary problems and widespread calls for further tax reductions, the Schröder government saw little leeway for greater national contributions. Instead it publicly supported discussions on innovative tax schemes which would make use of international transactions, such as international flights or arms exports. In a recent speech to the Davos World Economic Forum, the Chancellor even expressed some sympathy for the anathema of the global financial elites: a tax on international financial transactions. This rather peculiar initiative, however, only confirmed how much Germany's role in the reform of the world financial order had been declining. Given the well-known opposition of practically all relevant actors, including Schröder's own treasury and central bank, most observers did not regard it as a serious move. Instead, they interpreted the tax proposal above all as a half-hearted effort, which was only meant to please French President Chirac who had earlier voiced similar ideas.[52]

Conclusion: the sources of German conduct

Looking back at the lengthy international debates on the reform of the world's financial order,[53] it seems fair to say that Germany largely followed a consistent policy line that stressed the welfare-enhancing potential of well-regulated private competition. During all those years, the Bundesbank unflinchingly adhered to the neoclassical view, according to which sound money, healthy budgets, orderly liberalization, and clearly restricted public intervention provide the best policy mix for long-term growth. The treasury leadership briefly argued for a more active role of the official sector yet quickly closed ranks again with Frankfurt once the Lafontaine interlude was over. In the arcane field of international finance, experts in the bureaucracy had no difficulty in steering the state ship back into the mainstream of economic thinking. Only in the field of development finance and with regard to debt relief did the redistributional penchant of the Red–Green coalition leave a visible trace. The development ministry in particular took a more unorthodox position by stressing active solidarity with the poor, just as it was expected to do by the governing parties' activists. Ambitious reform proposals like the Tobin tax that are so dear to many globalization critics, however, did not meet significant support within the administration.

Frustrated as they may have been, grassroot activists may have found some consolation in the fact that the Federal Republic's financial sector hardly faired better. Whereas domestic-oriented institutions succeeded in making German negotiators pursue a Basel II accord more in line with the interests of smaller enterprises and local banks (if not necessarily with the interests of the economy as a whole), the financial sector utterly failed in changing the official stance on managing sovereign default. In spite of the banking community's vehement opposition against the Sovereign Debt Restructuring Mechanism, German authorities continued to push for this reform. It is only the US veto that so far has saved the private sector's interests.

By and large then, global financial policy can be considered as one of those issue areas where the Red–Green coalition stressed continuity over a new and distinct approach. It did not pursue some kind of "deutscher Weg" and soon realized that it was little use trying to face the US "auf gleicher Augenhöhe" (on an equal level) as a "partner in leadership"—to use a phrase coined by former president George H. Bush. Berlin's policy stances were primarily shaped by experts in the treasury and the Bundesbank who regarded the world financial order, in all its different facets, above all as a global public good in need of concerted and coordinated nurturing. From this perspective, there was neither much need nor much use for self-serving German initiatives. Thus, Germany's most distinct policy stances with regard to international financial issues resulted not so much from the pursuit of specific German interests but from particular ideas concerning the proper workings of international markets.

Acknowledgment

The author would like to thank Hanns Maull, Franz Neueder, Stefan Schirm, and Bernhard Speyer for their useful comments. As always, he claims responsibility for all remaining errors and omissions.

Notes

1 Heiner Flassbeck, "Wanted: An International Exchange Rate Regime. The Missed Lesson of the Financial Crisis," *International Politics and Society*, 3 (2000), pp. 282–91. Wolfgang Filc, *Gefahr für unseren Wohlstand. Wie Finanzmarktkrisen die Weltwirtschaft bedrohen* (Frankfurt: Eichborn, 2001), pp. 203–20.

2 Engelen, Klaus C., "Die neue Finanzwelt wird von ÇG1 und Freunden' regiert," *Handelsblatt*, October 1, 1999.

3 Filc, *Gefahr für unseren Wohlstand* (see note 1), pp. 204, 215.

4 "Schröder will G7-Gipfel im Kanzleramt planen," *Süddeutsche Zeitung*, November 16, 1998.

5 *Süddeutsche Zeitung* (see note 4); Flassbeck, *International Politics and Society* (see note 1).

6 "Warnung vor Wechselkurs-Zielzonen," *Frankfurter Allgemeine Zeitung*, October 28, 1998.

7 "Gegen Wechselkurs-Zielzonen und voreilige Zinssenkungen," *Handelsblatt*, November 19, 1998.

8 Gerhard Hennemann, "Der Einsame vom Petersberg," *Süddeutsche Zeitung*, February 20–21, 1999.

9 In the weeks before, Lafontaine tried to mitigate criticism by softening his original target zone ideas to a mere scheme for "flexible stability of exchange rates." One of his close confidants claimed that it had never been intended to straitjacket exchange rates or to subordinate US economic policy to the defense of target zones. According to Filc, *Gefahr für unseren Wohlstand* (see note 1), pp. 214–15, Lafontaine's near-term ambitions were limited to setting up a G-7 group that would have gathered, assessed, and interpreted currency market data. How such a less-stringent mechanism could have gained any credibility in the eyes of speculators remains a moot point. Presumably, markets soon would have tested the sincerity and resolve behind public "interpretations."

10 It is hard to tell if candidate Koch-Weser for his part improved his chances by publicly reproaching the US administration for its inadequate implementation of measures that had been agreed upon to reform the global financial architecture. See "Eichel legt sich in Tokio mit US-Finanzminister an," *Handelsblatt*, January 24, 2000.

11 Nikolaus Blome and Andreas Middel, "Schröder darf mit einem neuen IWF-Kandidaten aufwarten," *Die Welt*, March 14, 2000; Claus Hulverscheidt and Thomas Klau, "EU startet Werbefeldzug für IWF-Kandidaten," *Financial Times Deutschland*, March 14, 2000.

12   "Gläubiger schnüren gemeinsames Paket zur Entlastung hochverschuldeter Länder," *Süddeutsche Zeitung,* September 30, 1996; Roland Bunzenthal, "Briten wollen Gas geben—Franzosen bremsen," *Frankfurter Rundschau,* March 5, 1999.

13   "Relieving debt," *Financial Times,* January 22, 1999; "Bundesministerium der Finanzen, Die Kölner Schuldeninitiative—Umsetzung, Auswirkungen und Beitrag Deutschlands," Monatsbericht, September 2001, pp. 61–66. Available at: http://www.bundesfinanzministerium.de/Anlage8182/Die-Koelner-Schuldeninitiative.pdf.pdf. Accessed January 9, 2005.

14   John J. Kirton, "The Dynamics of G7 Leadership in Crisis Response and System Reconstruction," Shaping a New International Financial System. Challenges of Governance in a Globalizing World, Karl Kaiser, John J. Kirton, and Joseph P. Daniels, eds (Aldershot: Ashgate, 2000), pp. 65–93.

15   According to market-skeptic critics, continuity with the Kohl administration amounted to nothing less than a complete avoidance of serious reform proposals. See Filc, *Gefahr für unseren Wohlstand* (see note 1), p. 215; Barbara Unmüßig and Peter Wahl, "Stärkung der internationalen Finanzarchitektur—Überlegungen zur Reform des IWFs und der Finanzmärkte," Stückwerk oder konsequente Reform? WEED-Stellungnahme zum Papier des Bundesfinanzministeriums (Bonn: Weltwirtschaft, Ökologie & Entwicklung, 2001), pp. 2, 12.

16   I therefore share Stefan Schirm's opinion that Berlin's policies in this issue area are best explained by its worldview and value orientation. See Stefan A. Schirm, "The Divergence of Global Economic Governance Strategies," *New Rules for Global Markets: Public and Private Governance in the World Economy,* Stefan A. Schirm, ed. (New York: Palgrave Macmillan, 2004), pp. 12–3. However, in contrast to Schirm, I would give greater weight to the influence of such values as self-responsibility, lean government, and private competition.

17   Hans Eichel, "Der Einfluss der Finanzmärkte auf Wirtschaft und Beschäftigung," *Zur Globalisierung der Finanzmärkte und Finanzmarktstabilität,* Christa Ranzio-Plath, ed. (Baden-Baden: Nomos, 2001), p. 181; Bundesbank, Grenzüberschreitender Kapitalverkehr und die Rolle des Internationalen Währungsfonds, Monatsbericht, July 2001, pp. 21, 26, 30. Available at: http://www.bundesbank.de/download/volkswirtschaft/mba/2001/200107mba_kapitalverkehr.pdf. Accessed January 9, 2005; For a skeptical view within the government, see "Bundesministerium für wirtschaftliche Zusammenarbeit und Entwicklung 2004: Post-Washington-Consensus—Einige Überlegungen," Diskussionspapier, Berlin, April 2004. Available at: http://www.bmz.de/de/service/infothek/fach/diskurs/diskurs003 Kurzfassung.pdf. Accessed January 9, 2005.

18   Maria Heider, "Evaluation of the Recommendations of the 'Meltzer Commission' and German Guidelines for a Reform of the International Monetary Fund," *A Makeover for the Bretton Woods Twins? A Transatlantic Critique of the Meltzer Report and Other Reform Proposals* (Washington, DC: Heinrich Böll Foundation, 2000), pp. 17–22.

19   Hans Eichel, Statement to the International Monetary and Financial Committee Meeting, Prague, September 24, 2000 (quote). See also Bundesministerium der Finanzen, "Finanzmarktkrisen—Ursachen und Lösungsmöglichkeiten," Monatsbericht, April 2002, pp. 55, 58, Available at: http://www.bundesfinanzministerium.de/Anlage11655/Finanzmarktkrisen-Ursachen-und-Loesungsmoeglichkeiten.pdf. Accessed January 9, 2005; Bundesbank, "Die Rolle des Internationalen Währungsfonds in einem veränderten weltwirtschaftlichen

Umfeld," Monatsbericht, September 2000, p. 26. Available at: http://www.bundesbank.de/download/volkswirtschaft/mba/2000/200009mba_rolleiwf.pdf, Accessed January 9, 2005; Bundesbank, "Grenzüberschreitender Kapitalverkehr und die Rolle des Internationalen Währungsfonds," Monatsbericht, July 2001, pp. 23–5, Available at: http://www.bundesbank.de/download/volkswirtschaft/mba/2001/200107mba_kapitalverkehr.pdf, Accessed January 9, 2005.

20 Jürgen Stark, "Stellungnahme zum Thema Reform der internationalen Finanzmarktinstitutionen—Reformvorschläge und Verhandlungsstand anlässlich der Anhörung der Enquete-Kommission, Globalisierung und Weltwirtschaft," October 23, 2000, Berlin, p. 2.

21 Bundesministerium der Finanzen, "Finanzmarktkrisen—Ursachen und Lösungsmöglichkeiten" (see note 19), pp. 58–65; Bundesbank, "Die Rolle des Internationalen Währungsfonds in einem veränderten weltwirtschaftlichen Umfeld" (see note 19).

22 Bundesbank, "Die Rolle des Internationalen Währungsfonds in einem veränderten weltwirtschaftlichen Umfeld" (see note 19), p. 23; Bundesbank, "Grenzüberschreitender Kapitalverkehr und die Rolle des Internationalen Währungsfonds" (see note 19), p. 27; Bundesministerium der Finanzen, "Finanzmarktkrisen—Ursachen und Lösungsmöglichkeiten" (see note 19), p. 59.

23 Bundesministerium der Finanzen, "Finanzmarktkrisen—Ursachen und Lösungsmöglichkeiten" (see note 20), pp. 59–64; Stark, "Stellungnahme zum Thema Reform der internationalen Finanzmarktinstitutionen—Reformvorschläge und Verhandlungsstand anlässlich der Anhörung der Enquete-Kommission, Globalisierung und Weltwirtschaft" (see note 19), p. 3.

24 Klaus C. Engelen, "Funktionsfähigkeit der Märkte sichern," *Handelsblatt*, December 8, 1998.

25 Hans Tietmeyer, "International Cooperation and Coordination in the Area of Financial Market Supervision and Surveillance," Report by Hans Tietmeyer, president of the Deutsche Bundesbank, February 11, 1999; Bundesbank, Neuere institutionelle Entwicklungen in der wirtschafts- und währungspolitischen Kooperation, Monatsbericht, January 2001, p. 22. Available at: http://www.bundesbank.de/download/volkswirtschaft/mba/2001/200101mba_waehrungskoop.pdf. Accessed January 9, 2005.

26 Filc, *Gefahr für unseren Wohlstand* (see note 1), pp. 153–54; Paul Blustein, *The Chastening. Inside the Crisis That Rocked the Global Financial System and Humbled the IMF* (New York: Perseus, 2003), pp. 172–73.

27 Blustein, *The Chastening* (see note 26), p. 172.

28 *Frankfurter Allgemeine Zeitung* (see note 6); Bundesbank, "Neuere Ansätze zur Beteiligung des Privatsektors an der Lösung internationaler Verschuldungskrisen," Monatsbericht, December 1999, pp. 33–50, Available at: http://www.bundesbank.de/download/volkswirtschaft/mba/1999/199912mba_verschuldkrisen.pdf. Accessed January 9, 2005.

29 Stark, "Stellungnahme zum Thema Reform der internationalen Finanzmarktinstitutionen—Reformvorschläge und Verhandlungsstand anlässlich der Anhörung der Enquete-Kommission, Globalisierung und Weltwirtschaft" (see note 20), p. 13.

30 Bundesministerium der Finanzen, "Global Governance: Veränderungsprozesse in der globalisierten Wirtschaft," Monatsbericht, June 2004, p. 66; Ernst Welteke, Speech, IMF/World Bank 2002 Annual Meetings, Washington DC, September 29, 2002, pp. 4–5.

212   *Reinhard Wolf*

31   Hans Eichel, Statement to the International Monetary and Financial Committee Meeting, Washington, DC, April 12, 2003.

32   Stark, "Stellungnahme zum Thema Reform der internationalen Finanzmarktinstitutionen—Reformvorschläge und Verhandlungsstand anlässlich der Anhörung der Enquete-Kommission, Globalisierung und Weltwirtschaft" (see note 20), pp. 12–13.

33   Welteke, Speech (see note 30), 5; Hans Eichel, Statement to the International Monetary and Financial Committee Meeting, Washington, DC, September 28, 2002.

34   Bundesbank, "Die Rolle des Internationalen Währungsfonds in einem veränderten weltwirtschaftlichen Umfeld" (see note 19), pp. 26, 29; Blustein, *The Chastening* (see note 26), p. 334.

35   Eichel, Statement to the International Monetary and Financial Committee Meeting (see note 19).

36   As a matter of fact, the CCL had never been put to use.

37   Eichel, Statement to the International Monetary and Financial Committee Meeting (see note 19); Bundesministerium der Finanzen, "Global Governance: Veränderungsprozesse in der globalisierten Wirtschaft" (see note 30), pp. 64–5; Bundesministerium der Finanzen, "Verbesserung der Krisenbewältigung durch ein internationales Insolvenzverfahren für Staaten," Monatsbericht, December 2003, pp. 87–89. Available at: http://www.bundesfinanzministerium.de/Anlage21515/Teil-4-Monatsbericht-Dezember-2003-Verzeichnis-der-Berichte.pdf. Accessed January 9, 2005.

38   Deutscher Bundestag, "Gemeinsame öffentliche Anhörung des Finanzausschusses und des Ausschusses für wirtschaftliche Zusammenarbeit und Entwicklung zu dem Thema: 'Internationales Insolvenzrecht und präventive Politik zur Verhinderung von Finanzkrisen und zur Stabilisierung des Finanzsystems,'" Berlin, April 2, 2003.

39   Günter Bannas, "Schröder schilt 'Brüssel' und schielt auf Stoiber," Frankfurter Allgemeine Zeitung, March 7, 2002; Michael Scheerer, "Schröder weckt unerfüllbare Erwartungen," *Handelsblatt*, December 14, 2001; Detlef Fechtner, "Viel Buhei um Basel II," *Frankfurter Rundschau*, November 8, 2001.

40   *Frankfurter Allgemeine Zeitung* (see note 6).

41   Bundesministerium der Finanzen, "Fortschritte bei der Verhinderung von Geldwäsche," Monatsbericht, August 2003, pp. 75–87. Available at: http://www.wpk.de/pdf/wpk-news_geldwaesche-verhinderung.pdf. Accessed January 9, 2005; Eric Bonse and Christoph Nesshöver "OECD verlangt Reform der Finanzarchitektur," *Handelsblatt*, September 17, 2001; Werner Benkhoff, Klaus C. Engelen, and Michael Maisch, "Aktionsplan gegen Geldwäscher gefordert," *Handelsblatt*, October 19, 2001.

42   Christian Potthoff, "Sinnlose Verzögerung," *Handelsblatt*, September 19, 2003; K. Engelen and C. Potthoff, "Elite-Club vor der Bewährungsprobe," *Handelsblatt*, October 10, 2003.

43   Kirton, *Shaping a New International Financial System* (see note 14), p. 68; Benoît Cœureand Jean Pisani-Ferry, "Events, Ideas, and Actions: An Intellectual and Institutional Retrospective on the Reform of the International Financial Architecture," Paper presented for the CDC-CEPII-CEFI international conference on reshaping the architecture of the international financial system, Sienna, May 23–24, 2000.

44   Engelen, *Handelsblatt* (see note 2).

45 Werner Benkhoff, "Die Europäer? Ein Haufen von Egoisten," *Handelsblatt*, September 27, 1999; Robert Rubin, *In an Uncertain World: Tough Choices from Wall Street to Washington* (New York: Texere, 2003), p. 225.

46 Bundesbank (see note 19), 30–1; Ernst Welteke, (speech, IMF/World Bank 2003 Annual Meetings, Dubai, 23 September 2003); Eichel (see note 31).

47 Bundesministerium der Finanzen, "Global Governance: Veränderungsprozesse in der globalisierten Wirtschaft" (see note 30), p. 68.

48 Hans Eichel, Statement to the Interim Committee Meeting, Washington, DC, September 26, 1999; Stark, "Stellungnahme zum Thema Reform der internationalen Finanzmarktinstitutionen—Reformvorschläge und Verhandlungsstand anlässlich der Anhörung der Enquete-Kommission, Globalisierung und Weltwirtschaft" (see note 20), p. 4.

49 Heidemarie Wieczorek-Zeul, Statement to the Development Committee, Washington, DC, April 15, 2000, pp. 1–2.

50 Caio K. Koch-Weser, "Beitrag zum Thema, Reform der internationalen Finanzinstitutionen—Reformvorschläge und Verhandlungsstand," Public hearing of the Enquete commission "Globalisierung der Weltwirtschaft," Berlin, October 23, 2000, p. 2.

51 Wieczorek-Zeul, Statement to the Development Committee (see note 49), p. 6; "Bundesministerium für wirtschaftliche Zusammenarbeit und Entwicklung 2004: Post-Washington-Consensus—Einige Überlegungen" (see note 17), pp. 32–33; Hans Eichel, Statement to the International Monetary and Financial Committee Meeting, Washington, DC, April 29, 2001.

52 "Weltsteuer stößt auf breite Ablehnung", *Handelsblatt*, January 29, 2005; Nikolaus Piper, "Überraschender Vorstoß. Schröder will Finanzspekulationen besteuern," *Süddeutsche Zeitung*, January 29, 2005.

53 According to Germany's finance minister, Hans Eichel, the reform of the international financial architecture had almost been completed by 2003, although full implementation of agreed measures was still taking some time. See "Amerikaner müssen mittelfristig ihren Haushalt konsolidieren," *Frankfurter Allgemeine Zeitung*, September 19, 2003.

14
Germany's International Environmental Policy

Detlef F. Sprinz

The challenge of global environmental governance for Germany

Germany aspires to be a recognized leader in international environmental governance, and therefore takes ambitious positions in negotiations in this area. Given the growing competences of the European Union, an EU member can now also influence environmental governance in other member states—as long as those do not object too strongly and command sufficient support among other member countries. On the other hand, European legislation restricts domestic leeway, and the distribution of constitutional authority between the federal government and the *Länder* puts a strain on cohesiveness. Any German federal government will be challenged to be a lighthouse of global and national environmental governance that shines in the right directions and at appropriate intensity. This chapter will analyze how well Germany has been able to meet this challenge by looking at the two examples of global climate change and biodiversity.

Global climate change represents perhaps the most successful case of German international environmental policy. The country has managed to reduce its harmful emissions since 1990, and it has played a prominent role in the negotiations on and implementation of the UN Framework Convention on Climate Change (UNFCCC) and related policies at the European level. The relevant competencies for climate policy are concentrated at the federal level, though some of them are slowly being shifted to the European level. By contrast, while Germany is a clear supporter of the Convention on Biological Diversity (CBD), it has major problems adhering to core provisions of the convention. Competencies are fragmented with a major role played by the *Länder* for constitutional reasons.

Both the UNFCCC and the CBD belong to the major achievements of the 1992 UN Conference on Environment and Development (UNCED) at Rio de Janeiro. In successive rounds of negotiations, these two conventions were negotiated. Both opened for signature at UNCED and were augmented by the UN Convention to Combat Desertification (CCD) in 1994.[1] In the following, I will briefly review select aspects of German foreign policy within those two environmental domains and subsequently conclude with the role that the German nationstate can still play in the realm of global environmental governance.

Germany and the UN Framework Convention on Climate Change

Environmental challenges

Economic activities, such as the burning of fossil fuel for energy, release carbon dioxide; methane is emitted by rice paddies and cows, and cars as well as agricultural fertilizers release nitrous oxides.[2] Together, these form the three major greenhouse gases (GHGs) that are released into the atmosphere by human activities and contribute to the so-called greenhouse effect, which is responsible for the temperature on earth—and a prerequisite for life. The temperature record associated with GHG concentrations is not static over time; it has fluctuated during the earth's history. It is nevertheless feared that the anthropogenic addition of GHGs, leading to the enhanced greenhouse effect, is sufficiently disturbing the climate system to cause new dangers.

The Intergovernmental Panel on Climate Change was created in 1988 by the World Meteorological Organization and the United Nations Environment Programme to provide scientific, yet politically guided, expertise. Having corroborated the human impact on the climate system, the intergovernmental panel also synthesized the prospects for future climate development. Different emission scenarios were explored for the twenty-first century, some of them involving the phasing out of the fossil-fuel based energy system during this time period. Even in this case, the earth seems likely to experience a "globally averaged surface temperature [that] is projected to increase by 1.4 to 5.8°C over the period 1990 to 2100".[3]

Climate policy and energy policy are closely intertwined, as the latter has generated the emissions that the former wishes to curb. Projections of energy use into the future suggest substantial increases of GHGs, and developing countries (especially China) are expected to lead in emissions at some point during this century. Thus, the challenge will be to curb emissions while keeping the world's economies on a prosperous trajectory.

The UNFCCC and Kyoto Protocol frameworks

In five sessions, the Intergovernmental Negotiating Committee for a Framework Convention on Climate Change managed to compile a draft treaty in time for signature at the 1992 UN Conference on Environment and Development at Rio de Janeiro. The United Nations Framework Convention on Climate Change was signed by many countries at the 1992 conference and thereafter; it entered into force on March 21, 1994 and had been ratified by 189 countries as of May 24, 2004. The UNFCCC is a framework convention "plus"—that is, it follows the legacy of the regulations on stratospheric ozone depletion and transboundary air pollution by providing a general document that lays the foundations for future regulatory efforts. In particular, its Article 2 stipulates that the

> ultimate objective of this Convention and any related legal instruments that the Conference of the Parties may adopt is to achieve ... stabilization of greenhouse gas concentrations in the atmosphere at a level that would prevent dangerous anthropogenic interference with the climate system.[4]

The precise interpretation of this obligation is the topic of much important current research. No consensus has yet been found as to what "dangerous anthropogenic interference" means and how such dangers should be addressed. In addition to the ultimate goal, the UNFCCC advises industrialized countries to reduce their year 2000 emissions of GHGs to 1990 levels,[5] but the careful wording avoids setting clear obligations that could become the object of noncompliance procedures.

While the UNFCCC established an ultimate goal and an institutional architecture for achieving it, it does not include firm obligations for countries to control their emissions. At the first Conference of the Parties in Berlin in 1995, participants decided to start negotiations on a protocol to the convention that would lead to emission reductions in the industrialized countries (an agreement known as the "Berlin Mandate"). Subsequent rounds of negotiations ultimately led to the 1997 Kyoto Protocol to the UNFCCC, which includes a schedule for emission limitations by industrialized countries during the period 2008–12.

In contrast to the UNFCCC, the Kyoto Protocol is comparatively focused: for a range of industrialized countries, it stipulates legally binding emission reduction targets of six GHGs and groups of GHGs (in Annex B of the protocol). The 15 members of the European Union, as well as representatives from other European countries, accepted an 8 percent reduction goal of their average 2008–12 GHG emissions as compared to emissions in 1990, whereas the United States and Japan accepted reductions of 7 percent and 6 percent respectively. The Russian Federation is allowed to maintain its 1990 emission level, whereas Norway and Australia are allowed to increase their emissions by 1 percent and 8 percent respectively.

To achieve such emission reductions in an efficient way, countries are allowed to use the so-called Kyoto Protocol mechanisms, wherein a country with more emission rights than it anticipates using can sell this surplus to countries that would otherwise exceed their permitted amounts.

The Kyoto Protocol was concluded in 1997, yet only in late 2001 did countries agree on how to interpret the Treaty in more detail. Against US opposition, the Marrakech Accords of November 2001 represented an attempt under EU leadership to salvage the Kyoto Protocol. They finalized a compliance mechanism, made all types of greenhouse gas emission reduction efforts interchangeable, and tried to include Russia and other countries by granting generous allowances for the sequestration (binding) of carbon by forest resources and other types of so-called terrestrial sinks. Furthermore, the European Union, Canada, Iceland, New Zealand, Norway, and Switzerland announced to offer developing countries funding in the amount of € 450 million annually, starting in 2005.

These efforts ultimately proved successful as Russia ratified in late 2004 the Kyoto Protocol, which went into force on February 16, 2005. Whether it will prove successful at addressing the long-term challenge of climate change remains to be seen, especially since the United States withdrew from the Kyoto Protocol in 2001.

Germany and climate change

Germany has been an active player in formulating global climate policy since the early 1990s. It managed to reduce its GHG emissions by 18.9 percent between 1990 and 2002,[6] while the European Union achieved a mild overall reduction;[7] meanwhile, the remaining industrialized world and many developing countries have seen their emissions increase.

Germany's role in global climate policy owes much to its domestic foundations in the late 1980s and early 1990s. Several "inquiry commissions" (or Enquête Commissions) were established to design policies to protect the global atmosphere. Initiated by the Bundestag, the commissions include as members parliamentarians as well as scientists and strive to make policy suggestions that are supported by all participants. Following the first commission's advice, even before the results were published, the German government announced in 1990 that it would reduce its energy-related carbon emissions by 25 percent between 1987 and 2005, just five percentage points fewer than that suggested by the commission. The second commission focused on policies of implementation, yet was not able to maintain the same level of consensus as did the first commission.[8] Nevertheless, Chancellor Helmut Kohl in 1995 announced a 25 percent reduction target of carbon dioxide for all of Germany between 1990 and 2005. This goal was reconfirmed in 1998 by the government of Gerhard Schröder, but the target will be missed (a point explained in more detail later).

In support of such ambitious emission reduction targets, agreements between government and industry representatives were concluded in which industry promises to reduce its emissions in exchange for the government not imposing severe regulations of emissions. Prior to 1995, German industry agreed to a 20 percent reduction of energy-related carbon dioxide emission reductions between 1990 and 2005; with the Schröder government in power, this was upgraded in time for the Marrakech Accords to a 35 percent emission reduction of all GHGs for the period 1990–2012, thus covering the entire Kyoto Protocol compliance period.[9] While the Federal Ministry of the Environment has held responsibility for climate policy since 1990, it shares competencies with many other ministries, in particular the Ministry of the Economy, which is responsible for energy policy. In fact, understanding the antagonism that exists between both ministries is, at times, crucial for understanding policy outcomes: when Germany had to draw up an allocation plan in early 2004 for the trading of its industrial GHG emissions within the broader EU context, industrial leaders managed to exert influence over the plan, closely shaping it according to their own preferences (as compared to the plan originally crafted by the Federal Ministry of the Environment). Although climate policy is largely based on interparty consensus, the industry representatives are able to influence policy considerably in their own favor.[10] This effect cannot be counterbalanced by efforts of the environmental non-governmental agencies (NGOs).[11]

The Schröder government has implemented a range of policy programs and laws that should assist its climate goals, including an ecological tax reform, support for renewable energy provisions, and photovoltaic installations in particular, and support for cogeneration. These efforts were insufficient for reaching Germany's 25 percent emission reduction goal in 2005. To a large degree, this problem has been inherited from the Kohl government—and insufficient steps were taken since to rectify the situation. Overall, Germany is exploring and implementing limited climate-friendly policies, although they do not yet amount to a large-scale irreversible transformation of its energy system.

Second, competency for climate policy is shared between the European Union and its member countries. As a consequence, the country holding the council presidency speaks first and on behalf of the member countries in international fora. While European ministers are said to have shouted at each other during crucial negotiations on the Kyoto Protocol in 1997, the United States skillfully used "salami tactics" at Kyoto in 1997 and ultimately, slice by slice, shaped much of the Kyoto Protocol. Fortunately, the European Union has been much better represented on climate change since the turn of the millennium. Within the European Union, Germany has always actively pushed for early and substantial emission reductions. For example, in 1995 the country's representatives suggested a 15 to 20 percent EU-wide reduction of carbon dioxide during 1990–2010 as part of the preparations for negotiations on the Kyoto Protocol.[12] The European Union ultimately settled for a 15 percent proposal for the Kyoto negotiations, while members had distributed between them only a 10 percent reduction.[13] This allowed the European Union to act as the pusher in the international negotiations because the United States and Japan entered negotiations with more modest reduction goals. The resulting Kyoto Protocol obliges the EU 15 to reduce its emissions by 8 percent; the internal burden-sharing agreement allows for substantial variation in obligations across member countries. Germany has to reduce its GHG emissions by 21 percent by 2008–12 (as compared to 1990)—which amounts to approximately 80 percent of the total EU 15 reduction in emissions.[14,15] In essence, the emission reductions of Germany and the United Kingdom (while the latter's are substantially lower) take care of the net emission reductions of the European Union; but without Germany, the European Union would lose its leadership role on this issue.

Embeddedness is also double-edged: while Germany can use its weight within the European Union to play a more global role as a recognized team player, it took some time to abide by relevant EU legislation.[16] For example, the European emissions trading directive (Directive 2003/87/EC)[17] was agreed upon at the EU-level, yet once the national governments had to design an implementation plan for the initial allocation of allowances across industries, a serious conflict arose between the German ministries for the economy and the environment. As mentioned above, industry lobbyists skillfully used their connections to limit the impact of the Ministry of the Environment. Furthermore, the European Commission decided that the initial draft allocation plan (as those of several other countries) were not in full compliance with some of the directive's criteria.[18] Thus, European politics influences national climate policy and interministerial politics.

Third, Germany has prided itself on being an international leader in this area. In fact, the timing of some of its positioning is linked to international events. The country's 25 percent emission reduction goal occurred when the Kohl government took this stance on the occasion of the G-7 summit in 1990. Furthermore, the first voluntary agreement with industrial leaders was announced just prior to Germany hosting the first Conference of the Parties in Berlin in 1995;[19] Germany's current goal of a 40 percent emission reduction (which is contingent on the European Union taking on a 30 percent emission reduction for the period 1990–2020) is meant to provide a focal point for negotiations on the further development of climate policy beyond 2012.

While Germany is among the few nations championing proactive climate policy, some policy reversals have also occurred. At Kyoto, Germany (and other EU members) tried to limit the usage of the Kyoto mechanisms to 50 percent of a country's emission reduction obligation—as did many German environmental NGOs. The United States prevailed with a no-limit policy, and today, Germany is perhaps among the most enthusiastic supporters of their use—as are today's German environmental NGOs. Paradoxically, it is German industrial associations that have the most serious grievances over market-oriented policies as opposed to direct regulation. Sector-by-sector approaches, rather than universal rules and simple auctioning of allowances, characterize the present regulatory style.[20]

Fourth, transition management may be needed for the very substantial emission reductions called for to protect against major climate impacts. The German Advisory Council on the Environment suggests an ultimate goal of 450 ppm of carbon dioxide, which implies a nearly 80 percent emission reduction for Germany until 2050;[21] the German Advisory Council on Global Change advises the same environmental goal and suggests that a 45 to 60 percent emission reduction of energy-related carbon dioxide emissions would be needed.[22] More stringent emission reductions would be required toward the end of this century, especially for industrialized countries. Such ambitious reduction goals will only be possible if a transition takes place from a fossil fuel-based energy system to a system based on renewable sources. The German government is clearly an ambitious supporter of renewables—but the national plans just foresee to catch up with the European Union average. In essence, the German government lacks a long-term strategy to achieve its long-term goals, while Britain embarks on a bold 60 percent emission reduction strategy by 2050.[23]

Germany and the Convention on Biological Diversity

The environmental challenge[24]

The term "biodiversity" refers to all aspects of variability within the living world and encompasses ecosystem variety, diversity between species, and genetic variety within species. Apart from its intrinsic value, biodiversity provides manifold goods and services that are crucial to life on earth. Ecosystems such as forests, wetlands, oceans, lakes, and agricultural landscapes fulfill essential life-supporting functions such as climate regulation, soil conservation, mediation in the carbon cycle, and regulation of hydrological cycles. Genetic diversity is important as it provides the raw material of evolution and thus enables adaptation and change in organisms.[25] Recently, genetic diversity has become an important economic value with the development of modern biotechnology. Furthermore, biodiversity provides products such as fresh water, food, medicine, timber, and other materials.

Biodiversity is put under intense stress by numerous human activities. Humans permanently change the earth's landscape and ecosystems through, inter alia, deforestation, urbanization, conversion to croplands, and pollution. The world's forests, for example, are rapidly disappearing; about 45 percent of the earth's original forests have vanished during the past century.[26] Overharvesting, fragmentation, and degradation of habitats lead to the decline and extinction of species. While a natural rate of extinction has always been present, it is estimated that species now disappear at 50 to 100 times the natural rate.[27] With the loss of species and genetic variety, valuable genetic and physiological information is also lost, and consequently the

chances dwindle of using this information for biotechnological developments of agricultural and pharmaceutical products. Finally, various other
environmental problems, such as climate change, ozone depletion, water
degradation, and the accumulation of persistent organic pollutants, also
threaten biodiversity.

Besides the threats posed by the loss of biodiversity, the advances in
modern biotechnology in the last decades require international regulation.
Living modified organisms or, synonymously used, genetically modified
organisms are becoming part of an increasing number of products, including
foods and food additives, beverages, drugs, adhesives, and fuels. Biotechnology
may have the potential to improve efficiency, volume or quality in
agricultural and other production processes and hence contribute to food
security.[28] Little is known about the impacts of genetically modified products
on human health and the environment, including the risks to biological
diversity. For example, genes may be transferred to offsprings of the modified
individual through normal reproductive processes and thereby influence
the natural biodiversity. Therefore, in the last years public awareness and
concerns over the use and safety of genetic modification have increased
steadily.[29]

The CBD framework

The objective of the Convention on Biological Diversity (CBD) succinctly
summarizes many of the points of contention between industrialized and
developing countries:

> The objectives of this Convention ... are the conservation of biological
> diversity, the sustainable use of its components and the fair and equitable
> sharing of the benefits arising out of the utilization of genetic resources,
> including by appropriate access to genetic resources and by appropriate
> transfer of relevant technologies, taking into account all rights over those
> resources and to technologies, and by appropriate funding.[30]

The conservation aspect of the CBD directly responds to the ecosystem
approach preferred by natural scientists; the sustainable use aspect
addresses the tension between the economic use of ecosystems and the
threat of their destruction; while the equitable sharing aspect responds to
the observation that industrialized countries have appropriated much
of the knowledge in the past from developing countries without letting
the areas of origin—predominantly concentrated in the developing
countries—reap the resulting benefits for their agriculture and pharmaceuticals, for example. In fact, the industrialized world succeeded in grandfa-
thering past extractions of biodiversity with the help of the trade-related
aspects of intellectual property rights agreements within the World Trade
Organization.[31]

The CBD was signed by most countries in 1992 and became effective in late 1993. It was ratified by 188 countries, with the notable exception of the United States.[32] Given the challenges posed by modern biotechnology—that is, the possibility of creating genetically modified organisms as opposed to using traditional breeding techniques—the CBD served as the framework convention for the Cartagena Protocol on Biosafety. Its objective is

> to contribute to ensuring an adequate level of protection in the field of the safe transfer, handling and use of living modified organisms resulting from modern biotechnology that may have adverse effects on the conservation and sustainable use of biological diversity, taking also into account risks to human health, and specifically focusing on transboundary movements.[33]

In essence, this regulates trade in biotechnologically modified products. It also ensures that developing countries can use prior informed consent rules, which also guide international trade in hazard substances, to protect themselves against potential threats that they might not otherwise be aware of or could not manage within their territory. The Cartagena Protocol was concluded in 2000 at Montreal and went into effect in 2003. Both international treaties outline a set of institutional setups, reporting, compliance, and funding, as well as voting rules.[34] As the focus of this book is on Germany's foreign policy, I will now turn to select points of particular relevance to Germany.

Germany and biodiversity

As in the case of climate policy, the federal government serves as the point of reference for Germany's foreign policy on biodiversity.[35] However, in the case of biodiversity, the federal government only commands the right to pass framework legislation, with many of the remaining rights reserved for the *Länder*.[36] At the other end of constitutional governance, Germany is part of the European Union and therefore ought to honor EU law.

First, Germany's federal government lists the protection of biodiversity (under protection of nature) as one of its six priorities.[37] Its goal is that, by the year 2010, the loss of biodiversity will be halted worldwide, and biodiversity will be included in Germany's policy of sustainability. The Federal Ministry of the Environment is willing to commit to the 2010 deadline for halting biodiversity loss, whereas participants at the sixth meeting of the Conference of the Parties of the CBD in 2002[38] (Decision VI/26) and the World Summit on Sustainable Development at Johannesburg in 2002 only asked for a significant reduction in the current rate of biodiversity loss at the global, regional, and national levels.[39] Other parts of the German federal government seem content with the less demanding goal. More strikingly,

Germany seems to interpret biodiversity policy as a continuation of traditional policies of species protection (e.g., red lists of endangered species). The Federal Environment Ministry does not even have an informative website geared to biodiversity, while it does for many other issue areas. Again, traditional species protection appears to be the goal. In its 2002 sustainability report, the German federal government is embarking on the vague project to "achieve a stable condition at a high level for all species and the areas they represent".[40] As will be described further later, Germany essentially lacks a modern biodiversity strategy that complements the traditional protection of nature and is comprehensive in scope.[41]

Second, Germany provides generous amounts of funding for global biodiversity protection. This work is carried out via the Federal Ministry for Economic Cooperation and Development and its Deutsche Gesellschaft für Technische Zusammenarbeit GmbH. Much of the funds are channeled either through the Global Environment Facility (GEF)[42] or through bilateral aid. For the period 1991–2006, Germany has committed itself to a total of $US 903 million; as a share of total GEF funds, Germany will reduce its contribution from 13 percent in the early 1990s to 11 percent in the current phase for all topical domains.[43] A different pattern can be seen with bilateral aid directly aimed at biodiversity issues. Ranging from a modest start in 1982, passing €10 million annually in 1991 and increasing to over €70 million per year in 2003,[44] there is clearly an increase in dedicated bilateral expenditures—outpacing the multilateral aid given via the GEF. According to the Federal Ministry of the Environment, Germany currently finances forest projects in developing countries to the tune of €125 million per year.[45,46] What is striking is the input-orientation of public funds, as no postevaluation results are publicly communicated in the report; there is also a lack of European-wide cooperation in overseas assistance for biodiversity projects.

Germany's official policy on biodiversity is rhetorically ambitious, yet given the priority actually accorded to it (as described before), it is unexpectedly weak in terms of domestic implementation. The CBD and the Cartagena Protocol were quickly ratified by Germany. For example, Germany had already passed implementing legislation for the CBD in 1993, yet saw no basic need to adjust its legislation at the time—as Germany largely sees biodiversity in terms of the protection of nature rather than in the broader sense of biodiversity as stated in the CBD.[47] While Germany has delivered two national reports either late or during the grace period, it has not yet crafted a national strategy for biodiversity as mandated under Article 6 of the CBD. Such a strategy is now envisioned for delivery in 2006[48]— thirteen years after ratifying the CBD—following criticism by the German Advisory Council on Global Change.[49] The OECD (Organization of Economic Cooperation and Development) is less coy in its 2001 audit of

Germany's environmental policy performance. After listing some positive aspects of Germany's biodiversity policy, the audit states:

> Yet the fact remains that Germany's high population density and economic activity continue to generate such strong pressures that nature is not holding its own ... Loss of biodiversity has not been halted. Germany is among the cluster of central European countries with the highest shares of red-listed species for several classes. Only 6% of biotope types are classified as currently not threatened. Overall, nature conservation does not appear to have been given the thrust or resources commensurate with its status as one of the five priority themes of environmental policy ... There is no national biodiversity strategy. Neither the Federal Government nor any of the Länder has formally adopted or published a nature conservation plan with more detailed or quantified objectives in terms of desired results. Most important, national objectives are mainly informal and are not supported by political commitment on the part of the government or Parliament.[50]

For a benchmark, the German Advisory Council on Global Change suggests that 10 to 20 percent of the landmass should be protected.[51] The tension becomes perhaps most obvious when political goals and performance are compared. For example, Federal Environment Minister Jürgen Trittin strongly supports the creation of a global network of nature protection areas, yet when it comes to Germany's obligation to the European Union to build a European network of such protection areas, called Natura 2000, Germany is slow, underperforming, and in noncompliance with EU law. The European Court of Justice ruled in 2001 that Germany is insufficiently following community legislation on biodiversity.[52]

Part of the implementation dilemma may arise from the constitutional rights reserved by the *Länder* and their lack of enthusiasm for European legislation, which they cannot directly influence. Yet it remains a basic dilemma that German politicians want their international biodiversity policy to be ambitious, yet they too often lack credibility as leaders in this area because of Germany's own domestic policies. .

Germany's international environmental policy

We are now witnessing about 15 years of modern global environmental politics, and Germany aspires to play a major role in this field. Yet the space for maneuver and impact is limited. As former Federal Environment Minister Trittin summarizes,

> Of course, Germany does not participate in such negotiations as a nation state. We can only work within the European Union, and the EU Council

Presidency and the Commission act as "spokespersons" for the Union members. To put it in provocative terms: independent national environmental policy no longer exists inside the European Union ... In the field of environmental legislation, Brussels now has greater influence than any nation state in Europe.[53]

For nation-states who wish to act as innovators (such as Germany on shifting to renewable energy sources), there is still room to act. As this chapter shows, one sees an uneven performance in the two issues analyzed here. On global climate policy, Germany seems successful on the international stage, but when crucial decisions need to be made, the industries facing potential regulation know how to exert influence successfully. By contrast, biodiversity policy is not emphasized, although it officially shares the same priority status with climate change on the government's agenda. Which factors may account for the difference?

Federal authority on both issues is vested in the Federal Ministry of the Environment. While authority for climate policy rests solely at the federal level, responsibility for biodiversity is shared by federal and state governments. Furthermore, climate policy has long been an area to which either the chancellor or the federal minister of the environment attends. For example, Chancellor Kohl used several occasions to push the international agenda on climate change, and the former government under Chancellor Schröder expended considerable effort to salvage the Kyoto Protocol by assuring Russian ratification. The Schröder government even shifted its stance by allowing Russia to secure very substantial terrestrial sink allocations, though it originally believed that permitting sinks to control net emissions was premature due to the poor state of the research. Likewise, the Schröder government went from being a skeptic on the Kyoto mechanisms to one of its most fervent supporters, as did many environmental NGOs. Biodiversity never stood out as an issue on a comparable basis. In both cases, the Foreign Office plays an important role by providing coherence across policy issues and offering the services of its diplomatic missions, but this would not explain the difference in performance. Thus, distribution in competencies and varying de facto priorities appear to account best for the difference in Germany's good performance on global climate change and its modest performance on biodiversity.

Ultimately, the commonalities may be more striking than one would expect at first glance. In both cases, Germany lacks a long-term strategy. While it may sound banal to call for the development of a long-term strategy to deal with a long-term problem, this is exactly what is needed. Scientists would not attempt to fight smallpox with a short-term strategy, so why not apply such standards to climate change and biodiversity policies? In the field of biodiversity, Germany is planning to outline a national strategy—over a decade after it was due. And on climate policy, Britain appears more courageous in its outline of a strategy to reduce GHG emissions by about 60 percent by 2050.[54] While the latter announcement may have its weaknesses, it represents a start. Germany's lack of a long-term climate strategy is criticized by its German Advisory Council on the Environment[55] and academics[56] alike. Helmut Kohl's administrations were scolded for not solving fundamental problems with German economic and social policy. Thus, there could have been a chance for a Red–Green government to prove itself visionary and to lead on core "sustainability" issues such as climate change and biodiversity. Former Minister of the Environment Trittin suggests that

> [t]he simple truth is that politicians want to be re-elected. Hence we need voters with a global awareness for whom sustainability and the future of this planet is more important than current national politics ... In a democracy, it is always the citizen who is the sovereign. Global environmental governance needs a solid base: citizens with environmental awareness and commitment and with long-term thinking.[57]

While the quest for citizens with an ability for long-term thinking is laudable, why should a government be relieved of the obligation of forwarding credible suggestions for tackling major challenges? Unfortunately for the environment, this has been a common theme of both the Kohl and Schröder governments. It is time for Germany's international environmental policy to move beyond what Fischer and Holtrup called a "hectic stillstand."[58]

Acknowledgment

I am grateful to Hanns Maull and Christopher Kaan for comments on an earlier version of this chapter.

Notes

1 The official name is "UN Convention to Combat Desertification in Those Countries Experiencing Serious Drought And/Or Desertification, Particularly in Africa."
2 This subsection draws on Daniel Bodansky, "The History of the Global Climate Change Regime", *International Relations and Global Climate Change*, Urs Luterbacher, Detlef F. Sprinz, eds (Cambridge, MA: The MIT Press, 2001), and, in part verbatim, on Detlef F. Sprinz, Anja Bauer, Jette Krause, Kathrin Birkel, and Ruben Zondervan. *International Environmental Policy* (E-Learning Course), PolitikON, Available from http://www.politikon.org, 2004. Accessed on April 1, 2005.
3 John Theodore Houghton and Intergovernmental Panel on Climate Change. Working Group I, *Climate Change 2001 : The Scientific Basis: Contribution of Working Group I to the Third Assessment Report of the Intergovernmental Panel on Climate Change* (Cambridge: Cambridge University Press, 2001).
4 Article 2, United Nations, 2003, United Nations Framework Convention on Climate Change 1992, Available at: http://unfccc.int/resource/docs/convkp/conveng.pdf.

5 Ibid., Article 4 (2a).

6 *Umweltdaten Deutschland Online*, Available at: http://www.env-it.de/umweltdaten/open.do?navigation=%2Fumweltdaten%2Fjsp%2Fcatalogue.jsp%3Fevent%3Dload%26catalogueId%3D0%26termId%3D2344, Accessed on December 21, 2004.

7 European Environment Agency, *Greenhouse Gas Emission Trends and Projections in Europe 2004. Progress by the EU and its Member States Towards Achieving Their Kyoto Protocol Targets* (Copenhagen: European Environment Agency, 2004).

8 Guri Bang, *Sources of Influence in Climate Change Policymaking: A Comparative Analysis of Norway, Germany, and the United States*, vol. 43, 2004. (Oslo: Faculty of Social Sciences, The University of Oslo, 2003), quoted here p. 103; Christiane Beuermann, and Jill Jäger, "Climate Change Politics in Germany: How Long Will Any Double Dividend Last?," *Climate Change Policy. A European Perspective*, T. O'Riordan and J. Jäger, eds (London: Routledge, 1996); Alexandra Böckem "Umsetzungsprobleme in der deutschen Klimapolitik: Eine empirische Überprüfung polit-ökonomischer Erklärungsansätze," *HWWA-Report 189* (Hamburg: HWWA, 1999).

9 The environmental effects of these government-industry agreements are seriously questioned: Sachverständigenrat für Umweltfragen, *Umweltgutachten 2000, Schritte ins nächste Jahrtausend* (Stuttgart: Metzler-Poeschel, 2000), quoted: 323.

10 Guri Bang, *Sources of Influence in Climate Change Policymaking: A Comparative Analysis of Norway, Germany, and the United States*, vol. 43, 2004 (Oslo: Faculty of Social Sciences, The University of Oslo, 2003), quoted here pp. 220–21.

11 M. Schröder, M. Clausen, A. Grunwald, A. Hense, G. Klepper, S. Lingner, K. Ott, D. Schmitt, and D. Sprinz, eds, *Klimavorhersage und Klimavorsorge*, (Berlin: Springer, 2002), quoted here p. 149.

12 Guri Bang, *Sources of Influence in Climate Change Policymaking: A Comparative Analysis of Norway, Germany, and the United States*, vol. 43, 2004 (Oslo: Faculty of Social Sciences, The University of Oslo, 2003), quoted here p. 340.

13 M. Schröder, M. Clausen, A. Grunwald, A. Hense, G. Klepper, S. Lingner, K. Ott, D. Schmitt, and D. Sprinz, eds., *Klimavorhersage und Klimavorsorge* (Berlin: Springer, 2002).

14 Michael T. Hatch, *The Politics of Climate Change in Germany*, Unpublished Manuscript (Stockton, CA: Department of Political Science, University of the Pacific, 2004).

15 Minister for the Environment Trittin suggested that the German contribution is about two thirds of the net EU 15 emission reductions, see Fritz Vorholz "Fleisskärtchen mag ich nicht—Umweltminister Jürgen Trittin über Hyperaktivismus in der Klimapolitik, die Ökosteuer und Chinas Rolle beim Kampf gegen die Erderwärmung. Ein ZEIT-Gespräch." *Die Zeit*, December 16, 2004, p. 27.

16 Rüdiger K. W. Wurzel, *The Europeanisation of German Environmental Policy: From Environmental Leader to Member State Under Pressure?* (Berlin: Research Unit on Environmental Policy, 2002).

17 See: http://europa.eu.int/eur-lex/pri/en/oj/dat/2003/l_275/l_27520031025en 00320046. pdf. Accessed on December 22, 2004.

18 See: http://europa.eu.int/comm/environment/climat/pdf/germany_en.pdf. Accessed on December 22, 2004.

19 Michael T. Hatch, *The Politics of Climate Change in Germany*, Unpublished Manuscript (Stockton, CA: Department of Political Science, University of the Pacific, 2004).

20 Sachverständigenrat für Umweltfragen, *Umweltgutachten 2004—Umweltpolitische Handlungsfähigkeit sichern* (Berlin: Deutscher Bundestag, 2004), quoted here p. 111.

21 Sachverständigenrat für Umweltfragen, *Umweltgutachten 2004—Umweltpolitische Handlungsfähigkeit sichern* (Berlin: Deutscher Bundestag, 2004), quoted here p. 84.

22 German Advisory Council on Global Change, *Climate Protection Strategies for the 21st Century: Kyoto and Beyond* (Berlin: German Advisory Council on Global Change, 2003).

23 UK Government, *Energy White Paper: Our Energy Future—Creating a Low Carbon Economy* (London: UK Stationary Office, 2003).

24 This subsection is a revised version of Detlef F. Sprinz, Anja Bauer, Jette Krause, Kathrin Birkel, and Ruben Zondervan. *International Environmental Policy* (E-Learning Course), PolitikON, Available at: http://www.politikon.org, 2004.

25 Secretariat of the Convention on Biological Diversity, *Global Biodiversity Outlook* 2001, Available at: http://www.biodiv.org/gbo/gbo-pdf.asp#, quoted here p. 65. Accessed on April 1, 2005.

26 Ibid., p. 5.

27 Ibid.

28 Secretariat of the Convention on Biological Diversity. *Global Biodiversity Outlook*, 2001. Available at: http://www.biodiv.org/gbo/gbo-pdf.asp#, quoted here p. 67.

29 Ruth MacKenzie, Françoise Burhenne-Guilmin, Antonio G.M. La Viña, and Jacob D. Werksman. *An Explanatory Guide to the Cartagena Protocol on Biosafety* (Gland: IUCN, 2003), quoted here p. 6.

30 Secretariat of the Convention on Biological Diversity, *Convention on Biological Diversity*, 1992. Available at: http://www.biodiv.org/convention/default.shtml.

31 G. Kristin Rosendal. "Biodiversity: Between Diverse International Arenas," *Yearbook of International Co-operation on Environment and Development 1999/2000*, H. O. Bergesen, G. Parmann and Ø. B. Thommessen, eds (London: Earthscan, 1999).

32 See http://www.biodiv.org/world/parties.asp, Accessed on October 23, 2004.

33 Secretariat of the Convention on Biological Diversity. *Cartagena Protocol on Biosafety to the Convention on Biological Diversity* 2000. Available at: http://www.biodiv.org/doc/legal/cartagena-protocol-en.pdf.

34 Detlef F. Sprinz, "Comparing the Global Climate Regime with Other Global Environmental Accords," *International Relations and Global Climate Change*, Urs Luterbacher and Detlef F. Sprinz, eds (Cambridge, MA: The MIT Press, 2001).

35 Bundesministerium für Umwelt, Reaktorsicherheit und Naturschutz. *Schwerpunkte der Umweltpolitik bis 2006 (Main Goals for Environmental Policy Until 2006)*, Bundesministerium für Umwelt, Reaktorsicherheit und Naturschutz, without year, Available from http://www.bmu.de/das_ministerium/anschriften_aufgaben/schwerpunkte/doc/6510.php

36 Sachverständigenrat für Umweltfragen, *Umweltgutachten 2004—Umweltpolitische Handlungsfähigkeit sichern* (Berlin: Deutscher Bundestag, 2004), quoted here p. 172.

37 Bundesministerium für Umwelt, Reaktorsicherheit und Naturschutz. *Schwerpunkte der Umweltpolitik bis 2006 (Main Goals for Environmental Policy Until 2006)*, without year, Available from http://www.bmu.de/das_ministerium/anschriften_aufgaben/schwerpunkte/doc/6510.php

38 Decision VI/26, see: http://www.biodiv.org/decisions/?dec=VI/26, Accessed on April 29, 2005.

39   See http://www.biodiv.org/meetings/gbc-2010, Accessed on October 29, 2004. The EU sometimes asks for a halt of biodiversity loss by 2010 in its action plans. See Sachverständigenrat für Umweltfragen. *Umweltgutachten 2004— Umweltpolitische Handlungsfähigkeit sichern* (Berlin: Deutscher Bundestag, 2004) quoted here p. 120.

40   Die Bundesregierung, *Perspektiven für Deutschland—Unsere Strategie für eine nachhaltige Entwicklung*, 2002, Available from http://www.bundesregierung.de/Anlage585668/pdf_datei.pdf, quoted here p. 101, Translation by author.

41   Sachverständigenrat für Umweltfragen, *Umweltgutachten 2004—Umweltpolitische Handlungsfähigkeit sichern* (Berlin: Deutscher Bundestag, 2004), quoted here pp. 122–132.

42   The GEF concentrates its funding on project funding for biodiversity, climate protection, water bodies, and the stratospheric ozone layer in developing countries.

43   Bundesministerium für wirtschaftliche Zusammenarbeit und Entwicklung, *Biodiversity in German Development Cooperation* (Eschborn: Deutsche Gesellschaft für Technische Zusammenarbeit, 2002), quoted here p. 17, Available at: http://www2.gtz.de/biodiv/download/biodiv_conservation.pdf.

44   Ibid., p. 13.

45   Uschi Eid, *Rio + 10: Weltgipfel zur nachhaltigen Entwicklung—bisherige Erfolge und weiterer Handlungsbedarf*, 2002, Available at: http://www.uschi-eid.de/docs/020415Rio.htm.

46   The figures of the BMU and the Federal Ministry for Economic Cooperation and Development cannot be easily reconciled since the focus of German development outlays on biodiversity is thematically very broad; forestry certainly plays a major role.

47   Tanja Brühl, "*Bisherige Erfolge und Misserfolge der Biodiversitätskonvention— Gutachten im Auftrag der Enquete-Kommission," Globalisierung der Weltwirtschaft— Herausforderungen und Antworten*, (Frankfurt, am Main: Johann Wolfgang Goethe—Universität Frankfurt am Main: Institut für vergleichende Politikwissenschaft und Internationale Beziehungen, 2002), quoted here p. 33.

48   Sachverständigenrat für Umweltfragen, *Umweltgutachten 2004—Umweltpolitische Handlungsfähigkeit sichern* (Berlin: Deutscher Bundestag, 2004), quoted here p. 115.

49   German Advisory Council on Global Change, 2001. *Conservation and Sustainable Use of the Biosphere* (Sterling, VA: Earthscan, 2001).

50   See: http://www.bmu.de/en/1024/js/topics/environment/oecd, Accessed on October 23, 2004.

51   German Advisory Council on Global Change, 2001. *Conservation and Sustainable Use of the Biosphere* (Sterling, VA: Earthscan, 2001), quoted: 4.

52   Tanja Brühl, "*Bisherige Erfolge und Misserfolge der Biodiversitätskonvention— Gutachten im Auftrag der Enquete-Kommission," Globalisierung der Weltwirtschaft— Herausforderungen und Antworten* (Frankfurt am Main: Johann Wolfgang Goethe—Universität Frankfurt am Main: Institut für vergleichende Politikwissenschaft und Internationale Beziehungen, 2002), quoted here p. 40.

53   Jürgen Trittin, "The Role of the Nation State in International Environmental Policy", *Global Environmental Politics*, 4: 1 (2004): 23–28, quoted here pp. 24–25.

54   UK Government, *Energy White Paper: Our Energy Future—Creating a Low Carbon Economy* (London: UK Stationary Office, 2003).

55   Sachverständigenrat für Umweltfragen, *Umweltgutachten 2000, Schritte ins nächste Jahrtausend* (Stuttgart: Metzler-Poeschel, 2000).

56 M. Schröder, M. Clausen, A. Grunwald, A. Hense, G. Klepper, S. Lingner, K. Ott, D. Schmitt, and D. Sprinz, eds, *Klimavorhersage und Klimavorsorge* (Berlin: Springer, 2002).

57 Jürgen Trittin, "The Role of the Nation State in International Environmental Policy", *Global Environmental Politics*, 4: 1 (2004): 23–28, quoted here p. 27.

58 Wolfgang Fischer and Petra Holtrup, "Institutionelle Strukturen und Entscheidungsprozesse der Umweltaussenpolitik" *Deutschland neue Aussenpolitik: Institutionen und Ressourcen*, W.-D. Eberwein and K. Kaiser; eds (Munich: R. Oldenbourg, 1998).

Part V

The Outer Circle of German Foreign Policy

15

Germany's Development Policy since 1998

Peter Molt

Introduction

From its inception in the 1950s until the end of the east-west conflict, Germany's policy on development aid has shown a strong national bias. In addition to the country's interest in trading with developing countries and the wish to internationally isolate the German Democratic Republic (GDR), the focus on development aid seemed particularly useful for restoring Germany as a partner in international politics. This coincided with the expectation of the country's most important allies, the United States and France, that the burden would be shared for the stabilization of the newly independent countries as compensation for their support of German security interests.

After Germany's reunification, its aid policy declined in importance, demonstrated by the diminishing share of foreign aid as part of the gross domestic product. The general consensus of the political leaders, however, was that Germany now had to take on a greater responsibility, that it should act and be regarded as a reliable member of the United Nations. Toward this end, the German government under Chancellor Helmut Kohl has sought, since the middle of the 1990s, to obtain a permanent seat in the United Nations Security Council. The government under Chancellor Gerhard Schroeder reinforced these efforts. Germany's policy on development aid, which at least officially followed the recommendations of the Development Aid Committee (DAC)) of the Organization for Economic Cooperation and Development (OECD), was regarded as an important "soft power" issue that would help the country reach these goals.

Under the government of Chancellor Kohl, very few major disagreements arose about the general principles of German relations with the developing countries of Latin America, Africa, and Asia. An agreement was reached among the major parties—the Christian Democratic Union/Christian Social Union (CDU/CSU), the Social Democratic Party (SPD), and the Free Democratic Party (FDP) to consider development aid policy as a task requiring the consent of all parties and to avoid controversial discussions in this respect. The new orientation formulated in the 1990s in the framework of the UN conferences, the G-7 Summits, the international finance institutions, and the OECD met with the approval of the experts representing all parliamentary groups.

Global structural policy of peace and sustainable development as constituents of a new development aid policy

Erhard Eppler, the minister of economic cooperation and development under the socialist-liberal coalition formed in 1969, questioned for the first time the emphasis on foreign policy rather than aid policy. He underlined the ethical and humanitarian obligations to development cooperation. Eppler's resignation in 1974 underlined his failure to reconcile a foreign policy aligned with current national interests with a global, humanitarian conception of development aid. He succeeded, however, in extending the competence of the Federal Ministry for Economic Cooperation and Development (BMZ) and in disseminating among the broader public the notion that development aid is a humanitarian and ethical obligation. The public discourse since the 1980s in Germany has been more strongly stamped by a humanitarian and ethical understanding of development aid than it is in, for example, the United States, France, or England.

Twenty-eight years later, Eppler's ideas enjoyed a revival in the accord of SPD and the Alliance 90/ the Greens, when the Red–Green government was formed after the 1998 elections. The accord stated that development aid policy should be developed into an independent political field that aims for worldwide economic order and peace. The new, ambitious approach benefited from the fact that, through the debt-relief initiative for the Highly Indebted Poor Countries (HIPC-Initiative) and the UN-declaration of the Millennium Development Goals (MDG), the altruistic aspects of cooperation with developing countries had also gained international prominence.

Chancellor Schröder's appointee to the Ministry of Economic Cooperation and Development, Ms. Heidemarie Wieczorek-Zeul, has been primarily interested in this challenge. In her opinion, conventional development aid policy can only serve to support developing countries by designing their national structures to foster development and helping them adapt to the global economy.[1] Therefore, priority should be given to the redesign of international institutions and rules in favor of developing countries, as well as to the reduction of structural causes of conflicts, to non-violent conflict settlement, to promoting the ethical obligation of worldwide solidarity, global peace, and economic and social justice. Bilateral technical and financial cooperation, as well as the public subsidization of non-governmental organizations, should complement these aims in their programs and projects. With this program, Minister Wieczorek-Zeul based her policies essentially upon a memorandum of reform-oriented development experts and upon the decisions of the party conventions of the SPD and the Alliance 90/Greens.[2]

According to the coalition contract, development aid policy was considered an overarching task of the entire government. The BMZ became a member of the Federal Security Council for the first time. Political competencies relating to development in other departments were transferred to the BMZ, and a check of all bills whether they were corresponding to development aid goals, was introduced. As called for in the MDG-declaration, the federal government implemented in April 2001 "Action 2015," a program for combating global poverty.[3] It accorded to development aid a central role in its strategy for civilian crisis prevention, conflict solution, and peace consolidation. A non-governmental "Civilian Peace Service" was founded through which qualified peace workers are sent to mediate in the aftermath of conflicts and work for reconciliation. Permits for exports of arms are examined according to their effects on development. In accordance with the Department of the Environment, a high priority was granted to improving the environment and implementing policies to help curb global warming in developing countries. In EU committees, the BMZ became responsible for all matters concerning foreign aid, including the Cotonou convention on development cooperation between the European Union and the African, Caribbean and Pacific states group (ACP-states).

With the reassignment of competencies, frictions inevitably arose with other federal departments, primarily with the Foreign Office, which retained competencies for foreign policy regarding the United Nations, questions relating to the global order, international economic summits, European affairs, political relations with developing countries, and humanitarian aid. The conflict between the two departments had been latent and was not only caused by competence conflicts but also by differences in content. This schism became publicly apparent; in the spring of 2001, for example, the Foreign Office and the Federal Ministry for Economic Cooperation and Development announced at the same time their own diverging conceptions for Germany's policies on Africa.[4] In terms of its competencies, the BMZ suffered a setback when the EU council of development ministers was abolished in the summer of 2002, and its tasks were assigned to the EU ministerial council of foreign ministers.

But in spite of these internal quarrels, the Red–Green government did initially enjoy some success in the field of development policy. In the first half of 1999, when Germany held the EU presidency and hosted the G-7 Summit in Cologne, two important international projects had become ready for approval: the Cologne HIPC initiative and the EU–ACP Cotonou convention. Because of these successes, which were only possible because Germany's most important allies also supported them (the United States favored the HIPC Initiative, and France the Cotonou agreement), the German government gained an international profile as a supporter of far-reaching reforms.

The German government insists on the validity of this self-portrait to this day.

Financial freezing of aid

International expectations that, with the Red–Green coalition in power, Germany would embark on greatly increasing its overall allocation to foreign aid, however, were soon dissipated. Although the new government promised to reverse the trend of decreasing foreign aid, by the summer of 1999 it had become clear that the Treasury Department, announcing the intention of budget consolidation, was not willing to meet these expectations. Rather, it cut foreign aid by 8 percent for the year 2000, compared with the previous year's expenditures. The annual increase has remained under the rate of inflation ever since. Freezing the foreign aid budget is all the more critical, as the BMZ must finance numerous new programs, such as providing aid to southeastern European countries and the successor-countries of the Soviet Union. Funds must also be allocated for the HIPC Initiative and other promises made by the federal government, such as for the reconstruction of Afghanistan. Although the considerable transfers from Germany to the transition countries of Eastern Europe under the Kohl government have long since ceased, the resources freed were not transferred to the BMZ budget (Table 15.1).

Initially, the decreases in development aid "only" totaled just under € 100 million. Since the funds are spread across many countries and projects, the decline has only recently become noticeable. Internationally, however, the cuts have sent a signal to other donor countries and may ultimately weaken Germany's influence in the international organizations. Until the 2002 Monterrey World Conference for Development Financing, the Federal Republic could argue that other major donors also made small contributions. But since then, Germany's stagnating foreign aid stands in contrast to the increase in amounts spent by the United States and the other members of the European Union announced at the Monterrey meeting. The budget cuts of foreign aid have a considerable effect on the share of public foreign aid (ODA) compared with Germany's gross national product (GNP) (Table 15.2).

Table 15.1   Budget of the Federal Ministry for economic cooperation and development (in billions of Euros)

	1996	1997	1998	1999	2000	2001	2002	2003	2004	2005	2006	2007
Expenditures	4.034	4.010	4.052	3.997	3.675	3.797	3.672	3.695	3.744	3.783		
Expenditures planned											3.937	4.038
Share of fiscal budget	1.73	1.77	1.73	1.62	1.5	1.56	1.49	1.54	1.45	1.45		

Source: Federal Ministry of Finances: Financial Plan 2003–2007, August 2003 and Federal Budget 2004.

Table 15.2   Germany's Public Foreign Aid (ODA) as percentage of GNP

1982–83	1992–93	1998	1999	2000	2001	2002
0.53%	0.46%	0.26%	0.26%	0.27%	0.27%	0.27%

Source: OECD/DAC, Development Cooperation Review, Germany 1994 (Paris: OECD–DAC, 1995); OECD/DAC, Development Cooperation Review, Germany 1998 (Paris: OECD–DAC, 1999); OECD/DAC, Development Cooperation Review, Germany 2002 (Paris: OECD–DAC, 2003).

If the German government intends to fulfill the promise made at the 2002 Monterrey conference by Chancellor Schröder to increase aid to 0.51 percent of the GNP by 2010, the foreign aid budget would need to be expanded far beyond the amounts scheduled in the financial planning for the next few years.

Priority and partner countries

With the budget cuts in the year 2000, the BMZ took the opportunity to reduce its large number of recipient countries, which had been established according to foreign policy interests during the east-west conflict. The department hoped to achieve increased efficiency by narrowing its scope. The original plan foresaw 33 priority countries (with programs in three and more sectors) and another 37 partner countries (with programs in only one sector) (Table 15.3)

Table 15.3   Recipients of German development aid—priority and partner countries

	World			Sub-Saharan Africa	
	Total	German priority and partner countries	Share of ODA 1999 (%)	Total	German priority and partner countries
Least developed countries and territories	49	21	17	34	19
Other low-income countries and territories	18	18	34	7	5
Middle-income countries and territories	90	31	34	8	2
Total	157	70	85	49	26

Source: OECD/DAC, Development Cooperation Review, Germany 2002 (Paris: OECD–DAC, 2003). World Bank, World Development Report 2003 (Washington D.C.: The World Bank, 2003).

A general criterion for the choice cannot be discerned. This is shown in the example of Sub-Saharan Africa. The share of German Development Aid this region receives has remained unchanged for many years and is considerably below the average of the European Union and the share of France and England. In proportion to its poverty and unsolved problems, Sub-Saharan Africa is inadequately taken into account by German development aid.

Nor did Germany consult the other important donor countries in choosing its preferred recipients. Of the 40 out of 49 total countries of Sub-Saharan Africa that received aid in the year 2002, only 26 partner and priority countries shall remain on the list of recipients. Considerable aid is planned for countries such as Benin, Burkina Faso, Cameroon, Guinea, Mali, and Mozambique, all of which are also priorities for other donor nations. The choice of Ghana and Uganda demonstrate the powers of persuasion of the World Bank, which made these nations model countries in their new strategy. In order to achieve success, which was urgently needed for its credibility, the bank persuaded bilateral donors to allocate to those countries as much development aid as possible. Altogether, more than half of the countries chosen by Germany receive aid amounting to more than 10 percent of their GNP. The German share in these countries may reach up to 16 percent of the total aid received. On the other hand, 26 countries, which need help just as urgently, are left aside.

The emphasis given to poverty reduction was not taken into account either, apparently. In future, only 21 of the 49 Least Developed Countries (LDC) worldwide will receive German aid, and in Sub-Saharan Africa only 19 out of 34 countries will receive it. More than one-third of the population of Sub-Saharan Africa remains neglected.

This raises the question, does Germany prefer countries undertaking democratic reform? An examination of the 26 African partner and priority countries does not reveal any clear findings in this respect. A comparison with the Freedom House index[5] shows, that out of the 16 African countries, classified as "not free" seven are priority or partner countries. A further 12 of the selected countries are characterized as "partly free." In the other regions of the world, foreign trade and geostrategic interests as remnants of the east-west conflict or, as in Latin America, of long-existing traditional ties, influenced the setting of priorities even more than in Africa.

An objective political analysis on a country-by-country basis seems not to have been conducted, and the Foreign Office's findings for a strategy on Africa apparently were not properly taken into account. Hence it may be concluded[6] that the BMZ has based its selection on a mixture of explicit normative criteria, implicit strategic considerations, and individual country preferences at the level of the department and the organizations charged with executing these policies. As far as the BMZ bases its decisions and policies on normative criteria, there is growing public awareness that among the preferred countries, quite a few do not correspond to these norms. Thus, the BMZ's criteria for selecting aid recipients might in the end undermine the credibility of German development cooperation.

Doubt also exists as to whether a total of 70 partner and priority countries can be sustained in view of the shrinking resources. But to the contrary, already in 2002, based on promises made, the number of the countries had again increased to 80. Almost all countries considered in the past can again expect contributions, either through direct aid or regional programs already in place. Additionally, there are another ten countries in which development cooperation will likely need to be resumed, following changes in political conditions. Countries such as Zimbabwe, DR Congo, Togo, Sudan, Iraq, Haiti, Eritrea, and Somalia are prospective candidates. Soon, a figure as high as 110 could be reached for recipient countries, all of which fulfill the criteria for direct German bilateral cooperation.

Reforming German development aid: implementation and objectives

As the financial problems facing German development aid policy cannot be compensated by the described concentration, its alignment to new international conditions and concepts as outlined during the UN Monterrey conference would have been even more important. Substantial reforms with regards to organization and objectives were already claimed by the DAC review 1998 of German aid.[7] The recommendations of this review did not generate much response, however, due to the change of government and the overemphasis, given the BMZ's new direction, on global structural conditions. Therefore, the next, 2002 DAC review reiterated its criticism of the overall aspects of German development cooperation, stating that

> "despite these changes, Germany's development cooperation still appears to an outside observer as both centralized and hierarchical, while fragmented among the different institutional actors. While the diversity of actors within the German institutional architecture for aid is understandable, given the strong pluralistic precedent of the Federal State, the use of a multi-institutional system also creates challenges for coordination of effort. With different legal statutes, different political constituencies, different geographical locations, and a lack of operational leadership to coordinate in the field, it is a challenge to bring coherence to the design and implementation of German aid. While the diversity of semi-official and official institutions permits creative approaches to development and helps to avoid certain aspects of overly bureaucratic behavior, this diversity also offers opportunity for monopolistic behavior within the broader system, as well as overlapping parallel bureaucracy and corresponding issues of cost and inefficiency of management".[8]

The report also remarks that potential exists "to significantly improve upon the efficiency and the impact of Germany's assistance to the developing world." The report specifically notes that German foreign aid still concentrates on funding great infrastructure projects, supporting economic policy, capacity-building of institutions, and developing the private sector, therefore, it still essentially follows earlier conceptions of development aid. It states that it is still labor-intensive, an interchange of the technical aids with other donors does not take place, and the employment of local staff is limited, which also means that the capacity of the recipient country's administration is not adequately used or sufficiently strengthened. Technical aid is still provided predominantly by German experts and other expatriates, and therefore it is too broad and too expensive. The administrative requirements on the receivers' end remain high. The practice, to keep important program parts and particularly the financial management in their own hands goes counter to the principle of ownership by the receiver. The representation on the spot, where the coordination of the donors and the decision making should take place together with the recipient administration, is still inadequate. The decisions are centralized in Germany and remain, due to the various implementing organizations involved, fragmented. German embassies are not staffed to take over the coordination tasks; their "coherence mandate" is weak. The promised coordination between departments, primarily between the Foreign Office and the BMZ, apparently does not take place. A reorientation to a program-based approach, notwithstanding the claimed orientation of aid planning toward the World Bank Poverty Reduction Strategy Papers (PRSP) worked out with the recipient countries, has only been exercised exceptionally. The distribution of the German development cooperation has remained regionally and according to sectors essentially constant. An adaptation to the increased needs for the development of Africa and for the strategy of poverty reduction cannot be recognized.

This criticism of the policy of a important member country is rather harsh for an international organization such as the OECD. Whether the critique is warranted cannot be judged, since the available BMZ publications are not sufficiently detailed. The implementing organizations tend, quite understandably, to present a positive spin in their reports. The Red–Green government promised to improve and extend the evaluation of German development cooperation and indeed has put much effort into it. However, meaningful and verifiable analyses have not yet been published by the government.

The reform of the organizational structure got ahead only in edge areas. Thus, only the incorporation of the German Development Company (DEG) charged to promote joint ventures with private enterprises into the state-owned German Credit Bank for Reconstruction (Kreditanstalt für Wiederaufbau—KfW) took place, as well as the merger of Carl-Duisberg Society (CDG) working in the education and services sector with the German

Foundation for International Development and Cooperation (DSE). On the other hand, the restructuring of the core organizations of financial and technical aid, KfW and the German Technical Aid Agency (GTZ), whose respective activities are at this point undistinguishable, was left aside. The two organizations have a monopoly on the use of state technical and financial aid. But they may and shall pursue also entrepreneurial aims. This strengthens their interest, to channel the bulk of foreign aid to those areas and countries in which they have comparative advantages as enterprises or where the jobs of their employees can be safeguarded. These are not always the sectors or the countries of strategic importance.[9]

Another discussion refers to the priority placed on poverty alleviation, which the federal government declared the overarching goal of its new development policy. However, within the implementing organizations, there is no strong interest in making poverty-reduction a high priority in development aid. The contribution of German aid to direct measures of poverty alleviation is correspondingly rather small. The DAC Review 2002 notes that only 22 percent of the ODA in 1999 went to LDC countries and only 33 percent to low-income countries.

The report questions whether the share of 11 percent, which in 1997/1998 was used to support basic social services, was increased and the amount of credits, which with 24 percent of total foreign aid is relatively high in international comparison, reduced. New, reliable figures were apparently not available to the DAC, since the report suggests to prepare a detailed annual report on the use and the results of the German development cooperation with a view to provide more transparency. Interpreted generously, the measures of poverty alleviation may be projected onto about one third of total aid. Among them the campaigns against HIV-AIDS account already for almost 8%. In the non-availability of a detailed stocktaking of poverty alleviation it must be assumed, that the share of the income creating measures for the poor, basic health services and the basic education as well as for rural development is very small.

Assets of the German development cooperation continue to be only the political foundations, church services, and non-governmental organizations. After initially hesitating, the support of these organizations was increased cautiously by the Red–Green government. Although meaningful evaluations on these activities have yet to be made, there is sufficient evidence that the long-term efforts of these organizations have given important impulses to the strengthening of the civilian society, the respect of human rights, and the promotion of self-help. In particular, political foundations have successfully accomplished their task of promoting the political, intercultural, and scientific dialog and the exchange of views with liberty minded and peace oriented milieus.

A major challenge to German aid policies remains the adaptation to program-based approaches (PBA), stipulated by DAC and implemented so far mainly by the World Bank and the European Commission. The program-based approach means the support of programs of the partner countries by financial contributions to sector programs or by direct budget subsidies, preferably in a narrow coordination of all donors in the form of basket funding and common pools.[10]

The main obstacles for this strategy are obviously the poor performers, recently classified as LICUS (Low Income Countries Under Stress). The inherent problem to which extent the PBA can be followed through with notoriously bad performers has led to new efforts in international development strategy. The US government has started a worldwide program by its own for the best performers, the Millennium Challenge Account, judging the quality of the recipient countries by different independent indices including civil liberties. With the program, efforts by governments of the poor developing countries shall be rewarded: governments that "rule justly, invest into its population and encourage economic liberty."[11] The previous political conditionality as applied by the World Bank, the European Union, and many bilateral donors is replaced by a premium system for those countries that can prove measurable efforts in the mentioned areas. The G-8 action plan for Africa, adopted in the World Economic summit in Kanaskisis/Canada in 2002, points in the same direction. It is an attempt to concentrate on "good performers" of Africa. The G-8 industrial nations have promised up to US 4 billion per annum in addition to its regular aid for states, qualifying in the new strategic partnership for African development (NePAD) peer reviews.

All these programs, proposed or promoted by the United States, are based on the principle that the international community of states in its existing configuration must be preserved and that the proliferation of areas be without any actual state control, the more or less violent change of the existing borders and any further disintegration of states are highly problematic and therefore must be prevented by all means. The new American approach will force the other big donors to reconsider their own methods and strategies as regards foreign aid. Only England so far has reacted with the reform of its development agency. The German federal government has not yet clarified its policy with regard to these challenges. Will it follow the program-based approach of the World Bank, even if it reacted to it only hesitantly till now? A dissociation would contradict its professed support of the World Bank's goals. In which way will it limit its efforts to "good performers" and respond to the G-8 action plan for NePAD? What actions will it take to the poor performers?

German uncertainties versus America's claims for leadership

The shortcomings of Germany's development aid and the uncertainties in regard to its strategic directions contrast with the new US aid policy, focused after the events of September 11, 2001 on a reinforced fight against international terrorism and its origins. In its 2003 National Security Strategy,[12] the

US government claims international leadership in the areas of global economic order and the role of foreign aid policy. In its view the political instability and the economic problems of developing countries can be reduced only by an improved effectiveness of international cooperation, of the United Nations, and international finance institutions: "Decades of massive development assistance have failed to spur economic growth in the poorest countries. Worse, development aid has often served to prop up failed policies, relieving the pressure for reform and perpetuating misery. Results of aid are typically measured in dollars spent by donors, not in the rate of growth and poverty reduction achieved by recipients. These are the indicators of a failed strategy." Development aid policy is seen as an instrument of "soft power," being interwoven narrowly with the other instruments of American foreign policy.[13]

A first example of the new American claim to leadership was experienced by the other donor countries at the negotiations over the replenishment of the IDA Funds in July 2002. They had to give way to American pressure to increase considerably the volume of the thirteenth IDA (International Development Association) Fund and to concede in its lending policies a larger share of grants in relation to credits. The US demands were in line with their proposals for a comprehensive reform of international finance institutions, as already conceived by the Clinton administration.[14] The United States sees the World Bank's future role primarily in programs combating poverty, using the bulk of its means for measures that are not immediately economically profitable, but would improve the long-term prerequisites for development, like education and health. On the other hand, they wish that the IMF (International Monetary Fund) would stick to its core business, providing financial support for member states with balance of payment problems.

The Red–Green government did not oppose the American claim for leadership openly, but rather adopted an opposite standpoint, as can be seen in its concept of the reform of international financial institutions. In its view the scope of the World Bank's activities should not be cut back but enlarged, and the bank should be positioned as an international resource for "knowledge." It should, together with the IMF and WTO (World Trade Organization), be dedicated to the principles of partnership and multilateral cooperation and become a pillar of global governance. The organizations should be freed from the Anglo–American dominance. By means of structural changes promoted by them in the developing countries, they should influence the design of the global system. Moreover, new tasks should be assigned to them, such as the provision of global public goods, new financing facilities, promotion of environmental and social standards, support to renewable energies and care of gender questions. The engagement of the bank on the international capital markets should be directed to mobilize more funds for middle-level income countries. With the profits gained, the mentioned additional tasks in the least developed countries should be financed. The IMF should continue to commit itself with loans in the poorest countries. The weight of developing countries in both organizations should be strengthened.[15]

This ambitious concept, which contrasts with the American views, overestimates the international weight of Germany. As a middle-sized power it hardly has the chance to assert itself against the United States in fields they consider relevant for their security. It is also very difficult to form a coalition that presents opposing views to those of the United States. Whereas in the fields of security and foreign affairs, for example, close cooperation with France is possible, this is not likely in development politics. Traditionally the German administration's criticism and distrust of the French development aid policy is at least as profound as in the case of the United States, since French development aid is also seen as determined by narrow, postcolonial national interests.

At the beginning of her term in office in 1998, the Minister Wieczorek-Zeul hoped to mobilize support for her views by forming an alliance with the Scandinavian states, the Netherlands, and England. There is not much heard any more about this endeavor. Probably most European governments do not see European development aid policy as an appropriate tool for opposing the United States. Ongoing, serious internal management problems in European development cooperation are another reason that the European Union can hardly provide a platform on which to make development policy a pillar of the common European foreign policy. Till now, the European Union has not succeeded even in crafting a common African policy in spite of the summit meeting of European and African heads-of-state in Cairo in April 2000, the Cotonou convention with ACP countries, and the European Union's Mediterranean program. After the recent EU enlargement, the chances in this regard probably will be even more limited.

Results and prospects of Red–Green development aid policy

The various position papers of the BMZ on development issues, the gap between wishes and resources to fulfil them, the disputes between ministries, the lack of honouring internationally made promises, and the postponement of necessary reforms show the conceptional uncertainty, as well as a lack of leadership and coherence, in German development aid policy. It is vacillating between the ideal of a global policy and global governance, multilateral cooperation, the continuation of customary aid, a widespread scepticism about its aims, a reluctance to comply with international strategies, a distance to European development aid policy, and a misunderstanding of the nature of good transatlantic relations.

If the federal government would earnestly pursue its proclaimed goals of global solidarity and governance, it would have to start out with its so far unfinished European agenda. Closer cooperation of the European countries is an absolute must, since only through it can Europe gain the gravitas that might oblige the United States to seek closer multilateral cooperation. The challenges for international development aid, which result from state failure and state disintegration as well as from international terrorism, can only be met by a more coherent and intensified cooperation between the United States and Europe.

Despite the existing obstacles, Germany should therefore firmly continue to support a common EU development policy. Taking on a more active role for further design, however, presupposes that Germany was ready to intensify its political contribution and to increase its financial contribution. For this, almost all the institutional and financial prerequisites are currently missing. The streamlining of the political decision-making process by a greater coherence of the departments involved, the overdue reform of the management structures, clear and convincing priorities, an understanding of increasing efficiency, a realistic concept of the tasks attributed to the international organizations, and a solid financial base for such politics are imperative to meet adequately Germany's international obligations.

Notes

1 *Bundesministerium für wirtchaftliche Zusammenarbeit und Entwicklung: Elfter Bericht zur Entwicklungspolitik der Bundesregierung, Materialien 111* (Bonn: Bundesministerium für wirtschaftliche Zusammenarbeit und Entwicklung, 2001), pp. 61–68.
2 Eckhardt Deutscher, Gunther Hilliges, Manfred Kulessa, *Memorandum '98 für eine Politik der Nachhaltigkeit—Entwicklungspolitik als internationale Strukturpolitik* (Bonn: Memorandumsgruppe, 1998).
3 SPD Bundesparteitag Hannover, *Beschluss A1 zur Außen-, Sicherheits-und Entwicklungspolitik; Beschluss A19 Globalisierung und nachhaltige Entwicklung,* December 3, 1997 (Bonn: SPD, 1997).
4 Bundesministerium für wirtschaftliche Zusammenarbeit und Entwicklung (BMZ), *Armutsbekämpfung— eine globale Aufgabe. Aktionsprogramm 2015. Der Beitrag der Bundesregierung zur weltweiten Halbierung extremer Armut. BMZ Materialien 106* (Bonn: Bundesministerium für wirtschaftliche Zusammenarbeit und Entwicklung BMZ, 2001); Auswärtiges Amt, *Afrika-Strategie des Auswärtigen Amtes verfasst von den Referaten während des Jahres 2002.* Available at: http://www.auswaertiges-amt.de. Accessed December 15, 2003.
5 Freedom House, *Freedom in the World, 2003. Annual Global Survey of Political Rights and Civil Liberties.* Available at: http://www.freedom.org/research/survey2003.
6 Stefan Mair, *Künftige deutsche Afrikapolitik. Herausforderungen, Schwerpunktsetzung, Institutionen. Arbeitspapier Forschungsgruppe Naher/Mittlerer Osten* (Berlin: Stiftung Wissenschaft und Politik, Deutsches Institut für Internationale Politik und Sicherheit, 2003), p. 6.
7 OECD/DAC, Development Cooperation Review, Germany 1998 (Paris: OECD-DAC, 1999).

8   OECD/DAC, Development Cooperation Review, Germany 2002 (Paris: OECD-DAC, 2003).

9   Mair, *Künftige deutsche Afrikapolitik* (see note 6), p. 6.

10 Stefan Klingebiel, *Der internationale Diskussionsstand über Programmorientierung: Schlussfolgerungen für die deutsche Entwicklungszusammenarbeit. DIE Berichte und Gutachten 5/2003* (Bonn: DIE, 2003), p. 28.

11 USAID, *Millennium Challenge Account Fact Sheet*. Available at: http://www.usaid.gov. Accessed November 25, 2002.

12 US Government, The White House, *The National Security Strategy of the United States of America*. Available at: http://www.whitehouse.gov. Accessed March 3, 2003.

13 Joseph S. Nye Jr., *The Paradox of American Power. Why the world's only superpower can't go it alone* (New York: Oxford University Press, 2002), p. 146.

14 US Congress, United States Senate Foreign Relations Committee, *Hearing on the Future of the International Monetary Fund and International Financial Institutions*, February 29, 2000.

15 Bundesministerium für wirtschaftliche Zusammenarbeit und Entwicklung (BMZ), *Partnerschaft gegen die Armut—unsere Ziele in der Weltbank. BMZ aktuell 057* (Bonn: BMZ, 2003).

16
Business As Usual: Red–Green Policies toward Pacific Asia

Jörn-Carsten Gottwald

Introduction

German policy toward Pacific Asia under Chancellor Gerhard Schröder brought few changes to a foreign policy realm traditionally dominated by economic interests rather than high politics.[1] While crisis in Europe, the fight against terror, and the war in Iraq put heavy pressure on the decision makers of the German government, relationships with the states in Pacific Asia remained relatively relaxed. Within this general picture of continuity, there were, however, some new accents. While the chancellery increasingly focused on trade promotion and broader issues of world politics, it was left to the Foreign Ministry, other various ministries, or the European Commission to introduce more controversial topics such as human rights. In both spheres, that is, in trade promotion as well as in societal cooperation, the government seemed open to the influence of industry and nongovernmental organizations (NGOs). Having little global leverage except in its role as a trade power, the Red–Green coalition focused on improving relations with the most prominent economic powers in Asia, especially with the People's Republic of China. This pragmatic approach not only followed the broader normative requirements of a "civilian power" but also the growing awareness of Asia's importance in an interdependent world. It was also good public relations.

The importance of Pacific Asia in German foreign policy

Asia, especially Pacific Asia, remains economically the most dynamic region in the world, recovering fast from the so-called Asian Crisis of 1997–98; its population of approximately 1.7 billion people represents nearly one-quarter of the global population, constituting one of three global economic centers (next to North America and Western Europe). China had the highest average gross domestic product growth rates in the world between 1978 and 2003, and was seen as the most important "market of the future." The rise of

248   *Jörn-Carsten Gottwald*

Taiwan, South Korea, Singapore, Hong Kong, and later the Philippines, Indonesia, Thailand, and Malaysia, also gave important impulses to the global economy under the slogan of the "Asian Miracle." Additionally, Pacific Asia includes the second biggest global economy, that of Japan.

From the German (as well as European Union) perspective, Pacific Asia is important for both bilateral and broader global reasons (see tables 16.1 and 16.2). First, due to its sheer size, Pacific Asia is a huge consumer market, a very significant trading partner, and a global economic competitor for both Europe and the rest of the world. But it is also an important partner in managing growing global responsibilities and a hotbed for military and nuclear tensions.[2] In addition, a historically rooted cultural fascination plays

Table 16.1   Germany's trade with Pacific Asia: imports to Germany

Imports to Germany (in millions)	1990 (%)	1993 (%)	1996 (%)	1999 (%)	2003 (%)
Total	100	100	100	100	100
PR China	1.41	2.44	2.61	3.10	4.70
Japan	5.75	6.02	4.99	4.90	3.60
Republic of Korea	0.79	1.00	0.94	0.92	1.07
Taiwan	1.08	1.31	1.19	1.25	1.02
Singapore	0.52	0.71	0.63	0.63	0.64
Hong Kong	0.88	0.77	0.51	0.47	0.39
Taiwan	0.58	0.93	1.04	0.83	0.57

© Conrad / Gottwald 2004.
Source: Statistisches Bundesamt.

Table 16.2   Germany's trade with Pacific Asia: exports from Germany

Imports to Germany (in millions)	1990 (%)	1993 (%)	1996 (%)	1999 (%)	2003 (%)
Total	100	100	100	100	100
PR China	0.62	1.53	1.38	1.36	2.75
Japan	2.57	2.51	2.60	2.03	1.79
Republic of Korea	0.70	0.91	1.17	0.63	0.84
Hong Kong	0.47	0.79	0.81	0.65	0.60
Singapore	0.49	0.59	0.74	0.61	0.58

© Conrad / Gottwald 2004.
Source: Statistisches Bundesamt.

an important role in the perception of Asia among German political and economic decision makers.

The political programme: from the "Asia Concept" of 1993 to the "Regional Concepts" of 2002

After early but unsuccessful efforts to develop an active, independent policy toward Asia in the 1950s and 1960s, there was no cohesive Pacific Asia policy until 1993; when on his flight back from a state visit in Pacific Asia, practically in passing, the then Chancellor Helmut Kohl instructed members of the Foreign Ministry to work out an "Asia concept."[3] Published that same year, this concept also served as a model for the European Union's Asian policy, which was agreed upon one year later.[4] These two concepts formed the programmatic basis of German policy toward Pacific Asia when the Red–Green coalition, lead by Gerhard Schröder, came into power in 1998.

The European concept improved efforts to coordinate national Asian policies. Bilateral relations between the European Union and particular Asian nations evolved as part of specific state-related programs or cooperation agreements. Furthermore, the European Union fostered the institutionalization of multilateral roundtables, such as the ASEAN (Association of South East Asian Nations) Regional Forum and the Asia–Europe Meeting. The "strengthening of the EU's political and economic presence" according to the "growing global weight of an enlarged European Union"[5] remained the main interest behind the concept developed in 2001, which called for the promotion of a wide range of policies. In fact, however, interregional relations between Europe and Asia proved very path-dependent: national infighting between EU member states over Pacific Asian markets and the best way to gain access to them, as well as national efforts at trade promotion, still dominated, in stark contrast to the ambitious language of policy declarations. Indeed, national policies still dominate the supranational level when it comes to conducting European policies vis-à-vis Pacific Asia. Even for a "working paper,"[6] the European Union's "Asia concept" hardly satisfied the need for a coherent European approach.

Such was the situation when the Red–Green coalition, reacting to a profound change in the perception of Asia, at last presented a policy outline of its own. While fear of East Asian economic dominance had shaped the policy approach of the 1993 document, the new concept was fine-tuned in an atmosphere shaped by the aftermath of the Asian financial crisis and by the war against terror. The new "globalization of political and economic opportunities"[7] made the policy toward Pacific Asia a "central element of the global foreign and security policy of the EU."[8] Defining a set of priorities (such as the "peaceful solution of contradictory interests," "human rights, democracy, rule of law," "establishment of consultation and cooperation structures," as well as the "protection and support of our economic interests,"[9]) the document stresses the European Union's positive role in dealing with China and in the context of the Asia–Europe Meeting while the task of German foreign policy is explicitly described as providing "services," presumably for German commercial interests. In comparison with the earlier program, the prominent role of economic cooperation is now replaced by an emphasis on global security and bilateral human rights policy (the latter primarily as a rhetorical tribute to domestic pressures).

Continuing the traditional German focus on the relations with the People's Republic of China (PRC), the new program confirmed that Germany would stand by the one-China policy, hence withholding formal recognition of a democratic Taiwan, in spite of the fact that such recognition is a plausible step in fostering democracy, ostensibly one of the document's main objectives. With its emphasis on multilateral cooperation, human rights, and democracy, and its guideline for programs by particular ministries, the new policy outlines appear to be a catalogue of good but vague intentions directed at the public rather than a clear political agenda. Thus, not surprisingly, an empirical analysis of Red–Green policy vis-à-vis major Asian nations reveals a significant implementation gap.

Red–Green policy toward Pacific Asia: the case study of China

Policy toward Pacific Asia in fact largely means economic policy toward China, as some members of the Schröder government occasionally have admitted.[10] After early criticisms, especially by Foreign Minister Joschka Fischer, policy toward China quickly became the preoccupation of the chancellor. The chancellery's dominance of this issue was only interrupted once, when Schröder, trying to rush the export of a nuclear plant and the lifting of a European embargo against arms exports to China, came into conflict with the core values of his coalition partner, the Green party. In this case, parliamentary groups of the Red–Green coalition actively wrested Pacific Asia policy from the chancellor's grasp, thus scoring a victory that was humiliating for Schröder, who lost face with his Chinese counterparts to a certain degree. This shift turned out to be short lived, however. Most of the time, the Schröder administration followed the path laid out by its predecessors, catering carefully to industrial interests in Pacific Asia.

Shortly after its foundation in the 1950s, the Federal Republic of Germany tried to establish good trade relations with the PRC, but these efforts largely failed. After the two countries established formal diplomatic relations in 1972, political contacts proved relatively stable. In spite of a temporary setback caused by the 1989 Tiananmen massacre, when the Chinese authorities brutally suppressed political dissent and European governments reacted by imposing economic sanctions, bilateral relations grew ever deeper during the Kohl government.[11] When it came to power in 1998, the new coalition government led by Chancellor Gerhard Schröder inherited a broad program of German–Chinese cooperation, which it has since intensified further.

At first, however, there were few signs for continuity. When the Social Democratic Party (SPD) and the Greens were preparing to take charge in September 1998, Foreign Minister-designate Joschka Fisher declared that there would be "no further kowtowing toward the 'Peking dictatorship.' "[12] The prominent Chinese dissident Wei Jingsheng was invited to the chancellor's office, seriously annoying the Beijing leadership. Yet relations with China were quickly included among the chancellor's policy priorities, and as a result the focus shifted away from human rights and democracy and toward commercial relations.

While visiting the Chinese capital on May 12, 1999, during the Kosovo war, Schröder had to apologize for the accidental destruction of the Chinese embassy in Belgrade by NATO (North American Treaty Organization) air forces. This put an end to the active pursuit of advancing human rights policy. The chancellor managed this diplomatic balancing act well and established his office as the strategic actor in formulating policy goals vis-à-vis China. With its three regional policy outlines for East Asia, Southeast Asia, and South Asia articulated in May of 2002, the government officially stepped in line with the policy established by its predecessor—namely, according highest priority to the economic and political integration of the PRC, rather than to political change and democratization, and to the continuation of the cordial personal relationship that had developed between the German chancellor and then Chinese Prime Minister Zhu Rongji.

While the chancellor became a regular guest in the People's Republic, Foreign Minister Joschka Fischer seemed to avoid visits to the country. When he finally visited the PRC in the summer of 2004, he explicitly criticized his hosts on several occasions, arguing in public with his Chinese counterpart. The low profile of Fischer on China policy left ample room for maneuver for the state bureaucracy and nongovernmental organizations. But by no means did the Foreign Service help the Foreign Ministry challenge the chancellery's assertive stance in defining Germany's China policy. Having settled the Belgrade embassy crisis successfully, the government began to extend considerable support for German business activities in China. To win support for this among the German public, a "dialogue about the rule of law" was also established between the two countries. Relations were developing smoothly until the chancellor, in 2004, launched an "offensive"[13] to lift the European Union's ban on EU arms sales to China. In spite of the French president's strong support of this initiative, it failed to gain the necessary majority in the EU Council of Ministers. Interestingly, the initiatives of Jacques Chirac and Gerhard Schröder coincided with a shift in strategy of the Franco–German European Aeronautic Defence and Space Company (EADS), a major producer of weaponry, who declared China one of its most important future markets.[14]

As did his predecessor, Schröder claimed that his government was conducting a dialogue on human rights with China behind closed doors rather than in public. But this strategy seems to have met with very limited success,[15] beyond the symbolic release of a small number of political prisoners by the Chinese leadership in advance of state visits. What kept intra-party critics of the Red–Green coalition government at bay was the "outsourcing" of this sensitive question to the president, Johannes Rau, and to other bilateral and EU activities. The "dialogue on the rule of law" initiated in 1999 is often hailed as one of the major innovations of the Red–Green Asia policy, though various similar programs had been in place under the Kohl administration. Designed as a process of cooperation with a broad scope and long duration, the agreement will seek improvements in legal and judicial practices in China. The dialogue combines elements of careful public criticism,[16] frank discussions behind closed doors, and pragmatic cooperation at the bilateral and the European–Chinese level.[17] Remarkably, the 2003–2005 program does include a chapter concerning human rights.

This mixture of European initiatives and the occasional criticism of the Chinese government in public institutionalized a sophisticated twofold division of labor. While Chancellor Schröder assumed the part of the tireless trade promoter, Foreign Minister Fischer occupied the moral high ground by playing the occasional human rights conscience of the Red–Green coalition. This approach proved sustainable as long as the Chinese leadership tacitly approved, as it did in the confrontation with Fischer or after President Rau's critical remarks during his state visit to the PRC in September 2003. This was presumably not too difficult for them, as they knew full well that it was the chancellor who guided Germany's China policy. Concerning security policy, the Schröder government again followed its predecessor's example: while the SPD and the Greens had criticized Chancellor Kohl for supposedly exonerating the Chinese People's Liberation Army for its role in the Tiananmen massacre by paying the PLA a visit in 1995, it was the Social Democrat Rudolf Scharping who visited the PRC in 2001 as the first German minister of defense. With the establishment of the ASEAN Regional Forum, in which both China and the European Union participated, Germany also has a new, indirect forum to discuss security-related questions within a multilateral framework. In practice, Germany was content (as were the Europeans in general) to leave those issues to the US administration.[18]

The actors in Germany's China policy

While German diplomats in China tend to have rather low profiles, German business leaders often enjoy high visibility and great respect from the Chinese. For example, the CEO of Siemens, Heinrich von Pierer, and the former member of the Volkswagen board, Martin Posth, have established close relationships with members of China's core leadership. In their home countries, they are able to exercise considerable influence on Germany's policies toward China,[19] and they have managed to obtain significant political support for their activities in that country's market.[20] This close relationship between government and business serves mutual interests: the government receives advice and the opportunity to present itself as business-friendly, while Germany's big corporations obtain political and financial support in their hunt for large contracts.

The Red–Green coalition continued to fine-tune this system of public backing for commercial projects, occasionally even at the price of weakening the European Common Foreign and Security Policy. Like France, Britain, and most EU member states, Germany still tries to promote its "national champions" even while it pays lip service to free-market principles. As a result, European rivalry allows the Chinese side to play European offers against one another in search of the richest public finance component for European–Chinese trade and investment deals.[21] The German government's lobbying efforts on behalf of business also make it difficult for the government to link development aid—which de facto is often used to promote the country's commercial interests—to issues of human rights and good governance, as called for by its own (and the EU's) regional policies. Initial hopes that human rights NGOs would find the gates of the new administration wide open soon proved naïve: while many discussions took place, especially with the Foreign Ministry, important policy initiatives were coordinated by the chancellery with a clear bias in favor of industry. Yet although their policy impact in Berlin was strictly limited, German NGOs still play a prominent and important role in China itself. Thus, political party foundations—as well as experts of the German Association for Technical Cooperation, the German Foreign Exchange Service, the Goethe Institute, and the German Research Foundation—are very active. While quasi-governmental organizations like the German Association for Technical Cooperation usually keep out of the political spotlight, the work of the foundations is much more sensitive: in 1996, the Beijing office of the Friedrich Naumann Foundation was closed by the Chinese government in retaliation for a workshop on Tibet that the foundation had held in Germany. In fact, transnational commercial and cultural relations represent the most substantial and the most innovative aspect of German policy toward China.[22]

Fears that the prominent role accorded human rights issues in policy statements by the Green party would complicate bilateral relations between Germany and China proved unfounded. In reality, Red–Green policies showed little change and much continuity. The realities of German–Chinese relations often do not live up to the expectations created by the ambitious rhetoric of the German government. Thus, the broadened dialogue between human rights NGOs and the foreign ministry, and the creation in Germany of an office for a "human rights representative," had little effect on actual policies. Only when Schröder wanted to sell a nuclear plant to China did the opponents of his business-driven China policy in both coalition parties finally resist him successfully. In general, however, opponents acquiesced as the government claimed to promote human rights and democracy in China through enhanced commercial ties and EU policies. To criticize China from the EU level reduced the risks of retaliation by the Chinese government against German commercial interests. Compared to the turbulence in bilateral relations caused by the Tiananmen massacre during the tenure of Helmut Kohl, relations have experienced little public friction since 1998: tensions after the bombardment of the Chinese embassy in Belgrade were defused quickly, as was Chinese disappointment over Schröder's failure to push through the sale of the Hanau nuclear reprocessing plant and to lift the European arms embargo against China. Important questions of global scope, such as the implications of American plans to develop theatre missile defense systems for Pacific Asia and the conflict over the war in Iraq, largely remained outside the bilateral relationship. With China's 2001 admission to the World Trade Organization, which the European Union played a crucial role in bringing about, one of Germany's central policy goals with respect to China was achieved: the Middle Kingdom's integration into the international system took a big step forward. But this success also highlights that, despite all efforts to strengthen political dialogue between the two sides, economic exchange supported by the two governments remains the "backbone of the relationship."[23]

The surprisingly smooth evolution of bilateral relations had much to do with the groundwork laid by the predecessors of the Red–Green governments, which had removed various traps and pitfalls. Thus, the renunciation of a common European approach (which openly criticized Chinese human rights abuses), the build-up of official contacts with the Chinese military, participation in multilateral forums such as the ASEAN Regional Forum or the Asia–Europe Meeting (which allowed Germany to keep sensitive issues out of the bilateral framework), and the establishment of a strong German commercial presence cleared the way for a policy of continuity toward China. Part of this continuity was the strict adherence to the one-China policy, thus denying Taiwan any official support in its push for global recognition. While commercial relations with the young democracy in Taiwan developed rapidly, the Red–Green government avoided any steps that might be interpreted by Beijing as fostering Taiwan's ambitions for independence. Thus, economic and political relations with Beijing and trade relations with Taipei unfolded smoothly. This helped push forward the development of broad transnational relations.

Beyond China: Red–Green policy throughout Pacific Asia

Red–Green policies toward China are in fact similar to policies toward Pacific Asia as a whole. Generally speaking, they seem to have been set on autopilot since 1998, with bilateral relations largely dominated by transnational commercial activities. As in the case of China, relations with other nations in Pacific Asia were, at least from the German perspective, largely free from serious problems.

This is especially true for Japan; although the Foreign Ministry, regardless of the smooth bilateral relations with Japan, states that the "opportunities actually lying within the second and third biggest economies in the world are not depleted yet",[24] even if the intensity of bilateral economic ties is often underestimated.[25] It is exactly the lack of political controversies in German–Japanese relations that, in combination with the delegation of potential trade conflicts to the multilateral level, leads to a "lack of substance."[26] Again, the Red–Green government successfully continues the existing political, cultural, and social dialogue. As an economic and diplomatic partner that often shares Germany's broad outlook as a non-nuclear middle power, Japan is well regarded and integrated into German foreign policy through an extensive network of bi- and multilateral consultations. There also have been cases in which interests and objectives were so closely aligned as to produce significant policy coordination—for example, in the context of the Petersberg conference of December 2001, during which participants tried to coordinate international support for the rebuilding of Afghanistan; this was followed by a similar conference in Tokyo in January 2002, and a third in Berlin in 2004. Perhaps most importantly, both countries have been eager to join the UN Security Council as permanent members and have tried to coordinate their respective campaigns toward that goal. The depth of diplomatic cooperation is demonstrated in many venues, including annual meetings between German and Japanese heads of government and bi-annual consultation meetings between the foreign ministers, as well as the many supplemental talks to the G-8 and other international meetings, ministerial-level talks[27] and personnel exchanges,[28] and bilateral ambassador's conferences. The growing importance of global rather than bilateral questions is reflected in the agenda of "Japan and Germany in the 21st century—seven pillars of cooperation," an agreement signed on October 30, 2000 by German Foreign Minister Joschka Fischer and his Japanese counterpart, Yohei Kono. Despite this joint program, closely aligned interests and shared objectives, and the multitude of consultation arrangements, political cooperation seems ultimately devoid of substance. In the end, this bilateral relationship, as that with China, is therefore ultimately dominated by transnational activities.[29]

Security issues loomed largest on the Korean peninsula. Germany was among those nations to initiate the formal recognition of the Democratic People's Republic of Korea in 2000–2001.[30] The Red–Green government also kept an eye on the Korean Peninsula Energy Development Organization, through which the European Union supported efforts to disarm North Korea's nuclear capabilities. But EU involvement in managing the difficult issues posed by North Korea's nuclear weapons program has always been peripheral at best, and the European Union has not played any role in resolving the recent crisis over North Korea's secret nuclear enrichment program: "the six-party talks" that led to a suspension of the work in North Korea of the Korean Peninsula Energy Development Organization are taking place without any Western European participation. One important reason for this has been the lack of a coherent, closely coordinated approach by the European Union and its member countries. As showed by its recognition of the Democratic People's Republic of Korea, against all efforts and promises to follow a common, multilateral strategy, Germany was sometimes as much part of the problem in the European Union's Common Foreign and Security Policy as it was part of the solution. Germany had also pursued an individual course of action toward Indonesia after President Suharto's resignation.[31] Part of the Red–Green policy agenda toward Pacific Asia included efforts to intensify multilateral relations in the region, particularly in the context of the long-standing dialogue between the European Union and ASEAN, in the Asia–Europe Meetings, and the ASEAN Regional Forum. In all three contexts, however, matters have been complicated by controversies over the participation of Myanmar (formerly Burma), whose military junta refused to end its brutal suppression of the democratic opposition and release its leader, the Nobel Peace Prize winner Daw Aung San Suu Kyi. The question of whether Myanmar could become a member has overshadowed much of the discussions of the Asia–Europe Meetings, which represent a new approach to interregional cooperation. Still, the Asia–Europe Meetings have been reasonably successful in triggering a range of nongovernmental activities, including on the so-called track two, involving academics, journalists, and members of think tanks, as well as government officials in their private capacity, and track three, peoples-to-peoples exchanges. Although the official Asia–Europe Meetings have been used to raise issues of human rights violations and bad governance, it is difficult to see the "clear differences"[32] the government claimed for Germany's policies in this area in comparison to those of its predecessor.

Conclusion

Thus, continuity has been the watchword for German policy toward Pacific Asia: in more than one sense, it has been business as usual. This has also applied to process: most of the important decisions have been made in the chancellor's office rather than the foreign ministry. The influence of corporate leaders on the chancellor's activities in Asia has clear characteristics of a "policy capture." Human rights are highlighted rhetorically, but sidelined when it comes to policy implementation. The daily routine remains focused on trade and commercial support. The PRC has increasingly come to dominate Germany's approach to the region; other states get closer bilateral attention only during times of crisis.

The Red–Green government has continued to emphasize multilateral relations with Pacific Asia, through the Asia–Europe Meetings, for example; but its actual influence in shaping this process has remained limited.

In pursuing relations with Pacific Asia, the Red–Green government has established a twofold division of labor. While Chancellor Schröder has concentrated on trade promotion, President Rau, Foreign Minister Fischer, and others have occasionally voiced the kind of critical comments on Chinese human rights practices that both government parties had been calling for when in opposition. The second division of labor exists between the national and European levels. Participation in various fora on EU–Asia dialogues enables the Schröder administration to keep sensitive questions like market access or human rights at least partly out of bilateral relations. In this sense, the strategy to promote multilateralism in order to create new avenues to foster human rights[33] has been quite successful.

Thus, while Red–Green policies toward Pacific Asia have largely been set on autopilot, one of the most dangerous regional problems—the status of Taiwan—has practically been ignored by Germany, as well as by the other major European states in their rush to profit from the economic advance of the PRC. Whether this policy stance is prudent remains to be seen, but it clearly does not live up to the high-minded principles expressed in public documents and speeches.

On paper, Germany still follows the role model of a "civilian power." In practice, however, there has been little innovation, much path dependency, and the dominance of economic and commercial interests over normative considerations. Even in times of the threat of global terrorism, and against the expectations created by the policy stances of the SPD and Greens when they were in the opposition, under the Red–Green government trade promotion has remained the defining characteristic of Germany's policy vis-à-vis Pacific Asia.

Notes

1 Jörn-Carsten Gottwald, "Im Osten nichts Neues. Vier Jahre und vier Monate rot-grüne Ostasienpolitik," *Deutschland im Abseits? Rot-grüne Außenpolitik 1998–2003*, Hanns Maull, Sebastian Harnisch and Constantin Grund, eds (Baden-Baden: Nomos, 2004), pp. 133–47; quoted here p. 133.
2 Bundesregierung, "Asien-Konzept der Bundesregierung," *Internationales Asienforum*, 4/1993: 142–57.
3 Dieter Rothermund, "Perspektiven deutscher Politik—Chancen und Probleme", *Das Parlament*, June 9, 2000.
4 Commission of the European Communities, *Mitteilung der Kommission an den Rat. Auf dem Weg zu einer neuen Asienstrategie*, KOM(94), 314/endg./2, Brussels, July 27, 1994.
5 Commission of the European Communities, *Europe and Asia: A Strategic Framework for Enhanced Partnership. Communication from the Commission*, COM (2001) 469 final, Brussels, September 4, 2001.

6 Paul Lim, *Critique of the Commission's Communication, Europe and Asia: A Strategic Framework for Enhanced Partnership*, Available at: www.ased.org/content/eurasia/print.php?ch=1&id=1014604226.389423. Accessed November 10, 2002.

7 Auswärtiges Amt, *Aufgaben der deutschen Außenpolitik. Ostasien—Japan, Sued- und Nordkorea, Mongolei, China einschl. Hong Kong und Macau, Taiwan—am Beginn des 21. Jahrhundert.* Berlin, May 2002; quoted here 1.

8 Auswärtiges Amt, *Aufgaben der deutschen Außenpolitik* (see note 7), p. 3.

9 Auswärtiges Amt, *Aufgaben der deutschen Außenpolitik* (see note 7), p. 16.

10 Ludger Volmer, "Grundlinien der neuen deutschen Außenpolitik," Speech of Dr. Ludger Volmer, State Minister at the German Foreign Office at the "Politischen Forum Ruhr," November 12, 2001. Available at: http://www.ludger-volmer.de/arbeit/aussen p_visier/ index_ rede.htm. Accessed November 15, 2002.

11 Sebastian Heilmann, "Grundzüge deutscher Chinapolitik," *China Analysis No. 14*, August 2002, Available at: http://www.chinapolitik.de/studien/china_analysis/no_14.pdf. Accessed December 12, 2002.

12 Jürgen Kremb, "China-Politik. Ende des deutschen Kotau," *Spiegel-online*, November 13, 2002. Available at: http://www.spiegel.de/politik/ausland/0,1518,222622,00.html. Accessed January 16, 2003.

13 Sabine Muscat, "Bundesregierung tritt leise in der China-Politik," *Financial Times Deutschland*, March 16, 2004.

14 *Frankfurter Allgemeine Zeitung*, 26 February 2004.

15 Gerd Poppe, "Es muss weiterhin deutliche Kritik an China geben," *Die Welt*, October 4, 2002.

16 See *Rede von Bundeskanzler Schröder anlässlich der Verleihung der Ehrendoktorwürde der Tongji-Universität am 30. Dezember 2002 in Shanghai*. Available at: http://www.bundeskanzler.de/Energieversorgung-.9510.457033/Rede-von-Bundeskanzler-Schroeder-anlaesslich-der...htm. Accessed February 6, 2003.

17 Nicole Schulte-Kulkmann, "Der Einfluss westlicher Rechtsberatung auf die Rechtsreformen in der Volksrepublik China: Zur Rolle von Akteuren und Interessen in der chinesisch-westlichen Rechtsberatung," *China Analysis* No. 13 (July 2002). Available at http://www.chinapolitik.de/studien/china_analysis/no_13.pdf. Accessed December 12, 2002.

18 Sebastian Heilmann, "Grundzüge deutscher Chinapolitik." *China Analysis No. 14* (August 2002). Available at: http://www.chinapolitik.de/studien/china_analysis/no_14.pdf. Accessed December 12, 2002.

19 Both have prominent positions in influential NGOs: von Pierer chairs the APA, Posth the Asia-Pacific-Forum Berlin.

20 For example in the form of German Chambers of Trade and Commerce, Offices of Delegates of the German Economy, German Centers or a multitude of organizations, who take care of the interests of German corporations in China.

21 See R. Wong, *A Common European Policy on China? Economic, Diplomatic and Human Rights Trends since 1985*, Unpublished Draft, National University of Singapore, 2004.

22 Gudrun Zeeck, *Das ferne Interesse. Die deutsch-chinesischen Kulturbeziehungen. Bestandsaufnahme und Empfehlungen.* Ifa//dokumente/1/2002 (Stuttgart: Institute for Foreign Relations, 2002).

23 Matthias Nass and Michael Taubmann, "Schrecklich normale Verhältnisse," *Die Zeit*, 16 (2002).

24 Auswärtiges Amt, *Deutsch-japanische Beziehungen*. Available at: www.auswaertiges-amt. de/www.../laender_ausgabe_html?type_id=14&land_id=6. Accessed January 14, 2003.

25 Werner Pascha, "Economic Relations between Germany and Japan—An Analysis of Recent Data," Duisburg Working Papers on East Asian Economic Studies No 61 / 2002. Available at: http://www.uni-duisburg.de/FB5/VWL/OAWI/ ARBEITSPAPIERE/paper61.html. Accessed December 14, 2002.

26 Nadine Leonhardt and Hanns W. Maull, "Deutschland und Japan," *Handbuch zur Deutschen Außenpolitik*, Herbert Dittgen and Siegmar Schmidt, eds (to be published in 2006).

27 Institutionalized for several ministries, that is BMF, BMWi, BMVg, BMJ, BMFSJ, BMU.

28 German participants are the Foreign Ministry, the Ministry of Justice, Ministry of Defence, and the Ministry for Education and Research.

29 Leonhardt and Maull, *Handbuch zur Deutschen Außenpolitik* (see note 26); Angelika Viets, "Thema: die deutsch-japanischen Beziehungen: Zu wenig Probleme?," Paper presented at the Centre for Pacific Asian and Pacific Studies, University of Trier, February 2, 2004. Available at: http://www.zops.uni-trier.de/files/ Vortrag_Vietz.pdf. Accessed May 21, 2004.

30 See S. Bersick, *Zur Politik der interregionalen Beziehungen. Das Beispiel des ASEM-Prozesses*. PhD thesis, Free University Berlin, 2002, 277.

31 Rüdiger Siebert, "Auch Deutschland hat die indonesische Diktatur indirekt unterstützt. Die Männerfreundschaft zwischen Kohl und Suharto," *Das Parlament*, June 9, 2000.

32 Ludger Volmer, "Staatsminister Dr. Ludger Volmer über das Treffen der Außenminister der EU und ASEAN," *Berliner Morgenpost*, December 10, 2000.

33 See for example Wolfgang Ischinger, "Der politische Dialog zwischen Asien und Europa nach Seoul," Speech held at the European-Asian Forum 2001, Berlin, May 5, 2001. Available at: http://www.auswaertiges-amt.de/www/de/ archiv_print?archiv_id=1510. Accessed September 22, 2004.

17
Germany and the Israeli–Palestinian Conflict

Martin Beck

Introduction

The end of the east–west conflict and the reunification of Germany gave rise to a lively political and scientific discussion as to whether a normalization of German foreign policy was ahead. Would Germany maintain its postwar tradition of being a self-restrained "civilian power" whose foreign policy is driven by certain norms, social roles, and identities rather than by egoistic self-interests? Or, would the release from the constraints of being a "front state" in the conflict with the Soviet Union and the newly acquired territory and population lead the henceforth fully sovereign Germany to pursue the foreign policy of a regular European great power? When the first academic balances were drawn around 2000, most scholars, especially those whose contributions were based on the sound application of foreign relations theories, came to the clear conclusion that German foreign policy after reunification would continue to be one of civilian power.[1] It is noteworthy that this conclusion was not confined to scholars whose normative orientation was more or less in favor of Germany being a civilian power.[2] Rather, authors who regretted the postwar German tradition of power aversion also agreed that the structural changes of the late 1980s did not result in a reorientation of German foreign policy.[3]

Despite the above-mentioned findings, recent major decisions and statements from Berlin indicate possible alterations of Germany's foreign policy. In 1999, for the first time since Second World War, the German army participated in an out-of-area NATO (North American Treaty Organization) mission; during Anglo–Saxony war preparations against Iraq in 2002–2003, again for the first time since 1949, Germany took a stand against the United States in relation to a major issue of security politics, thereby triggering a serious crisis in its transatlantic relations; recently, Germany has continuously violated major obligations of the European Stability Pact, and finally, Chancellor Gerhard Schröder, in a campaign speech in Hanover on August 5, 2002, perplexed many observers when he declared that his policy stands for a "German way," opposing the American "adventure" of waging war on Iraq. Possibly, these and other events and statements would not have been of major concern if they had been sporadic. However, the accumulation of deviant behaviors by a civilian power poses the question among scholars and politicians alike as to whether German foreign policy is currently undergoing a major change. Actually, this question was of particular interest for those who had argued a few years earlier that Germany was still a civilian power.[4] The present contribution aims at analyzing German foreign policy toward the Israeli–Palestinian conflict since the 1990s, in light of the tradition and, possibly, crisis of Germany as a civilian power. To what degree does Germany's Middle East policy support the thesis that Germany is a civilian power? Does the case under consideration give evidence to the hypothesis that Germany has become less of a civilian power after the East-west conflict?

For this purpose, the civilian-power concept, which has rarely been applied explicitly to (German) foreign policy toward the Middle East, must be briefly presented. Moreover, the framework of the target region will be clarified, that is, what kind of political environment does a civilian power meet in the Middle East (see section "The Concept of Civilian Power and the Middle Eastern framework")? The task of section "Germany as a Civilian Power toward the Israeli–Palestinian Conflict?" is, first, to describe the German policy toward Israel and Palestine since the 1990s—preceded by a historical overview of the previous period in order to have a standard of comparison—and, second, to assess German policy in light of Germany's status as a civilian power. In the last section, a conclusion is presented.

The concept of civilian power and the Middle Eastern framework

Definition and methodological challenges

In essence, the civilian-power concept is derived from the constructivists' claim that political actors follow the *homo sociologicus'* logic of appropriateness rather than the *homo economicus'* logic of consequentiality.[5] In other words, the policy of a civilian power does not reflect an actor who attempts to choose the best means available to achieve a certain aim based on egoistic self-interest. Rather, according to constructivism, the most important independent variables defining the interests pursued by a state's foreign policy are norms.[6] Norms exert their impact on the behavior of states as a result of a socialization process that, due to the Janus-faced nature of the modern nation-state, has both internal and international dimensions.[7]

Constructivist analysis of foreign policy exposes serious methodological problems. For example, norms can be identified on different levels. Moreover, they can be followed in an imperfect way, in specific situations different norms may require different actions, and sometimes actors may meet expectations as a result of internalization rather than out of a conscious decision, and so on. Thus, a constructivist virtuoso will always be able to select among available norms to explain the behaviors of any actor.[8] To avoid this problem of arbitrary selection, the analysis presented here will be based on an ideal-type model of a civilian power. To subject constructivism to such a hard test seems appropriate, given that German foreign policy, according to the findings of leading scholars such as Knut Kirste and Hanns W. Maull, is understood to be an easy case for constructivism.[9]

The aspirations and convictions of an ideal-type civilian power are based on Dieter Senghaas' idea of the "civilizational hexagon."[10] Accordingly, the foreign policy of a civilizational power seeks "effective control of private violence through the monopolization of force; a culture of non-violent resolution of political disputes; rule of law; development of social division of labour and institutions; participation in decision making by those affected by them; and social justice."[11]

The political framework of a civilian power in the Middle East

The foreign-policy options of a civilian power, as well as the effectiveness of its policy, depend considerably on the political environment it faces in the target region, because the civilizational hexagon cannot be realized without international cooperation.[12] Thus, the question arises as to whether the political character of international relations in the Middle East are favorable or hostile for cooperation. Not only in comparison to Europe but also contrary to other developing regions, especially Asia and Latin America, the Middle East is underinstitutionalized. Although there are some long-lived institutions in the Middle East, such as the Arab League founded in 1944, regional-wide institutions aiming at close security and/or economic cooperation, such as Mercosur or ASEAN, have not emerged in the Middle East.

In addition to the lack of regional institutions to facilitate the policies of a civilian power, the way external actors have penetrated the Middle East constitutes a hostile environment for a civilian power. In the early nineteenth century, the Middle East became the object of rivaling European power politics.[13] In the 1950s and 1960s, the United States and the Soviet Union gradually displaced the European powers—that is, Britain and France—as the dominant external powers in the rapidly modernizing subregion of the near east, defined as Israel and its Arab neighbors. During this period, the east–west conflict overshadowed development in the Middle East. However, with the oil revolution of the early 1970s, the rent-based petrolistic system was established, and, by the 1980s, the United States was the only major external power in the Middle East, with the Soviet Union's influence limited to a few, fairly weak Arab countries, such as South Yemen.[14] Thus, although the end of the east-west confrontation certainly enlarged the United States' potential influence on regional developments, the United States had already largely enjoyed the privilege as the only remaining superpower in the region for more than a decade before the dissolution of the Soviet Union. The United States took advantage of this situation by enlarging its ties with hand-picked, regional strong states, especially Israel and Saudi Arabia—so-called special relationships—thereby influencing the regional development in an indirect but very efficient way. Because the basic idea behind these special relationships was strict bilateralism, no regional institutions of major significance were established, and no other actors, not even US allies in Europe, became involved. Thus, during the period under special review for this contribution, the 1990s, the US administration was basically not interested in altering a reliable system based on strong bilateral ties with individual actors in the region. Moreover, the same is true of the American partners in the region: all of the Arab allies of the United States stood out for having a highly problematic record in terms of the civilizational hexagon because the regimes contradicted basic principles of civil and political freedom to a much higher degree than in any other world region.[15] Even the only democracy in the Middle East, Israel, has been violating basic principles of human rights, democratic rights of freedom and participation, as well as international law in the occupied Palestinian territories, since 1967. Because the United States tolerated the occupation regime, Israel had no intrinsic interest in granting a civilian power an independent role in the Middle East.[16]

Germany as a civilian power toward the Israeli–Palestinian conflict?

The period before the unification of Germany

Germany's troublesome negotiations with Israel on indemnification payments starting in early 1952 and the delayed ratification of the agreement, which had been reached in Luxembourg in September 1952, was the only Middle East foreign policy issue ranked in March 1953 as a top priority by Germany[17] between 1949 and 1990.[18] To date, it is debatable whether the German government was guided by civilizational norms, such as paying tribute to the Jews killed in the Holocaust and/or the desire to support Israel (facing a difficult financial situation in the 1950s), or whether Bonn reacted to the more or less direct American pressure that non-ratification could delay or even endanger Germany's track of so-called *Westintegration*.[19]

Be it as it was, the September 1951 speech delivered in the German Bundestag by the then German Chancellor, Konrad Adenauer, stated that Germany felt deeply obliged to support Israel—a message well received in the United States. This speech laid the foundations for a continuous tradition of special German relations to Israel that, despite diplomatic self-restraint, manifested itself when all major German political parties were unified in their sympathy for Israel in the June War of 1967.[20] At the same time, a new challenge for German Middle Eastern policy came into being with the triumphal victory of Israel over Egypt and Syria. It became obvious that Israel's military survival as a state was no longer especially precarious. Furthermore, the Six Day War initiated a major change in US policy; Washington gave up its cautious policy of a balanced stand in the Arab–Israeli conflict, replacing it with a strong special relationship with Israel, including major diplomatic, military, and financial assistance. Henceforward, the significance of Germany's declarations to support Israel's survival was only symbolic—albeit with far-reaching implications, as will become apparent in the following. At the same time, as a result of Israel's occupation of the Palestinian territories, German foreign policy had to deal with the development of a quasi-colonial system denying self-determination to the Palestinians, who met all defining criteria of a people by the mid-1970s.[21]

The European Union (EU) was the first actor beyond the Third World to acknowledge the status of the Palestinians as a people and their right to self-determination. With significant German support,[22] the European Council, in its Venice Declaration on the Middle East[23] on June 13, 1980, declared that the Palestinian issue was not just a refugee problem and that the Palestinian Liberation Organization (PLO) "will have to be associated with the negotiations." Thereby, the European Council contradicted both the Israeli interpretation of Resolutions 242 (1967) and 338 (1973) of the UN Security Council and Israel's position of the PLO as a "terrorist organization." Moreover, although the European Union did not explicitly demand a Palestinian state in 1980, the formulation that "the Palestinian people, which is conscious of existing as such, must be placed in a position, by an appropriate process defined within the framework of the comprehensive peace settlement, to exercise fully its right to self-determination" did not really leave room for different conclusions, especially considering the Israeli settlements in the Palestinian territories were condemned as "illegal under international law." In several declarations thereafter, the European Union consistently confirmed its position. Finally, in its 1999 Berlin Declaration,[24] the European Council officially opted for the two-state solution by "(reaffirming) the continuing and unqualified Palestinian right to self-determination including the option of a state."

The period since the unification of Germany

The widespread allegation that the European Union lacks the quality of a unified actor capable of formulating consistent and trendsetting foreign policies does not apply to declarations on the Israeli–Palestinian conflict, especially when compared to official US statements, which suffer from a significant degree of inconsistency.[25] Again, contrary to US foreign policy, the declarations of the European Union before and after the reunification of Germany have given direction to what is currently viewed as common sense in the international community, namely the two-state solution as approved in UN Security Council Resolution 1397 (2002).

However, in two ways, the European Union, and especially Germany, contradicted its self-imposed standards. First, several times, Germany (in alliance with the Netherlands, and, to a lesser degree, Britain) impeded a unified European appearance toward the Israeli–Palestinian conflict in major international institutions. For example, in 1997, Germany abstained from two resolutions of the UN General Assembly condemning Israeli settlements.[26] Moreover, Germany was not active in the removal of the European self-imposed blockade, which prevented making the EU policy toward the Arab–Israeli conflict a truly common one. In addition, at the summit in Feira in June 2000, when the European Union agreed on a "Common Strategy of the European Union on the Mediterranean Region," decisions related to the peace process in the Near East were excluded from majority votes—thereby contradicting the aim of enhancing the tool developed in the frame of the Common Foreign and Security Policy (CFSP).[27] All in all, it seems appropriate to state that Germany's Near Eastern policy was, to a high degree, oriented toward the vague formula of so-called *Ausgewogenheit* (even-handedness) triggering inconsistencies with the principles of the civilizational hexagon.[28]

Second, the policies implemented by the European Union lagged far behind the policies envisioned on the level of declarations, especially in Germany's case. Despite the official European condemnation of the Israeli settlement policy, Germany hesitated to enforce a policy that would exclude commodities produced in settlements from privileged access to the European market (a privilege enjoyed by regular Israeli products on the basis of the European–Israeli association agreement).[29] Thus, only after significant delay, in December 2003, Israel finally accepted that it had to identify products exported from the settlements to the European Union. Moreover, especially since the outbreak of the Al Aqsa Intifada and Israel's military reaction to it, there can be few doubts that Israel is situated in the middle of an "area of tension," which is considered a disqualifying criteria for German arms exports. However, to date, German military exports to Israel have proceeded. When in early 2002—in light of Israeli military activities in the Palestinian territories—the German government put on hold arms deliveries to Israel, especially spare parts and drive units for tanks, the confidential decision was revised immediately after it was leaked to the Israeli press.[30] Although the military significance of German weapon deliveries to Israel is disputable, it should be noted that, according to Israeli scholar Shlomo Shipro, the German submarines exported to Israel in 1999 and 2000 might be capable of launching long-range weapons that could target aims in Iraq and Iran.[31] Moreover, although German arms exports to Israel do not significantly alter the distribution of power capabilities between Israel and Palestine, it is possible that German exports to Israel were used for military campaigns against the Palestinians, many of which, according to standards and official positions of the European Union (and independent nongovernmental organizations such as Human Rights Watch), contradicted international law.[32]

As long as Israel, backed by the United States, refrained from negotiations with the Palestine Liberation Organization, Germany's profile toward the subregion of the Near East, particularly regarding the Palestinian issue, was low in comparison to other European actors, especially France. Yet, in the 1990s, the Israeli–Palestinian peace process codified in the Oslo Accords opened the door for Germany to pursue an active policy in the Near East. Inspired by the concept of the World Bank,[33] which stated that the main condition for peace process success depended, especially for the Palestinians, on a "peace dividend," the European Union and Germany in particular—fully approved by Israel—was assigned an important role as donator of aid to the Palestinians. In fact, in terms of aid received per capita, the Palestinian people became the major recipient of German foreign aid.[34] In order to promote a Palestinian state-building process based on accountability, the European Union established a fairly sophisticated formula of pledging, committing, and disbursing financial aid related to well-defined projects.[35] However, by the mid-1990s, the peace process began to crumble and, despite fairly high foreign aid donations, the Palestinian peace dividend proved to be very low, in some fields even negative.[36] Consequently, the Oslo process became more and more unpopular in the Palestinian territories—so much so that it became increasingly apparent to Western actors that it could only be stabilized if the newly established Palestinian Authority (PA) was relieved from standards of accountability and from observing human rights in dealing with the growing Islamist opposition as a result of the crisis of the peace process. When torn between the conflicting aims of strengthening the peace process and democratizing Palestine, the European Union and Germany—fully approved by the United States—went for the first option.[37]

Already by the 1990s, the labor-sharing formula between European and US foreign policies toward the Middle East (the United States being the "player" and the European Union the "payer"[38]) proved to be problematic. Primarily, this outcome was because the United States was too closely allied with Israel and did not put pressure on Israeli governments to make concessions to the Palestinians regarding crucial conflict issues such as settlement policy and the reign over Jerusalem. Despite discord, no open conflict between the United States and the European Union on the peace process occurred at that time, because—apart from the fact that the European Union eschewed conflict with the United States and Israel on their roles in the Middle East—the stalemate between the parties still seemed to be manageable and the US administration under the leadership of then US President Bill Clinton was engaged in the Near East to such a high degree that, despite the troublesome development on the ground, considerable hope remained that the peace process could result in a final agreement. However, this hope eventually disintegrated when the negotiations at Camp David (2000) and Taba (2001) failed, leaving the Palestinian people with a paralyzed leadership. The violent uprising known as the Al Aqsa Intifada and the Israeli militant response to it sounded the death knell for the Oslo peace process.[39]

The first year of the Intifada coincided with a period of significant American disengagement from the Palestinian–Israeli conflict under its new president, George W. Bush. With the growing force and counterforce of Palestinians and Israelis, the European Union, including Germany headed by its foreign minister, Joschka Fischer, attempted to fill in the gap by embarking on active crisis management in the Near East. However, rather than basing themselves on a coherent strategy, European and German interventions relied mainly on ad hoc reactions, as is obvious when considering one of the major achievements of German policy during this period. In an impressive way, Fischer managed to persuade Palestinian leader Yasser Arafat to read a television speech in Arabic condemning the suicide attack committed at the Dolphin discothèque on June 2, 2001, and Israeli Prime Minister Ariel Sharon rewarded this gesture by refraining from a direct military response. However, beyond his personal engagement, there can be few doubts that Fischer's success depended on the coincidence that he was witnessing the suicide attack in Tel Aviv; moreover, his activities exerted only a suspension in hostilities rather than structural change.

When the terrorist attacks of September 11, 2001 forced President Bush to give US foreign policy toward the Middle East the highest priority, the European Union aimed to convince the United States to refresh the Israeli–Palestinian peace process through a joint initiative under American leadership. In terms of procedures, this aim was achieved by establishing the so-called quartet composed of the United States, the European Union, the United Nations, and Russia, in April 2002. Germany preceded the initiative by presenting an "idea paper," drafted by Fischer, on April 15, 2002.[40] The basic idea of the plan was to turn the Oslo process upside down by starting the peace process with the declaration of a Palestinian state with provisional borders, and then negotiating a final settlement. Even though Germany did not manage to convert Fischer's plan into an official EU proposal, and the United States stuck to the Oslo formula of a graduated scheme ending with a Palestinian state instead of starting with it, the "Road Map"[41] drafted by the quartet comprised of some European and German ideas, especially reforming the PA and monitoring the peace process by the quartet. Moreover, the mere fact that the European Union was officially and visibly included in the new peace initiative may be considered a major achievement. Yet, the American leadership in the quartet was undisputed, so much so that, from the German perspective, it diminished the effective influence of the European Union and Germany on decisive issues. For instance, the European Union could not push the United States to walk the talk of democratizing Palestine (which would first require a serious relaxation of occupation). Moreover, the European Union could exert virtually no influence on Israel, either in a direct way or through the United States. Thus, though already drafted in 2002, the Road Map was put on hold by the United States because of its preoccupation with preparing for the war against Iraq. This circumstance left time for Israel to create new facts on the ground, for instance, by accelerating its settlement policy. Moreover, when President Bush, in his speech on the Middle East delivered on June 24, 2002, decided to adopt the Israeli position of declaring Arafat irrelevant while simultaneously demanding a democratization of Palestine, the European Union as a member of the quartet ended up in a very delicate situation. Being aware of the conflicting facts, that on the one hand Arafat was one of very few Arab leaders elevated through free elections,[42] and, on the other, his established authoritarian regime, the European Union's approach was to lay the foundations for new elections. Yet, because Israel effectively blocked elections by sticking to its aggravated occupation policy, the European Union decided to continue its relations with Arafat, thereby offending Israel and the United States. Furthermore, it is doubtful whether the—limited—political influence that the European Union gained through the establishment of the quartet contributed to the productive management of the previously mentioned player-payer issue.

In contrast to the 1990s and since the Al Aqsa Intifada, being one of the major payers of the PA has had severe repercussions on the European political role. On one hand, public order in the occupied territories could only be maintained because the European Union was ready to resume direct budget subsidies to the PA after the beginning of the Intifada and the Israeli military response to it. On the other hand, by supporting the PA, as well as funding emergency projects to the impoverished Palestinian society, the European Union bore the costs of the Israeli occupation to a considerable degree, supported an authoritarian Palestinian regime and, despite its critical position toward the PA, was accused, by Israel, of facilitating terrorist structures.

Assessment in light of Germany as a civilizational power

As described in the section "The concept of civilian power and the Middle Eastern framework" the political environment of the Middle East is hostile to a civilian power, especially in the Near East. Thus, the European Union and Germany are hardly to blame entirely for the fact that the effectiveness of their policy was very limited. Indeed, the high degree of ineffectiveness could have been avoided only if Germany had been ready to challenge American predominance in the region—again with extremely questionable prospects for success. Nevertheless, Germany was among those members of the European Union who blocked possible institutional advancements of European foreign policy toward the Middle East, thereby contributing to its limited effectiveness. Moreover, both on the level of bilateral policies toward actors of the Near East, especially Israel, and in its voting behavior in multilateral institutions, particularly the United Nations, several times Germany contradicted basic ideas of the civilizational hexagon, such as the principle of promoting a culture of non-violent resolution of political disputes and facilitating social justice. That said, regarding policies beyond direct bilateral relations with Israel, it must also be mentioned that, after 2000, the German government showed a higher degree of commitment to civilizational principles, even when Israel felt offended. This change in behavior may be rooted in the change of government in Germany in 1998 or in the fact that after the termination of the Oslo peace process, a civilian power could hardly avoid of being critical of both conflict actors.

Conclusion

With the exception of Israel in the 1950s, the Middle East was not a major target region of the foreign policies of the two German states until Germany's reunification. Also, in 2004, the Middle East is not among the major foci of German foreign policy. Though still "in quest of a concept,"[43] Germany's Middle Eastern policy deserves this label much more than 15 years ago.

Constructivism had to perform a difficult task in the analysis presented. Thus, it is not surprising that a number of the German foreign policies targeting Israel and Palestine did not fully meet the requirements of a civilian power, which was, for the purpose of this chapter, defined as an actor whose policy is committed to the civilizational hexagon.

The initial assumption that the Middle East is a difficult region for a civilian power, due to the absence of well-established regional institutions crossing national border lines and the power-oriented US policy in the region, has been confirmed in the course of the analysis. Yet, it also became apparent that Germany is not immune to power-oriented politics. Several indicators were found that Germany's policy toward the parties of the Israeli–Palestinian conflict was (partially) motivated by an attempt to bandwagon with the United States.

The fact that German policy toward the Near East is only partially consistent with the ideal-type model of a civilian power may be considered a blow to constructivism. However, if the assumption is made that Germany's behavior toward Israel and Palestine was torn between competing norms, constructivism may claim a fairly high degree of plausibility. Constructivism may argue that, due to the history of Nazi Germany, a special norm emerged resulting in postwar Germany's support of Israel as the only state that guarantees the survival of the Jewish people—even if this very state contradicts the values of the civilizational hexagon through occupation. Furthermore, since norms sometimes exert a life of their own, Germany may still be driven by the norm to support Israel's survival as a state, despite Israel's superior power capabilities vis-à-vis its adversaries. Moreover, it is arguable that the incomparable suffering imposed by Germans on the Jewish people has shaped German identity to such a high degree that Germany is hesitant to draw any conclusions from the Holocaust other than support for Israel—even though a sound interpretation of the civilizational hexagon would suggest a more complex approach of German Near Eastern policy.[44]

Acknowledgment

A longer version of the present article, which covers several subregions of the Middle East and includes a discussion of neorealism and liberalism, has been published in *Orient*, 45: 3 (2004): 401–22.

Notes

1 Ingo Peters, "Vom 'Scheinzwerg' zum 'Scheinriesen'—deutsche Außenpolitik in der Analyse," *Zeitschrift für Internationale Beziehungen*, 4: 2 (1997): 361–88.

2 Christina Schrade, "Machtstaat, Handelsstaat oder Zivilstaat? Deutsche Entwicklungspolitik nach dem Ende des Ost-West-Konflikts," *Zeitschrift für Internationale Beziehungen*, 4: 2 (1997): 255–94; Helga Haftendorn, *Deutsche Außenpolitik zwischen Selbstbeschränkung und Selbstbehauptung* (Stuttgart: DVA, 2001); Sebastian Harnisch and Hanns W. Maull, eds, *Germany as a Civilian Power? The Foreign Policy of the Berlin Republic* (Manchester: Manchester University Press, 2001); Wolfgang Wagner and Volker Rittberger, "German Foreign Policy Since Unification: Theories Meet Reality," *German Foreign Policy Since Unification: Theories and Case Studies*, Volker Rittberger *et al.*, eds (Manchester: Manchester University Press, 2001), pp. 299–325.

3 Christian Hacke, *Die Außenpolitik der Bundesrepublik Deutschland: Weltmacht wider Willen?* (Berlin: Ullstein, 1997).

4 See Gunther Hellmann, "Sag beim Abschied leise servus. Die Zivilmacht Deutschland beginnt, ein neues 'Selbst' zu behaupten," *Politischen Vierteljahresschrift*, 43: 4 (2002): 498–507; Hanns W. Maull, "Editorial: Deutschland auf Abwegen?," *Deutschland im Abseits? Rot-Grüne Außenpolitik 1998–2003*, Hanns Maull, Sebastian Harnisch, and Constantin Grund, eds (Baden-Baden: Nomos, 2003), pp. 7–18; Volker Rittberger, "Selbstentfesselung in kleinen Schritten? Deutschlands Außenpolitik zu Beginn des 21. Jahrhunderts," *Politische Vierteljahresschrift*, 44: 1 (2003): 10–8.

5 Henning Boekle, Volker Rittberger, and Wolfgang Wagner, "Norms and Foreign Policy: Constructivist Foreign Policy Theory," *Tübinger Arbeitspapiere zur internationalen Politik*, 34 (2000), Available at: http://www.uni-tuebingen.de/uni/spi/taps/tap34a.htm. Accessed June 14, 2004.

6 Hanns W. Maull, "Germany and the Use of Force: Still a Civilian Power?" *Survival*, 42: 2 (2000): 56–80.

7 Boekle, Rittberger, and Wagner, *Tübinger Arbeitspapiere zur internationalen Politik* (see note 5).

8 Boekle, Rittberger, and Wagner, *Tübinger Arbeitspapiere zur internationalen Politik* (see note 5).

9 Knut Kirste and Hanns W. Maull, "Zivilmacht und Rollentheorie," *Zeitschrift für Internationale Beziehungen*, 3: 2 (1996): 299–303.

10 Dieter Senghaas, "Frieden—Ein mehrfaches Komplexprogramm," *Frieden machen*, Dieter Senghaas, ed. (Frankfurt am Main: Suhrkamp, 1997), p. 573.

11 Hanns W. Maull, "German Foreign Policy, Post-Kosovo: Still a 'Civilian Power'?" *German Politics*, 9: 2 (2000): 14–5.

12 Henning Tewes, "Das Zivilmachtkonzept in der Theorie der Internationalen Beziehungen: Anmerkungen zu Knut Kirste und Hanns W. Maull," *Zeitschrift für Internationale Beziehungen*, 4: 2 (1997): 348–50.

13 L. Carl Brown, *International Politics and the Middle East: Old Rules, Dangerous Games* (Princeton: Princeton University Press, 1984), Part 1.

14 Martin Beck, *Friedensprozeß im Nahen Osten: Rationalität, Kooperation und politische Rente im Vorderen Orient* (Wiesbaden: Westdeutscher Verlag, 2002), pp. 240–48.

15 Freedom House, *Country Ratings* (2003). Available at: http://www.freedomhouse.org/ratings/index.htm. Accessed June 14, 2004.

16 Martin Beck, "Jenseits globaler Trends: Zur Bedeutung der israelisch-amerikanischen Allianz für das palästinensische Herrschaftssystem," *Religion, Kultur und Politik im Vorderen Orient: Die islamische Welt im Zeichen der Globalisierung*, Peter Pawelka and Lutz Richter-Bernburg, eds (Wiesbaden: VS Verlag für Sozialwissenschaften, 2003), pp. 93–106.

17 The following presentation will be confined to the Federal Republic of Germany. For the foreign policy of the German Democratic Republic toward the Middle East, see Angelika Timm, "The Middle East Policy of East Germany," *Germany and the Middle East: Past, Present, and Future*, Haim Goren, ed. (Jerusalem: Hebrew University Magnes Press, 2003), pp. 245–62.

18 The diplomatic disturbances triggered when, in 1964, Egypt learned about secret German weapon deliveries to Israel were, to a high degree, related to the *Hallstein Doctrine*, which is beyond the scope of this article. See Friedemann Büttner, "Germany's Middle East Policy: The Dilemmas of a 'Policy of Even-Handedness' (*Politik der Ausgewogenheit*)," *Germany and the Middle East: Past, Present, and Future* (see note 17), 127–35.

19 Michael Wolffsohn and Douglas Bokovoy, *Israel: Grundwissen-Länderkunde Geschichte Politik Gesellschaft Wirtschaft (1882–1996)* (Opladen: Leske und Budrich, 1996), pp. 237–40 and 450–52; Martin Beck, "Israel," *Handbuch der Außenpolitik von Afghanistan bis Zypern*, Jürgen Bellers, Thorsten Benner, and Ines M. Gerke, eds. (München: Oldenbourg, 2001), 789–799; Dominique Trimbur, "American Influence on the Federal Republic of Germany's Israel Policy, 1951–1956," *Germany and the Middle East: Past, Present, and Future* (see note 17).

20 Büttner, *Germany and the Middle East: Past, Present, and Future* (see note 19), p. 136.

21 Beck, *Der Friedensprozeß im Nahen Osten* (see note 14), pp. 227–30; Beck, *Religion, Kultur und Politik im Vorderen Orient* (see note 16); Martin Beck, *Prospects for and Obstacles to Achieving a Viable Palestinian State: What Can an Actor with Inferior Power Capabilities Do in a Graduated Prisoner's Dilemma?* (Birzeit: Birzeit University, 2004), pp. 7–9.

22 Udo Steinbach, "Naher und Mittlerer Osten," *Handbuch zur Deutschen Außenpolitik*, Siegmar Schmidt, Gunther Hellmann, and Reinhard Wolf, eds (Wiesbaden: VS Verlag für Sozialwissenschaften, forthcoming). For the harsh Israeli diplomatic response, targeting especially Germany, see Kinan Jaeger, *Quadratur des Dreiecks! Die deutsch-israelischen Beziehungen und die Palästinenser* (Schwalbach/Ts.: Wochenschau Verlag, 1997), Chapters 9–10.

23 Venice Declaration on the Middle East, (June 13, 1980). Available at: http://domino.un.org/unispal.nsf/0/fef015e8b1a1e5a685256d810059d922?OpenDocument. Accessed June 8, 2004.

24 Berlin European Council, Presidency Conclusions (March 24–25, 1999). Available at: http://europa.eu.int/council/off/conclu/mar99_en.htm#ME, Accessed June 8, 2004.

25 Muriel Asseburg, "Die EU und der Friedensprozeß im Nahen Osten," *SWP-Studie*, No. 28 (Berlin: Stiftung Wissenschaft und Politik, 2003), p. 24.

26 Muriel Asseburg, "Der Nahost-Friedensprozess und der Beitrag der EU—Bilanz und Perspektiven," *Die Friedens-Warte*, 76: 2–3 (2001): 257–88.

27 Asseburg, *SWP-Studie* (see note 25), p. 25.

28 Büttner, *Germany and the Middle East: Past, Present, and Future* (see note 18); Steinbach, *Handbuch der Deutschen Außenpolitik* (see note 22).

29 Asseburg, *SWP-Studie* (see note 25), pp. 24–25 and 33.

30 Christian Sterzing, "German Arms Exports: A Policy Caught Between Morality and National Interest," *Germany and the Middle East. Interests and Options*, Volker Perthes, ed. (Berlin: Heinrich-Böll-Stiftung and Stiftung Wissenschaft und Politik, 2002), pp. 181–82.

31 Shlomo Shipro, "Communicating Interests Across History: German-Israeli Security Cooperation," *Germany and the Middle East. Past, Present, and Future* (see note 17), p. 327.

32 See Sterzing, *Germany and the Middle East* (see note 31).

33 World Bank, *Developing the Occupied Territories: An Investment in Peace* (Washington: World Bank, 1993).

34 Asseburg, *SWP-Studie* (see note 25), p. 8.

35 Rex Brynen, *A Very Political Economy: Peacebuilding and Foreign Aid in the West Bank and Gaza* (Washington, DC: United States Institute of Peace Press, 2000), Chapter 4.

36 Beck, *Friedensprozeß im Nahen Osten* (see note 14), Chapter 6.

37 Martin Beck, "The External Dimension of Authoritarian Rule in Palestine," *Journal of International Relations and Development*, vol. 3, no. 1 (2000): 47–66.

38 See Asseburg, *SWP-Studie* (see note 25), pp. 279–81; Christian Sterzing and Jörn Böhme, "German and European Contributions to the Israeli-Palestinian Peace Process," *Germany and the Middle East: Interests and Options* (see note 30), p. 40.

39 Helga Baumgarten, *The Myth of Camp David or the Distortion of the Palestinian Narrative* (Birzeit: Birzeit University, 2004); Martin Beck, "The Political and Scientific Relevance of the Failed Camp David and Taba Negotiations (Comment)," *The Myth of Camp David or the Distortion of the Palestinian Narrative* (Birzeit: Birzeit University, 2004), pp. 73–8.

40 *Germany and the Middle East: Interests and Options* (see note 30), pp. 220–21.

41 For a description and evaluation of the Road Map, see Muriel Asseburg, "Von Aqaba nach Genf—Herausforderungen für die europäische Politik," *Sicherheit und Frieden*, 21: 3–4 (2003): 121–27; Martin Beck, "Aussicht auf Frieden in Nahost? Fahrplan und Genfer Abkommen im Lichte konflikttheoretischer Überlegungen," *Sicherheit und Frieden*, 21: 3–4 (2003): 115–20.

42 Helga Baumgarten, "Die palästinensischen Wahlen," *Orient*, 36:4 (1996): 599–618.

43 Udo Steinbach, "German Foreign Policy and the Middle East: In Quest of a Concept," *Germany and the Middle East: Past, Present, and Future* (see note 17), p. 85.

44 For instance, since there is, first, evidence that the Holocaust had a direct impact on the international support for establishing the state of Israel, and, second, the Palestinians were victims of the Israeli state-building process in 1948, Germany could have drawn the conclusion that it has specific obligations to both the Jewish and the Palestinian people.

Organization (as shown in Chapter 2 by Miskimmon and Paterson, Chapter 4 by Marco Overhaus, and Chapter 6 by Harnisch and Schieder). Serious persistent deficiencies are also found in foreign economic policies (Chapters 11–13 by Friedemann Müller, Andreas Falke, and Reinhard Wolf), in policies toward development assistance (Peter Molt, Chapter 15), toward Pacific Asia (Jörn-Casten Gottwald, Chapter 16), and even with regard to key bilateral relations (see Chapter 7 by Hans Stark on Franco–German relations for the low points in that relationship, Chapters 8 and 9 by Stephen Szabo and Peter Rudolf on US–German relations, and Chapter 10 by Günter Joetze on policies toward the Balkans and Russia). Some of those policies (such as those concerning energy security, development, the Israeli–Palestinian conflict, and Pacific Asia) have considerable historical depth. In other policy areas, the performance seems to have deteriorated more recently (such as in the case of trade, international financial policies, and, most importantly, in policies toward Europe and the United States).

How can we explain those "deficiencies"? One important set of answers is provided by changes in Germany's foreign policy environment and its resource endowment. From the perspective of the ideal type civilian power role concept, which intrinsically relies on arrangements for the international division of labor and shared sovereignty, civilian powers importantly depend on certain external and internal conditions, such as:[6]

- a congenial (i.e., non-violent, heavily institutionalized) environment;
- vibrant and effective international institutions; and
- reliable and cooperative partners.

Civilian powers can work most effectively in such an environment. Germany's largely successful foreign policy as a civilian power in the past depended heavily on such favorable external conditions, as well as on considerable skill and expense by German policy makers. Those successes, in turn, also contributed to sustaining and developing this favorable policy environment, with the ability of German foreign policy to generate trust in Germany as a key asset to exercise influence in multilateral contexts.

While I will not attempt to summarize here the changes in Germany's regional and global international environment that have been described in our analyses, it is clear that these changes have been extensive. In retrospect, the years from November 1989 to September 2001 appear as an intermediate period in which international relations were in a state of flux; since September 11, 2001, the central structural elements of the post-Cold War world have become quite clear. Two key factors in this context are (1) a growing diffusion of power in the international system as a consequence of the dynamics of globalization, and (2) the revolution in US foreign policy under George W. Bush.[7]

The notion of diffusion of power implies a rise of entropy in international relations as a whole. This tendency has manifested itself above all in the growing fragility of political structures at all levels of the international system, most importantly at that of the nation-state, which generally has been weakened in its ability to shape the future autonomously. States thus have come under strong pressure to adjust. Beyond the developed world, this has made statehood increasingly fragile and precarious, sometimes even to the extent of state implosion. But even in consolidated industrialized democracies, the pressures have been felt strongly, contributing to widespread difficulties of "governance."

One response to this development has been to enhance regional and global cooperation and integration so as to regain national influence over events through arrangements of shared power. Perhaps the most notable example of this counterstrategy has been the European Union's realization of Economic and Monetary Union and the successful introduction of the euro. Yet those (and other) efforts at strengthening the formal and informal arrangements of regional and global governance arguably have not compensated for centrifugal and fissiparous tendencies in those arrangements. In the case of European integration, the effects of "deepening" have been more balanced, at least in the short and medium term, by the complexities of EU enlargement and a widespread trend toward renationalization, reflecting the difficulties and reluctance of governments to honor their self-imposed obligations.

Those changes have been particularly painful for Germany, as its traditional foreign policy has always relied heavily on effective multilateral institutions and reliable partners. In fact, German foreign policy as a civilian power has developed, as role concepts generally do, through processes of learning and socialization, which, in the case of Germany, have been heavily influenced by external expectations and interventions. Thus, Germany's postwar foreign policy guidelines, which were developed during the 1950s, were initially as much imposed by the victors' policies and the circumstances of the Cold War in Europe as they reflected the policy preferences of a small group of decision makers. It took at least a decade before those policy guidelines had been internalized by a clear majority of West Germans. Even after that, however, strong external anchors, represented by the expectations of Germany's key foreign policy partners and allies about how the country's foreign policy should be conducted, as well as by vibrant international institutions (in particular, the European Communities and NATO), continued to provide pillars of support for Germany's foreign policy orientation from the outside.

After unification, those external supports progressively became weaker, as international institutions lost some of their strength and Germany's key foreign policy partners began to adapt their own foreign policies to the new environment. Germany has been hit particularly hard by changes in

US foreign policy, which, as Marco Overhaus shows in chapter 4, undermined the very foundations of Germany's traditional policy of equidistance and mediation between Paris and Washington. Moreover, some of the policies that Germany itself had been instrumental in securing after 1990, as a way of reinforcing traditional anchors, came with a steep price tag. Thus, as Reinhard Wolf shows in Chapter 13, Germany lost one of its key foreign policy assets, the deutsche Mark, through its own efforts to "deepen" European integration via European Monetary Union during the first half of the 1990s, which was a way to reassure Germany's partners and to retain (shared) power over Germany's currency.

Yet our analyses suggest that changes in the external environment are only part of the story of Germany's declining foreign policy effectiveness. The other part is found in what the country does—or does not—contribute to regional and international governance. Given its economic and political importance within Europe and in the world economy, a Germany that does not pull its weight will certainly affect the ability and goodwill of other countries to cooperate and will ultimately impair the performance of regional and global institutions. In fact, the growing deficiencies of German foreign policy may well already have contributed to a deteriorating foreign policy environment.

Thus, it is not only changes in the external environment that account for the country's deteriorating foreign policy performance, but also changes in Germany itself. Those can be analyzed along three foreign policy dimensions: power, purpose, and process. "Power" refers to the hard and soft power resources at the disposal of German foreign policy and the skill, effectiveness, and efficiency with which they are deployed to secure desired outcomes. "Purpose" not only deals with the specific objectives pursued, but also with the intangibles of political will, such as commitment, determination, and perseverance. "Process" concerns the mechanics and politics of formulating and implementing foreign policies. Our analyses show that, on balance, German foreign policy performance has suffered along all those three dimensions.

Fragile power

Globalization produces complexity and the diffusion of power in international relations. Under such circumstances, the ability to affect outcomes often depends upon a high level of concentration of power resources. Yet, since unification, Germany's underlying power resource base has become weaker rather than stronger, for several related reasons:

- deteriorating economic performance and low growth;[8]
- the burden of financing unification (net transfer payments to eastern Germany continue at a level of about 5 percent of the gross national

product (GNP) cumulatively. For the period 1990 to 2004, net transfers are estimated to have totaled about €1500 billion, representing approximately 4 to 5 percent of the GNP annually;[9]

- sharply rising public debt, and concomitant, severe budgetary constraints, which have had obvious implications for Germany's ability to use "checkbook diplomacy";[10]

- loss of "soft power" resources; while the *Modell Deutschland* used to be admired and emulated because of its ability to forge effective institutions, such as the Bundesbank, the dual system of professional education, or consensus-oriented industrial relations, with the loss of socioeconomic dynamism and accumulating difficulties to manage change (*"Reformstau"*), this ability to exercise influence through serving as a model has been lost.

Thus, Germany has become less powerful overall in terms of its power resources. But even if it had been otherwise, this would not change the simple fact that Germany on its own, in most instances, would not have been able to secure desired outcomes in international relations—that is, to mobilize on its own what we might call proactive power. On the other hand, Germany continues to hold veto power—that is, the ability to block others and prevent developments considered undesirable by German foreign policy makers; in fact, this veto power may well have increased as a result of changes in international relations.

Use of proactive power relies on pooling resources effectively and efficiently, and on developing a sense of shared interests and objectives through accommodating divergences among actors; in short, it depends on the art of coalition and consensus building. This requires leadership, but also discretion and above all the ability to keep common objectives and interests firmly in mind. Proactive power, both for purposes of conflict prevention and crisis management, therefore needs "effective multilateralism." German foreign policy has achieved this very successfully in the past, even within the last few years: recent examples are Germany's major contribution to the political settlement of the Kosovo war, its pivotal role in setting up the Stability Pact for South Eastern Europe, as well as important initiatives and leadership in the context of nuclear nonproliferation policies (cf. Chapter 3 by Harald Müller) and international climate policy (cf. Chapter 14 by Detlef Sprinz). Germany also lead the coalition that eventually managed to launch the International Criminal Court against US objections, and it initiated and contributed significantly to negotiations for the EU Constitutional Treaty.

Yet those successes need to be put in perspective. Overall, the assessment of the preceding chapters points to a declining performance. In recent years, one finds many examples of Pyrrhic victories, such as the appointment of Horst Köhler as IMF managing director (see Chapter 13 by Reinhard Wolf) and the Stability and Growth Pact for Europe (see Chapter 6 by Harnisch and Schieder), and failed initiatives, such as on currency target zones, and on the choice of the commission president to succeed Romano Prodi. The most recent major initiative by Germany, the quest for a permanent seat in the UN Security Council, may well become another Pyrrhic victory, if not an outright debacle.[11]

Our analyses indicate that, in recent years, German foreign policy has been focused more on veto power (e.g., on Iraq, on limiting financial commitments to the European Union, and on preventing a common European immigration and asylum policy) than on proactive power, more on situative (e.g., on personnel decisions such as the Intentional Monetary Fund (IMF) managing director, the South Eastern European Stability Pact, and the European Community presidency) than on structural decisions (such as the future development of NATO, of international financial order, or the future role of the European Union in international relations). This shift has been accompanied by a changed foreign policy rhetoric, particularly by Chancellor Gerhard Schröder, emphasizing a more self-confident pursuit of German national interests. In fact, however, what was presented as self-confidence and often perceived as assertiveness seems to reflect, and may even serve to camouflage, Germany's diminishing power in affecting outcomes.

Uncertain purpose

Power is needed in the pursuit of (foreign) policy objectives against obstacles and opposition. Conceptually, as we have seen, power can be used either defensively, as in a veto, or proactively. In this latter context, we can distinguish specific objectives ("situative goals") to "shape the milieu"[12] and enhance institutions in ways conducive to German foreign policy objectives and influence ("milieu goals"). Situative goals are generally less demanding in terms of power resource inputs and efforts than milieu goals. The former concerns specific decisions—such as how to vote on draft resolutions before the UN Security Council, whether to contribute troops to multilateral interventions, or how to secure an important commercial contract in China through publicly subsidized credit arrangements. Milieu goals, on the other hand, concern generic or constitutive acts: what national authority will be devolved to the European Commission and Parliament, whether to create an International Criminal Court or introduce target zones for currency exchange rates, enhance the WTO (World Trade Organization), or enlarge the European Union.

In the case of German foreign policy, our analyses note a shift from proactive to defensive goals, and within the former from milieu to situative goals. The principal reason for this shift seems to have been a combination of a more difficult international environment and a diminishing ability or commitment to the traditional foreign policy role concept. The latter allowed domestic actors such as the *Länder*, the Bundestag, and the Constitutional

Court to push for their own limited agendas more effectively, causing the "domestication" of foreign policy (see Chapter 6 by Harnisch and Schieder). The same applies to NGOs (Non-governmental Organizations) and business interests, notably the automotive and utility companies, which repeatedly have been able to "colonize" German foreign policies ("commercialization").

In other instances, it seemed to be political reflexes and short-term calculations, rather than strategy, that shaped policy, reflecting a more shallow understanding of and commitment to the civilian power role concept. Thus, in the Iraq crisis, German foreign policy succeeded in preventing a mandate for regime change by the UN Security Council, but failed to halt the US-led invasion, the deterioration of the overall situation in the Middle East, and a severe crisis in transatlantic relations. Berlin also allowed itself to become the follower of France, thus forfeiting an important traditional source of influence from its ability to mediate between Washington and Paris. On the use of military power and the development of multilateral frameworks for power projection—NATO and European Security and Defense Policy (ESDP)—Germany since 1995 has only rarely pursued its own strategies (e.g., in its efforts to integrate the Franco–British initiatives on security cooperation in the European Union or to develop the political and institutional dimensions of ESDP); most of the time, German security and defense policies, including the use of the Bundeswehr, appear to have been shaped by others, while Germany followed.

Fragmented process

The lack of consistency over time and coherence between different actors, which we repeatedly noted in recent German foreign policy, is unlikely to reflect only individual failings of key decision makers, such as chancellors or foreign ministers. Rather, we need to look beyond the personality factor to structural changes in foreign-policy decision making and implementation processes. Our analyses do reveal important changes here, too. They have been the result of (1) the end of the Cold War, which had long occupied the attention of German foreign policy makers; (2) the deepening impact of globalization on German politics, economics, and society, which introduced new actors and interests into foreign policy decision making; (3) the progress of European integration; and (4) inherent tendencies toward gridlock in the complex and consensus-oriented decision-making machinery of Germany's polity.

The end of the Cold War and the rising tide of globalization have brought a reorientation of politics toward domestic and economic issues in most, if not all, major industrialized countries (though, after 9/11, the United States clearly shifted its policy focus to the war against international terrorism). In that sense, the "domestication" and "commercialization" of German foreign policy after 1990 is hardly exceptional. The result, as we have seen, has been

Conclusion 281

a closer involvement of domestic political and commercial actors. This has facilitated centrifugal tendencies within government (see, especially, Chapters 12 and 15 by Andreas Falke and Peter Molt). The result has been a net loss of foreign policy consistency and cohesion and, therefore, of policy effectiveness.

In reaction to those tendencies, there have been efforts to strengthen the role of the chancellery in foreign policy making, to the detriment notably of the Foreign Ministry, the Ministry of Economics, and the Ministry of Defense, and to develop common European foreign, security, and defense policies. At the same time, the chancellery's coordination capacity is limited; this may have contributed to the shift from proactive to reactive policies and to policy inconsistency. It certainly also facilitated the instrumentalization of foreign policy (as seen in the conflict over Iraq and Germany's opposition to US policies) for domestic political purposes ("politicization"), notably in the election campaigns for the Bundestag in September 2002 and for the parliament in Lower Saxony in February 2003.

The other remedy, that of "Europeanizing" foreign policy, also turned out to have limited utility in improving Germany's foreign policy performance. As the Iraq crisis, among many other incidents, revealed, on most important foreign policy issues there simply is as yet no coherent or consistent European position, let alone an effectively coordinated implementation of common decisions and strategies. While the need for such policies is largely undisputed, they have to be forged and followed through with persistent political efforts by determined member states, with Germany in a key position. Thus, rather than providing solutions to German foreign policy dilemmas, Europeanization in fact represents an important additional charge and challenge to the German foreign policy process and thus poses new dilemmas, notably those related to the gap between German ambitions for the Common Foreign and Security Policy and the available financial resources, between its demands and expectations on others and its ability and willingness to meet its own standards and obligations. Those awkward realities of truly common European foreign and security policies tended to be overlooked, however, by the political class and the foreign policy bureaucracies in Germany, who tended to confuse a common European position with a practical joint-policy stance, and a new institutional arrangement to a solution with the problem at hand.

Germany: the uncertain power

The emergence of protracted foreign policy problems may have become most evident during the tenure of the Red–Green governments since 1998, but the *"Reformstau"* in Germany's foreign policy has been in the making for some time. During the 1990s, the government of Helmut Kohl shied away from deepening the European Union vigorously enough to prepare it for the accession of Central Middle Eastern European countries. Instead, at the Amsterdam summit it blocked deeper integration in the areas of Justice and Home Affairs over questions such as asylum rules and Germany's public regional banks. Paradoxically, this may have damaged rather than stabilized the traditional "permissive consensus" on European integration in general and German support for the European Union's eastern enlargement in particular. In the area of security policy, the Kohl government reformed Germany's army-based Cold War forces only slowly and half-heartedly. As a consequence, rather than preparing the Bundeswehr in time for emerging security challenges and postconflict peacekeeping, one of Western Europe's biggest armed forces is now under enormous strain as it tries to keep pace with ever increasing, and more difficult, assignments.

The erosion of Germany's power, the weakening of its commitment to conduct foreign policy from the perspective of a clearly conceived and defined strategy[13] (i.e., its lack of purpose), and the fragmentation of decision making and policy implementation thus reflect long-term trends, not just political realignment. Those symptoms have sometimes been interpreted as a renationalization of German foreign policy.[14] The first observation to make in this context is that these problems are hardly confined to Germany alone; rather, they are "normal." Thus, the alleged renationalization in no way represents a return to a German *Sonderweg*;[15] it is, for that reason alone, rather misleading to draw parallels with the late nineteenth century. However, there is a second, even more important, reason to consider this label of renationalization as completely misleading. While it is true that German foreign policy, as that of other countries, has tended in recent years to accord higher priority to specific "national" interests (i.e., to promote objectives considered particularly important by the government of the day), much of this has been defensive and reactive, trying to protect the domestic status quo and cater to special interests of particular political salience. This has nothing in common with earlier, virulent forms of European nationalism, which reflected completely different demographic, socioeconomic, and cultural circumstances and, as a result, were viciously expansionist, imperialist, and militaristic. Then, the notion of "national interests" meant territorial expansion, revisionism, and the search for military balance, if not superiority. Today, what is presented as Germany's national interests is the desire to limit contributions to the European budget, to halt European efforts to pry open some of the cosseted arrangements of German corporatism, and to protect the commercial and social status quo in an aging and rather risk-averse German society. The epithet "re"-nationalization is therefore simply wrong and even misleading: the thrust of this so-called nationalism is not expansive and revisionist, nor does it focus on comprehensive domestic mobilization and the enhancement of national power resources. Rather, the pursuit of alleged national interests often turns out to be special pleading for protection from the forces of change, hence an expression of weakness.

In one sense, this is good news: the ghosts of Germany's nationalist past have, it seems, been put to rest by the weight of the last 55 years of German history (a period, we should recall, longer than the history of the "second" Wilhelminian Reich, let alone the Third Reich). The bad news concerns the ability of German foreign policy to deliver its contribution to reconstructing and enhancing arrangements of regional and global governance. The turbulences of globalization and their impact on US foreign policy, in particular, make this an uphill task for international politics and the states called upon to play key roles in that context. Germany is one of them; its experience since 1955 as a civilian power, its central position in Europe and in European integration, and its weight in international relations in the past allowed the country to "punch above its weight" by forging consensus and, on that basis, effective coalitions; it allowed Germany to build, invigorate, and develop international institutions to "civilize" international relations and enhance international stability. Today, a much more difficult policy environment, as well as an eroding power base, a lack of focus and commitment, and a fragmenting policy process have all made Germany an uncertain power.

Overall, this survey of continuity and change in Germany's foreign policies since the mid-1990s underlines the central importance of policy performance in analyzing foreign policy—performance defined by power, purpose, and policy process. "Performance" starts with actors having a clear sense of purpose, in other words, a strategy. Germany's foreign policy strategy has not changed in substance, but it is showing signs of erosion and disintegration. Admittedly, Germany today has to cope with a much more demanding and less favorable external environment, in which many of the traditional external anchors of German foreign policy have been weakened. Yet this alone does not offer a satisfactory explanation for the declining performance of Germany's foreign policy since the mid-1990s. It is hard to avoid the conclusion that the country has not tried very hard, and sometimes has not even tried at all, to stem itself against the tide, and thus has become part of the problem of, rather than the solution for, a deteriorating international environment. Neglect of foreign policy by Germany's political class and society as a whole are at the heart of this problem. Yet it matters a great deal how well Germany conducts its foreign policy. Just as in economics, the country still occupies a critical position in Europe and, throughout Europe, in the international order. If it neglects its foreign policy, this will have consequences—for Germany as well as for others. Therefore, the "German problem" may well have returned for Europe and the world, albeit in a new, unexpected incarnation.

Notes

1 According to our previous comparative analysis of German, Japanese, and US foreign policies, the willingness to remain committed to agreed principles, norms, and rules, even if they do not in the short-term coincide with perceived national interests, represents one of the three core aspects of the ideal type civilian power. See Ulf Frenkler et al.: "Deutsche, amerikanische und japanische Außenpolitikstrategien 1985–1995: Eine vergleichende Untersuchung zu Zivilisierungsprozessen in der Triade," DFG-Projekt "Zivilmächte": Schlussbericht und Ergebnisse (Trier, 1997). Available at: http://www.uni-trier.de/fb3/politik).

2 At issue are not occasional deficiencies but whether foreign policy behavior persistently contradicts core elements of the ideal type. This would suggest that foreign policy is being shaped by some other role concept. Examples for insufficient compliance with the ideal type include nonproliferation policies until 1990 (see Chapter 3 by Harald Müller) and policies toward Eastern Europe before 1990, which arguably neglected some of the normative guidelines inherent in the civilian power role concept. See Timothy Garton-Ash, *Im Namen Europas. Deutschland und der geteilte Kontinent* (Munich: Hanser, 1993). Michael Staack has argued that German foreign policy generally has been closer to the role concept of a "trading state" than to that of a civilian power, but his case rests on an insufficient understanding of the role concept and dubious empirical evidence (Michael Staack, *Handelsstaat Deutschland, Deutsche Außenpolitik in einem neuen internationalen System* [Paderborn: Schöningh, 2000]). His claim that Germany's development policies have not been consistent with a civilian power role concept, for example, has been effectively refuted by the study of Engel on Germany's Africa policy during the 1990s. See Ulf Engel, *Die Afrikapolitik der Bundesrepublik Deutschland, 1949–1999* (Hamburg: Lit Verlag, 2000).

3 Cf. Emil J. Kirchner, "Germany and the future of European integration," *Germany and fifty-five, Berlin ist nicht Bonn?*, James Sperling, ed., *Issues in German Politics* (Manchester: Manchester University Press, 2004), pp. 450–73.

4 Gunther Hellmann, Rainer Baumann, Monika Bösche, Benjamin Herboth, and Wolfgang Wagner, "De-Europeanization by Default? Germany's EU Policy in Defense and Asylum," *Foreign Policy Analysis*, 1 (2005): 143–64.

5 The terms "role concept" and "grand strategy" are used interchangeably in the following pages; both refer to the principal norms, objectives, strategies, and preferred instruments which together define basic foreign policy orientations and shape specific decisions, although those terms are linked to fundamentally different "schools" of international relations theory. This need not detain us here, though. "Political culture" describes the attitudes and beliefs of a society that relate to its foreign relations. Foreign policy role concepts or grand strategies are held and pursued by governments; they will reflect, but also help shape, the (societal) foreign policy cultures in which they are embedded.

6 Cf. Hanns W. Maull, "Allemagne et Japon: deux pays à suivre," *Politique étrangère*, 60: 3 (summer 1995): 477–96.

7 Cf. Ivo M. Daalder and James M. Lindsay, *America Unbound: The Bush Revolution in Foreign Policy* (Washington, DC: Brookings Institution, 2003). "Diffusion of power" really is a net concept; it describes a negative balance between the diffusion of power among existing actors and the rise to power of new actors, on the one hand, and the result of countervailing efforts to concentrate power through power expansion strategies and/or successful coordination of behavior between actors.

Table C.1 Economic performance of Germany in relation to France, UK and the EU

Year	GNP (Germany : France ratio)	GNP (Germany : UK ratio)	GNP (Germany : EU ratio)	Military expenditure (Germany : France ratio)	Military expenditure (Germany : UK ratio)	ODA expenditure (Germany : France ratio)	ODA expenditure (Germany : UK ratio)	ODA expenditure (Germany : EU ratio)
1995	1.58 : 1	2.17 : 1	0.29 : 1	0.86 : 1	1.23 : 1	0.92 : 1	2.25 : 1[a]	0.23 : 1[a]
2003	1.48 : 1	1.93 : 1	0.27 : 1	0.77 : 1	0.82 : 1	0.94 : 1	1.08 : 1	0.15 : 1

Note: [a]1991–92.

Source: OECD Statistics, IISS Military Balance.

8   As a result, the ratio between the size of the German economy and those of France and the United Kingdom has been declining since the mid-1990s. The decline is much more pronounced still in terms of defense expenditure (see Table C.1).

9   These estimates are based on calculations by the Institut für Wirtschaftsforschung in Halle. Quoted in: http://www.faz.net/s/RubFC06D389EE76479E9E76425072B196C3/Doc~E54C5B83922734DA4B3C813D21EAFF477~ATpl~Ecommon~Scontent.html#top. Accessed February 10, 2005.

10 The positive importance of this ability to facilitate compromise through financial incentives should not be underestimated. "Checkbook diplomacy" hardly deserves the dubious reputation it has come to enjoy.

11 Thomas G. Weiss, "The Illusion of UN Security Council Reform," *The Washington Quarterly*, 26: 4 (2003): 147–61. Available at: http://www.twq.com/03autumn/docs/03autumn_weiss.pdf. Accessed February 12, 2005.

12 Bulmer, Simon, Jeffery, Charlie and Paterson, William E., *Germany's European Diplomacy, Shaping the Regional Milieu*, (Manchester: Manchester University Press, 2000).

13 It is telling that the most recent comprehensive document on German foreign policy, which could be taken as setting out the basic elements of Germany's strategy, is the White Paper on Defense of 1994.

14 Cf. Adam Krzeminski, "Zwischen Renationalisierung und Europäisierung, Ein polnischer Blick auf Deutschland," *Internationale Politik und Gesellschaft*, 1 (2004): 11–26; and Anne-Marie LeGloannec, "The Unilateralist Temptation, Germany's Foreign Policy after the Cold War," *Internationale Politik und Gesellschaft*, 1 (2004): 27–40.

15 Ibid.

Index